HUMAN RELATIONS
A JOB ORIENTED APPROACH

HUMAN RELATIONS
A JOB ORIENTED
APPROACH

ANDREW J. DuBRIN

College of Business
Rochester Institute of Technololgy
Rochester, New York

Reston Publishing Company, Inc.
Reston, Virginia
A Prentice-Hall Company

Library of Congress Cataloging in Publication Data

DuBrin, Andrew J.
　　Human relations.

　　Includes bibliographies and indexes.
　　　1. Industrial sociology.　　2. Personnel management.
3. Organizational behavior.　I. Title.
HD6955.D82　　　658.3　　　77-15039
ISBN　0-87909-371-4

To my daughter Melanie

© 1978 by
Reston Publishing Company, Inc.
A Prentice-Hall Company
Reston, Virginia　22090

10　9　8　7　6　5　4　3　2　1

Printed in the United States of America.

CONTENTS

PREFACE

Does the world need another book about human relationships on the job? One answer is "Yes, because few of the major problems have yet been solved. Perhaps this book will be the one to reduce the waste, inefficiency, dissatisfaction, and strife present in so many places of work." From a less grandiose standpoint, it is important to note the six intended features of this book that the author believes justifies its writing.

First, human relations is a continuously expanding body of knowledge. Older books quickly become dated. The present book is a concise analysis of understanding and dealing effectively with human problems at work. It includes traditional topics, plus a range of newer topics that have infrequently appeared in texts. Among these topics are job stress, job politics, coping with a bureaucracy, assertiveness training, and managing your career.

Second, the emphasis in this book is upon the reader (whether a manager, individual contributor, or student) and what he or she can do to handle situations. In contrast, most management books emphasize how managers should handle subordinates.

Third, the approach to writing this book resembles that used in a nontechnical, popular book. An attempt has been made to maintain reader interest by writing in a style suited both to a general audience and students. It is styled somewhat after my popular books about people at work.

Fourth, classical topics that have suffered from overexposure, such as the Hawthorne studies, Maslow's need hierarchy, and Herzberg's two-factor theory, receive short mention. In their place, this book emphasizes modern developments stemming from these keystone ideas.

Fifth, virtually every concept presented in this text will be illustrated with an example. My experience has been that people respond best to concepts and ideas when the latter are translated into a concrete "for instance."

Sixth, an attempt will be made to explain how many of the concepts in this book can be used to enhance individual or organizational effectiveness. Such application of knowledge is woven into the body of the book rather than placed in a separate application section.

My target audiences for this book are students of human relations in colleges and participants in supervisory and management training courses. People interested in the field of organizational behavior or industrial psychology stripped of its theoretical and research underpinnings should also find this book of value.

A book of this nature requires the cooperation of many people to write and publish. My primary thanks goes to my editor, A. Stuart Horton, who suggested that I consider writing a book about human relations for Reston Publishing Company. Students of mine at the Rochester Institute of Technology have been helpful in contributing case ideas and examples about human behavior on the job. Many of these contributions have found their way into this text. A number of examples in this book stem directly from organizations that I visited as a consultant or speaker. Although an attempt has been made to appropriately cite all authors whose ideas I have used, many people are undoubtedly not given sufficient credit.

The several anonymous reviewers of the first version of this manuscript receive my appreciation for their penetrating candor. Although at times painful, such honest criticism helps produce a well-balanced text. K. Lois Smith turned in her customary superior performance as my manuscript typist. Kathy Kulp provided me prompt and enthusiastic clerical service.

My wife Marcia and my children Drew, Douglas, and Melanie receive my thanks for helping to create a peaceful and joyful family life, so essential for the concentration required of a textbook writer.

ANDREW J. DuBRIN

ACKNOWLEDGMENTS

Although all quoted material in this book is indicated by footnotes, those sources granting us permission to reproduce material frequently request, and deserve, separate acknowledgment. These special permissions and copyrights are listed next, arranged by type of source (journals and magazines, book publishers, and individuals). Citations are used as requested by the various publishers.

JOURNALS AND MAGAZINES

Business Horizons: Donald F. Crane, "The Case for Participative Management," April 1976, p. 19.

Business Week: "The 'Humanistic' Way of Managing People," July 22, 1972, p. 148.

Dun's Review: Lee Smith, "What Kills Executives?" March 1975, p. 37. Reprinted with the special permission of *Dun's Review*, March 1975. Copyright 1975, Dun and Bradstreet Publications Corporation.

Harvard Business Review: (1) George M. Prince, "Creative Meetings Through Power Sharing," July–August 1972, p. 72. (2) Henry Mintzberg, "The Manager's Job: Folklore and Fact," July–August 1975, pp. 49–61. (3) Abraham Zaleznik, "Power and Politics in Organizational Life," May–June 1970, p. 47. All three articles copyrighted by the President and Fellows of Harvard College; all rights reserved.

Industry Week: (1) Thomas J. Bouchard, "What Ever Happened to Brainstorming?" August 2, 1971, p. 29. (2) J. David Else, "Treat or Treatment for Alcoholics," April 26, 1971, p. 50.

International Management: David Clutterbuck, "General Motors Strives to Motivate Its Workers," January 1975. Reprinted by special permission from the January 1975 issue of International Management. Copyright McGraw-Hill International Publications Company Limited. All rights reserved.

Nation's Business: (1) Ralph G. Nichols, "Listening Is a 10-Part Skill," from undated brochure, "Managing Yourself." (2) Eugene Raudsepp, "Ideas: Test Your Creativity," June 1965, p. 80.

Personnel Journal: Verne Walter, "Self-Motivated Career Planning," March 1975, p. 115. Reprinted with permission *Personnel Journal,* copyright March 1975.

Personnel Psychology: Leonard V. Gordon, "Measurement of Bureaucratic Orientation," Spring 1970, p. 3.

Product Marketing: (1) Ed Roseman, "The Myth of the Powerless Product Manager," February 1976, p. 34. (2) Ed Roseman, "How to Play Clean Office Politics," May 1976, p. 33.

Rochester Gannett Newspapers: (1) Meryl Gordon, "A Case of Financial 'Patients'," September 15, 1976, p. 8D. (2) "9-Year Headache a Lot of Trouble," June 23, 1976, p. 1A.

BOOK PUBLISHERS

Addison-Wesley Publishing Company: Muriel James, *The OK Boss,* 1975, pp. 92–95. Reprinted by special permission from *The OK Boss* by Muriel James. Copyright Addison-Wesley Publishing Company, Reading, Massachusetts. All rights reserved.

Brooks/Cole Publishing Company: Marvin D. Dunnette, editor, *Work and Nonwork in the Year 2001,* 1973, pp. 91, 92, and 93. Copyright 1973 by Wadsworth Publishing Company, Inc. Reprinted by permission of the publisher.

Business Publications, Inc.: James L. Gibson, John M. Ivancevich, and James H. Donnelly, Jr., *Organizations: Structure, Process, Behavior,* revised edition, 1976, p. 62.

Delacorte Press: Lynn Z. Bloom, Karen Levin Coburn, and Joan Crystal Perlman, *The New Assertive Woman,* 1976, pp. i, 175–176.

Gulf Publishing Company and Scientific Methods, Inc.: Robert R. Blake and Jane Srygley Mouton, *The Managerial Grid,* copyright 1964, p. 10. Reproduced with permission.

International Personnel Management Association: Felix M. Lopez, *Evaluating Employee Performance,* 1968, p. 12. Reprinted by permission of the International Personnel Management Association, 1313 East 60th Street, Chicago, Illinois 60637.

Richard D. Irwin, Inc.: (1) Joe Kelly, *Organizational Behavior: An Existential–Systems Approach,* revised edition, p. 716. (2) Ross A. Webber, *Management: Basic Elements of Managing an Organization,* 1975, p. 653. (3) George F. Wieland and Robert A. Ullrich, *Organizations: Behavior, Design, and Change,* 1976, p. 504.

Major Books: Andrew J. DuBrin, *Survival in the Sexist Jungle,* copyright 1974, pp. 215–220. Books for Better Living. Reproduced with permission.

McGraw-Hill Book Company: (1) Keith Davis, *Human Relations in Business,* 1957, p. 244. (2) Fremont Kast and James F. Rosenzweig, *Organization and Management: A Systems Approach,* second edition, 1974, p. 110. (3) Douglas McGregor, *The Human Side of Enterprise,* 1960, pp. 33–48.

Pergamon Press, Inc.: (1) Andrew J. DuBrin, *Fundamentals of Organizational Behavior: An Applied Perspective,* 1974, pp. 249–255. (2) G. Singer and Meredith Wallace, *The Administrative Waltz,* 1976, p. 3.

Prentice-Hall, Inc.: (1) William H. Newman, *Administrative Action: The Techniques of Organization and Management,* second edition, 1963, p. 88. (2) Edgar H. Schein, *Organizational Psychology,* 1970, p. 12.

Scott Foresman and Company: Alan C. Filley, Robert J. House, and Steven Kerr, *Managerial Process and Organizational Behavior,* second edition, 1976, p. 229.

INDIVIDUALS

Thomas J. Bouchard, "What Ever Happened to Brainstorming?" *Industry Week,* August 2, 1971, p. 29.

James D. Christie, "Murdock the Maneuverer," unpublished case.

John David Else, "Treat or Treatment for Alcoholics," *Industry Week,* April 26, 1971, p. 50.

Charles R. Garbowski, "The Hard Working, Dissatisfied Engineer," unpublished case.

Thomas Iten, "The Frustrated Chairman," unpublished case.

Paul R. Paulson, "The Tarnished Company Image," unpublished case.

Gerald J. Soltas, "Making Eight Is a Hassle," unpublished case (excerpted).

Paul G. Toner, "The Aims Game," unpublished case.

PART ONE
INTRODUCTION TO HUMAN RELATIONS

Our introduction to the study of human relations begins with a framework, or organized method, for viewing the broad subject matter of this topic. Included are a modern definition of the field, a historical perspective, and an illustration of how research contributes to human relations knowledge. In addition, we present a brief guide to help you derive the most personal benefit from reading and studying this book.

1

A FRAMEWORK FOR HUMAN RELATIONS

Learning Objectives

After reading and studying this chapter, you should be able to

1. Define what human relations is and give an example of the practice of human relations.
2. Give one example of what human relations is not.
3. Describe the behavioral model of human beings.
4. Discuss how scientific research contributes to knowledge of human relations.
5. Explain why human relations is not simply common sense.
6. Provide a brief historical sketch of the human relations movement.

At the height of the summer vacation season, a waiter named Waldo walked into the office of Cynthia Cambridge, dining room manager at the posh Towering Pines Hotel. With a dismayed look on his face, he exclaimed:

"Cynthia, I'm packing my bags and leaving for home today. I can't take another day of this job. As a waiter I don't even feel like a human being. The guests are ordering me around in the dining rooms. When I go into the kitchen I get flak from the kitchen help and the head waiter. I feel like a rubber band being stretched from both ends. And I'm about to snap."

"But Waldo, you can't walk out now. It's July 1 and 600 guests will be arriving this weekend. Leave me now, and you'll never get another job as a waiter again. Are you a man or a mouse?"

"Insult me all you want, but my sanity is more important than my job as a waiter."

A Shop Superintendent.   Back from a seminar in job motivation, Tony Demarco decided to better motivate his shop supervisors by enriching their jobs. His decision was to give his foremen and forewomen the opportunity to visit customer locations to see how the machines built in Tony's department were actually being used in the field. Tony first approached Bernie, one of his foremen, with his new plan of job enrichment:

"Bernie, I've decided that your job has a couple of missing links. You could use a better understanding of how your job fits into the total picture. Toward that end, I'm authorizing you one trip a month to visit customer installations."

Bernie thought over in his mind for a minute the idea proposed by Tony and then reacted: "Tony, that sounds to me as if my job would be even more complicated. As it is I have more work to do than I can possibly handle. You could do me a favor by giving me less work to do, not more."

The managers involved in the above interchanges were both encountering human relations problems. So were their subordinates. Cynthia was insensitive to the pressures as perceived by Waldo; he was doing a poor job of managing stress. Tony was trying out a widely used technique of job motivation—job enrichment—without tailoring it to the individual situation of a given subordinate. Bernie was having a human relations problem to the extent that somebody thought he needed to exhibit a higher level of job motivation.

Anytime anybody confronts a problem at work dealing with people, either individually or in groups, he or she is *potentially* making use of human relations. We emphasize the word potentially because not everything done to cope with the human element in work organizations can rightfully be considered human relations. If human relations were conceived in this manner, it would be a field of knowledge and practice without bounds.

What then is human relations? From our viewpoint, human relations is the art and practice of using systematic knowledge about human behavior to achieve organizational and/or personal objectives. Since human relations borrows ideas from several fields (to be described shortly) to accomplish its work, it is also a body of knowledge in addition to being a practice or art. An effective U.S. senator is a practitioner of human relations. So is an effective night supervisor at McDonald's. When the president of your company or college deals productively with human problems on the job, he or she is also practicing human relations. Both managers and nonmanagers practice human relations in their work.

The subject of human relations is broad enough to encompass several different approaches to its study and definition. Fred J. Carvell has arrived at a workable definition of human relations that he builds from the ideas of Keith Davis.[1] Carvell holds that "human relations is motivating people in groups to develop teamwork which effectively fulfills

their needs and achieves organizational objectives." An important difference between this definition and ours is that we stress individuals as well
as groups. In addition, human relations deals with many different human
processes aside from motivation. Being creative on the job, communicating with people, and using office politics in a sensible way are among
the many different aspects of human relations worthy of consideration.

A BEHAVIORAL MODEL OF HUMAN RELATIONS

Almost any reader of this book will have had some exposure to psychology or a closely related field that provided a model of the basic nature
of human behavior. It is therefore unnecessary to provide here a full
conception of what people are like, yet a few anchor points are necessary.
To deal effectively with individuals or small groups in a job environment,
you need a basic framework for understanding human beings. Even if
the framework you choose is not the most sophisticated available, it is
better than no framework at all. A framework gives you a starting point
for arriving at conclusions about people, but it should not be an intellectual straitjacket that prevents you from making spontaneous observations.

To use a sports analogy, in developing tennis strategy you might
use the general assumption that the best way to beat (deal effectively
with) an opponent is to keep him or her running. According to your basic
framework about human behavior on the tennis court, a person kept on
the move hits more erratically than a person who has the opportunity to
hit from essentially one position. You might find this the best strategy to
use against most people, but now and then you might have to reformu-
late your strategy. You might encounter a player who returns the ball
best when he or she is kept running about the court. When forced to hit
many balls from the same position, that particular opponent feels too
constricted and therefore becomes more erratic in his or her tennis
stroking.

The behavioral model of human beings presented here stems from
a conception developed by Henry L. Tosi and Stephen J. Carroll.[2] Shown
in Figure 1.1, the model can be brought to life by applying it to a case
history of a young man who tackled a challenging assignment.

Stimulus, Cue, Force, or Pressure. Tom received a phone call from a
stranger, offering him this proposition. "Hello, this is Mr. Orbaker. A
friend of yours referred you to me. I have an old building that has been
messed up pretty badly by the two families who have been living there.
Both families have left and the place is in shambles. Would you be interested in patching the place for me so it's suitable for people to live in?"

Tom responded, "I've never tackled anything that big before on my
own. Right now I'm doing some free-lance work for other contractors.

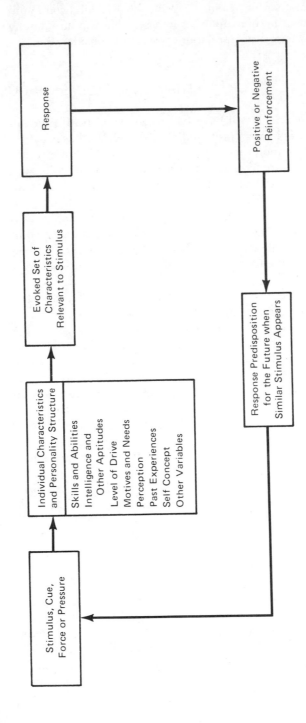

FIGURE 1.1
A behavioral model of human beings.

But I'd like to meet with you and inspect what has to be done."

"Okay," replied Orbaker, "Let's you and I meet next Thursday evening at 6 P.M. Here's my address. . . ."

Tom had thus received a stimulus (or even pressure) from the environment. He had been invited to become an independent contractor for refurbishing a two-family building.

Individual Characteristics and Personality Structure. How (the manner in which) Tom responds to this stimulus from the environment depends upon many things about him as a person. Each stimulus, or environmental force, brings forth (or awakens) different aspects of our personal makeup. A stimulus, cue, force, or pressure evokes only the particular set of the many elements that the individual associates with the stimulus, cue, force, or pressure.

For instance, Tom's *self-concept* includes many different elements. He prides himself in being a good softball player and a good lover, but these aspects of his self-concept will not come into play in his decision whether or not to tackle this assignment. Also, these aspects of his self-concept will not influence to any measurable extent how well Tom performs if he should undertake the assignment.

Tom's *past experiences* will contribute selectively to Tom's acceptance or rejection of this assignment and to how he performs. Many aspects of his past experience will be called to mind by the stimulus of the contracting job, but certainly not every aspect.

Tom's past history of success and failure in handling independent work will influence his decision. So will his past history in relating to an authority figure like Mr. Orbaker. If Orbaker reminds him of an unfriendly high school teacher, Tom may hold back just a little in entering into a business relationship with him. Tom, or anybody else, may not be consciously aware of the profound influence of past experience on present decisions. Thus they serve as an automatic, semiconscious influence.

Evoked Set of Characteristics Relevant to Stimulus. As Tom inspects the building with Mr. Orbaker, many elements of his personal makeup come into play. For example, his *level of drive* toward accomplishing worthwhile tasks is higher than average. He wants to succeed as a business person. His drive level impels him toward a decision such as "Yes, Orbaker, I'll tackle this assignment if we can agree on a satisfactory price."

Before Tom could proceed to take on the assignment, other aspects of his functioning were evoked. His *intelligence* and numerical ability were crucial. Tom arrived at an estimated cost of $1100 plus supplies. If Tom provided too high an estimate, Orbaker might take his business to a licensed, established contractor. If Tom estimated too low, he might find himself working at wages so low that he would not be able to cover his living expenses.

Many of Tom's *needs* and *motives* were also evoked by Orbaker's proposition. A need is a deficit within an individual, such as a craving for water or recognition. A motive is a need or desire coupled with the intention to attain an appropriate goal. Tom has a strong need to be independent, and his motive for taking on such an assignment (and performing well) might be to experiment with self-employment.

Response. As already hinted, Tom did say yes to the offer. He contacted his close friend, Pete, to work with him on the assignment. Tom and **Pete** worked diligently for twelve days, with a three-day rest break in the middle for camping. In Orbaker's opinion and their own, Tom, accompanied by Pete, performed admirably well.

One objective index of their positive *response* to this *task* (*stimulus, or cue*) was that the Bureau of Property Conservation removed the entire list of twenty-four violations on the property that existed before Tom and Pete began their renovation work. Tom and Pete applied a wide range of skills to the assignment, including carpentry, painting, electrical, and plumbing.

Positive or Negative Reinforcement. In this situation, Tom and Pete received almost all positive reinforcement. Performing the task well was a reward in itself; it helped to strengthen the self-confidence of both men. (A *reward* is anything that acts as a positive reinforcer.) The money received by the men, including a $50 bonus for exceptional performance, was also rewarding. Among the other rewards was an immediate additional assignment to paint another building owned by Orbaker.

Response Predisposition for the Future. As a consequence of the substantial positive reinforcement received by Tom, he is now predisposed to bid on any construction or renovation contracts that might come his way. Ten days after completing the Orbaker job, Tom was awarded a contract to renovate two run-down, two-family buildings owned by a local savings bank. Ecstatic about the good work performed by Tom and Pete, Orbaker mentioned them in conversation to an acquaintance who worked in the mortgage foreclosure section of a savings bank. Through foreclosure, the bank had acquired many more distressed properties than it wished to own. As a profit-minded institution, it was seeking economical ways of restoring them to the point of being suitable for occupancy by tenants. On the basis of Orbaker's testimonial, hiring Tom and Pete looked like a possible solution to the problem of economically restoring distressed properties.

Where Does Human Relations Fit In? To the extent that Orbaker used systematic knowledge about human behavior to achieve his objectives, *human relations* was practiced. Orbaker did rely on systematic knowledge about people in a variety of ways to achieve his objectives. Orbaker was intuitively effective with people, but he was also a consumer of knowledge about human relations and industrial psychology!

Orbaker chose the right leadership approach to handle Tom and Pete. Sensing that they were responsible, mature young adults, he gave them considerable freedom to do the job as they saw fit. He provided them with general guidelines of what he wanted done but allowed them to choose the method. Orbaker made no pretense about being a skilled tradesman.

Orbaker recognized that Tom and Pete were in need of money. His response was to make $275 payments as they completed each quarter of the project. As a form of nonfinancial reinforcement, Orbaker provided Tom and Pete with large quantities of praise and reassurance. To wit, "You fellows are doing a terrific job. You're saving me from going down the tubes with this building. Keep up the good work and you'll see a lot more work from me in the future."

Tom and Pete practiced good human relations by reinforcing Orbaker's faith in them. Orbaker established charge account privileges for them at a large hardware store located several blocks from the building site. They were instructed to charge whatever supplies they needed to accomplish the job. Aside from stocking themselves with an ample supply of paint brushes and brooms (in all fairness, a reasonable informal token reward), Tom and Pete ordered only those supplies needed to accomplish their job.

Working together as employer and employees, Orbaker, Tom, and Pete created an organizational climate of trust and openness—a very helpful condition in achieving both organizational and personal objectives. Tom demonstrated to himself that he could handle an assignment without close supervision and that he could work effectively with a close friend as a quasi-subordinate. His self-concept now enlarged, Tom was well on his way to a career of self-employment.

HUMAN RELATIONS AND BEHAVIORAL SCIENCE

Human relations is a field and skill that gathers much of its systematic knowledge from the social and behavioral sciences.[3] Classification schemes differ, but the social sciences are now generally considered to be economics, history, and political science. Behavioral sciences are primarily anthropology, sociology, and psychology. If a diligent scholar were to trace the sources of most scientific studies undergirding human relations principles, he or she would discover that psychologists and sociologists are the largest contributors. More specifically, most of the body of knowledge now called human relations stems from the findings and observations of industrial and organizational psychologists.

Personnel administration is a hybrid field similar in scope to human relations. Personnel administration differs from human relations primarily because it is concerned with the application of personnel research. A person who practices personnel administration must use human relations, but also be conversant with personnel testing, wage and salary administration, and attitude surveys, among numerous techniques.

How Research Helps Human Relations. An example of the relationship between human relations and science is found in a study about improving job performance through training in goal setting published in the *Journal of Applied Psychology.*[4] Conducted by Gary P. Latham and Sydney B. Kinne III, this study is considered relevant because many practitioners of human relations believe that goal setting is a vital ingredient of good supervision. Reliable information about goal setting in a work environment would thus help the practitioner of management and the human relations specialist make more sound pronouncements about goal setting.

Purpose of the Study. The researchers wanted to determine the effects of a one-day training program on the job performance of pulpwood workers. Criteria used for measuring the effectiveness of the program were cords-per-sawhand hour and cords-per-crew hour of production. Additional criteria included measures of turnover, absenteeism, and injuries, all indirect indexes of worker job satisfaction or dissatisfaction.

Method and Procedures. Twenty-six producers and their crews were selected and matched on such considerations as past production records. One crew from each pair was randomly assigned to the training group. The remaining participants in the study were used as a comparison group, a crucial requirement of a scientific study.

Seven experienced company foresters were given instruction in training. A three-hour program was conducted that carefully explained the purpose of the experiment and its underlying assumptions. An intensive discussion program period was held after the program.

Each of the seven foresters contacted the selected producers and requested their participation in the study. Each producer was told that they would be participating in a research program of three-month duration, but that they could leave at any time. However, the *experimental groups* (those who received training) were given slightly different instructions than the *control group* (no training).

The experimental subjects were told that the purpose of the study was to give them a one-day training program in learning to set production goals and to determine its effects on performance—the absolute truth. The control subjects were told that the study was designed to determine the effects of injuries, absenteeism, and turnover on production—a deceptive statement considered necessary for the sake of science!

As noted by the experimenters,[5]

Training in goal setting was based on the premise that increasing the performance of the sawhand results in an increase in the productivity of the crew. This premise was based on the fact that the felling of a tree is vital to achieving the remaining tasks in pulpwood harvesting.

By means of complicated statistical analysis, production tables were constructed to systematically establish production goals. These tables allowed for factors that could affect production owing to differences in harvesting stand conditions.

A production goal in trees-per-sawhand hour was determined for each day and week. This goal was stressed as a minimum standard of acceptable performance. However, no penalties were established for failure to reach the goal. Producers in the control group (and their sawyers) were not informed of the goal established for the experimental groups.

Production levels were measured by means of tally meters assigned to sawyers in the experimental groups—the people who actually cut down the trees. Producers in both groups were given a form to record production, turnover, absenteeism, and injuries. Producers in the experimental group had an item on their form requesting information concerning the production goal.

Key Results of the Study. The difference in production between the group of sawyers who received training in goal setting was slightly higher than the production of the control group. A more striking difference was found between the performance of the crews trained in goal setting and the nontrained groups. A third important result of the study was that absenteeism was significantly higher in the control group than in the experimental group.

Implications for Human Relations. Experimenters Latham and Kinne concluded that training in goal setting can lead to an increase in production and a decrease in absenteeism (at least for a very well-defined type of job). A manager can now more confidently devote ample amounts of time to setting specific production goals for people. Of equal significance, this experiment provides new support for the widespread belief that people perform better when they keep a tally on how well they are going (i.e., receive feedback on their performance). You as an individual might be able to produce more and find your job more interesting if you keep accurate records of your own performance.

HUMAN RELATIONS AND COMMON SENSE

A computer scientist complained angrily, "Why did my company send me to this workshop on human relations? Anybody with half a mind knows how to be nice to people. Don't they know that human relations is just common sense?"

This computer scientist's first charge can be dismissed quite readily. Human relations sometimes involves "being nice to people," but more importantly it involves dealing with people in such a manner that individual and organizational goals are fostered. For instance, in some situations it might be helpful to fire a drug abuser if she refuses to undergo treatment for her problem. Firing in this instance might have a therapeutic value in that it dramatically demonstrates the idea that she is responsible for the implications of her behavior. This woman's drug-abuse problem had impaired her ability to perform satisfactorily as a sales representative.

Common Sense Is Uncommon. A minority of people are highly effective in dealing with other people either on the job or in personal life. Aside from those rare individuals who intuitively know how to cope with a variety of people in an effective manner, most people are plagued with interpersonal problems. Virtually all organizations have many problems involving people. Thus, if common sense (meaning natural wisdom, not requiring formal knowledge) were widely held, there would be fewer problems involving people.

Since few people have such common sense in matters dealing with people, human relations training is necessary to help improve upon the chaos found in some organizations. Human relations training for personal life might help reduce the number of people chronically dissatisfied with their spouses, children, and themselves. Our present concern, however, is job-oriented behavior.

Common Sense Requires Experience. Louis, an accounting supervisor with three months of experience, reported to his boss, Barney, that he was having vexing problems with two accountants in his office: "They spend so much time in my office complaining about each other that it is difficult for me to take care of my other work. Besides, they are wasting precious time. I've about given up on the problem. Do you have any suggestions?"

Barney instructed Louis to bring the two combatants together in his office (Louis's) and hold a three-way discussion about the problem. Barney also urged Louis to make sure that each accountant clearly laid out the nature of his complaint to the other one.

Louis returned to Barney's office one week later with this comment: "Your approach worked like a charm. They shook hands after the conference and I haven't had a complaint from either of them in days. How did you figure that one out?"

Barney replied, "It's just a matter of common sense."

True, Barney has learned how to resolve conflict through trial and error and now has common sense about such problems. By happenstance, he passed on some of his wisdom to Louis. If Louis had supervised people long enough, he too would probably learn good techniques of resolving office conflicts. A more efficient approach would be to read a reliable source about conflict resolution before the problem occurred. Reading about human relations (or any subject) is an economical way of gaining experience. Study an applied subject and you will capitalize upon the experience—and common sense—of others who have been there first. Before skiing down a mountain, why not read a book about skiing or take lessons from a professional?

Human Relations Sharpens and Refines Common Sense. People with the most common sense often derive the most personal benefit from human relations training. They build upon strengths, which in general has a bigger payoff than overcoming weaknesses. Through common sense, the interpersonally competent individual may be able to handle many situations involving people. With a few refinements, his or her handling of people may be even more effective.

Anne, a sales manager, prided herself in her sales-conference techniques. She felt that more was accomplished in her meetings than in most meetings. Yet Anne was still not satisfied. As she told her human relations consultant, "I figure we can still get more out of our meetings. I detect that people are not really talking to each other about the problems facing them. I want communication to flow even better than it does now."

The human relations consultant asked about the physical arrangements in her conferences. Anne explained how people sat around a table with their notebooks, ashtrays, and water pitchers placed in front of them. "Now I see what you are doing wrong," said the consultant. "You are setting up a few structural barriers to communication. Get the people out in the middle of the room, seated in a circle. Let them put their notebooks aside. Get them physically closer to each other."

Anne tried this technique in her next sales conference and it worked. Communication barriers broke down as people no longer psychologically hid behind their tables, notebooks, ashtrays, and name placards. Anne was already effective with people, but by introducing the concept of *overcoming physical barriers to communication* to her repertoire, her effectiveness multiplied.

Human Relations Sometimes Disproves Common Sense. A final major reason that having common sense does not make the study of human relations superfluous is that common sense can be wrong. Instances exist in which the commonsense explanation to a problem is inferior to the explanation provided by systematic knowledge about human behavior. A situation involving a school superintendent in the Midwest serves as a case in point.

Laird, a school superintendent, surprised many of his friends and professional colleagues by his decision to leave school administration. He informed people that effective this upcoming September he would be teaching at a school for mentally retarded children in the South. Several of his colleageus commented, "Laird must be flipping his lid. Why would anybody leave a job as good as his for a lesser job?"

In commonsense terms, Laird's colleagues were correct. Commonsense knowledge tells us that a *good* job is a high-paying job. True, Laird was making in excess of $33,000 as a school superintendent, but to him it was a *bad* job. Therefore, he left to take what for him constituted a *good* job.

From a human relations point of view, what Laird did made sense. Job-motivation theory tells us that a good job is one that meets our particular needs at the time. Job satisfaction stems from contentment with the nature of the work we are doing. Laird regarded his administrative job as interfering with his directly helping people. Working in one-to-one relationships with retarded children, even if the job paid only half as much as his present job, was therefore a rational decision. In this instance, common sense provided the wrong analysis of a person's job behavior, whereas systematic knowledge about human behavior provided the right explanation.

THE HUMAN RELATIONS MOVEMENT

The historical development of human relations knowledge applied to job settings warrants some attention in any book about human relations. Any history of the application of systematic knowledge about human behavior to the job must use some arbitrary milestones. For instance, the crew chiefs concerned with constructing the Egyptian pyramids must have had useful informal concepts of leadership available to them.

The Hawthorne Studies. As described in virtually every book written about management,[6] the human relations or behavioral school of management began in 1927 with a group of studies conducted at the Hawthorne plant of Western Electric, an AT&T subsidiary. Curiously, these studies were prompted by an experiment carried out by the company's engineers between 1924 and 1927. Following the scientific management tradition, these engineers were applying research methods to answer job-related problems.

Two groups were studied to determine the effects of different levels of illumination on worker performance. One group received increased illumination, while the other did not. A preliminary finding was that, when illumination was increased, the level of performance also increased. Surprisingly to the engineers, productivity also increased when the level of illumination was decreased almost to moonlight levels. One interpretation made of these results was that the workers involved in the experiment enjoyed being the center of attention; they reacted positively because management cared about them. Such a phenomenon taking place in any research setting is now called the *Hawthorne effect*.

As a result of these preliminary investigations, a team of researchers headed by Elton Mayo and F. J. Roethlisberger from Harvard conducted a lengthy series of experiments extending over a six-year period. The conclusions they reached served as the bedrock of later developments in the human relations approach to management. Among their key findings were the following:

1. Economic incentives are less potent than generally believed in influencing workers to achieve high levels of output.
2. Leadership practices and work-group pressures profoundly influence employee satisfaction and performance.
3. Any factor influencing employee behavior is embedded in a social system. For instance, to understand the impact of pay on performance, you also have to understand the climate that exists in the work group and the leadership style of the superior.

Leadership Styles and Practices. As a consequence of the Hawthorne studies, worker attitudes, morale, and group influences became a concern of researchers. A notable development of this nature occurred shortly after World War II at the University of Michigan. A group of social scientists formed an organization, later to be called the Institute for Social Research, to study those principles of leadership that were associated with highest productivity.[7]

Based upon work with clerical and production workers, an important conclusion was that supervisors of high-producing units behaved differently than those of low-producing units. Among the differences in style noted were that supervisors of productive groups in comparison to their lower producing counterparts were

1. More emotionally supportive of subordinates.
2. More likely to play a *differentiated role*—plan, regulate, and coordinate the activities of subordinates, but not become directly involved in work tasks.
3. More likely to exercise general rather than close or "tight" supervision.

Similar studies were conducted at Ohio State University. Among their key findings also was that people-oriented leadership was generally more effective than production-oriented leadership. Today it is recognized that the requirements of the situation dictate the best (or optimum) leadership style. However, the historical significance of the studies cannot be dismissed. From these researchers emanated leadership-training programs designed to make first-line supervisors more aware of the feelings, attitudes, and opinions of their subordinates. Unfortunately, many of the earlier leadership-training programs overemphasized people awareness and paid insufficient attention to the other aspects of a supervisor's job.

Organization Development.   Another major development in the human relations movement is the proliferation of programs and techniques designed to move organizations toward more honest and authentic ways of dealing with work problems and each other. Today the majority of large business organizations (and numerous school systems) participate in some form of organization development (OD) with the hope of improving organization effectiveness.

Sensitivity training, the first widespread formal OD technique, owes its historical roots to the work of Kurt Lewin.[8] In the mid-1940s, Lewin formalized the technique of bringing a group of people together and helping them examine how their attitudes were received by other members of the group. Additionally, group members were presented information about group dynamics. This activity was undertaken as part of a project to make local leaders from several communities understand and implement the new Fair Employment Practices Act.

The group discussion and feedback to members involved in this project became formalized as the T-group (a central aspect of sensitivity training). In 1947, the National Training Laboratory was established at Bethel, Maine, by a group of social scientists from the Massachusetts Institute of Technology and the National Education Association.

Today, an intriguing array of OD techniques are used to improve human relations effectiveness, including the widely mentioned managerial grid, team building, and conflict-resolution exercises. Management by objectives (MBO), a system of management that holds people accountable for their results, is sometimes considered to be part of the OD movement.

The Human Potential Movement.   Concurrent with the growth of human relations in work organizations, has been the burgeoning of techniques and programs to foster human growth off the job. In the last two decades, millions of people seeking personal growth (or sometimes simply emotional arousal) have participated in programs such as encounter groups, marriage enrichment groups, Erhard seminar training, couples groups, and transactional analysis.

During the early 1970s, the human potential (meaning development of one's potential) movement began to appear in work settings. A prime example is the popular use of transactional analysis (TA) training programs for managers and specialists. In one airline training program, stewardesses were taught how to handle difficult passengers by use of TA. If a passenger were to yell out in flight, "Make me a scotch and soda," the stewardess was instructed to relieve tension by responding, "Poof, you're a scotch and soda."

17

A Framework for
Human Relations

Management awareness training and assertiveness training represent two other techniques related to the development of human potential. Both are designed to deal with the problem of job discrimination against women. In management awareness training, managers are made more sensitive to their sexist attitudes (such as thinking of all engineers as male) and helped in changing their attitudes. Assertiveness training has been widely used to help women be more direct in making known their demands for equal opportunity.

Career-development programs in industry are more prevalent today than at any time in the past. Although varying widely in content, all these programs are designed to help the individual make career decisions that will move him or her toward self-fulfillment. In the process, it is assumed that the person will make a better contribution to the organization.

HOW THIS BOOK WILL HELP YOU

A person who carefully studies the information in this book and incorporates many of its suggestions into his or her mode of doing things should attain five objectives (and more importantly derive five benefits). People vary so widely in learning ability, personality, and life circumstances that some people will be able to attain some objectives and not others. For instance, you might be so shy at this stage of your development that you will not want to try some of the conflict-resolution techniques. Or you may be locked into a family business and therefore uninterested in career-planning techniques.

Awareness of Relevant Information. Part of feeling comfortable and making a positive impression in any work organization is being familiar with relevant general knowledge about the world of work. By reading this book you will become conversant with many of the buzz words at work, such as *leadership style, theory X manager,* and an *OK boss.*

Development of Human Relations Skills. Anybody who aspires toward higher-level jobs needs to develop proficiency in such human relations skills as how to motivate people, how to communicate, and how to counsel subordinates with substandard performance. Studying information about such topics in this book, coupled with trying them out now or when your job situation permits, should help you develop such skills.

Coping with Job Problems. Almost everybody who holds a responsible job inevitably runs into human problems. Reading about these problems and prescriptions for coping with them could save you considerable inner turmoil. Among the job-survival skills you will learn about in the following chapters are coping with job stress and dealing with conflict between yourself and your boss.

Capitalizing Upon Opportunities. Many readers of this book will spend part of their working time capitalizing upon opportunities rather than resolving daily problems. Every career-minded person needs a few break-through experiences in order to make his or her life more rewarding. Toward this end we have included a separate chapter on job creativity and career planning. Improving your creativity can multiply your effectiveness, while planning your career could be your path to life satisfaction.

Awareness of Subtle Factors. Hard work and intelligence will only carry you so far at work. You also need an awareness of subtle undercurrents in order to climb the organization ladder or even get good assignments at your present level. To help you accomplish this objective, this book contains information about job politics and dealing with a bureaucracy. Job politics can be practiced in a sensible, ethical manner. Learning more about how bureaucracies operate will lessen some of your frustrations in dealing with a large, complex organization.

*Summary
of Key Points*

1. Human relations is the art and practice of using systematic knowledge about human behavior to achieve organizational and/or personal objectives.
2. A model presented here for understanding people incorporates these elements: an outside stimulus acts upon a person to call forth certain aspects of his or her personal makeup, such as intelligence and self-confidence. The person's response to the stimulus will be positively or negatively reinforced by others, thus influencing that person's later response to a similar stimulus.
3. Human relations derives most of its knowledge from the social and behavioral sciences, and is not simply common sense.
4. The human relations movement began with the Hawthorne studies, and now includes such approaches as organizational development (OD) and transactional analysis (TA).
5. A formal study of human relations should increase your effectiveness in dealing with yourself and other people.

*Questions
for Discussion*

1. Based on what you have read so far, does it appear that human relations could help a person's social and family life? Explain your answer.

2. Describe how a present or former boss practiced *good* human relations.

3. Describe how a present or former boss practiced *poor* human relations.

4. If you were Tom (the free-lance contractor described in this chapter), would you have taken on the renovation assignment? Why or why not?

5. If you were Orbaker, would you have granted Tom and Pete charge account privileges at the hardware store? Why or why not?

6. Does human relations seem to be a science? Explain your answer.

FOOTNOTES

[1] Fred J. Carvell, *Human Relations in Business*, Macmillan, 1975, p. 2.

[2] Henry L. Tosi and Stephen J. Carroll, *Management: Contingencies, Structure, and Process*, St. Clair Press, 1976, pp. 58–60.

[3] Two overviews of the behavioral science literature particularly relevant to students of human relations are Andrew J. DuBrin, *Fundamentals of Organizational Behavior: An Applied Perspective*, 2nd ed., Pergamon Press, 1978, and Paul Hersey and Kenneth H. Blanchard, *Management of Organizational Behavior: Utilizing Human Resources*, 3rd ed., Prentice-Hall, 1977.

[4] Gary P. Latham and Sydney B. Kinne III, "Improving Job Performance Through Training in Goal Setting," *Journal of Applied Psychology*, April 1974, pp. 187–191.

[5] *Ibid.*, p. 188.

[6] An original source of information about the Hawthorne studies is Elton Mayo, *The Human Problems of an Industrial Civilization*, Viking Press, 1960. A useful summary and synthesis of these classic studies is found in Tosi and Carroll, *op. cit.*, pp. 46–48.

[7] Arnold S. Tannenbaum, *Social Psychology of the Work Organization*, Wadsworth, 1966, p. 74.

[8] Robert J. House, "T-Group Education and Leadership Effectiveness: A Review of the Empiric Literature and a Critical Evaluation," *Personnel Psychology*, Spring 1967, p. 2.

SUGGESTED READING

CARROLL, STEPHEN J., and TOSI, HENRY L. *Organizational Behavior*, St. Clair Press, 1977, Chapter 1.

CARVELL, FRED J. *Human Relations in Business*, 2nd ed., Macmillan, 1975, Chapters 1–3.

DAVIS, KEITH. *Human Behavior at Work*, 5th ed., McGraw-Hill, 1977.

GELLERMAN, SAUL W. *The Management of Human Relations*, Holt, Rinehart and Winston, 1966.

GEORGE, CLAUDE S., JR. *The History of Management Thought*, 2nd ed., Prentice-Hall, 1968.

PERROW, CHARLES. *Complex Organizations: A Critical Essay*, Scott, Foresman, 1972.

ROETHLISBERGER, FRITZ J., and DICKSON, W. J. *Management and the Worker*, Harvard University Press, 1939.

SANFORD, AUBREY C. *Human Relations Theory and Practice*, Merrill, 1973, Chapters 1–2.

TAYLOR, FREDERICK W. "The Principles of Scientific Management," in H. F. Merril (ed.), *Classics in Management*, American Management Association, 1960, pp. 82–113.

WREN, DANIEL A. *The Evolution of Management Thought*, Ronald Press, 1972.

PART TWO
WORKING WITH
INDIVIDUALS

An understanding of human relations obviously includes an understanding of individuals. This part of the book covers key aspects of human behavior that are likely to manifest themselves on the job. Among these complex aspects of behavior are motivation, creativity, stress, conflict, and office politics. Arbitrarily, we have decided not to include an overview of introductory psychology. Thus the reader will not find long discussions of how people learn, think, and perceive.

Although the focus here is on individuals one at a time, the reader must not forget that human behavior on the job is also influenced by group and organizational forces. For instance, a devious person might behave in a more straightforward manner if he or she were placed in a group that provided him or her with ample emotional support. In turn, that same group might be more supportive if the total organization in which it operates had higher morale.

2
JOB MOTIVATION

Learning Objectives

After reading and studying this chapter, you should be able to

1. Explain why high motivation does not always lead to good performance.
2. Understand the difference between job motivation and job satisfaction.
3. Explain how rewards or incentives can be systematically used to improve job performance.
4. Understand how people's expectations influence their work motivation.
5. Understand how job enrichment often leads to improved performance.
6. Develop a strategy for increasing your own level of motivation.

Scheduled to leave town the next week to begin his new position as regional sales manager, Brian was giving some last-minute tips to his replacement, Heidi. In giving her a rundown of his perceptions of the sales force, Brian made these parting comments:

"I've purposely left my opinion about Earl and Roger for last, because they are my extreme cases. Roger is a blockbuster. He'll keep on knocking on customer doors until every potential customer has closed for the day. He takes his paperwork home at night and is always caught up on everything. The best way to treat Roger is to get out of his way. He's on his way to becoming a big success in life.

"Earl is a different story. He has a tendency to start the day strong but by noon he's on the phone chatting with friends. He tells a good story about wanting to become a professional sales representative, but he doesn't back it up with hard work. You have to keep close tabs on Earl and make sure he's putting in an honest day's work."

Sales manager Brian was expressing two fundamental truths about job motivation. People vary extensively in how hard they work, and these differences influence how they are treated by their superiors. The concept of job motivation as used in this text refers to the amount of effort directed toward attaining goals desired by the organization. Many other concepts of job motivation also exist. One frequently quoted definition proposes that motivation deals with (1) the direction of behavior, (2) the strength of the response (effort) once a direction or course of action is chosen, and (3) the persistence or duration of the behavior exhibited by the person.[1]

A clue to why Roger works harder (has more motivation than) Earl is provided by the meaning each person attaches to work. Earl says that the primary reason he works is "Because I need money to live and have fun." Roger contends, "I want to make my mark in this world. My work is my way of telling the world who I am."

The few generalizations made about job motivation so far hint at the complexity of this subject. No human relations topic has received more attention in technical and popular writings. As an introduction to this topic, this chapter will help answer such questions as the following:

1. Why do people work?
2. Why do some people work harder than others?
3. How can you get yourself or others to work harder?

HARD WORK AND JOB PERFORMANCE

Motivation—the expenditure of effort toward achieving an objective the organization wants accomplished—is an important concept about people. Yet it does not fully explain why some people accomplish a lot of work while others are not nearly as productive. Clyde is a highly motivated writer, yet he is a complete flop as an author. He has written six short stories and one novel in the past three years, all of them unpublished. Clyde tries hard, but he does not succeed. Every year countless thousands of people try hard (are motivated) to bowl 300 in one game, but the reasons for their failure lie outside of motivation.

Performance is of much more importance to management than is motivation. The former refers to some outcome that can be used by others, such as units of production or service.[2] Performance can only happen when someone works either mentally or physically. Performance is the result of the application of effort. Technically, performance refers to the multiplication of effort and ability ($P = E \times A$).

Nonmotivational Characteristics.   Many well-motivated, hardworking individuals fail to achieve work objectives because they are deficient in such characteristics as problem-solving ability, skills, and appropriate training.[3] To perform a task well, you need to be bright enough to do the task and have the appropriate underlying skills. Such skills are usually acquired through training or direct job experience. Oscar's demise as a staff assistant is a case in point.

> Shortly after graduating from high school, Oscar secured a job as an office boy in a bank. His diligence, good work performance, and business-like appearance quickly won the attention of his supervisors. Within one year Oscar was promoted to a clerical position. Oscar continued to perform well, and gradually developed the idea that he would like to become a bank officer someday.
>
> Two years later Oscar received a promotion to the position of staff assistant. Now he was part of the exempt payroll—the equivalent of a professional position in his bank. Part of Oscar's responsibilities in his new position was to prepare written reports about the bank's consumer loan program. Oscar's reports were roundly criticized by his immediate superior. As hard as Oscar tried, his reports were still deficient. Finally, Oscar was transferred to a clerical position in another department because, in his supervisor's judgment, he was not properly trained for the position.
>
> Oscar failed in his first try as staff assistant, but his drive level prevented him from permanently failing. Through self-study combined with appropriate night courses, Oscar eventually developed the skills and abilities required of a staff assistant.

Group Factors. Another reason well-motivated people sometimes are not high producers is that the work group may influence them to hold back on their performance. Group norms may discourage some people from being superior performers even if they are well motivated. In such situations, the group acts as a constraining influence on the person (providing he or she is concerned about group acceptance).

> Frank was hired as a laboratory technician in a medical laboratory that ran diagnostic tests for individual physicians, group medical practices, and clinics. Wanting to elevate himself to a supervisory position, Frank worked up to nearly his capacity. Within one month, he was approached by Al, the informal group leader in the lab. Al admonished Frank, "Cut out the showboating. You're running more urine analyses than two of us combined. If you want to be one of us, cool off on that mass production mentality of yours."
>
> Frank gradually reduced his output about one third, reasoning (or rationalizing) that the work pace he originally set for himself could lead to diagnostic errors.

Technological Factors. The old adage, "You need the right tools to accomplish the job," sheds light on the relationship between motivation and performance. Unless people have the appropriate tools, machines, facilities, and equipment to accomplish their job, desire alone will not get the job done. Thus management, through its control of resources, creates the conditions whereby a well-motivated person can accomplish his or her work objectives.

> A plant manager showed a 10 percent decrease in salvage rate and a 40 percent decrease in delayed orders in comparison to the previous year. A personnel specialist from the home office visited his plant to talk about the significant improvements. "You must be taking those management development programs very seriously. It appears you're now doing a better job of motivating your staff."
>
> "Not particularly," replied the plant manager. "I finally got authorization to put in some of the equipment we've needed for years. Now a person can put in a decent day's work without having to worry about machine breakdown."

ARE YOU SATISFIED, MOTIVATED, OR BOTH?

Job satisfaction and motivation are not identical. Satisfaction refers to satisfaction of a need often resulting in a state of contentment; motivation refers to expending effort toward a goal. One way to visualize the relationship between satisfaction and motivation is by use of a four-way diagram indicating the extremes—highs and lows with the middle conditions omitted. These four different possibilities are shown in Figure 2.1.

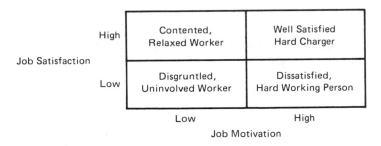

FIGURE 2.1
Four relationships between job satisfaction and motivation.

Contented, Relaxed Worker. Many people who have worked into a comfortable rut in a bureaucratic organization fall into this category. Some people derive job satisfaction from working in a relaxed, nonpressured atmosphere. If they had to work too hard, they would experience job dissatisfaction. Family businesses, too, have their share of contented individuals who expend very little effort toward achieving company goals.

Disgruntled, Uninvolved Worker. People who fit into this category are often under stress. They dislike their jobs yet work just hard enough to prevent being fired or receiving serious reprimands. Involuntary enlisted men often fall into this category. However, there are occasional people in managerial positions who dislike their jobs and are not particularly interested in working. Economic necessity (such as the need to pay bills) forces them to work.

Dissatisfied, Hardworking Person. Many people with a professional orientation work hard even if they are currently dissatisfied with their company, management, or working conditions. Often people with technical training find themselves in jobs that do not properly challenge their capacities. They nevertheless persevere, believing that conditions will improve or they can change jobs later. A professionally oriented person would not want to damage his or her reputation by performing poorly, even if a particular job was unsatisfying.

Well-Satisfied, Hard Charger. A person in this category is usually on the path toward self-fulfillment. A quarterback on a winning professional football team fits neatly into this category. Many branch managers and successful small-business persons are also well satisfied and hardworking. A young man with a small but busy and profitable landscaping business said of his work, "I happily work ten hours a day because landscaping is my thing."

JOB MOTIVATION AND HUMAN NEEDS

For several decades, need theories have been used to explain work motivation. In simplest form, people work to satisfy needs. You will thus work hard to satisfy needs of yours that are currently not being satisfied. The two most popular need theories will be described here because they are (1) historically significant and (2) the forerunners of newer approaches to underwork motivation.

Maslow's Self-Actualizing Model of People. Abraham Maslow[4] reasoned that human beings have an internal need pushing them on toward self-actualization (fulfillment) and personal superiority. However, before these higher-level needs are activated, certain lower-level needs must be satisfied. A poor person thus thinks of finding a job as a way of obtaining the necessities of life. Once these are obtained, that person may think of achieving recognition and self-fulfillment on the job. When a person is generally satisfied at one level, he or she looks for satisfaction at a higher level.

A major misinterpretation of Maslow's theory is that people behave as they do because of their quest to satisfy one particular need. In reality, many different motives are dominant at any one time. A draftsman may satisfy a number of needs (for instance, recognition, esteem, and self-satisfaction) by developing a design that works in practice.

Maslow arranged human needs into a five-level hierarchy. Each level refers to a group of needs—not one need for each level. These need levels are described next in ascending order.

Physiological needs refer to bodily needs, such as the requirements for food, water, shelter, and sleep. In general, most jobs provide ample opportunity to satisfy physiological needs. Nevertheless, some people go to work hungry or in need of sleep. Until that person gets a satisfying meal or takes a nap, he or she will not be concerned about finding an outlet on the job for creative impulses.

Safety needs include actual physical safety as a feeling of being safe from both physical and emotional injury. Many jobs frustrate a person's need for safety (policeman, policewoman, taxi cab driver). Therefore, many people would be motivated by the prospects of a safe environment. People who do very unsafe things for a living (such as racing-car drivers and tightrope walkers) find thrills and recognition more important than safety. Many people are an exception to Maslow's need hierarchy.

Love needs are essentially social or belonging needs. Unlike the two previous levels of needs, they center around a person's interaction with other people. Many people have a strong urge to be part of a group and to be accepted by that group. Peer acceptance is important in school and on the job. Many people are unhappy with their job unless they have the opportunity to work in close contact with others.

Esteem needs represent an individual's demands to be seen as a person of worth by others—and to himself or herself. Esteem needs are also called *ego* needs, pointing to the fact that people want to be seen as competent and capable. A job that is seen by yourself and others as being worthwhile provides a good opportunity to satisfy esteem needs.

Self-actualizing needs are the highest levels of needs, including the need for self-fulfillment and personal development. True self-actualization is an ideal to strive for, rather than something that automatically stems from occupying a challenging position. A self-actualized person is somebody who has become what he or she is capable of becoming. Few of us reach all our potential, even when we are so motivated.

Not every self-actualized person is a nationally or internationally prominent individual. A woman of average intelligence who attains an associate's degree and later becomes the owner–operator of an antique store might be self-actualized. Her potential and desire may both have been realized by self-employment as an antique dealer.

Maslow's need hierarchy appears to be a convenient way of classifying needs, but it has limited utility in explaining work behavior. Its primary value has been the fact that it highlights the importance of human needs in a work setting. When a manager wants to motivate another individual, he or she must offer that individual a reward that will satisfy an important need. Another criticism of the hierarchy approach is that career advancement may be the true factor underlying changes in need deficiencies.[5] Researchers found in one study that, as managers advance in organizations, their needs for safety decrease. Simultaneously, they experience an increase in their needs for affiliation with other people, achievement, and self-actualization.

Herzberg's Two-Factor Theory. Over two decades ago Frederick Herzberg reported research suggesting that some elements of a job give people a chance to satisfy higher-level needs.[6] Such job elements are called *satisfiers* or *motivators*. Although individuals and groups vary somewhat in the particular job elements that they find satisfying or motivating, they generally refer to the *content* (guts of) the job. Specifically, they are achievement, recognition, challenging work, responsibility, and the opportunity for advancement. Following this theory, if you want to motivate most people, provide them with the opportunity to do interesting work or receive a promotion.

In contrast, some job elements appeal more to lower-level needs; they tend to be noticed primarily by their absence. For instance, you may grumble about having to work in a hot, cramped office with no windows. Because of it you may experience job dissatisfaction or even be demotivated. But a cool, uncrowded office with a view of the ocean will probably not increase your level of job satisfaction or motivation.

Herzberg and his associates also noted that dissatisfiers relate mostly to the *context* (the job setting or external elements). Specifically, they are company policy and administration, supervision, physical working conditions, relationships with others on the job, status, job security, salary, and personal life.

The motivation–hygiene theory of Herzberg has had a considerable impact upon practicing managers. As discussed later in this chapter, job enrichment owes its origins to the thinking of Herzberg. Nevertheless, a large body of research evidence has accumulated which indicates that Herzberg's ideas are not as universally correct as originally thought. Abraham K. Korman observes that Herzberg erred by assuming that most, if not all, individuals are at the higher-level needs.[7] A complex, challenging, variable, and autonomous job is motivating for all people who are *operating at higher-level needs*. Many factory workers and clerical workers are operating at higher-level needs, but many are not.

Salary is a prime example of a job element that acts as a motivator for some people and a *hygiene* (used to prevent dissatisfaction) for others. When you currently are worried about money you will work hard, given the chance to earn the amount of money you want. Another confounding factor is that money satisfies so many different needs. Given enough money you can buy status, recognition, and at times even accomplishment. To illustrate, money can lead to accomplishment because it can buy education or a small business venture.

The theories of Maslow and Herzberg support each other. As shown in Table 2.1, satisfiers and motivators relate to the higher-level needs. Similarly, dissatisfiers and hygiene factors relate to lower-level needs. One major difference between the Maslow and Herzberg theories is that, according to the former, an appeal to any level of need can be a motivator. Herzberg contends that only appeals to higher-level needs can be motivational.

TABLE 2.1.   A COMPARISON OF THE MASLOW AND HERZBERG THEORIES.

Maslow	Herzberg
	Motivational Factors
Self-actualization	Work itself
	Achievement
	Responsibility
Self-esteem	Recognition
	Advancement
	Status
	Hygiene Factors
Love (belonging and affiliation)	Interpersonal relations
	Supervision–technical
Safety and security	Company policy and administration
Physiological needs	Job security
	Working conditions
	Salary
	Personal life

Whatever need theory of motivation you find useful, it is essential to recognize that needs are dynamic, not static. The same individual may have a different need hierarchy at different stages in his or her life. A man preoccupied with softball may want a nonchallenging job so that he can reserve most of his energy for softball competition. Later in life this same man may be searching for self-fulfillment on the job and thus be motivated by challenging work.

MEETING PEOPLE'S EXPECTATIONS (EXPECTANCY THEORY)

A realistic way of looking at job motivation is that how hard a person works essentially depends upon what he or she expects to get out of it. An elaborate theory of work motivation, expectancy theory, stems from this basic idea. One type of expectancy is the relationship between effort and performance. People expect that hard work will lead to the type of performance desired by the organization. Another type of expectancy is the relationship between performance and reward. People expect that good performance will result in some type of reward, or outcome, sanctioned by the organization.

Expectation also means that people assign subjective probabilities (or hunches) to the tie-in between effort and performance (or reward). If a bank guaranteed you $1.50 for every John F. Kennedy half-dollar you turned into them, you would probably work diligently collecting those half-dollars *if $1.50 satisfied an important need of yours* (a woman whose child needed milk would probably persist in finding Kennedy half-dollars under these conditions). Your belief in the bank might allow you to conclude that there was an almost 100 percent chance that you would receive $1.50 for each Kennedy half-dollar.

Figure 2.2 outlines a basic version of expectancy theory. Human needs figure prominently into this analysis of worker motivation. Six conditions or factors figure prominently into expectancy theory.[8] Applying Figure 2.2 to a live situation, assume that Todd, a computer programmer,

---

Person Will Expend Effort Under These Conditions

A. Hard work leads to favorable performance.
B. Favorable performance leads to a reward.
C. Reward satisfies an important need.
D. Need satisfaction is intense enough to make effort seem worthwhile.
E. Subjective probability is high that effort will lead to favorable performance and that favorable performance will lead to reward.
F. If probability of reward is low, payoff must be big.

FIGURE 2.2
Expectancy theory of job motivation.

is told by his boss, Shirley, that he has a good chance of being promoted to systems analyst. "However," notes Shirley, "we would have to see some good results from you for at least a year."

Condition A is met if Todd believes that he is capable of turning in a good performance. Todd probably believes that he has the capability of performing well in his job.

Condition B is met. Todd has learned that good performance will lead to a reward, promotion to systems analyst. But human motivation is more complex than that. Simply offering somebody a reward does not automatically lead to effort. If that were true, everybody would get an A in every course.

Condition C is also probably met. A promotion to systems analyst would satisfy several of Todd's needs: recognition, status, and perhaps even a step toward self-fulfillment.

Condition D might be met, depending upon how much Todd values (the *valence* he attaches to) a promotion. If working as a systems analyst is a big thrill for Todd, that would give him an intense amount of recognition, status, and so forth.

Condition E gets to the heart of expectancy theory. If Todd perceives Shirley and the company as being trustworthy, he would attach a high probability to two years of hard work leading to a promotion. Todd also bases his probability on the confidence he has in his own abilities. In his work as a computer programmer, he comes into contact with systems analysts. His self-estimate is that "I have just as much talent as those high-paid systems analysts. All I need is a little more experience." Thus Todd attaches a high probability to his chances of being able to (1) turn in a good performance as a computer programmer and, (2) do the work of a systems analyst, once promoted.

Condition F is important if expectancy theory is to explain much about human behavior. People will work long and hard at a task with a low probability of success if the potential payoff is enormous. Thousands of people work away diligently at an invention or a novel with the hope of instant fame and wealth. However, they also recognize that their chances of success are slim indeed. For example, only 1 in 300 first novels ever gets published.

In Todd's situation, he might work very hard toward becoming the president of his company, even though he knows that his chances are very small. Perhaps even 0.001!

Expectancy theory can be explained from a still more basic perspective. Assume that you want to motivate another person (or yourself). The chances of that person or you putting forth effort increase if answers are supplied to three basic questions:

1. What's in it for me?
2. How hard will I have to work to get what's in it for me?
3. What are my real chances of getting that reward if I do what you (or they) want?

BEHAVIOR MODIFICATION ON THE JOB (REINFORCEMENT THEORY)

Armed with knowledge about what job factors an individual finds rewarding, it is possible to influence people to repeat desired behavior. For instance, if your manager knows that you have a strong need for praise, he or she can increase the probability that you will work harder by giving you appropriate praise. Correspondingly, if he or she withholds praise when you do not work hard, this too may increase the probability of your working harder. Influencing behavior by dispensing rewards—and occasionally punishments—is the key ingredient to behavior modification.

A much publicized application of behavior modification to increase worker efficiency at Emery Air Freight Corporation has given impetus to other programs of this nature.[9] Supervisors are given training in knowing how and when to reinforce productive behavior. Applying behavior modification to problems of work motivation has a broad appeal because of its logical, step-by-step nature. Behavioral modification is now a field in itself, yet a few key principles help explain its basic nature.[10]

Choose an Appropriate Reward or Punishment. The Motivation theories discussed so far all point to the idea that the way to motivate people is to use a reward that is meaningful to each particular person. A status-hungry supervisor might work hard just for the opportunity to have a parking space adjacent to the president's parking space. A medical technician might boost her output if given the chance to do a laboratory workup on an occasional rare disease.

Each reward listed in Table 2.2 can be related back to the need categories mentioned earlier in the chapter. Most of these rewards relate to higher-level needs. People display individual differences with respect to which reward will satisfy which need. For instance, one culturally deprived person might feel virtually self-fulfilled by achieving the status symbol of membership in the company country club. Most people could only achieve self-fulfillment through a highly challenging work assignment. Despite these individual differences, a couple of illustrative generalizations are in order. The need for self-fulfillment or self-actualization might be met partially by rewards such as praise, recognition, favorable performance, receiving a favorable performance appraisal, challenging work assignments, or a promotion. Needs for belonging and affiliation might be met by approval, comradeship, or good co-workers.

When holding out positive rewards does not work, it is sometimes necessary to use mild forms of punishment (negative motivators) to motivate people. For instance, criticizing a salesman for attending baseball games during working days may be enough to make him stop such behavior. Motivation enters the picture, because it is hoped that he will now spend more time calling on accounts rather than wasting company time.

Table 2.2 lists a group of rewards and punishments that are feasible in a job environment.[11] Without a knowledge of potential rewards and punishments, it is difficult to make effective use of behavior modification. The last item listed under rewards, "desired behavior itself," requires careful attention. Critics of behavior modification contend that it is a system of manipulating defenseless people by dangling carrots in front of them (or sticks in back of them). When behavior modification is truly effective, good work itself becomes its own reward.

TABLE 2.2.   A CHECKLIST OF REWARDS AND PUNISHMENTS OF POTENTIAL USE IN A JOB SETTING.

Rewards	*Punishments*
Feedback on desired behavior	Feedback on undesired behavior
Praise, encouragement, and related rewards	Criticism
	Withdrawal of privileges
Approval	Probation
Recognition	Suspension
Comradeship	Fining
Job security	Undesirable assignment
Money	Demotion
Favorable performance appraisal	Withholding of any of the rewards listed to the left
Privy to confidential information	
Challenging work assignments	
Promotion	
Improved working conditions	
Capable and congenial co-workers	
Status symbols	
Desired behavior itself	

Assume that early in your working career you detest making out your income tax form. Yet the threat of punishment (fine, imprisonment, or both) motivated you to do an honest and accurate job of completing the required tax form. As the years passed, you may gradually take pride in preparing your own tax return, and perhaps delight in finding all your rightful deductions. What you originally did only at the threat of punishment (preparing your tax returns) ultimately becomes challenging work that is self-rewarding.

Find Some Constructive Behavior to Reinforce.   To help another person learn a new behavior, or to keep on repeating an already learned behavior, you have to begin somewhere. Assume that Ken, an individual working for you, keeps a desk so messy that he loses important files. Although you are not obsessed with orderliness, you recognize that Ken's sloppy work habits are interfering with productivity. Following the precepts of behavior modification, when Ken makes any progress toward keeping his desk in order, reinforce that behavior. For instance, if you notice that he no longer has old coffee cups on his desk, you might comment to Ken, "I can already see the improvement in your work area.

Keep up the progress." Although this process sounds elementary, *shaping* of behavior toward a planned-for objective increases the probability that larger-scale changes will be forthcoming.

Schedule Rewards Intermittently.   Rewarding a person for constructive work involves the dual consideration of (1) how frequently to give a positive reinforcement and (2) how close in time rewards should follow the constructive behavior. Behavior modification often fails as an approach to motivating people because these considerations are neglected.

Years of experimentation with behavior modification indicates that people should be rewarded often but not always. If you worked as a shoe store manager, it might be rewarding to you if on an occasional visit to your store your boss told you, "Everything looks just fine around here. The customers seem pleased. Your volume is up and the store looks first class. Keep this up and you'll notice a difference in your salary." However, if your boss gave you the same pep talk every week, the reward would lose its impact.

For maximum effectiveness, rewards (or punishments) should follow close in time to the motivated behavior. Assuming that money motivated you (a safe assumption for about 80 percent of the people studying human relations), you would be more likely to sustain your drive level if hard work led to quick cash. If you were selling life insurance, you would tend to keep on prospecting much more readily if you received your commission in one month rather than six.

A major criticism of behavior modification is that it manipulates people against their will. Perhaps this is true of retarded people in institutional settings, but most adult workers will only respond to rewards that they find satisfying or valuable. For instance, if you find the work of a finance company collection agent demotivating, the finance company is unlikely to come up with a reward strong enough to keep you going. Behavior modification at its best is simply a systematic way of dispensing rewards and punishments. A leader cannot escape modifying behavior and perform his or her job well.

MAKING JOBS MORE MEANINGFUL (JOB ENRICHMENT)

A direct application of much of the motivation theory we have discussed so far is to increase the productivity of workers by giving them the chance to perform more interesting tasks. By increasing the attractiveness of the *intrinsic* aspects of a job, less reliance need be placed on *extrinsic* factors (such as praise from superiors). However, the ideal combination is to increase both the extrinsic and intrinsic rewards associated with a job. An enriched job will not be looked upon with favor if the individual whose job is enriched perceives it as a substitute for a salary increase. Nor does an enriched job mean that people will no longer care about hygiene factors such as having properly ventilated work areas or clean washrooms.

Job enrichment can take a variety of forms, limited only by the imagination of those designing the jobs, the constraints of making a profit (or staying within budget), and the willingness of people to have enriched jobs. Three examples of job enrichment are the following:

1. An accountant is offered the opportunity to accompany his boss to staff meetings with higher levels of management. In the past the accountant analyzed figures for his boss, while his boss made presentations to the next level of management. In the first staff meeting the accountant attended, his boss said, "Now we are going to hear from Glen. He's the person closest to the figures. I don't see why I should serve as a funnel for his ideas. His figures might lose something in the translation." Glen's job satisfaction and work output increased with this new arrangement.

2. In an electronics company, final assembly of components was considered a different function from testing whether or not the components worked.[12] As an approach to job enrichment, assemblers were trained in and given responsibility for testing the devices. Previously, the testing was done by highly skilled test technicians.

After two months the testing performance of the assemblers equaled that of the technicians. The assemblers developed a more positive attitude toward their jobs. Improvement in job attitudes was also evident among the technicians. As a consequence of enrichment, they were now free to do less testing (which they considered routine) and more troubleshooting.

3. A publicity assistant in a major publishing company performed the detail work necessary to arrange publicity tours for the leading authors who published books with her firm. Although working in a glamour field, Beverly began to feel that working as an administrative "gopher" (go for coffee, go for airline reservations, and so forth) was unglamorous. After discussing the problem with her boss, Beverly was assigned the task of personally escorting a few of the top authors around on publicity tours, often in a rented limousine.

Beverly's spirits raised, and so did her productivity. She noted, "Now I'm getting to see what these TV and radio personalities are like in person. I feel I'm part of show biz."

Despite its logical appeal and sound psychological underpinnings, job enrichment has not been widely applied. Less than 5 percent of leading industrial companies had formal programs of job enrichment operating in 1974.[13] Mitchell Fein has noted that there are few, if any, genuine cases where job enrichment has been applied successfully to a large, heterogeneous work force. Most applications of job enrichment have been either commonsense job redesign or done with select groups of workers who are well motivated and satisfied anyway. Fein further notes that the intrinsic nature of the job is secondary to most production workers.[14] Their primary interest is in receiving external rewards (such as money), which enable them to lead a comfortable life.

The experience of General Motors with team approaches to automobile assembly illustrates how job enrichment does not always work as planned. (People working in small teams of generalists, rather than performing specialized, routinized functions, is considered the ultimate in job enrichment.) Stephen H. Fuller, vice-president of personnel administration, made these comments:[15]

> The GM assembly division has built Chevrolet vans for many years, and this has become a fairly simplified product. They took four men and women to a separate building and tried to educate them to build a van. They had the assistance of an engineer who worked with them to get them started. Building a van on the assembly line takes eight man-hours per man. At first these people were taking 13 to 14 man-hours. But eventually they got to the point where they could build the van in a little less than one and a half hours per man. Finally we put that van assembly job in Detroit with another team alongside the ordinary moving assembly line.
>
> Some people on the team soon decided they preferred working on the assembly line, and the department had to juggle its personnel until it had a group that liked teamwork. We intended to put the team building approach through the whole plant. But when we surveyed the workers, they just didn't want it.

In conclusion, job enrichment can work well in situations where workers want more interesting, exciting, or challenging work assignments. As a starting point, job enrichment should be voluntary. Those people who are motivated by extrinsic factors should be left to perform routinized, repetitive work.

HOW DO YOU MOTIVATE YOURSELF?

People often interpret theories about work motivation as basically a way to motivate others to accomplish their jobs. Of equal importance, a study of human motivation should help you in energizing yourself to accomplish worthwhile tasks. In general, applying the theories discussed in this chapter to yourself should help you to understand the conditions under which you are likely to work hard. Following are several specific suggestions about self-motivation.

Set Goals for Yourself.   Goals are fundamental to human motivation. Set yearly, monthly, weekly, daily, and sometimes even morning or afternoon goals for yourself. For example, "By noontime I will have emptied my in-basket and made one suggestion to improve safety practices in our shop." Longer-range, or life, goals can also be helpful in gathering momentum in spurring yourself on toward higher levels of achievement. However, these have to be buttressed by a series of short-range goals. You might have the long-range goal of becoming a prominent architect, but first it would be helpful to earn an A in a drafting course.

Identify and Seek Out Your Motivators.   Having read this chapter, combined with some serious introspection, you should be able to identify a few job elements that turn you on (your personal motivators). Next find a job that offers you them in ample supply. You might have good evidence from your past experience that the opportunity for close contact with people (comradeship or good interpersonal relationships) is a personal motivator. Find a job that involves working in a small, friendly department.

Owing to circumstances, you may have to take whatever job you can find, or you may not be in a position to change jobs. In that situation try to arrange your work so you have more opportunity to experience the reward(s) that you are seeking. Assume that solving difficult problems excites you, but your job is 85 percent routine. Develop better work habits so that you can more quickly take care of the routine aspects of your job. This will give you more time to enjoy the creative aspects of your work.

Get Feedback on Performance.   Few people can sustain a high level of drive without getting an objective or subjective opinion on how well they are doing. Even if you find your work exciting, you still need feedback. Photographers may be enamored with the intrinsic aspects of their work. Yet photographers, more than most people, want their work displayed. A display delivers the message, "Your work is good enough to show to other people."

If your boss or company does not recognize the importance of feedback (or simply forgets to tell people how they are doing), don't be hesitant to ask an occasional question such as:

"Is my work satisfactory so far?"

"How well am I doing in meeting the expectations of my job?"

"I haven't heard anything good or bad about my performance. Should I be worried?"

*Summary
of Key Points*

1. Job motivation refers to effort expended to meet an organizational objective.
2. High motivation does not inevitably lead to high performance. To achieve goals, intelligence, ability, and appropriate resources are also necessary.
3. Job satisfaction refers to feelings of contentment. Not all satisfied workers are well motivated and not all well-motivated people are satisfied.
4. A popular conception of motivation is that people work to satisfy needs. People are best motivated by the opportunity to satisfy higher-level needs, but there are wide individual differences in this regard.

5. A useful strategy for motivating people is to offer them meaningful incentives for achieving specific goals. People also need to know the likelihood that effort will lead to reward. Feedback on performance is also essential in motivating people.

6. Much of the motivation theory described in this chapter can be applied to yourself as well as others.

1. What are three job elements or factors that would make you work harder?

2. What human needs can be satisfied in a prison setting?

3. How could an instructor use behavior modification to improve the level of class performance?

4. How could students in a class use behavior modification to improve the instructor's level of performance?

5. Use expectancy theory to explain why some people bet on 200 to 1 shots at the racetrack or buy lottery tickets.

6. Think of a specific method whereby a "lazy" person could motivate himself or herself to work harder.

A Human Relations Incident
TWO SILVER DOLLARS FOR TWO MILLION DOLLARS

As plant personnel manager, your boss (the plant manager) often consults with you about problems of job motivation. One day he asks your opinion on a major program he has been mulling over for several weeks:

"I think I have an idea on how we can get this plant to raise productivity. For two years now we've had some kind of psychological barrier about shipping two million dollars worth of product in one month. Many times we have gotten close to shipping that figure but we fall down in the final few days.

"My plan is to set up an incentive system. If in any one month the plant ships two or more million dollars of product out the door, everybody in the plant will get two silver dollars. We'll mail them right to their homes so the whole family can share in their achievements. Every month our people reach two million dollars, they will get two more silver dollars. Everybody likes silver dollars and everybody likes recognition.

"But before I go ahead and announce the campaign, I want your opinion. Will my plan work?"

What would you tell your boss about his motivational scheme?

THE HARDWORKING, DISSATISFIED ENGINEER*

Gary Burns, manager of value analysis at Bristol Electronics, was conducting an informal six-month performance review with Sid Green, an engineer who had been promoted to Gary's group six months ago. The review showed high performance in terms of reaching agreed upon objectives, a fact that did not surprise Gary. Sid had come to the group with an impressive record as a person who achieved his objectives and was highly motivated. In addition to rating people on a management basis by objectives system, Bristol Electronics also included as a standard practice ratings of and comments about knowledge and motivation. A portion of the review session proceeded in this manner:

Gary Burns: Your overall review is very impressive. You accomplished what you set out to do, and you did it in a manner acceptable to the company. It's obvious that you quickly grasped the concepts so vital to our operation in value analysis. I see clear evidence that you have both good job knowledge and good potential for further growth in the company. Sid, how do you feel about my review of you?

Sid Green: Gary, thanks for all those nice things I hear you saying about me; I'm very pleased with the review. It's the job that's giving me trouble, not your evaluation of me. Frankly, I'm very frustrated in this job. When I accepted the promotion to your group, I had high hopes for an exciting assignment. I expected to do a lot more than collect information, crank out numbers, and distribute the numbers in report form every week. I wanted something big to strive for. Something that would provide me a little professional growth. Who wants to turn out projects that almost anybody could do? When I'm done with one of your assignments I get the feeling that any competent clerk could have done the same assignment equally well."

Gary was taken back by Sid's comments. It wasn't easy for him to believe that such a hardworking engineer could really be dissatisfied with his job. Recently, Gary had completed a short course in organizational behavior sponsored by his company. Intellectually, he could accept the principle that "motivation and satisfaction are different—there is no one-to-one correspondence between motivation and productivity." Yet, emotionally, he was not ready to accept this finding of behavioral science.

Gary felt that in general there was always a split between the information that the company said was important and the information that was actually reflected in management decisions. It was the same for quantitative decision making. The company would beat the drums for using sophisticated methods of making objective decisions. When it came time for a decision, they would revert to intuition. In Gary's evaluation, they seemed

* Charles R. Garbowski conducted the research for this case and is responsible for most of its writing.

to be saying that this is the way it should be done; however, *this* is the way we do it. Gary shared some of his thoughts with Sid:

"It's still hard for me to accept the fact that motivation and satisfaction can really be different for you or anybody else. How can you work so hard yet not like your job? I worked myself up from very humble beginnings. Getting ahead was the big carrot in front of me. Getting ahead in the world was my source of satisfaction. If it satisfies me to get ahead, and I have to be motivated in order to be satisfied, then motivation and satisfaction are the same thing. Anyone who is motivated should therefore also be satisfied.

"Sid, maybe you are just an exceptional case. Anyway, you're the first living example I've ever seen of a person who worked so hard and so well, yet wasn't satisfied."

His managerial curiosity heightened by this incident with Sid Green, Gary decided to follow his new insights through to a logical conclusion. Three weeks later Sid was given a special project in addition to his normal reporting duties. His assignment was to review a particular area that had been included in his reports and had been added to the reporting systems of the value analysis group only a year ago.

Sid was to review the areas so he would know how and where the information came from, the forms the information was summarized on, and to audit the counts to ensure reliable reporting of actual events. Sid's analysis was also to identify any deviations from what was supposed to be happening, potential trouble areas, and make recommendations. Once the review and audit were completed, it was distributed to the people concerned. Gary made sure Sid's analysis was included in that week's progress report which listed significant actions taken by his group.

Gary followed up this assignment with another additional task. Sid's next project was a joint project with another member of the group on fork-truck utilization. Again, this was in conjunction with Sid's normal reporting tasks. However, Sid now perceived the reporting function quite differently since he discovered all the detail involved in the reporting system. Sid and his partner had to first set up a reporting system to determine how many trucks were being used and for how long. Detailed reports were kept on each truck in the maintenance department as to how often each truck required repair, the type of repair, and the probable cause. Four months were required to complete this project. Based upon the limited amount of information collected, combined with information that had been haphazardly collected in the past, Sid and his partner entered their findings into a formal report.

Sid's report was similar to previous reports with the important exception that this type of project lent itself to making recommendations that included dollar figures. Based on their recommendations, which ranged from specifying hoses (leaks were a major cause of downtime, necessitating keeping additional trucks available) to considering a different manufacturer with an excellent repair record that sold a less expensive truck, the company was able to realize an annual savings of $250,000.

When Sid's form review took place six months later, he was pleased to relate to his manager the satisfaction that he now derived from his work compared to his feelings six months before. Gary was both pleased and amused that his subordinate was satisfied with his work and still a productive person making an important contribution to the company. He was also pleased that he had been able to emotionally understand that motivation and satisfaction are different.

1. How generally applicable is the observation that motivation and job satisfaction are different? Are there any particular groups of people to whom this generalization fits (or does not fit) well?

2. What concerns do you have that Gary Burns is establishing an awkward precedent? Might other engineers in the department conclude that a sure way to obtain a more interesting job is to perform your job well but gripe?

3. Is Gary naive in his beliefs about human behavior? What is the opinion of experienced managers about the relationship between motivation and productivity?

4. Was Sid being unreasonable in complaining about his position after working in the department only six months? Explain your reasoning.

5. How else might Gary have handled Sid's complaints about job dissatisfaction? Do you agree with Gary's approach (giving him a challenging assignment)?

FOOTNOTES

[1] John P. Campbell, Marvin D. Dunnette, Edward E. Lawler III, and Karl E. Weick, *Managerial Behavior, Performance, and Effectiveness*, McGraw-Hill, 1970, p. 340.

[2] Stephen J. Carroll and Henry L. Tosi, *Organizational Behavior*, St. Clair Press, 1977, p. 128.

[3] Our discussion of these factors borrows from two sources: Henry L. Tosi and Stephen J. Carroll, *Management: Contingencies, Structure, and Process*, St. Clair Press, 1976, pp. 127–136; and Edgar F. Huse and James L. Bowditch, *Behavior in Organizations: A Systems Approach to Managing*, Addison-Wesley, 1973, pp. 52–55.

[4] Virtually exery text in organizational behavior, human relations, or introduction to management has a discussion of Maslow's need hierarchy. An original source is Abraham Maslow, *Motivation and Personality*, Harper & Row, 1954, p. 13 cf.

[5] Douglas T. Hall and K. E. Nougaim, "An Examination of Maslow's Need Hierarchy in an Organizational Setting," *Organizational Behavior and Human Performance*, Feb. 1968, pp. 12–35.

[6] Herzberg is also quoted in the general sources mentioned in footnote 4. An original source is Frederick Herzberg, *Work and the Nature of Man*, World Publishing Co., 1966.

[7] A good synthesis of the research criticism of Herzberg's theory is found in Abraham K. Korman, *Organizational Behavior*, Prentice-Hall, 1977, pp. 140–145.

[8] An original exposition of expectancy theory is Victor H. Vroom, *Work and Motivation*, Wiley, 1964. The six conditions mentioned here follow the

reasoning presented in Ross A. Webber, *Management: Basic Elements of Managing Organizations*, Irwin, 1975, p. 97. An excellent technical overview of expectancy theory is George P. Wieland and Robert A. Ullrich, *Organizations: Behavior, Design, and Change*, Irwin, 1976, pp. 148–157.

[9] *Organizational Dynamics*, "At Emery Air Freight Positive Reinforcement Boosts Performance," Winter 1973, pp. 41–50.

[10] An exposition of the principles of behavior modification most applicable to job motivation is found in Andrew J. DuBrin, *Managerial Deviance: How to Handle Problem People in Key Jobs*, Mason/Charter, 1976, pp. 126–133.

[11] *Ibid.*, Chapters 7 and 8.

[12] David Sirota and Alan D. Wolfson, "Job Enrichment: Surmounting the Obstacles," *Personnel*, July–Aug. 1972, p. 14.

[13] Fred Luthans and William E. Reif, "Job Enrichment: Long on Theory, Short on Practice," *Organizational Dynamics*, Winter 1974, p. 30.

[14] Mitchell Fein, "Job Enrichment: A Reevaluation," *Sloan Management Review*, Fall 1973, pp. 69–88.

[15] David Cluterbuck, "General Motors Strives to Motivate Its Workers," *International Management*, Jan. 1975, p. 37.

SUGGESTED READING

CASS, EUGENE L., and ZIMMER, FREDERICK G. (eds.). *Man and Work in Society*, Van Nostrand Reinhold Co., 1976.

DuBRIN, ANDREW J. *Managerial Deviance: How to Handle Problem People in Key Jobs*, Mason/Charter 1976, Chapters 6–8.

FEIN, MITCHELL. "Job Enrichment: A Reevaluation," *Sloan Management Review*, Fall 1973, pp. 69–88.

HAMNER, W. CLAY. "Reinforcement Theory and Contingency Management in Organizational Settings," in Henry L. Tosi and W. Clay Hamner, *Organizational Behavior and Management: A Contingency Approach*, St. Clair Press, 1974, p. 112.

HAMNER, W. CLAY. "Worker Motivation Programs: Importance of Climate, Structure, and Performance Consequences," in W. Clay Hamner and Frank L. Schmidt, *Contemporary Problems in Personnel*, St. Clair Press, 1974, pp. 280–308.

HAWORTH, J. T., and SMITH, M. A. (eds.). *Work and Leisure*, Princeton Book Company, 1976.

HUNT, J. G., and HILL, J. W. "The New Look in Motivation Theory for Organizational Research," in Henry L. Tosi and W. Clay Hamner, *Organizational Behavior and Management: A Contingency Approach*, St. Clair Press, 1974, pp. 226–239.

LAWLER, EDWARD E., III. *Pay and Organizational Effectiveness*, McGraw-Hill, 1971.

MASLOW, ABRAHAM H. *Motivation and Personality*, Harper & Row, 1954.

YUKL, GARY A., LATHAM, GARY P., and PURSELL, ELLIOT D. "The Effectiveness of Performance Incentives Under Continuous and Variable Ratio Schedules of Reinforcement," *Personnel Psychology*, Summer 1976, pp. 221–231.

3
JOB CREATIVITY

Learning Objectives

After reading and studying this chapter, you should be able to

1. Explain the concept of creativity.
2. Develop preliminary insight into your own level of creative potential.
3. Identify several types of creativity.
4. Describe several methods of improving job creativity.
5. Develop a plan for improving your own creativity.
6. Understand how organizational climate influences creativity.

Creativity helps you succeed in a wide variety of jobs, including jobs that are basically routine. A creative person, one who has the ability to process information in such a way that the result is new, original, and meaningful, is a valuable contributor.[1] For example, a clerk in the circulation department of an eastern newspaper noticed that, although the cost of first class mail kept increasing, the number of complaints about service also kept increasing. His conclusion was not to figure out a way of revamping the postal system but to have his newspaper take over part of the postal system's job. Subsequently, the newspaper he worked for was the first to insert advertising flyers previously sent by mail inside their newspaper. That simple combination of ideas helped that individual eventually to become circulation director.

As a prelude to our examination of the job-related aspects of creativity, two misconceptions need to be dispelled. One myth is that people can be accurately classified as creative or uncreative. In fact, creativity is like height, intelligence, and strength. People vary considerably in these dimensions, but everybody has *some* height, *some* intelligence, and *some* strength. Creativity appears to be normally distributed.

Another misconception about creativity is that it can only be exercised in a limited number of fields, such as physical science, the arts, and photography. An accurate analysis reveals that creativity can be exercised in any field and in almost any setting. You can be creative in such diverse places as an art design studio or on a farm.

CREATIVITY AND JOB PERFORMANCE

In Chapter 2 it was mentioned that high motivation does not inevitably lead to high job performance. A similar situation exists for creativity. Raw creativity alone may not necessarily lead to productive results. Creativity needs to be buttressed by support from the organization and good follow-through in order to obtain good results. A noted management writer, Ross A. Webber, draws a useful distinction between creativity and *innovation*.[2]

> Because creativity is merely the generation of new ideas, much of it exists. Real innovation is rarer, for it includes the application of any idea, borrowed or original, to a situation where it has not been employed before. Innovation, then, is creativity followed by entrepreneurial management action to the point where it has an economic impact. Indeed, the creator and the innovator may be different persons, for the creator may lack the desire or means to innovate. . . .

Webber has put into formal words what marketing executives have known for many years. Creative ideas are plentiful. Many people can think of farfetched ideas for new products or services, but few people have the skills and/or courage to carry these ideas through to fruition. Another reason that raw creativity alone is a mixed blessing is that your creative idea may be something that has been unsuccessfully tried in the past. Unless you are familiar with other people's past experiences in your field, you may be wasting time on pursuing ideas that have already proved unworkable. Ramsey, a marketing research associate, is a case in point.

> Ramsey requested a meeting with his new boss, Mike, to discuss his job situation. With considerable emotion he told Mike, "One thing I didn't like about my last boss is that he discouraged creativity. I fed him all sorts of good ideas for moving this company in a new direction, yet nothing ever happened to them. I think that maybe even the company has no room for creativity. Three years ago I said we should be marketing an instant camera or finding a way to computerize picture taking. I told Ted that we should develop a camera to take identification pictures low enough in cost so every supermarket and bank could own one.

"In fact I have a file of over fifty suggestions I have given the company in the last three years and not one has been acted upon."

Sympathizing but not agreeing, Mike reported his conversation with Ramsey to his former superior, Ted. Ted replied, "Mike, I wish the best for Ramsey. Maybe you can help him. I wish he would take one of his ideas and do something with it besides throw it in somebody else's lap. His idea about computerizing picture taking would have cost us about fifteen million dollars in developmental and startup costs. Even if we had invested the money, we would have no way of forecasting the demand for such a product. Ramsey has to learn that there is a lot more to business than blurting out a half-processed idea. It takes a lot of time and money to do justice to even a simple idea."

WHAT IS YOUR CREATIVE POTENTIAL?

A logical starting point in studying creativity is to gain a tentative awareness of your creative potential in comparison to other people. Psychologists have developed standardized tests (not for use by the general public) to measure creativity. Here we shall confine our measurement of creative potential to several illustrative exercises. Do not be overly encouraged or dejected by any results you achieve on these tests. They are designed to give only preliminary insights into whether or not your thought processes are similar to those of creative individuals.[3]

Unusual Uses Test. Write down ten uses for each of the following objects, allowing yourself five minutes per object.

Red brick
Paper clip
Pencil eraser
Household spoon

A glance at several answers given by other people might be helpful to you in examining your own creative potential. A guidance counselor thought of these uses for a red brick: "Doorstop, bookend, paperweight, grind up and make stones for an aquarium, use to settle marital disputes, put behind rear wheel of car when fixing flat, step for reaching on top of refrigerator, insulator for putting pizza on table, newspaper weight when reading at beach or lake."

A college student thought of these uses for a paper clip: "Tie clip, abortion instrument for very small girl, ear cleaner, roach clip, bookmark, typewriter key cleaner, temporary screwdriver, cocktail stirrer, toothpick, money clip."

A purchasing agent thought of these uses for an eraser: "Something to play with while tense, ear plug, toy for kitten, small wire insulator, pellet for harmless gun, poker chip, goldfish bowl decorative float, something to have a catch with, low-calorie chewing gum, place in mouth instead of smoking."

A shoe salesman thought of these uses for a spoon: "Screwdriver, plant and gardening tool, child spanker, shoehorn, sharpen and use for weapon, infant toy, discharge electricity before shaking hands with another person on thick carpet, drumstick, use as a catapult for small objects by pressing quickly at large end, postman signal for rural mail-box."

Interpret your scores in this manner: if you were able to arrive at close to ten uses for each object (other than repeating the obvious, such as using a paper clip for a tie clip), you show good creative potential. If the entire task left you stymied, you need work in loosening up yourself intellectually. Keep on trying exercises of this nature (and study the rest of this chapter).

Unusual Consequences Test. Anticipate at least three of the consequences if the following things were to happen:

> We all had a third arm sticking out from our stomach.
>
> The law of gravity did not work on Monday.
>
> Weeds became the only digestible food for human beings.

Here are some typical answers to these unlikely events: The "third arm" question elicits responses from mature adults such as these: "Tailors would go crazy modifying shirts, sweaters, and overcoats." "A person could grab the other guy by the belt while punching him with his two other hands." "Shoplifting would be an even bigger problem. People could be lifting goods while distracting a sales clerk with their own two hands."

The "law of gravity" question troubles people, yet brings forth responses such as, "People would have to stay home on Mondays to hold on to their belongings." "All cars would have to be off the streets of San Francisco on Sunday night. Otherwise, they might roll up the hills." "You could do all your cleaning on Monday's because it would be easy to lift up heavy furniture." "Don't sweat it. There would only be one of these Monday's. The world would come to an end after the first Monday without gravity."

The "weed" question puzzles and concerns many people. A sample of the answers: "The A & P would go out of business forever." "People who owned old vacant lots would suddenly become rich. At the same time all the grass-people from the suburbs would be cursing themselves for having spent so much of their lives getting rid of weeds." "Every pet in this country who wanted it would be fed a diet of the best table foods. At least until the supply ran out."

If you were not able to think of more than one consequence to these unlikely events, it could mean that you need considerable practice in taking a suppositional ("what if") point of view. If consequences came readily to you, it shows a healthy degree of flexibility in your thinking.

Word Hints to Creativity.[4]   The object of this exercise is to find a fourth word that is related to *all* three words listed below. For example, what word is related to these?

cookies   sixteen   heart   _____

The answer is "sweet." Cookies are sweet; sweet is part of the word "sweetheart" and part of the phrase "sweet sixteen."

What word is related to these words?

poke   go   molasses   _____

Answer: slow.

Now try these words:

1. surprise	line	birthday	_____
2. base	snow	dance	_____
3. rat	blue	cottage	_____
4. nap	rig	call	_____
5. golf	foot	country	_____
6. house	weary	ape	_____
7. tiger	plate	news	_____
8. painting	bowl	nail	_____
9. proof	sea	priest	_____
10. maple	beet	loaf	_____
11. oak	show	plan	_____
12. light	village	golf	_____
13. merry	out	up	_____
14. cheese	courage	oven	_____
15. bulb	house	lamp	_____

If you were able to think of the "correct" fourth word for ten or more of these combinations of words, your score compares favorably to that of creative individuals. A very low score (about one, two, or three correct answers) suggests that performing such remote associations is not yet a strength of yours. Here are the answers:

1. party	5. club	9. high	13. make
2. ball	6. dog	10. sugar	14. Dutch
3. cheese	7. paper	11. floor	15. light
4. cat	8. finger	12. green	

Creative Personality Test.   The following test will help you determine if certain aspects of your personality are similar to those of a creative individual. Since our test is for illustrative and research purposes, proceed with caution in mind. Again, this is not a standardized psychological instrument. Such tests are not reprinted in general books.

Directions: Answer each of the following statements as "mostly true" or "mostly false." We are looking for general trends; therefore, do not be concerned if you answer true if they are mostly true and false if they are mostly false.

		Mostly True	*Mostly False*
1.	Novels are a waste of time. If you want to read, read nonfiction books.	_____	_____
2.	You have to admit, some crooks are very clever.	_____	_____
3.	People consider me to be a fastidious dresser. I despise looking shaggy.	_____	_____
4.	I am a person of very strong convictions. What's right is right; what's wrong is wrong.	_____	_____
5.	It doesn't bother me when my boss hands me vague instructions.	_____	_____
6.	Business before pleasure is a hard and fast rule in my life.	_____	_____
7.	Taking a different route to work is fun, even if it takes longer.	_____	_____
8.	Rules and regulations should not be taken too seriously. Most rules can be broken under unusual circumstances.	_____	_____
9.	Playing with a new idea is fun even if it doesn't benefit me in the end.	_____	_____
10.	So long as people are nice to me, I don't care why they are being nice.	_____	_____
11.	Writing should try to avoid the use of unusual words and word combinations.	_____	_____
12.	Detective work would have some appeal to me.	_____	_____
13.	Crazy people have no good ideas.	_____	_____
14.	Why write letters to friends when there are so many clever greeting cards available in the stores today?	_____	_____
15.	Pleasing myself means more to me than pleasing others.	_____	_____
16.	If you dig long enough, you will find the true answer to most questions.	_____	_____

is as follows:

1. Mostly False
2. Mostly True
3. Mostly False
4. Mostly False
5. Mostly True
6. Mostly False

7. Mostly True
8. Mostly True
9. Mostly True
10. Mostly True
11. Mostly False
12. Mostly True

13. Mostly False
14. Mostly False
15. Mostly True
16. Mostly False

Give yourself a plus one for each answer you gave in agreement with the keyed answers.

How Do You Interpret Your Score?   As cautioned earlier, this is an exploratory test. Extremely high or low scores are probably the most meaningful. A score of 12 or more suggests that your personality and attitudes are similar to that of a creative person. A score of 5 or less suggests that your personality is dissimilar to that of a creative person. You are probably more of a conformist (and somewhat categorical) in your thinking, at least at this point in your life. Don't be discouraged. Most people can develop in the direction of becoming a more creative individual.

TYPES OF CREATIVITY

As suggested by the several ways of measuring it, creativity manifests itself in different forms. When one person says he or she is creative, he or she may have something different in mind than another person making the same claim. The first person might be skillful in generating new ideas; the second might have a knack for recombining the ideas of others. We shall consider four types of creativity.[5]

Origination.   Most people think that innovative or original thinking is synonymous with creativity. Thinking of something new is an important manifestation of creativity although it is not the only form of creativity. Newness, of course, is difficult to prove. Patent attorneys hassle for many months over whether or not a given invention can be considered *new*. What many people consider new is simply a variation of something old— "old wine in new bottles."

   To originate an idea, you have to break with tradition, exemplified by the development of instant photography or the ball-point pen. When you do produce an original idea, your innovation may be resisted by your co-workers and superiors. People have a tendency to reject most ideas that depart radically from tradition. However, if you persevere, you might think of the modern-day equivalent of a Model T Ford or canned beer.

Synthesis.   Combining ideas from several different sources and integrating them into a useful pattern is not only a worthwhile contribution; it is also a key manifestation of creativity. Perhaps more people become rich and famous from synthesis than from origination. David Reuben's first book, *Everything You Always Wanted to Know About Sex But Were Afraid to Ask* (which sold about 8 million copies) is a germane example. Reuben's was not the first popularly written sex manual but a synthesis of currently available information. Reuben's ticket to success (his books still sell in the millions) was synthesis, not origination.

Combining computer knowledge with medical knowledge about symptoms of various diseases has led to advances in medical diagnosis. By this synthesis of computer science and clinical judgment, a new field has been created. Diagnosis of medical problems is now becoming a much more objective process because of computerization.

Extension.   Sound innovations are sometimes increased in value by the process of extending their boundaries. Hicks and Gullett note that "much research and development work is concerned with expanding a previously recognized discovery."[6] A breakthrough scientific idea, the laser beam, has now been extended into many different areas of application, such as drilling holes in metals and eye surgery. Another example is the use of atomic fission not only for nuclear warheads but also for home and industrial sources of power.

A less exotic example of *extension* is the search for low-cost plastic components for a variety of products. The original idea of replacing key metal parts with plastic has now been extended into thousands of every-day applications, such as plumbing supplies and fishing equipment.

Duplication.   Many people live by the credo "If you can't be original, at least copy good ideas." Many business firms are creative in the sense that they introduce products which are new to them but borrowed from others. Much of the growth of Japanese manufacturing stems from duplication, rather than origination. One way for any person to behave creatively on the job is to collect ideas from other people, and sort out those which you believe could be applied to your job. For instance, one junior executive earned himself a promotion and a raise by convincing his company to recycle scrap parts from its manufacturing activities. Asked by a friend how he thought of such a brilliant idea, the young man replied, "I read about it in the business section of the local newspaper."

Combined Types of Creativity.   Many instances of creativity are really a combination of two, three, or four of the basic types of creativity. If this were not the case, patent attorneys would have much less work to perform. A few years ago an unidentified person thought of the idea of offering a new service to the public, a traveling van that made emergency repairs and routine servicing (tune-ups, tire changes, and so forth). An automobile service station that made house calls was in a sense something new, something synthesized, something extended, and something duplicated.

Offering the service while people were working (by driving the van to company parking lots) was new, but house calls and road service were certainly old. An element of extension was present because emergency automobile service has been in existence for a long time.

CHARACTERISTICS OF CREATIVE PEOPLE

To understand creativity, you have to understand creative people. A wide range of studies about creative people (including some of the author's experiences in working with creative people) points toward one distinguishing characteristic. Creative people in general are more emotionally loose and open than their less creative counterparts. Thus the creative person is more loose than tight, open than closed, flexible than rigid.

Ten conclusions about the creative individual can be reached based upon extensive studies and observations.[7] Several of these characteristics support the popular stereotype of the creative person as somewhat of a maverick, both intellectually and socially.

1. Creative people tend to be bright rather than brilliant. Extraordinarily high intelligence is not required to be creative, but creative people are good at generating many different ideas in a short period of time.
2. Creative people tend to have a positive self-image; they feel good about themselves.
3. Creative people are emotionally expressive and sensitive to the world around them and the feelings of others.
4. Creative people, almost by definition, are original in their thinking.
5. Creative people tend to be interested in the nature of the problem itself; they are stimulated (motivated) by challenging problems.
6. Creative people usually suspend judgment until they have collected ample facts about a problem. Thus they are more reflective than impulsive.
7. Creative people are frequently nonconformists. They value their independence and do not have strong needs to gain approval from the group.
8. Creative people lead a rich, almost bizarre, fantasy life. They are just "crazy" enough to serve their creative ends.
9. Creative people tend to be flexible and not authoritarian. Faced

with a problem, they reject black and white (categorical) thinking and look for the nuances.

10. Creative people are more concerned with meanings and implications of problems than with the small details.

Having read these characteristics about creative people, think about how well they fit your personality. If it does not appear that you have as many of these characteristics as you would like, pessimism is not in order. Techniques are available that can help an individual develop his or her creative potential (assuming you want to become more creative).

IMPROVING YOUR CREATIVITY

Creativity can sometimes be improved through formal training programs. At other times, do-it-yourself techniques can be equally beneficial. Here we shall present information about both self-help and formal techniques. Even if you were to attend a creativity improvement program, self-discipline would still be required for the benefits to be long lasting.

Loosen up Emotionally and Intellectually. Methods of creativity improvement are generally based on the same underlying principle: in order to become more creative, you have to loosen up emotionally and intellectually. As long as you remain a "tight" individual, it is difficult to give free rein to your creative potential. Alcohol and other drugs sometimes provide the user with a temporary state of emotional looseness that can conceivably stimulate the creative process. However, the loss of intellectual alertness usually more than offsets the advantage of emotional looseness.

Overcoming perceptual blocks is a mechanism by which a person can become emotionally and intellectually looser.[8] People frequently cannot solve problems in a creative manner because they are bound by preconceived ideas, which tend to block out new ways of looking at familiar things (a perceptual block). Until a person can look beyond the normal way of doing things, he or she will probably not find a creative solution.

Larry was marketing head of a building maintenance firm. The service they offered was to perform maintenance for small office buildings. Larry and the president, June, suddenly realized that they needed to cut down the cost of doing business in order to stay profitable. June and Larry both agreed that they could not pay their maintenance help any lower wages, nor could they get by with fewer workers.

In an agonizing two-hour cost-cutting conference, Larry experienced a sudden insight. Said he, "Why do we need sales representatives? We have three people on our staff earning about $18,000 each including benefits. Why not have one person arranging telephone conferences with business prospects working right out of our office?"

The plan worked. Larry spent four hours per day on the telephone soliciting new business and servicing old business (mostly asking about the quality of service and handling complaints). One salesman took over as a field supervisor on two major contracts. Another quit, and the third salesman was terminated.

To Larry and June, the most surprising offshoot from their new plan was that prospects preferred a phone call to an in-person appearance from a sales representative. It consumed less of their time.

Discipline Yourself to Think Creatively. Self-discipline is required for all forms of self-development, including the improvement of your creativity.[9] An important starting point toward becoming more creative is to develop the attitude that creativity is both important and desirable. Faced with a job or personal problem calling for a creative response, one effective starting point is to sit quietly with a pencil and pad and begin to generate possible solutions. For example, "How can I prove to my boss that I'm worthy of a 10 percent salary increase?"[10] Few people have developed the self-discipline to concentrate on a problem in this manner for more than a few moments at a time.

The type of exercises designed to measure your creativity described earlier in the chapter can also develop effective approaches for improving creativity. By disciplining yourself to perform such exercises as "Think of ten uses for a brick," you will develop more fluency in your thinking. After conducting these warm-up exercises, you should be able to tackle job problems requiring creativity more readily. One example would be, "What are five different things my laboratory could do with our used chemicals?"

Brainstorming. This widely known technique is used both as a creativity training program and as a method of finding solutions to real-life problems.[11] In simplest form, a group of people assemble in a room and more or less simultaneously call out solutions to a problem facing the organization. Any group member is free to enhance or "piggyback" upon the contribution of any other member of the group. Anything goes, however bizarre it sounds at the time. Later, somebody may be assigned the task of sorting out and editing some of the unrefined ideas.

Two men and a woman assembled to think of a method of introducing opposite-sexed people that could be offered as a service to unattached individuals. They were hoping to think of a matchmaking service that was not simply a duplication of computer dating or a singles club. Here are some of the ideas that flowed from the brainstorming session:

"Hold a two-dollar purchase raffle. If they lose they get nothing. If they win they get a chance to date one of us."

"What about phone-a-date? Whenever you're lonely call us and we'll immediately give you a number of another lonely person to call. Each number costs four dollars."

"What about spin-a-date? You get about fifty fellows and gals together. Each person pays five dollars and gets assigned a number. You then spin the roulette wheel three times. You then go over and introduce yourself to the person whose number you have spun. Males spin the female wheel and females spin the male wheel to avoid wasting each other's time."

"What about video taping brief interviews with people who enroll in our dating service. Instead of simply reading about another person you get a chance to see him or her on the video tape. That way it's one step beyond a blind date."[12]

Whether brainstorming in a group has any particular advantage over private brainstorming sessions is an issue of considerable debate. Groups differ so much from one another that research results from one study to another are difficult to evaluate. Thomas J. Bouchard, a person long associated with research about brainstorming, has shown that under the right conditions brainstorming is more effective than individual methods in arriving at solutions to problems. One of the *right* conditions is that people make their contributions in sequence rather than simultaneously ("free for all").

By adding the sequencing procedure to typical brainstorming instructions, group performance becomes as good as individual performance. Even if group solutions were slightly inferior to individual solutions, they might be chosen by some organizations. People will be more willing to implement a solution to a problem that stems from a group meeting than from a unilateral decision. Bouchard makes the following analysis:[13]

> Why does group sequencing procedure have such a profound effect?
> The procedure makes it difficult for any one individual to dominate the discussion (often with trivia).
> It forces the discussion to stay directly on the problem, and in such a way that the group's thought processes are channeled along relevant lines.
> It promotes and forces greater involvement by all members.
> It does not allow, or at least makes it more difficult for, one member to take the role of expert and inhibit the performance of other members.

Synectics. Another popular way of improving creativity is a group of methods developed by William J. Gordon of Synectics, Inc.[14] The synectics process involves two complementary procedures: (1) making the strange familiar, and (2) making the familiar strange. Making the strange familiar means developing an understanding of a problem. For instance, how would you feel if you were a drain pipe that kept on clogging? Once the problem is understood, it is made strange again by adding an unusual twist. In the drain pipe problem it might be assumed that water will flow up the pipe without an outside force. A crucial part of the synectics method is the *personal analogy* method; the person must psychologically identify with an object (as with the drain pipe). Here is an example:

If the problem is finding a new way to open a particular kind of container, each member of the group in turn plays the role of the container (bottle, box, can), and the remaining members question him (or her) about the best way to get in.

An exchange between two participants in the above exercise might go this way: "Hey, you container head, what's a good way to open you?"

"You might try unzipping me or popping me open from the top."

"But then how would I tighten you back up when I was finished with you for awhile?"

"Good point. I had better think of another solution."

THE CREATIVE CLIMATE

To achieve creative solutions to problems (and to think of new opportunities) an organization needs more than creative people. Creativity is the combined influence of creative people working in an environment that encourages (or at least does not discourage) creativity.

Brad, an engineering technologist, joined a screw machine company as a production engineer. After three months on the job he informed the head of manufacturing (a self-made man) that he had a good idea for reducing turnover and enhancing worker interest. "Why don't we experiment a little with job enrichment or at least job rotation?" said the production engineer. His boss replied, "Take those dumb college ideas of yours some place else. This is a business, not a social agency."

Brad's situation is an extreme example of how the wrong organizational environment can inhibit creativity. In general, it is easier to discourage than encourage creative responses from members of an organization. Organizations that are able to capitalize upon much of the creative potential of their members have generally certain characteristics in common. As you read the following list, notice that many of the characteristics of creative organizations are similar to those of creative people.[15]

1. A trustful management that does not overcontrol people.
2. Open channels of communication among members of the organization; a minimum of secrecy.
3. Considerable contact and communication with outsiders to the organization.
4. Large variety of personality types.
5. Willing to accept change, but not enamored with change for its own sake.
6. Enjoyment in experimenting with new ideas.

7. Little fear of the consequences of making a mistake.
8. Selects people and promotes them primarily on the basis of merit.
9. Uses techniques for encouraging ideas, such as suggestion systems and brainstorming.
10. Sufficient financial, managerial, human, and time resources to accomplish its goals.

*Summary
of Key Points*

1. Creativity is the processing of information in such a way that the result is new, original, and meaningful.
2. People show a normal distribution of creative potential.
3. Creativity can be divided into four types: origination, synthesis, extension, and duplication.
4. With appropriate support from the organization, creativity should improve job performance.
5. Creative potential can be measured with some degree of accuracy by psychological tests. Taking such tests can give you valuable experience in attempting creative responses to problems.
6. Creative people differ from less creative people in characteristics such as being more emotionally loose and open, sensitive, and prone to rich fantasy lives.
7. You can improve your creativity by techniques such as brainstorming and making a conscious effort to think creatively.
8. Organizations that encourage creativity from their members have some characteristics similar to those of creative people (such as being loose rather than tight).

*Questions
for Discussion*

1. Based on your own observations of creative people, what are their most distinguishing characteristics?
2. Give two examples of higher-level jobs that you think do not require creativity. Why?
3. If you wanted to hire a creative person, how could you determine whether or not that person was creative?
4. Do you know anybody who is very creative yet unsuccessful by conventional standards? What accounts for his or her lack of success?
5. Were you surprised by your score on the creative personality test? Why or why not?
6. Does your present place of work (or school) encourage or discourage creativity? On what basis did you reach your conclusion?

You are the marketing manager in a commercial bank. One of your objectives is to devise novel advertising and promotional campaigns to attract new bank customers. To help you achieve this objective, you place Ellis (a management trainee) in charge of developing new advertising and promotional strategies. He accepts the assignment with enthusiasm.

After returning from a three-day trip, you are shocked by the appearance of Ellis's work area, which is located in an open space visible to customers. Two mobiles with multicolored pieces of glass dangling from them hang from the ceiling over his desk. So do three exotic plants. Ellis is wearing faded blue jeans and a bright red shirt with a deep V cut in the front. A tiffany lamp sits on his desk as does an oversized fruit basket. Almost in disbelief, you ask Ellis what is going on. He replies:

"What can you expect? You put me on a creative assignment, so I want to get into the right mood. Things have to be set right to think creatively. Don't you realize that creativity requires the right surroundings?"

You sympathize with Ellis, but you believe that his work area decor is out of keeping with the bank image. How should you handle the situation?

Ralph Benson, president of Mainline Food Service, Inc., looked forward with anticipation to his Monday morning staff meeting with his five key subordinates. Ralph spoke to his secretary, "I hope this morning will be it. We certainly need a breakthrough in our thinking about Mainline. I've keyed up the staff for today's meeting."

After the usual exchange of pleasantries on Monday morning, Ralph introduced the major topic of the meeting: "I'm glad you could all be here today. We have some heavy thinking to do. The way I see the problem, Mainline Food Service needs to diversify a bit. For over thirty years we've been offering vending machine and cafeteria service on a nationwide basis. As you all know this is a tough, competitive business with very slim margins of profit.

"Because of the many cost-cutting procedures I've suggested—sometimes over your objections—we've been able to stay profitable. Our profit as a percentage of sales is two percent, which may not sound like much to the person on the street, but we're doing much better than our competitors. Yet it's obvious to me that we have to diversify. We're too heavily concentrated in the food service business. As I see the problem, we should be using some of our capital to get into the restaurant business.

"And that's why I have called this meeting. As I informed you in my memo, the purpose of today's meeting is to decide upon what type of restaurant business we should enter."

Naomi Miller, manager of customer service, spoke first: "Ralph, you've made the assumption that we should be entering the restaurant business. Isn't that kind of limiting our choices? Suppose I said we should be opening up a chain of garden stores? Why are we restricting ourselves to restaurants?"

"Naomi, enough of your philosophizing," replied Ralph. "It only takes common sense to realize that a company in the food business should stick to the food business. As my father told me many times, 'Shoemaker, stick to thy last'."

"Could be, Ralph, but we don't find too many shoemakers around anymore. Maybe they stuck to their lasts too long."

Appearing mildly irritated, Ralph asked for somebody to make the first specific suggestion about Mainline entering the restaurant business. Buzz Owens, institutional sales manager, complied: "Let's go all the way Ralph. I'm suggesting we open up a chain of ten posh restaurants called the Executive Club. You could only eat there if you had a membership card that cost about fifty dollars per year. All our waitresses would be well spoken and physically attractive. Grand dining has sort of slipped by the wayside, but I think there is still a big demand for that kind of fine, elite restaurant."

"Buzz, I would hardly call that a novel idea. It's been tried many times in the past and failed," answered Ralph. "Does anybody else have a more novel idea?"

Chuck Adams, manager of vending operations, spoke next: "Ralph, you asked for a novel suggestion, so I'm taking you at your word. My brainstorm for a new restaurant chain would be to set up a franchise of fast-food restaurants called Jet Service. Each restaurant would have a fiberglass front that would look like the nose cone and cockpit of a Boeing 747. The help would all wear airplane personnel uniforms. We'd have travel posters on the walls, and jet-turbine-shaped salt and pepper shaker. Even our rest rooms would be styled after those found in an airplane."

"Thanks so much, Chuck. If we ever merge with Eastern Airlines or Pan Am, I'll be back in touch. Maybe you need an airplane trip yourself. Maybe you've been working too hard. Next suggestion please."

John Rubright, operations manager, looked around at his colleagues self-consciously before making his suggestion. "Ralph, I've given a lot of careful thought to our problem. I detect a new era of conservatism and nostalgia sweeping the country. I'm recommending that we open a chain of simple country restaurants called G.O.F.F. That stands for Good Old Fashioned Food. Get it? We would have knotty pine chairs and tables and our waitresses would wear colonial uniforms. Even though the Bicentennial has passed, the interest in America should not pass away for years."

"Thanks for the suggestion," said Ralph. "It's not half-bad, but it seems to me that type of restaurant has been tried in New England for many years. It stands no more chance of succeeding than the average roadside beanery. We haven't heard yet from Dinah Malone. As director of quality control, she should have a good idea about the restaurant business."

"My idea is so basic, that it might be dismissed as too simple," said Dinah. "Yet I think I'm on to something very important. The United States is tired of McDonald's and the like. But most people can no longer afford to eat in first-class restaurants. I'm saying let's bring back the old-fashioned, aluminum exterior diner. But let's do it in a big way with smiling porters and authentic railroad whistles. Let's call this chain, 'Dinah's Diner.' Kind of tricky, don't you think?"

"I could see why you would want a chain of restaurants named after you, Dinah, but is the Ford Motor Company bringing back the Model T? Maybe we've gone far enough in today's meeting. Let's all try again next Monday. During the week try to be at your creative best. I'm eager to get some new suggestions."

As the last member left the room, Ralph said to his secretary, "Why can't our people be more creative?"

1. In what way might Ralph be discouraging creativity?
2. Whose suggestion do you think is the most creative? Why?
3. What approach should Ralph take to bringing forth creative suggestions for a new business venture from his subordinates?
4. Do you see Ralph as rigid or flexible? Why?
5. Should Ralph have offered a prize for the best suggestion? Why or why not?

FOOTNOTES

[1] This definition of creativity comes from *Understanding Psychology*, CRM Books, 1974, p. 71.

[2] Ross A. Webber, *Management: Basic Elements of Managing an Organization*, Irwin, 1975, p. 653.

[3] The unusual uses and unusual consequences tests, along with the personality test of creative potential, follow closely their presentation in Andrew J. DuBrin, *Survival in the Office: How to Move Ahead or Hang On*, Mason/Charter, 1977, pp. 202–204.

[4] This test, developed by Eugene Raudsepp, is quoted from "Ideas: Test Your Creativity," *Nation's Business*, June 1965, p. 80.

[5] Herbert G. Hicks and C. Ray Gullett, *The Management of Organizations*, McGraw-Hill, 1976, pp. 209–211. However, these authors use the term *innovation* where we use *origination*.

[6] *Ibid.*, p. 210.

[7] Two sources are Donald W. MacKinnon, "The Nature and Nurture of Creative Talent," in *Readings in Managerial Psychology*, University of Chicago Press, 1964, pp. 90–109; and Gary A. Steiner (ed.), *The Creative Organization*, University of Chicago Press, 1965, pp. 22–23.

[8] Andrew J. DuBrin, *Fundamentals of Organizational Behavior: An Applied Perspective*, Pregamon Press, 1974, p. 87.

[9] *Ibid.*, p. 89.

[10] The best answer here is to prove to your boss that your accomplishments are worthy of more money than you are presently receiving.

[11] The original source is Alex F. Osburn, *Applied Imagination,* rev. ed., Scribner, 1957.

[12] Videotaping was agreed upon and formed the basis for a new business that has spread around the United States.

[13] Thomas J. Bouchard, "What Ever Happened to Brainstorming?" *Industry Week,* Aug. 2, 1971, p. 29.

[14] *Ibid.,* p. 30.

[15] Two good sources here are Carl E. Gregory, *The Management of Intelligence,* McGraw-Hill, 1967, pp. 188–199; and Steiner, *op. cit.,* pp. 22–23.

SUGGESTED READING

BOUCHARD, THOMAS J., JR. "A Comparison of Two Brainstorming Procedures," *Journal of Applied Psychology,* Oct. 1972, pp. 418–421.

CUMMINGS, LARRY L., HINTON, BERNARD L., and GOBDEL, BRUCE C. "Creative Behavior as a Function of Task Environment: Impact of Objectives, Procedures, and Controls," *Academy of Management Journal,* Sept. 1975, pp. 489–499.

DUBRIN, ANDREW J. *Casebook of Organizational Behavior,* Pergamon, 1977, Chapter 3.

DUBRIN, ANDREW J. *Survival in the Office: How to Move Ahead or Hang On,* Mason/Charter, 1977, Chapter 12.

ELLIS, WILLIAM D. "Creativity: A Path to Profit," *Nation's Business,* Mar. 1973, pp. 70–72.

HICKS, HERBERT G., and GULLETT, C. RAY. *The Management of Organizations,* McGraw-Hill, 1976, Chapters 11 and 12.

HINTON, B. L. "Personality Variables and Creative Potential," *Journal of Creative Behavior,* vol. 3, 1970, pp. 210–217.

MAIER, NORMAN R. F. *Problem Solving and Creativity in Individuals and Groups,* Brooks/Cole, 1970.

PRINCE, GEORGE M. "Creative Meetings Through Power Sharing," *Harvard Business Review,* July–Aug. 1972, pp. 47–54.

STEINER, GARY (ed.). *The Creative Organization,* University of Chicago Press, 1965.

4
JOB STRESS

Learning
Objectives

After reading and studying this chapter, you should be able to

1. Explain how job stress can harm people and impair job performance.
2. Explain how job stress can help people and improve job performance.
3. Identify major sources of stress that people create for themselves.
4. Identify the major sources of stress that are found in organizations.
5. Know about current methods of reducing stress.
6. Develop a strategy for preventing harmful job stress in your career.

Work is a dominant source of satisfaction and reward for many people. In the extreme, some people find more tranquillity on the job than in the home. It is not unknown for a career-minded person to leave the house and head toward the office in search of peace and tranquillity. Despite such rewards that are potentially available in a job environment, the world of work can have an opposite effect upon an individual. Job stress occurs at every level in the organization. From the window washer to the company president, nobody is immune to job stress. The window washer may gradually develop a fear of heights; the president may fall prey to excessive worry about the competition.

To effectively manage your career or manage others, it is thus important to identify sources of stress, and to be familiar with methods of reducing and preventing job-related stress. Fortunately, a wide array of techniques is available to help people cope with stress. A discussion of several of them will follow an examination of the nature and sources of stress.

People vary widely in their capacity to withstand stress. Your personality characteristics, emotional health, physical health, and past experiences in coping with stress are among the factors that determine your response to stress. We can only determine if a particular source of stress is harmful to an individual after measuring his or her response to stress. For instance, one man might find employment as a door-to-door vacuum cleaner sales representative. After one month of cold canvassing, he finds himself a victim of stress. He experiences nervous indigestion, sweats profusely, and argues repeatedly about trivial events. Another young man takes the same job and thrives on this type of stress. He says, "I love the challenge of knocking on strange doors. You never know who you are going to meet or whether or not they are going to be your next purchaser of a deluxe model."

An optimum amount of stress theoretically exists for each person. Many people believe that they perform best on tests or the athletic field when they are placed under pressure. Yet too much pressure, of course, may produce undesirable reactions. William R. Cunnick, Jr., an insurance company medical director, makes this observation:[1]

> We all need stress. The goal is not a state of nirvana where the executive is suspended in an emotional nothingness. But we have to distinguish between satisfying and unsatisfying stress. It is satisfying when you are running around achieving goals. It is unsatisfying when everything gets out of control. That's when people develop symptoms such as headaches, diarrhea, and heart palpitations.

Generalizations about how much stress is harmful are difficult to reach. Some sources of stress will have adverse consequences for most people. Among these are losing one's job, going through a divorce, or receiving conflicting directions from two bosses. Some forms of stress tend not to be harmful. Among them are engaging in reasonable competition, being criticized by a boss, or losing a set of keys.

STRESS AND JOB PERFORMANCE

As already suggested, an optimum amount of stress can improve job performance, whereas an overload of stress can impair performance. Figure 4.1 is an overview of the relationship between job performance and stress. When stress has positive consequences for an individual, job per-

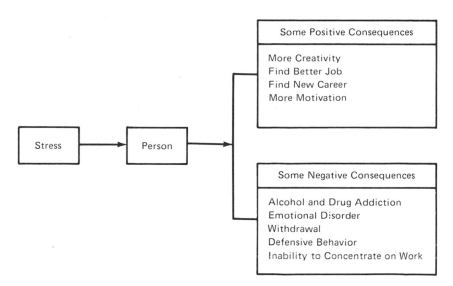

FIGURE 4.1
Relationship between stress and job performance.

formance will most likely be improved. For example, a woman owned a flower shop in a small village. The uncertainties of business combined with the necessity for paying bills was a source of stress to her. Her solution was to find a secure job in a child-care center. (Of course, she was subject to a period of discomfort until she sold her business and found new employment.) This woman improved her job performance, although she had to change jobs to do it.

The negative consequences section of Figure 4.1 illustrates the traditional thinking about stress. Included here is the stereotyped advertising executive who develops an ulcer as a reaction to the instability of his business. Because of his concern about his ulcer and his general agitation, his decreased ability to concentrate hurts his job performance.

In this chapter the adverse consequences of stress will be emphasized. Few people would be concerned with finding methods of preventing or reducing stress that actually helped their job performance.

STRESSES PEOPLE CREATE FOR THEMSELVES

Often an individual will succumb to stress in a job situation primarily because of his or her basic personality. Nancy, a hypothetical executive in the garment industry, might relish the competitive spirit of that line of work. Despite the heavy demands placed upon her, she will not exert herself beyond her breaking point. Her counterpart, Roxanne, might be an intensely competitive person who works so long and hard, and becomes so frustrated with every setback, that she eventually suffers a heart attack. Who is to blame, the company or Roxanne?

Type A Behavior.   Meyer Friedman and Ray H. Rosenman have identified several personality characteristics of people who are the most prone to heart disease. Such individuals tend to gravitate toward occupations that encourage heavy work. In addition, they tend to be heavier cigarette smokers. Labeled "type A" individuals, their distinguishing characteristics are as follows:[2]

> Chronic and severe sense of time urgency. For instance, they become particularly frustrated in traffic jams.
>
> Constant involvement in multiple projects subject to deadlines. Somehow they take delight in the feeling of being swamped with work.
>
> Neglect all aspects of life except work. *Workaholics* live to work rather than work to live.
>
> A tendency to take on excessive responsibility, combined with the feeling that "Only I am capable of taking care of this matter."
>
> Explosiveness of speech and a tendency to speak faster than most people. Type A people are thus prone to ranting and swearing when upset.

Lack of Relevance.   In recent years young people, and some members of the older generation, have become acutely concerned with the social value of their work. When they perceive their work as having no socially redeeming value, this situation can create stress (and thus tension). Usually it is the person's subjective opinion as to what constitutes a socially relevant product or service. For instance, a young man finds employment as a designer in a toy factory. After one year of work he might say to himself, "What a way to spend my working days. I'm simply adding fuel to a waste economy. How purposeless to design new and better toys for children. I think they would be better off playing with pots and pans."

Another design engineer working for the same company for a year might say to himself, "I'm glad my job is a useful one. Think of all the young minds I'm helping to develop as they play with these creative toys. Not only am I giving children an opportunity for enjoyment, but I'm helping them grow intellectually. Few other engineers can say the same thing."

Another problem with the concept of social relevance is that some occupations seem socially relevant to an outsider but socially irrelevant from many an insider's perspective. One woman left a job as an editorial assistant in a book publishing company to become a caseworker. Her objective was to do something of social relevance. To her chagrin, she found her experiences as a caseworker less relevant than her work as an editorial assistant.

> What I objected to the most was being ripped off by these clients. I could cite you one hundred examples. Our social agency has a policy of providing moving allowances for welfare recipients when they are forced to move. This happens frequently when the building in which they live is considered unsuitable for occupancy by the city.
>
> At least one half the time the clients pocket the moving money and have a friend move them. Even more frequent is the practice of people collecting welfare who have live-in partners who could afford to contribute their share and keep the woman off public assistance. After one year as a caseworker, all my idealism is gone.

Robert L. Kahn and his associates in their large-scale research uncovered a variation of the stress caused by lack of relevance.[3] People in creative jobs frequently complained of conflict between their nonroutine creative activities and their routine administrative duties. Paper work, according to these people, is time consuming, disrupts their creative work, and is generally unpalatable. As such, its relevance is indirectly challenged.

Frustrated Ambitions.   Most organizations need large numbers of people who are content to work hard at their assignments without being overly concerned about climbing the organizational ladder. Approximately 1 percent of jobs in any organization is truly executive (policy-making) positions. Thus, when a person is bitterly frustrated because he or she fails to become an executive, the organization should not be blamed. It is mostly a problem of a person aspiring toward a goal with an exceedingly small chance of success.

The stress created by not becoming wealthy and powerful is virtually a pure case of culturally induced stress. As sex-role liberation becomes more complete, it is probable that a smaller proportion of males will be obsessed with the pursuit of "success."[4] Male consciousness-raising groups, the hippie philosophy of life, and the new Eastern religions all emphasize that people should be pursuing the "good life." In contrast, the organization person of the 1960s and 1970s felt that high rank and the accumulation of material goods were the true sources of satisfaction.

ORGANIZATIONAL SOURCES OF STRESS

In many instances, the place where you work must receive the primary blame for creating stress that leaves you tense and anxious. We use the term *primary* because neither the person nor the organization is fully to blame when a person succumbs to stress. A person subject to stress usually has the option to speak up and deal with the problem in a constructive manner.

Exorbitant Work Demands.   A burdensome workload can create stress for an individual in two ways. First, the person may accumulate fatigue and thus be less able to tolerate annoyances and irritations. Think of how much easier it is to become provoked over a minor incident when you lack proper rest. Second, a person subject to exorbitant work demands may feel perpetually behind schedule, which in itself creates an uncomfortable, stressful feeling.

Heavy work demands are considered part of an executive's life. However, many people of lesser rank and income are also asked to give up much of their personal freedom and work under continuous pressure during working hours. Jody, a phone solicitor, describes an unfavorable work experience that illustrates the problem of exorbitant work demands.

> My plans were to enter sales as a career, but it wasn't easy getting a full-fledged sales job with my limited experience. So I did the next best thing—at least I thought so at the time—and took a job as a phone solicitor. The company I joined sold home improvements, but mostly aluminum siding and basement waterproofing. My job, along with five other women, was to phone every homeowner on our list and request that they grant one of our sales representatives an appointment.
> Business was slow, so we were asked to make more and more calls. We sat down in little booths. Our supervisor, Mr. Delbert, was a tyrant. He would prance up and down the office making sure that nobody was taking a rest break. If he saw any of us pausing, we would be subject to a verbal reprimand. Every once in a while he would come over close to us to make sure that we weren't making social calls.
> In the three months I was there we must have replaced twenty women. The last straw for me was when Mr. Delbert asked us all to show up early one morning to hear a special announcement. He informed us that since business was down ten percent we would each have to make ten percent more calls to make up for the loss in business. He said that if we didn't like the idea, we could leave. So I left.

Conflicting Demands and Confusing Directions.   "I'm really not sure I know what I'm supposed to be doing around here" is a common lament, even at higher-level jobs. People in large and small, profit and not-for-profit organizations are often placed in a situation where their job expectations are sloppily defined. In addition, they receive conflicting demands from two or more people. Daniel Katz and Robert L. Kahn have labeled such conditions role conflict and role ambiguity, two conditions that create substantial stress for many people.

Role conflict is the "simultaneous occurrence of two or more role sendings such that compliance with one would make more difficult compliance with the other."[5] Four types of role conflict have been identified:

Intrasender conflict occurs when one person asks you to accomplish two objectives that are in apparent conflict. If your boss asked you to hurry up and finish your work but also decrease your mistakes, you would experience this type of conflict (plus perhaps a headache!).

Intersender conflict occurs when two or more senders give you incompatible directions. Your immediate superior may want you to complete a crash project on time, but company policy temporarily prohibits authorizing overtime payments to clerical help.

Interrole conflict results when two different roles that you play are in conflict. Your company may expect you to travel 50 percent of the time (in order to be promoted), while your spouse threatens a divorce if you travel over 25 percent of the time.

Person–role conflict occurs when the role(s) your organization expects you to occupy are in conflict with your basic values. Your company may ask you to fire substandard performers, but this could be in conflict with your humanistic values.

Confusing directions (role ambiguity) are closely related to role conflict. A man was hired into a management-training program and given the elegant title of "assistant to the general manager." After three days of reading company manuals and taking plant tours, he pressed for an explanation of what he was supposed to be doing in the assignment. His boss told him, "Just try to make yourself useful. I'll be going out of town for two weeks. If you have any questions, ask my secretary for help."

Underutilization of Abilities. A major stress facing people early in their careers is that of being underutilized.[6] Not only was the assistant to the general manager described above subject to unclear directions; he also had no challenging work to perform. Gerald J. Soltas, now a manager, describes his experience with underutilization:[7]

> When I was released from the service, I was looking forward to finally getting a chance to be a "real engineer." I guess you could say I was gung-ho. I took a job with a large shipyard in Virginia that had several contracts to build navy warships. I had almost four years of sea duty as a missile fire control and systems officer, and I felt I could apply my education and experience to building those ships and their missile systems. It was a rude shock to me when I was assigned to antisubmarine systems about which I knew very little.
> It is worse to realize a few weeks later that I wasn't expected to know or do very much. I read more than one novel and many magazines just to have something to fill the hours. I was not alone in my frustration either. Numerous other engineers referred to their time-filling activities as "making eight." To compound the aggravation, we were occasionally required to put in overtime because "the project is behind." Talk about waste, a master's degree in automatic control systems engineering, four years of experience on the navy's newest missile systems, and I was reduced to checking plans from some jerk in Washington who probably had never seen the inside of a college or a ship.
> It really got to me. I was coming home from work frustrated and

discouraged. I've never been particularly easy to get along with, but my wife said I was becoming even more of a grouch. I had to do something!

Creating stress for people by underutilizing their abilities is rarely a conscious plot on the part of large organizations. Two factors underlie many cases of underutilization. First, large organizations have a difficult time perfectly matching human resources and job requirements at any given point in time. Thus an automobile manufacturer may have a few hundred excess technicians in a six-month period. It would be wasteful to fire everybody who was not fully occupied at the moment. Second, few organizations have enough challenging and exciting jobs to stretch the potential of every person in the firm who is seeking self-fulfillment.

REACTIONS TO JOB STRESS

Analyzing what people do under stress encompasses the field of abnormal psychology. Here we shall highlight a few of the adverse reactions that organizational members frequently exhibit to severe stress. Such reactions range from temporary emotional outbursts (such as shouting at another worker) to a complete change in a person's life style (such as a harassed executive becoming a potato farmer). Underlying all reactions to stress are physiologic responses within the body. Stress stimulates our glands to produce hormones that better equip us to combat the stress. For instance, a surge of adrenalin helps the person encountering stress to call forth an unusual amount of physical energy.

Stress Arouses Emotion. When faced with stress, people typically react with some form of emotional response. Among the most significant emotional patterns for job-related behavior are anger, fear, and anxiety.[8] The expression of these emotions can be both direct or indirect. A manager who has been demoted may express his anger directly by telling other people in the company how thoughtless the company has become. He may express his anger indirectly by taking an inordinately long time to learn his new job (and make frequent errors in the process).

Fear is displayed in response to several job-related stresses. In times of recession many people fear losing their jobs. Their fear reaction typically is to become more and more hesitant to take risks that involve innovative solutions to problems. People fear making mistakes because they fear the penalty associated with having made them. When threats of job loss are high, people fear being fired as a consequence of having made a mistake.

"Anxiety is a feeling of apprehension and fearfulness in the absence of specific danger."[9] People experience anxiety when the source of stress is felt, but its implications are not exactly known. A male middle manager in a bank talked about his anxiety this way:

I'm not sure what all these changes mean to me personally, but they have made me so tense that my stomach is churning. I know the bank is trying to promote more women into officer positions. That must mean that fewer men will be promoted but nobody has said that for sure. Also, a good number of New York City banks have moved into our area. That could have some bad implications for us, but I have seen no problems yet.

Emotional Disorder.   Everybody has some emotional problems, many of which are precipitated by work pressures. Sometimes the latter are severe enough to precipitate an actual emotional illness. The Menninger Foundation has developed a checklist of questions, the answers to which help a person determine if he or she is in fact experiencing an emotional disorder:[10]

At the end of this self-examination, a person should have a good idea of whether there are serious problems in his or her career or personal relationships. Being honest with oneself, the experts emphasize, is the first step toward problem solving.

1. What are my goals in life and how realistic are they?
2. Is my use of time and energy helping me to reach these goals?
3. Do I have a proper sense of responsibility, or do I try to do too much and fail to acknowledge my limitations?
4. How do I react to disappointments and losses?
5. How am I coping with stress and anxiety?
6. What is the consistency and quality of my personal relationships? Are my contacts with others superficial, meager, and unrewarding?
7. From whom do I receive and to whom do I give emotional support? Do I avoid getting support from others for fear of appearing weak?
8. What is the role of love in my life? How much time do I give to listening to and caring for others?

Alcoholism and Drug Addiction.   Although people should not ordinarily blame their alcoholism or drug abuse on their employers, certain job pressures can precipitate a person toward such maladaptive behavior. A publishing executive told me that he was leaving his firm because "I have not had a drink in over one year. If I put up with these people another week, I know I'll go back to drinking."

Alcoholism continues to be a major behavior problem in business, industry, government, and education. About 5 to 9 percent of the work force in the United States has a serious drinking problem. Alcoholism costs the government and industry about $35 billion annually (expressed in terms of a 1978 dollar).[11]

Randy Taylor of the National Clearing House on Alcohol Information has noted that her agency's rule of thumb is that, in an average company with 500 employees, about 25 are alcoholics, and the company is losing $60,000 a year to absenteeism, lowered efficiency, work dodging, medical treatment, and work accidents.[12]

Drug abuse has now become a problem at managerial and worker employee levels, although the problem is still more pronounced at lower levels in the organization. Drug abusers in management tend to use soft drugs such as marijuana and amphetamines and not hard drugs. The fatigue associated with certain routine, repetitive jobs is one stress that appears to precipitate some people toward energizing drugs.[13]

Defensive Behavior. As is well known to anyone who has ever read an introductory psychology text, people use defense mechanisms to help them lessen anxiety or preserve self-respect. Defensive behavior also manifests itself in many ways in reaction to job stresses. A few such coping behaviors are particularly relevant.

Denial is an extreme form of defensive behavior in which the person exposed to severe stress denies that a problem exists. An executive was forced into early retirement at age 60 by his firm. He reacted to the forced retirement by taking regular trips to the office for two months. During the day he would busy himself with activities such as reading in the company library and taking plant tours open to the public. In addition, he would confer with his stockbroker and banker. Coaxing by his wife and former boss finally convinced him to accept the fact that he had now entered a different stage in life—that early retirement was no disgrace.

Fantasy represents a type of behavior in which the individual achieves his or her goals and needs through imagination. Denied many times by his company an opportunity to work as an executive (the stress of frustrated ambitions), Jeff decided to establish his own "marketing research firm" which he operated during nonworking hours. By judicious use of industrial directories he was able to build up a correspondence file with a number of marketing professors in the United States, Canada, and Europe. His transactions with these people amounted to an occasional exchange of informational letters. Despite the objective facts of the situation, Jeff represented himself to people as the executive director of Market Research International. Close friends tolerated Jeff's fantasy behavior because it amounted to no more than a harmless prank.

Rationalization is widespread in the world of work. Many individuals search out socially approved reasons to explain why they behaved as they did. A manager of a stenographic pool illustrates how people under stress sometimes resort to rationalization.

> Vivian supervised the stenographic pool in an insurance company. An extensive time and motion study of the company's operations suggested that the stenographic pool could operate efficiently with a 20 perecnt reduction in personnel. Vivian had no choice but to go along with management's edict. She dismissed several poor performers and did not replace three women who requested maternity leave.
> Vivian was now subject to two sets of pressures. Her company expected higher productivity with fewer people. Her subordinates com-

plained about excessive workloads. Vivian's solution was to instruct her typists to pay less attention to proofreading, thus freeing up more of their time for typing. Within a few weeks time, serious proofreading errors were found in company correspondence. For instance, a letter addressed to a Mr. A. L. Bandass, was typed as "A. L. Badass."

When Vivian was confronted by management with the increase in errors in her department, she replied that she thought the company was primarily concerned with effectiveness, not nitpicking over typographical errors.

Projection is another familiar defense mechanism that may surface in response to job related stress. In projection the individual under pressure will protect himself or herself from awareness of undesirable or unacceptable feelings by attributing them to others. Ned, a production control clerk, might aspire toward becoming a manufacturing superintendent. Underneath, he would like to block the progress of better qualified competitors for such a position. Instead of admitting these feelings to himself, Ned projects them on to others. He contends that the reason he is not being promoted is that others are out to "get him." Projection can lead to paranoid thinking.

METHODS OF REDUCING OR COPING WITH STRESS

Because stress is such a widespread problem, many techniques have been used to help reduce or at least cope with stress. Among them are psychotherapy, yoga, working out in a gymnasium, rolling a smooth stone between your fingers, and religious confessionals. The distinction between methods of reducing versus preventing stress is somewhat arbitrary. For example, transcendental meditators contend that TM not only reduces stress, it gives you a way of life that helps you prevent stress. Similarly, physical exercise helps you reduce accumulated tensions, but it also helps you ward off some of the adverse effects of future tension.

Take Constructive Action. Underlying any approach to reducing stress is this key principle. Until you take constructive action about reducing stress itself or removing the causes of stress, you will continue to suffer. One value of chemical approaches to reducing stress (such as tranquillizing medication) is that they calm down a person enough that he or she can deal constructively with the source of stress.

A dentist was under considerable stress because he was scheduled to make a presentation to the county dental society. Among his discomforting symptoms were digestive disturbances and continuous sweating under the arms. After taking Valium, he made the rational decision to read a book about public speaking and follow some of its suggestions.

At times, the first step taken to overcome a source of stress or to reduce the discomfort of stress may seem modest. However, the fact that you are now working toward a solution to your problem may make you feel better about the problem. To illustrate, if you find that working Saturday mornings is creating problems between you and your spouse, it behooves you to deal constructively with that problem. Discuss the problem with your boss and/or your spouse. One man facing this problem spoke to his supervisor and was pleased to learn that he could substitute working late on Thursday nights for his Saturday assignment.

Transcendental Meditation and Other Relaxation Approaches. By 1976 an estimated 700,000 Americans had been trained to meditate by using TM, the so-called McDonald's of meditation.[14] Introduced in the United States by Maharishi Mahesh Yogi, TM is officially defined as a process of establishing a physiological state of deep rest; it is practiced twice daily for about 20 minutes, morning and evening, by sitting comfortably with eyes closed. During the sessions the subject meditates by quietly repeating a meaningless syllable called a mantra. TM trainees agree not to reveal their mantra to any other person. One such secret syllable is "malra."

TM provides relaxation by providing the mind with the opportunity to temporarily cease the activity of the waking state, while cultivating a high degree of awareness and alertness. During meditation the body carries out needed repairs and adjustments that are not possible during activity and not accomplished during deep sleep.

The burgeoning of TM has spurred considerable research about its effectiveness in coping with personal and job-related stress. David R. Frew, conducting research in a job setting, reached these conclusions:[15] (1) TM appears to improve productivity; (2) people at higher-level jobs tend to derive the biggest boosts in productivity from using TM; (3) gains in productivity are more apparent in a democratic than an autocratic job environment.

Although TM trainers often look upon their program as a way of achieving a tension-free existence, the testimony of meditators is more modest. A young woman who left the garment business suffering from ulcers made this comment: "I would say that meditating has helped me relax a bit more. I feel fine today. Things don't bother me as much as they used to, but I still have problems to face every day. But it does get kind of boring sitting off in a corner and meditating right in the middle of a day."

Herbert Benson, a cardiologist from Harvard, is one of many researchers and practitioners who question the claims of exclusivity made for TM. His best-selling book, *The Relaxation Response*, offers a simple (and apparently workable) method of relieving stress.[16] By getting yourself quietly comfortable and thinking of the word "one" (or any simple prayer) with every breath, you can duplicate the antistress effects of TM.

Concentration. For those individuals who feel uncomfortable about joining what appears to them to be a religious cult (TM), or even going through formal exercises to relieve stress, an alternative exists. Learning to concentrate on a meaningful activity for thirty-minute periods can be stress reducing. For example, you might concentrate so hard on what you are studying that the book in front of you (and its contents) is your only touch with reality. Should you prefer tennis as a way of practicing concentration, stare so hard at the ball that it appears to be grapefruit sized. Furthermore, you should be able to read the trademark with clarity—even while playing.[17]

The principle underlying concentration as a method of tension reduction is probably similar to the underlying principle behind other relaxation approaches. Your muscles and brain seem to be energized by carefully focusing them on something quite specific. Even if tension is not reduced, performance in the task at hand is improved!

Biofeedback Control. Among the most scientific of relaxation techniques are electronic machines that help you develop an awareness of muscle sensations throughout the body. After awareness comes the ability to control impulses that are ordinarily considered involuntary. For instance, through biofeedback you might be able to slow down your breathing rate. Assume then that you are making a presentation to department heads in your company. As they challenge you, it is apparent that your breathing rate is increasing and that you are losing control of the situation. By slowing down your breathing rate you may be able to regain your composure and increase your effectiveness in the meeting.

A widely followed concept of biofeedback is simple, as are many breakthrough ideas.[18] Body processes generate their own particular specific electrical waves. These waves are picked up by sensors and reported on a speedometer-like device. By observing the indicator, an individual can follow many of the processes taking place inside the body. You might be able to detect churning inside your stomach, emotional arousal, or heavy thought activity in your brain.

Sensory feedback to the person is essentially a form of communication with the body. We communicate with our internal processes and learn to exert control over them. One explanation is that human *will* brings about this control. A dietician reports on an interesting application of biofeedback:

> I was so overweight that I was in danger of losing my job. The company thought it kind of ludicrous that a food expert was 150 pounds overweight. I tried everything from Yoga to hypnosis. Then a friend got me into biofeedback. It taught me how to relax. Once I was less tense I had much less need to eat in response to my tension. My compulsive eating was almost cured because I overcame the tension that caused me to be a compulsive eater.

Shared Decision Making. At times the best response to stress is one involving individuals at many levels in the organization. By soliciting their opinions about what should be done in response to stress facing the organization, management may arrive at a superior solution. Douglas T. Hall and Roger Mansfield studied organizational and individual changes resulting from severe environmental stress (such as reduced budgets) in three research and development organizations.

Hall and Mansfield observed that the managers in the organizations studied assumed that the professionals were interested mainly in their work and did not want to be bothered with helping the organization cope with its financial stress.[19] One idea would be for management to share stress and responsibility for coping with the researchers. The researchers reasoned that, if the professionals felt that they had the ability to help the organization cope with stress, there would be greater organizational identification. Previous research suggested that employees had identified with the organization when they and management mutually coped with stress.

A logical question at this point is whether or not different coping approaches are particularly helpful for different types or sources of stress. In other words, which method is best for coping with which source of stress? This author is not aware of any evidence that answers this question. Coping methods have to be tried until you find one that is effective. Even tranquillizing medication is rarely related to particular sources of stress. People who are tense for many different reasons take the same brand and type of tranquillizer.

METHODS OF PREVENTING STRESS

An offensive strategy is usually superior to a defensive one. Creating a situation for yourself that aids you in being resistant to many sources of job-related stress is thus an effective career strategy. Working for an organization whose management knows how to avoid creating needless stress is another useful approach to preventing stress.

Strengthen Your Personal Qualifications. Many stresses that you might face in your career stem from the fact that you can readily be replaced by another individual or that there are a limited number of jobs for which you qualify.[20] A person may have to endure a frustrating, dissatisfying job for many years unless he or she can find another more satisfying job. A person with strong qualifications (one with a unique contribution to the organization) is much less subject to threats of job security than is his or her less qualified counterpart.

One way of enhancing your qualifications is through formal means. Thus attaining an advanced degree, a certificate of competency, or a license in your field of speciality increases your potential value to employers. Career education rests upon the premise that formal knowledge increases your job effectiveness.

Qualifications may also be strengthened through informal methods. The most effective approach is to develop a solid reputation for achieving results. Positive statements made about you on performance appraisals, such as "I think this person has good potential for management," are distinct assets. Membership in trade and professional organizations also strengthens you as an individual. Acquiring diverse job experience and performing well in those tasks is another significant way of making yourself a more valuable member of your firm. Publishing an article in a trade magazine is considered by many to be another important approach to enhancing your reputation.

Practice Good Management. What constitutes good management is a book-length subject in itself. One example of the relationship between stress prevention and good management will suffice for now. Many of the job-related stresses that people face concern the fact that they feel unchallenged by their positions. This situation is particularly true of young, ambitious individuals. One relatively new principle of management would be helpful in preventing such stress.

As part of a management-by-objectives program (see Chapter 13), a person is supposed to establish some *stretch* objectives—those that take a person beyond the normal expectations of his or her position. For instance, if an accountant were to establish an objective of "Attach a dollar figure to the human resources in our department," he would be amply challenged for the next six months. Having at least one exciting portion to your job helps ward off the stress of feeling underutilized or experiencing chronic job dissatisfaction.

1. Stress is an inevitable part of work and often results in negative consequences to the individual and organization.
2. People create stress for themselves by means such as their own competitive striving, restricted definitions of relevant work, and lofty personal goals.
3. Organizations create stress for people by such means as placing exorbitant work demands upon them, giving them conflicting demands and confusing directions, and underutilizing their abilities.
4. People react to stress in diverse ways, including displaying emotion, developing an emotional disorder, overusing alcohol and drugs, and exhibiting defensive behavior.
5. Methods of reducing stress include taking constructive action,

transcendental meditation (TM), learning to concentrate, and bio-feedback control.

6. Among the methods of preventing stress are strengthening your qualifications and belonging to organizations that practice good management.

1. Recall a period in your life when you were exposed to harmful stress. How did you handle the situation?

2. If you are a meditator (or use another relaxation technique), tell other members of your discussion group (or class) what this technique has done for you.

3. What ambitions or personal characteristics of yours do you think are presently (or will in the future) creating stress for you?

4. What stresses does your place of work (or school) create for you? Why isn't something done about the problem?

5. How does a person know when he or she might be experiencing an adverse reaction to stress?

6. What are you doing to prevent being subjected to harmful job-related stress?

A Human Relations Incident
KEEP THE HELP ON THEIR TOES

Marlene, a hotel administration major, found summer employment at White Mountain Inn, a Rocky Mountain resort. Two weeks into the summer, Marlene noticed that the waiters, waitresses, and busboys spent considerable time bickering with each other about the use of cups and saucers. Apparently, when the inn was filled to near capacity, there were not enough cups and saucers for everybody. Marlene immediately brought this problem to the attention of Cyrus, the dining room manager.

"Are you aware, Cyrus," explained Marlene, "that we have useless fighting over this easily rectified problem?"

"Young lady," replied Cyrus, "I intentionally have a shortage of cups and saucers. I've been doing that for years with pretty good results."

"You mean it saves the hotel money on cups and saucers?"

"I don't know about that," answered Cyrus, "but it's good for the help. It keeps them on their toes. This way they come into the dining room early just to get their share of cups and saucers. Kind of a clever ploy on my part, don't you think?"

How should Marlene respond to Cyrus? What should be her recommendations?

Paul was delighted when he learned of his appointment to the faculty of one of the nation's leading colleges of photographic technology. Although he did not have an academic background and little classroom teaching experience, he was told not to worry; his professional expertise would carry him through the rough spots, and he could rely on his colleagues for support and encouragement in learning the ropes. Since Paul was an intelligent person and conscientious worker, he soon learned about goals, behavioral objectives, lesson plans, and the necessary mechanics to make his classroom presentations effective.

Paul's superior proved to be right; his professional expertise helped immensely when teaching methodology and theory. He was soon recognized as being one of the better teachers and was credited with instilling his students with high levels of motivation. Paul's yearly merit evaluations read like the Marine Corps citations he had received while a young Marine. He was appointed to many department committees because of his easygoing manner coupled with the ability to make perceptive analysis of situations and intelligent recommendations. The switch from professional photographer to college professor, which had been prompted by a bad heart and the doctor's admonishment to get out of the rat race, seemed to be bearing fruit. Paul was appointed to the position of department chairman.

The administrative job began a new phase in Paul's academic life. In one respect, it was a new challenge; at the same time it deprived him of some of the leisure he had come to welcome as a needed benefit of switching from professional photographer to teacher. His superiors, the director of the school and the dean of the college, promised him their support and cooperation and wished him well in his new endeavor. Paul was the first chairman in his department.

Part of Paul's responsibility as chairman was to evaluate the performance of the teachers in his department for purposes of advancement and merit pay raises. There were ten teachers in the department, many of whom were senior to Paul and longtime friends of the school's director. Paul was objective in his evaluation, but it soon became apparent that merit pay raises were anything but that. Seniority often overshadowed competence, and friendship seemed to overrule any input Paul had given the director, even though the evaluation form was specifically formulated by the college to take into account variables of tenure, seniority, time in rank, classroom observation, and student and peer evaluation.

Paul's responsibility as department chairman also entailed selecting a replacement for a faculty member who had died suddenly. It was Paul's task to review the applications that were submitted in response to an ad placed by the school. Quite familiar with the job description of the vacated position, Paul made a selection while the director was on vacation. Upon the director's return, Paul was chagrined to find that the director had contacted an old acquaintance (and past president of a professional photog-

* Case contributed by Thomas P. Iten.

rapher's association) and offered him the position. It was clear to everyone in the department that Paul's selection was in the better interest of the department (indeed, the school) than that of the director's; but the director insisted upon bringing his friend to school, wining and dining him, and waiting until just before the start of the fall term for his reply. The director's friend turned down the position; subsequently, Paul's selection was hired, but only after much needless duplication of effort in checking references and qualifications by the director. Paul was subjected to extensive questioning of his ability. He then experienced chest pains for the first time in years.

Several weeks later, Paul became aware of a problem that was a long time in the making. One of the younger faculty members was accused of gross misconduct in the classroom. Paul had frequently been approached by students of this particular faculty member and been told of his improper advances towards some of the female members of the class, as well as his lack of preparation and surly attitude while in the classroom. Paul had tried counseling the teacher, listening to his problems, and making suggestions to improve his work performance and classroom behavior, but to no avail. The teacher was clearly jeopardizing the effectiveness of Paul's department. Because of rising resentment among the students and threats of a lawsuit by the parents of an outraged female student, dismissal of the faculty member was the only workable solution. Paul made an appointment with the director to discuss the termination of the faculty member's appointment. Since these were sufficient grounds for dismissal and the faculty member was not tenured, Paul did not anticipate any resistance to his recommendations.

Paul left the director's office the following day, stunned by the decision of the administration. In spite of Paul's documentation of the case and his recommendation for dismissal of the erring faculty member, he was told that the teacher in question would be retained until the director could ascertain whether the matter had been dealt with properly. When the other members of the department heard the decision, they threatened to go to the president of the college; they could not bear to see the effectiveness of the department suffer nor accept the behavior of the errant faculty member any longer. Paul became physically ill and was placed under the care of a doctor for a week.

While recuperating at home, Paul was informed that the matter was investigated by the provost of the college and the guilty faculty member was dismissed from his job. The investigation was prompted by a petition from the student body forwarded to the dean of academic affairs. The director was chastised for his decision and Paul was vindicated; but he resigned his position as department chairman on the advice of his physician.

1. What was the dominant source of stress for Paul? How could this stress have been prevented?
2. Should Paul have resigned? What else could have been done to cope with this problem?
3. Was Paul overreacting when his decision to dismiss a faculty member was reversed? Why or why not?
4. What do you think of Paul's decision to enter college teaching as a way of avoiding stress?
5. What should Paul do now?

[1] Quoted in Lee Smith, "What Kills Executives," *Dun's Review*, Mar. 1976, p. 37.

[2] Meyer Friedman and Ray H. Rosenman, *Type A Behavior and Your Heart*, Fawcett, 1975, pp. 100–103.

[3] Robert L. Kahn, "Stress from 9 to 5," *Psychology Today*, Sept. 1969, p. 37.

[4] A clear exposition of this theme is Warren Farrell, *The Liberated Man: Beyond Masculinity, Freeing Men in Their Relationships With Woman*, Random House, 1975.

[5] Daniel Katz and Robert L. Kahn, *The Social Psychology of Organizations*, Wiley, 1966, p. 184.

[6] Andrew J. DuBrin, *Fundamentals of Organizational Behavior: An Applied Perspective*, Pergamon Press, 1974, pp. 111–112.

[7] Gerald J. Soltas, "Making Eight Is a Hassle," unpublished case.

[8] James C. Coleman, *Abnormal Psychology and Modern Life*, 4th ed., Scott, Foresman, 1972, p. 120.

[9] *Ibid.*, p. 121.

[10] Quoted in "Cracking Under Stress," *U.S. News & World Report*, May 10, 1976, p. 59.

[11] Andrew J. DuBrin, *Managerial Deviance: How to Handle Problem People in Key Jobs*, Mason/Charter, 1976, p. 28.

[12] Tendayi Kumbula, "Alcoholism on the Job—A Major Headache," *Rochester Democrat & Chronicle* and *Los Angeles Times*, July 27, 1976, p. 14C.

[13] W. Clay Hamner and Frank L. Schmidt (eds.), *Contemporary Problems in Personnel*, St. Clair Press, 1974, p. 480.

[14] Dan Goleman, "Transcendental Meditation Goes Public," *Psychology Today*, Nov. 1975, p. 90.

[15] David R. Frew, *The Management of Stress: Using TM at Work*, Nelson-Hall, 1976, p. 280.

[16] Reviewed in Goleman, *op. cit.*, p. 91.

[17] A thorough description of how concentration can improve performance in sports is W. Timothy Gallwey, *The Inner Game of Tennis*, Random House, 1974.

[18] T. George Harris, "Barbara Brown's Body," *Psychology Today*, Aug. 1974, p. 45.

[19] Douglas T. Hall and Roger Mansfield, "Organizational and Individual Response to External Stress," *Administrative Science Quarterly*, Dec. 1971, p. 545.

[20] DuBrin, "Fundamentals," p. 128.

SUGGESTED READING

DuBrin, Andrew J. *Survival in the Office: How to Move Ahead or Hang On*, Mason/Charter, 1977, Chapter 4.

Frew, David R. *The Management of Stress: Using TM at Work*, Nelson-Hall, 1976.

GOLEMAN, DAN. "Transcendental Meditation Goes Public," *Psychology Today,* Nov. 1975, pp. 90–91.

IVANCEVICH, JOHN M., and DONNELLY, JAMES H., JR. "Relationship of Organizational Structure to Job Satisfaction, Anxiety-Stress, and Performance," *Administrative Science Quarterly,* June 1975, pp. 272–280.

KAY, EMMANUEL. *The Crisis in Middle Management,* AMACOM, 1974.

KELLER, ROBERT T. "Role Conflict and Ambiguity; Correlates with Job Satisfaction and Values," *Personnel Psychology,* Spring 1975, pp. 57–64.

McLEAN, ALAN (ed.). *Occupational Stress,* Charles C Thomas, 1974.

PALM, J. DANIEL. *Diet Away Your Stress, Tension and Anxiety: The Fructose Diet Book,* Doubleday, 1976.

SMITH, LEE. "What Kills Executives," *Dun's Review,* Mar. 1976, pp. 37–39.

WALTON, RICHARD E. "Quality of Working Life: What Is It?" *Sloan Management Review,* Fall 1973, pp. 11–21.

5
JOB CONFLICT

Learning Objectives

After reading and studying this chapter, you should be able to

1. Summarize the major reasons we have so much job conflict.
2. Explain how job conflict can sometimes be beneficial to both individuals and organizations.
3. Identify several harmful consequences of job conflict.
4. Know why line versus staff conflict is so common in work organizations.
5. Develop insight into ways of resolving conflict on your own.
6. Explain how proper organizational design can reduce or prevent conflict.

"**I**f you can't stand the heat, get out of the kitchen," states a popular management cliche. Similarly, if you can't stand conflict and are unwilling to learn methods of resolving it, avoid jobs that involve interaction with people. Every organization has some conflict between individuals and groups.

The term *conflict* has developed several popular meanings. Among them are controversy, strife, battle, quarrel, and incompatibility. To a specialist in human relations, the term *incompatibility* points to the true nature and meaning of conflict. A conflict occurs when two goals are incompatible or mutually exclusive. When you achieve one, you are unable to achieve the other. Assume that you are a ski buff who also likes money. You are made two job offers, one in Colorado at low pay and one in Miami at high pay. If your interest in skiing is satisfied, your need for money will be partially frustrated. If your money needs are satisfied, your skiing interest will be frustrated. Your conflict will persist until you find a constructive solution, such as taking up water skiing!

Another example of job-related conflict occurs when two departments want the same program under their jurisdiction. In a food company, the marketing and home economics departments asked for jurisdiction over the newly created position of consumer representative. The incumbent would represent the voice of the consumer to the company. Conflict occurs because when one department gets the prize (the consumer representative position) the other department will automatically not get the prize.

Conflict ties in closely with the topic of job stress. As discussed in Chapter 4, conflict is a source of stress for many individuals. When a person learns effective ways of managing conflict, he or she can reduce one more source of stress in his or her life. When a manager learns effective ways of reducing conflict within the organization, he or she is reducing one more source of stress within the organization.

THE JOB CONFLICT QUESTIONNAIRE

To help you develop an appreciation of the symptoms of job conflict, complete the questionnaire shown in Figure 5.1. Apply it to a place you presently work or have worked in the past. As with many other questionnaires or checklists that you complete for study or research purposes, candor is important. As before, we are not dealing with a scientifically validated instrument.

Directions: Check each of the following statements "mostly agree" or "mostly disagree" as it applies to your place of work.

	Mostly Agree	*Mostly Disagree*
1. A few of our departments do not talk to each other.	_____	_____
2. You frequently hear bad things said about other departments.	_____	_____
3. We seem to have more security guards than do most places.	_____	_____
4. You find a lot of graffiti about management in the restrooms.	_____	_____
5. People are fearful of making mistakes around here.	_____	_____
6. Writing nasty memos takes up a lot of our time.	_____	_____
7. A lot of people at our place of work complain about ulcers or other psychosomatic disorders.	_____	_____

8. We have considerable turnover in management. _____ _____

9. We have considerable turnover among employees. _____ _____

10. "Finger pointing" and blaming others happens frequently around here. _____ _____

11. We have a lot of strong cliques. _____ _____

12. You can almost feel the tension in some departments. _____ _____

13. A widely used expression around here is "They are a bunch of fools." _____ _____

14. We have had several incidents of vandalism and sabotage during the last year. _____ _____

15. We have a lot of bickering over such matters as who should do what job. _____ _____

16. Many people around here say, "That's not my job," when asked to do something out of the ordinary. _____ _____

17. Some departments in this organization are practically hated. _____ _____

18. Our organization seems more like a roller derby than a team. _____ _____

19. People rarely help you out because they actually want you to look bad in the eyes of management. _____ _____

20. We disagree more than we agree in our office (or factory). _____ _____

FIGURE 5.1
Job conflict questionnaire.

Interpretation of Scores. Use this questionnaire primarily as a guide to sensitizing you to the presence of interpersonal and intergroup conflict in a job environment. However, as a measure of conflict you might use this rough scoring system: if you agreed with fifteen or more statements, it probably indicates that you work in a conflict-ridden environment. If you agreed with three or less items, it could mean that too little conflict exists; perhaps people in your company are in danger of becoming too complacent. Scores from four to fourteen, those outside of the extremes, probably indicate that your organization is a mixture of conflict and cooperation. Most work organizations fall into this category.

A number of reasons[1] why so much conflict is found in organizational life have been identified. We shall discuss five of them. All these reasons or *sources* of conflict stem from the same underlying theme of two incompatible events discussed earlier in this chapter.

Interdependence of People or Departments. People who are dependent upon each other almost inevitably come into conflict. Similar to marital partners or roommates, departments requiring the cooperation of each other tend to find reasons for conflict. The operations and maintenance units of an airline are thus frequently in conflict with each other because they are interdependent. Without an airplane to service, the maintenance department is out of business. Without a properly serviced airplane, the operations department can quickly go out of business.[2]

Differences in Objectives. When two groups have major differences in objectives, the potential for conflict is high. Although one might argue that everybody working for the same organization should have the same ultimate objective, the success of the organization, this does not always happen in practice. Frequently, smaller units in the organization have different aspirations and desires than does management.

An example of conflict caused by differences in objectives was a four-day strike by New York City physicians.[3] In the tradition of conventional trade unionists, they marched in picket lines and demanded improvements in pay, hours, and working conditions. Professionals who work for large bureaucratic organizations (such as the hospital interns and residents just mentioned) believe that they should have considerable control over their working conditions. Often they want the right to choose what problems they will and will not work on. In contrast, the administration wants to maintain control over such matters.

A study conducted with 264 certified public accountants in large public accounting firms provides more evidence of differences in objectives as a source of conflict.[4] Those accountants with the most professional ideals felt the most frustrated by working in a bureaucratic organization. When a professional felt he or she was in conflict with the organization, it frequently resulted in his or her quitting.

Competition for Limited Resources. A fundamental reason so much conflict between groups exists in organizations is that not every department can get all the money, material, and human resources it wants. Conflict develops because most departments (or any other organizational unit) believe that their cause is the most worthwhile. Even when a company is prospering, resources have to be divided in such a manner that not everybody gets what he or she wants.

A special staff meeting was called to discuss an emergency situation as perceived by Pete, the corporate treasurer of a prefabricated housing company. He made this plea to the rest of the staff: "I don't think you gentlemen realize the gravity of the situation. We are in danger of not meeting our next payroll. We owe the banks $17 million and our receivables aren't coming in fast enough to pay off our notes. I told you people several months back that we need to begin cutting back on a few of the luxuries. We may be a glamour company to the world outside, but we need some restraint internally."

The marketing vice president interrupted with his notes: "But, Pete, we have cut back in many areas at your suggestion. We decided to postpone the construction of our southern plant for the time being. We've cut down on overtime except for emergency situations. We've even discontinued the practice of paying for spouses on company trips."

Replied Pete, "What irritates the heck out of me, Harold, is the gluttony of marketing. You're as aware of our need for restraint as anybody on the management team. I've been denied the right to hire an additional cost accountant who would have probably paid for himself anyway. I learned yesterday that the president has authorized the purchase of another corporate jet without even consulting me. Why can't the marketing department impress our potential customers with the two jets we already have?"

"There you go again, Pete, taking an accountant's view of the world," retorted Harold.

Role Theory and Role-Based Conflict. Roles are crucial in understanding conflict within organizations. Roles determine what people *ought* to do as a function of their position. Thus the carpenter who prefers not to fix a leaky faucet can rightfully claim, "It's not my job." The airport security officer who frisks you in search of contraband can suppress complaints by noting, "I'm just doing my job."[5]

Joe Kelly defines role as a set of behaviors or attitudes appropriate to a particular position in any organization, irrespective of who occupies the position. A manager's role in part is to exercise control and evaluate performance. It would therefore be unrealistic for a subordinate to object to having his or her performance evaluated by management. Nevertheless, people's positions or *roles* do sometimes contribute to conflict.

When interpersonal conflict is found in an organization, it is frequently related to the roles people occupy rather than to their differences in personality. Certain jobs have built-in conflict in the sense that people tend to resent the activities performed by the holder of that job (his or her role). An informal survey of students on one college campus revealed that many of them disliked the campus security officers. One student expressed the very nature of role conflict in her comments about the security officers:

It's nothing personal. Those guys are paid to be bastards. Most students can't afford the type of cars that you can count on to start when you want them to. The result is that during a cold spell we often have to abandon our cars for a couple of days. Often you get a ten dollar ticket that you can't afford. Worse is when you get the car towed away.

Auditors, quality-control experts, safety advisors, equal employment opportunity officers, and industrial engineers are among other occupations that are faced with role conflict. When your job involves criticizing or improving upon the work of others, the potential for conflict exists.

As described in Chapter 4, role conflict can be a source of stress. It can also be a source of general job dissatisfaction. When people experience considerable role conflict, the result is often dissatisfaction with many aspects of the job, including the quality of supervision, pay, and opportunities for promotions.[6]

Personal Differences. A variety of personality and cultural differences among people contributes to job conflict.[7] One contributor to conflict is the differences in values that stem from differences in age. The *generation gap* can lead to conflict because members of the different generations may not accept the other group's values. Cooperation is sometimes difficult to achieve between older and younger members of a department because older workers question the seriousness of purpose of the younger workers. Simultaneously, the younger workers believe that the older workers are resistant to change and are blindly loyal to the company.

Some people are more predisposed toward conflict because of their aggressive or hostile nature. A person with a strong need to bully other people may use the job situation to express such hostility. Prison guards, for instance, are frequently people with such aggressive impulses. People with other types of problems also contribute to job conflict. A person with low self-esteem may overcompensate by being belligerent toward others.

A clerk in a motor vehicle department was noted for her frequent altercations with people applying for license plate renewals. She would intimidate customers by her critical questioning of information contained on their applications. She seemed to take pleasure in sending people to the back of the line while they searched for additional information to correct their applications.

So many complaints were made that this woman was sent for counseling to a psychologist employed by the state. Counseling revealed that the woman herself was severely punished for mistakes she made as a child, both by her parents and a punitive teacher in a one-room schoolhouse. Unconsciously, she was using license plate applicants as a scapegoat for her own inadequacies. She finally learned that by treating others with respect she would receive the respect from them that she needed to build her self-esteem.

Most people can recall an incident in their lives when conflict proved to be beneficial in the long run. Perhaps you and your boss hammered out a compromise to a problem troubling you only after you bitterly complained about working conditions. Properly managed, moderate doses of conflict can be beneficial.

1. Talents and abilities may emerge in response to conflict. When faced with conflict, people often become more innovative than they would be under a tranquil situation. When a department is fighting with management to justify its existence, it may provide a creative explanation of what it can do for management. One such community relations department faced with a serious reduction in staff sold top management on the idea of the department developing an ecology task force.

2. Conflict can satisfy a variety of psychological needs. Among them are a desire to express aggressive urges and to be aroused by something in the environment. Instead of entering into physical combat with others, an aggressive person may be satisfied to argue about work procedures.

3. Conflict can lead to innovation and change. When the Equal Employment Opportunity Commission at first demanded that companies develop Affirmative Action Programs for integrating women and minority groups into management, minor instances of conflict emerged. The net effect was to create many good opportunities for these groups that had been underrepresented in key jobs. Conflict about these matters has also appeared to diminish.

4. As an aftermath to conflict, organizations often learn useful methods of resolving and preventing conflict. Executive rap sessions are a case in point. Top management first held informal discussion sessions with lower ranking employees because of the latter wanting more of a voice in company matters. Now such rap sessions have become institutionalized in many places. Top management learns of problems before they fester into larger problems.

5. Many individuals are bored with their jobs, and thus find interdepartmental squabbles a refreshing pause in their day. Office conflicts tend to add sparkle to coffee break conversations, even if the discussants are not personally involved in the dispute.

6. Conflict can provide diagnostic information about problem areas in an organization. For instance, if quality control and manufacturing are in constant conflict, it might indicate that manufacturing was using inferior methods or quality control was being unrealistic. Either condition requires an adjustment.

7. As an aftermath of conflict, unity may be reestablished. The drama of childhood is frequently reenacted in complex organizations.

Two adolescents engaged in a fist fight may emerge bloodied but good friends after the battle. Two warring departments may also become more cooperative toward each other as an aftermath of confrontation.

DETRIMENTAL ASPECTS OF CONFLICT

As common sense would suggest, conflict can have a multitude of harmful consequences to both individuals and organizations. Five of the major *dysfunctional* consequences of conflict will be mentioned here.

1. Conflict often results in extreme demonstrations of self-interest at the expense of the larger organization. Units of an organization or individual people will place their personal welfare over that of the rest of the organization or customers. Several times in recent years air traffic controllers were in dispute with their management about salary and miscellaneous working conditions. The controller group expressed their conflict by literal compliance with every air traffic regulation on the books at the time.[8] As a result, air traffic slowed down to almost a standstill because regulations liberally interpreted in the past were now strictly enforced.

2. Prolonged conflict between individuals can be bad for some people's emotional and physical well being. Many an individual has suffered psychosomatic disorders as a consequence of the intense disputes taking place within their companies.

3. Time and energy can be diverted from reaching important goals (such as making a profit) when people are in conflict. In addition, money and material can be wasted. One such example is a meeting called more for the purpose of settling interdepartmental disputes than for discussing how to achieve company goals. A headquarters personnel staff scheduled a weekend conference at a resort with a personnel group from a company division. The underlying purpose of the meeting was for the headquarters representatives to convince the division people that they (not the corporate group) should conduct management-development programs. During the conference, almost no mention was made of the technical quality of the program. Both groups were more concerned about who should have responsibility for the programs.

4. The aftermath of conflict may have high financial and emotional costs. Sabotage might be the financial consequence. Concomitantly, management may develop a permanent distrust of many people in the work force, even if only a few of them were saboteurs.

5. Another extreme consequence of conflict is the falsification of data and the distortion of reality. To win a point, people may present an untrue picture of their position. One group of highly specialized quality-control people were called superfluous by a manufacturing group. The quality-control group enlisted the help of allies in the field to document

their value to the company. Such friends were told to submit anecdotes about the worst quality-control problems that they had encountered. A convincing, but unrepresentative, presentation was then made of the importance of a supraquality control group for keeping equipment in the field running smoothly.

LINE VERSUS STAFF CONFLICT (WHO ASKED FOR YOUR ADVICE?)

A comprehensive form of conflict in most large organizations is that of line generalists versus staff specialists. Such conflict stems from most of the reasons for conflict described earlier. Line–staff conflict is given separate attention here because it represents a pervasive form of intergroup conflict in work organizations.[9]

Territorial Encroachment.   In general, the staff person advises the line person. The latter may accept or reject this advice as he or she sees fit in getting things accomplished. In some instances a staff person has considerable power. For example, if the company lawyer says a particular sales contact is absolutely illegal, management will probably draw up a more acceptable contract. At other times a staff person may be ignored. A personnel research specialist might inform management that its methods of selecting employees are unscientific and unsound. Management may ignore his advice.

An underlying reason that staff specialists and line personnel so often find themselves in dispute is that the line person may resent staff encroachment. In the personnel research example just cited, the plant manager and his personnel manager may say to each other, "Who does this character from the home office think he is, telling us how to select people? Our plant is running well. We have a work force of good people. We have no problems for him to solve. Why is he bothering us?"

Line people see staff people as encroaching on their territory in another important way. Whenever a staff specialist (such as an industrial engineer) makes a suggestion for improvement to a manager, it automatically infers that present conditions need improvement. If the industrial engineer says, "My methods will improve your efficiency," it implies that the manager is not perfectly efficient in his or her current mode of operation.

Conflicting Loyalties.   A good number of staff specialists come into conflict with line personnel over the issue of loyalty to their discipline versus their organization. The staff person feels this role conflict because he or she may want to adhere to a professional code that conflicts with tasks assigned by the firm. An accountant in an electronics firm faced this dilemma when he disapproved of the company's earnings statement. He felt that the company was using almost fraudulent accounting practices, yet his company pressured him to approve the statement. He finally approved the financial manipulations asked for by the president, but simultaneously wrote a letter of protest. His guilt about violating accounting ethics finally led him to resign from the company. Four months after he resigned, the company declared bankruptcy.

Separation of Knowledge and Authority. In large organizations few executives have sufficient knowledge to carry out their responsibilities. They are dependent upon lower-ranking staff advisors to furnish the appropriate information. A company president (or political candidate) usually does not even prepare his or her own speeches. In other instances an executive may have to choose a course of action based upon technical advice that he does not fully understand. His interdependence with the staff specialist may become a source of conflict.

Another source of conflict arises when the specialist resents being evaluated by a generalist whom he or she feels lacks the appropriate background to fairly evaluate his or her work. A performance appraisal of an engineering technician by a construction superintendent led to a confrontation. The superintendent told the technician he was performing "barely adequately" in his job. In response the technician replied, "What makes you think you are qualified to evaluate my technical work? You have no specialized background in engineering."

Formal Versus Informal Authority. When a line manager wants something accomplished, he or she often has the formal authority to influence the behavior of others.[10] When the department manager requests that the maintenance department repair a venetian blind, the maintenance department usually recognizes this as a proper (legitimate) request. Should the same request be made by an engineer in the department, the maintenance department might feel that the request is unauthorized. Staff specialists, and sometimes staff managers, must often go beyond their formal authority in getting things accomplished. Staff and line thus conflict over one more basic aspect of organizational life.

To compensate for their limited formal authority, staff personnel frequently resort to informal authority (personal or referent power) to get things accomplished. When a staff person is perceived as misusing informal authority, the result can be intensified conflict. One personnel manager attempted to enhance his informal authority by intimating to line managers that he worked closely with the president, and therefore indirectly held much power. One of his frequently used phrases was "Today when I was talking to Mr. Walker (the president). . . ." One day the head of manufacturing asked Mr. Walker if he had seen the personnel manager recently. Walker replied, "I hardly ever see him. He reports two levels below me." From that point on few people listened to the requests of the personnel manager in question.

In the past, more so than today, line and staff were distinctly different in personal style. Staff people tended to be better educated, more "modern," more style conscious, and more professionally oriented.[11] Such differences tended to breed conflict. Although many of these differences are probably less pronounced today than when they were originally noted by researchers, many differences still exist. Specialists with advanced formal education are often described by line management as being "ivory towerish." In response, staff personnel contend that line management is "resistant to change" or "old-fashioned."

RESOLVING CONFLICTS ON YOUR OWN

Because of the inevitability of conflict in work organizations, a career-minded person must learn practical, uncomplicated ways of resolving conflict with other people.[12] In recent years much attention has been paid to resolving conflict between marital partners or between parents and children. Job disputes must also be resolved to keep you free from excessive preoccupation with problems.

Gentle Confrontation.   A recommended starting point in settling any dispute between yourself and another individual is to openly discuss the problem with your adversary. Assume that Mary, the person working at the desk next to you, loudly cracks chewing gum while she works. You find the gum chewing both distracting and nauseating. If you don't bring the problem to Mary's attention, it will probably grow in proportion with time. Yet you are hesitant to enter into an argument about something that a person might regard as a civil liberty (the right to chew gum in public places).

A psychologically sound alternative is for you to approach the person directly in this manner:

> *You:* Mary, there is something bothering me that I would like to discuss with you.
>
> *She:* Go ahead, I don't mind listening to other people's problems.
>
> *You:* My problem concerns something you are doing that make it difficult for me to concentrate on my work. When you chew gum you make loud cracking noises that grate on my nerves. It may be my hang-up, but the noise does bother me.
>
> *She:* I guess I could stop chewing gum when you're working next to me. It's probably just a nervous habit.

An important advantage of gentle confrontation is that you deal directly with a sensitive problem without placing yourself in a position that will jeopardize the chances of forming a constructive working relationship in the future. One of the many reasons gentle confrontation works so effectively is that the focus is on the problem at hand (in this instance distracting noises) and not upon the individual's personality.

Disarm the Opposition. In many instances of interpersonal conflict the other individual has a legitimate complaint about specific aspects of your behavior. If you deny the reality of that person's complaint, he or she will continue to harp on that point and the issue will remain unresolved. By agreeing with that criticism of you, the stage may be set for true resolution of the problem.

An everyday example of this technique in action is found in an oft-repeated scenario on the highway. Perhaps you are driving slightly in excess of the speed limit (maybe 60 miles per hour in a 55 mile per hour zone). You notice a highway patrol car following you, sounding its siren, and flashing it's rotating light. Here are two ways to handle the situation when the policeman (or woman) walks up to the door of your car:

> *Usual Defensive Approach:* What's the problem? I wasn't speeding. My friend sitting right here will vouch for me.
>
> *Police Officer:* Don't tell me that. My speedometer doesn't lie.
>
> *Disarming the Opposition:* Officer, thank you for stopping me. When I heard your siren it made me realize that I was exceeding the speed limit by five miles per hour. That is clearly in violation of the law.
>
> *Police Officer:* I'm glad you realized it. Be careful the next time or you might be cited for a violation.

Agreeing with criticism made of you by a superior is effective, because by doing so you are then in a position to ask for his or her help in improving the situation. Most rational managers realize that it is their responsibility to help subordinates overcome problems, not to merely criticize them. Imagine that you have been chronically late with reports during the last six months. It is time for a performance review and you know you will be reprimanded for your tardiness. You also hope that your boss will not downgrade all other aspects of your performance because of your tardy reports. Here is how disarming the opposition would work in this situation:

> *Your Boss:* Have a seat. It's time for your performance review and we have a lot to talk about. I'm concerned about some things.
>
> *You:* So am I. It appears that I'm having a difficult time getting my reports in on time. I wonder if I'm being a perfectionist. Do you have any suggestions?
>
> *Your Boss:* Well, I like your attitude. I think you can improve in getting your reports in on time. Maybe you are trying to make your reports too perfect before you turn them in. Try not to figure everything out to five decimal places. We need thoroughness around here, but we can't overdo it.

Appeal to a Powerful Third Party.   At times gentle approaches to resolving interpersonal conflict do not work. The party with whom you are in a dispute may be unwilling to compromise; or he or she may use his or her organizational power (rank) to settle the conflict. In those instances, power tactics are necessary. Thus worker–management conflicts are often solved by an appeal to a labor union, problems of sexism and racism are resolved by an appeal to the Equal Employment Opportunity Commission, and disputes with an insurance company over a claim are resolved by appeal to legal authority.

The powerful third-party approach can also be applied to job-conflict situations in which you do not file a formal grievance or hire yourself a lawyer (a time-consuming and expensive process). Because of the ill will it usually creates, the powerful third-party tactic is only recommended when winning your dispute is very important to you. One such incident follows:

> Tim believed that a course in art appreciation would be helpful to him in his work as a company photographer. He found the course that he wanted at a tuition fee of $250. Being short on cash, Tim requested that his immediate superior authorize this course under the company Tuition Refund Program.
>
> Ralph, Tim's boss, disagreed. He believed that the company should only sponsor courses directly related to an employee's work. In Tim's situation this would be courses such as photographic science, business administration, or human relations. Tim and Ralph discussed the problem for twenty minutes, but Ralph would not change his mind.
>
> Tim then suggested that the request for the art appreciation refund be sent to the tuition refund coordinator. Tim telephoned her and was given authorization to take the course at company expense. Ralph refused to discuss the matter further. He never even inquired about how Tim liked to course.

ORGANIZATIONAL METHODS OF RESOLVING CONFLICT

During the last decade, behavioral and social scientists have developed an elaborate technique for resolving conflict between people and groups. Aside from working out techniques that relate to feelings and attitudes, many approaches have been developed for designing organizations to lessen conflict. One technique from both the confrontation and the organizational design approach will be presented here.

Organization Confrontation Meeting.   All techniques for resolving conflict by having people openly discuss their points of difference involve an element of confrontation.[13] Such confrontation approaches tend to work better when the parties confronting each other have approximately equal power in the organization. People are much less hesitant to confront peers than superiors. Often a confrontation meeting between superior and subordinates is stiff and contrived, particularly when the superior is not trusted.

A representative organization confrontation meeting was conducted in a manufacturing company between manufacturing line personnel (mostly foremen and superintendents) and manufacturing services (groups such as production engineering and production scheduling). A consultant suggested these meetings when he was asked to help "decrease some of the feuding between manufacturing and manufacturing services."

Step one involves each group meeting by itself to list their complaints about the other group. Both manufacturing and manufacturing services sent about half their total number to this meeting. A leader was appointed for each side to collect and condense the perceptions of the group.

Manufacturing had these five major complaints about manufacturing services:

"Too bossy; act as if we worked for them."

"Think that because they went to college, they know all the answers."

"Take our best ideas and feed them back to us without giving us any credit."

"Really don't know what's going on down here. Lack practical experience."

"Make too much money in comparison to us."

Manufacturing services had these five major complaints about manufacturing:

"Won't listen to advice, even when they need it."

"Overvalue practical experience. Tend to shut out new knowledge."

"Won't accept necessity for planning. Prefer to manage by crisis."

"Basically are opposed to our function. We have to fight to get their cooperation."

"Insist on bad-mouthing us to higher management."

Step two involves the representatives (leaders) from the two groups exchanging the list of complaints made about each other and asking questions to clear up ambiguities. In this situation, both team leaders received a clear message of what each side meant by its comments.

Step three involves the leaders bringing the images (or list of complaints) back to their groups for discussion about how some of these issues could be resolved. This stage took several hours.

Step four involves the leaders exchanging with each other the action plans developed by their groups to overcome some of these complaints.

Manufacturing had these two suggestions for overcoming the objections of manufacturing services:

"In the future if we have any complaints about your group we'll discuss them with you first."

"We'll listen more carefully to your suggestions, including those made about how we can plan better."

Manufacturing services had these two suggestions for overcoming the suggestions of manufacturing:

"Each staff member would spend one week during the upcoming year performing a routine production job in order to gain some practical experience."

"Any time that we use an idea for efficiency furnished us by a member of manufacturing we will put a written memo in his file to that effect."

Step five involves the team leaders bringing these action plans back to their groups for final discussion. Both sides agreed that the action plans were reasonable and feasible.

Confrontation approaches of this nature tend to have a short-lived effect unless there are some follow-up sessions or reminders. After a few months people usually retreat into their former habits, and the benefits of the conflict resolution procedure are lost. In this instance the consultant made two follow-up trips to meet with the groups and discuss progress. The reminder approach seemed to work. An acceptable level of inter-group conflict was present in comparison to the unacceptable level prior to the confrontation meeting.

Changing the Organizational Design. A widely used approach to conflict resolution is to change the shape or design of an organization in such a way that the sources of conflict are minimized. The underlying assumption in reducing or preventing conflict by modifying the structure is that personality clashes are not at the root of certain conflicts.

Modifying the organizational design is a useful way of reducing or eliminating many forms of role-based conflict. Manufacturing and marketing are so frequently in conflict that resources are wasted in settling their disputes. Manufacturing accuses marketing of being willing to sell anything to a customer even if the product cannot be manufactured at a profit. Furthermore, manufacturing contends that marketing wants everything accomplished on an unrealistically short schedule. Marketing, in turn, accuses manufacturing of being inflexible and unresponsive to the demands of customers.

A common solution to this problem has been the creation of a buffer position between manufacturing and marketing. Called something like "marketing liaison specialist" or "demand specialist," this individual becomes the communications bridge between the two groups. He or she interprets the demands of both groups to each other. The plan works except when the interface person feels that he or she has a superfluous job.

A modern approach to facilitating the resolution of conflict between supervisor and subordinate is the ombudsman.[14] Usually a person selected because of his ability to listen, the ombudsman takes the problem of lower-level personnel (usually factory workers) to somebody higher in management. His or her function is considered necessary because often factory workers do not feel that they have sufficient power to handle disputes with their immediate superior. When an organization has a labor union, employees might first take their grievances to a shop steward.

An ombudsman is granted the right to speak to anybody at any level in the company. He or she is sometimes seen as a lay therapist or a priest. Unlike an arbitrator, the ombudsman does not have the power to make a decision, but he or she can bring a problem to the attention of higher management.

What kind of conflict can an ombudsman help resolve? In one company an employee and his supervisor had a heated discussion about whether or not the supervisor was discriminating against the employee because he was black. Claimed the supervisor, "It's your attitude, not your race, that is holding you back from good assignments in my department." The employee brought the problem to the attention of the ombudsman (himself a black man). After the ombudsman brought the problem to higher management, the plant superintendent, ombudsman, and supervisor conferred about the problem. The employee was given a trial favorable assignment (night supervisor on a rotating basis). His attitude improved because of his favorable treatment, and the problem of perceived discrimination seemed to disappear.

*Summary
of Key Points*

1. Conflict occurs when two or more alternatives are incompatible.
2. Among the many reasons we have job conflict are the interdependence of people, differences in objectives, competition for limited resources, roles that conflict by design, and personal differences among people.
3. Job conflict can be beneficial or detrimental to both people and organizations. For instance, conflict can make people more creative; but it can also lead people to wasting resources while they fight their battles.
4. An almost inevitable form of conflict in complex organizations is that between staff specialists and line generalists. One contributing reason is that line personnel resent having their authority usurped, while staff people must justify their existence by keeping busy.
5. Among the many individual approaches to conflict resolution are gentle confrontation, disarming the opposition, and appeal to a third party.

6. Organization approaches to conflict resolution include the organization confrontation meeting and modifying the organization structure (or design) to lessen conflict.

1. What is the biggest conflict in the place you work or attend school? Can it be resolved?
2. Is a prize fight a conflict? Why or why not?
3. What is your usual approach to resolving conflict? How effective is it?
4. Which technique described in this chapter is best suited to resolving conflict in personal life (such as working out disagreements with a spouse or partner)?
5. Hockey players are notorious for engaging in physical combat during a game. How might such conflict be reduced?
6. Can you think of any organization that would probably score a 19 or 20 on the Job Conflict Questionnaire? Describe that place. What seems to be its major problem?

A Human Relations Incident
HOW DO WE MAKE COLLECTION AGENTS MORE LOVABLE?

Barney Wingate, regional manager at Worthwhile Financial Corporation, was studying the personnel research reports furnished him by Edie McGovern, corporate personnel manager. "Edie, it looks like we have a terrible turnover problem with our collection agents," said Wingate. "From your reports it looks like we can't recruit agents fast enough. Why do you think the problem is as bad as it is?"

"We don't know for sure, but I have some hunches. It seems that nobody likes a collection agent. When we send an agent out to track down a delinquent customer, he gets very little cooperation from anybody. I heard a story the other day about an agent who was lost in a poor neighborhood, trying to find a particular address. Strangers kept sending him off in the wrong direction. People seemed to know he was an outsider.

"We've tried tough guys, clean-cut kids, and executive-looking types. The results are always the same. Complaints and high turnover."

"Edie, have you ever thought," countered Barney, "that we're just not picking the right agents. Maybe we should just look for lovable types. Maybe they would get better cooperation."

If you were Edie, how would you respond to Barney's suggestion? Does he seem to be on the right track?

When Peter Tonnelli applied for a position in the Production Planning Department of the G. J. West Company, he inquired about the cooperative spirit in the department. Gordon Shaw, the manager, replied: "The cooperative spirit is the greatest asset of our department. In fact, the esprit de corps is so great that we were able to promote about one third of our staff over the last three years in recognition of the contribution they made to the department's goals." Being promoted as a reward for sustained cooperative effort appealed to Pete. He accepted a position in the department as a production planner.

Pete's first job related to consumer products. Later he was transferred to the position of production planner for the Graphic Arts Marketing Division. He is responsible for supplying finished product to the Marketing Division in accordance with the finished film schedule that the division provides. For Pete to fill the orders he receives for film from his marketing division, he must compete with each of the other planners for space and time in the film-coating alleys. This condition exists due to the complex nature of the products and the policy of company management.

It is the responsibility of the Production Planning Department to prepare production plans and schedules to optimally utilize all production facilities and produce the proper mix of products on time to meet customer demand. According to company philosophy, any customer should be able to order any catalog product at any time and it will be available.

During the last few years, demand for the company's products has been very high, and production facilities have been taxed to capacity. The company policy of austerity budgets has kept the capital expenditure budget tight, and money for new production facilities will not be made available for at least two more years.

John Sears, a planner in the emulsion coating planning group, is responsible for coordinating the coating of products. Each month John receives from each planner information on his or her requirements for film. All the requirements are added together and an inventory adjustment is made, the intent of which is to require all groups to have their inventories at a predetermined level of "normal," based on strategy guidelines determined by the management of the Production Planning Department and the Distribution Center Planning Department, which represents all the marketing areas. "Normal" is a statistical model that smooths demand and production variations, and gives an inventory position that will theoretically cover fluctuations in demand. When this calculation is complete, a computer program allocates a certain amount of coating footage to each planner known as an *aim*. The aim is divided by week over a three-month span and updated each month.

When Pete receives his aim, he utilizes several statistical techniques available to him to allocate his share of the pie among the various products for which he is responsible. Pete then schedules the products he needs for

* Case researched and written by Paul G. Toner.

the next three months and submits this schedule to John Sears. John aggregates the schedules and then runs a computer program that loads the schedules to determine whether or not the mix of products compares favorably with the capacity constraints in the coating alleys.

This process has come to be referred to among the planners as the "aims game." The following sketches are typical of incidents that have occurred:

1. When Pete receives his aim and schedules his products, he realizes that the strategy he was planning to use for product A won't fit his aim for week 1. He then goes to Pat who plans movie film. "Say, Pat, I need more aim in week 1 to schedule product A; can you underrun week 1 and I'll return the aim in week 4?" "Sorry, Pete, I'm already over and was hoping you could help me in week 1. Why don't we see if Glen and Morris can help us." Since capacity is tight, it is unlikely that anyone can help them.

2. Pete sees that he has extra aim in week 2, but doesn't really wish to give it away since he sees this as an ideal chance to build inventory for a future week when he may be tight.

3. John comes to Pete and says, "Pete, got a problem. The load is over in alley A in week 2. You will have to take 200,000 feet out of your schedule."

4. A meeting is called by Lou, the supervisor of the emulsion planning group with all the product planners; he says, "We ran the load program and find that we can add 500,000 feet to week 5 and 700,000 feet to week 7. Who needs more and how much can you take?" After the noise dies down, he arbitrarily assigns numbers to each planner.

5. Pat runs into John's office. "John, you've just got to give me more aim. I can't get all the products coated I really need to have." "Sorry, Pat, but if I give you more, I have to take it from someone else. Everybody says they need more."

6. When she leaves, Keith comes in to see John. "John, I just lost my last coating of product X due to dirt contaminant. If I don't replace it right away, we'll lose a big order." "O.K. Keith, I haven't heard Nancy complain this week. I'll tell her she'll have to give you 200,000 feet to cover that order."

7. Betty wears a basic black ensemble on the days that aim comes out since she knows that John is attracted to women in black; her desk is situated so that each time he looks up he will see her.

8. Morris, Glen, and Pete seem to have a constant battle to get enough aim, while Nancy and Rick never complain. Morris begins to feel that Nancy and Rick must be "fat" due to John's padding their aims for personal favors.

Pete sees the game being played and wonders what Gordon Shaw was talking about. He thinks to himself, "Cooperation? Team spirit? This is really a bag of snakes. No wonder we've lost so many planners to jobs at headquarters or out in the field. Who can stand this rat race; maybe I should look around too."

1. What is the underlying cause of the conflict described in this case?
2. What kind of behavior is Pete exhibiting by his decision to "look around"?

3. What might Pete do about the conflict he observes?

4. What kind of behavior is Betty exhibiting? Is it a fair technique for getting her share of aim?

5. What can be done about the practice of "John padding people's aims in exchange for personal favors"?

FOOTNOTES

[1] Summaries of the reasons for conflict in organizations are found in Andrew J. DuBrin, *Fundamentals of Organizational Behavior: An Applied Perspective*, 2nd ed., Pergamon Press, 1978, Chapter 10; and Ross A. Webber, *Management: Basic Elements of Managing Organizations*, Irwin, 1975, Chapter 25.

[2] James D. Thompson, *Organizations in Action*, McGraw-Hill, 1967, p. 55.

[3] Dennis Chamot, "Professional Employees Turn to Unions," *Harvard Business Review*, May–June 1976, p. 119.

[4] James E. Sorenson and Thomas L. Sorenson, "The Conflict of Professionals in Bureaucratic Organizations," *Administrative Science Quarterly*, Mar. 1974, p. 98.

[5] Joe Kelly, *Organizational Behavior: An Existential-Systems Approach*, rev. ed., Irwin, 1974, p. 320.

[6] Robert T. Keller, "Role Conflict and Ambiguity: Correlates with Job Satisfaction and Values," *Personnel Psychology*, Spring 1975, pp. 57–64.

[7] Webber, *op. cit.*, p. 590.

[8] DuBrin, *op. cit.*, Chapter 10.

[9] The analysis presented here follows part of the outline presented by Webber, *op. cit.*, pp. 590–593.

[10] Alan C. Filley, Robert J. House, and Steven Kerr, *Managerial Process and Organizational Behavior*, 2nd ed., Scott, Foresman, 1976, p. 391.

[11] *Ibid.*, p. 392.

[12] Andrew J. DuBrin, *Survival in the Office: How to Move Ahead or Hang On*, Mason/Charter, 1977, Chapter 5.

[13] One of many useful sources about confrontation meetings and related methods of resolving conflict is Newton Margulies and J. Wallace, *Organization Change: Techniques and Applications*, Scott, Foresman, 1973.

[14] Webber, *op. cit.*, p. 597.

SUGGESTED READING

ALINSKY, SAUL. *Rules For Radicals*, Random House, 1971.

BERNARDIN, H. JOHN, and ALVARES, KENNETH M. "The Managerial Grid as a Predictor of Conflict Resolution Method and Managerial Effectiveness," *Administrative Science Quarterly*, Mar. 1976, pp. 84–92.

BUTLER, ARTHUR G., JR. "Project Management: A Study in Organizational Conflict," *Academy of Management Journal*, Mar. 1973, pp. 84–101.

DuBrin, Andrew J. *Survival in the Office: How to Move Ahead or Hang On,* Mason/Charter, 1977, Chapter 5.

Filley, Alan C. *Interpersonal Conflict Resolution,* Scott, Foresman, 1975.

Johnson, Thomas W., and Stinson, John E. "Role Ambiguity, Role Conflict, and Satisfaction: Moderating Effects of Individual Differences," *Journal of Applied Psychology,* June 1975, pp. 329–333.

Kochan, Thomas A., Huber, George F., and Cummings, L. L. "Determinants of Intraorganizational Conflict in Collective Bargaining in the Public Sector," *Administrative Science Quarterly,* Mar. 1975, pp. 10–23.

Renwick, Patricia A. "Perception and Management of Superior–Subordinate Conflict," *Organizational Behavior and Human Performance,* June 1975, pp. 444–456.

Sorenson, James E., and Sorenson, Thomas L. "The Conflict of Professionals in Bureaucratic Organizations," *Administrative Science Quarterly,* Mar. 1974, pp. 98–106.

Zacker, Joseph, and Bard, Morton. "Effects of Conflict Management Training on Police Performance," *Journal of Applied Psychology,* Apr. 1974, pp. 202–208.

6
JOB POLITICS

After reading and studying this chapter, you should be able to

1. Provide several reasons why so much job politics exists in organizations.
2. Understand the major types of power.
3. Identify several ways of increasing your power in work organizations.
4. Identify several ways of gaining favor in an organization.
5. Recognize ways in which job politics can be controlled.
6. Acquire insight into your present tendencies toward being an office politician.

$\mathbf{B}$eing competent in your job is still the most effective method of achieving success. After skill comes hard work (motivation) and luck (being in the right place at the right time) as important success factors. A fourth ingredient is also necessary for success in both work and social organizations—political know-how. Few people can succeed in their work without having some awareness of the political forces around them and how to use them to advantage. A manager must be alert to political ploys used by his or her subordinates.

Political maneuvering, or the art of office politics, refers to so many different sets of behaviors that it would be difficult to integrate them all into one chapter or even one book. Job politics (a more inclusive term than office politics, since not everybody works in an office) can be subdivided into three somewhat overlapping categories: (1) methods of gaining power, (2) strategies for impressing your boss and other key people, and (3) career-advancement strategies. In this chapter we deal with gaining power and impressing others by means other than merit or skill.

Chapter 16, about managing your career, discusses several strategies for career advancement.

WHY WE HAVE JOB POLITICS

Politicking is all around us. People jockey for positions and try a variety of subtle maneuvers to impress their boss in almost every place of work. To understand the nature of job politics, it is important to understand why such actions on the part of rational people are ever-present.

Competition for Power. The very shape of large organizations is the most fundamental reason people jockey for position and power. Only so much power is available to distribute among the many people who would like more of it. As you move down the organization chart, each successive layer of people has less power than the layer above. At the very bottom of the organization, people have virtually no power.

Abraham Zaleznik, an organizational psychologist and psychoanalyst, makes this analysis of the inevitability of power struggles in business organizations:[1]

> Whatever else organizations may be . . . they are political structures. This means that organizations operate by distributing authority and setting a stage for the exercises of power. It is no wonder, therefore, that individuals who are highly motivated to secure and use power find a familiar and hospitable environment in business.

Lack of Objective Standards of Performance. Assume that you are a commercial artist. Your firm informs you that in order to become a supervisor you must first complete 500 assignments acceptable to clients. Your path to a promotion would be so clear-cut that you would not need to use political maneuvers to attain a supervisory position. Few organizations have such clear-cut measures of performance or well-defined steps for promotion. Because of this fact, people resort to job politics in an attempt to move ahead or gain advantage.

People resort to company politics because they do not believe that the organization has an objective (fair) way of judging their suitability for promotion.[2] Conversely, when management has no objective way of differentiating effective from less effective people, they will resort to favoritism in making promotions. The adage, "It's not what you know but who you know," does apply to organizations that lack clear-cut work objectives.

> Arnie, a junior executive working for an electronics company, was also a Little League coach. One of the three pitchers on his team, Heather, had much less accuracy than the other two pitchers. Nevertheless, Arnie per-

sisted in appointing Heather as the starting pitcher. Puzzled and mildly irritated, his assistant coach, John, asked Arnie why he relied so heavily on the erratic arm of Heather. He explained, "John, how can you be so naive? I know Heather isn't as good as my other two pitchers. But her father happens to be a vice-president in my company. Every time he sees me in the hall he gives me a big smile and tells me how great I am not to be prejudiced against female athletes. I'm sure it's going to lead to a promotion for me."

"But what about your record at the company? Isn't that more important?" asked John. Arnie noted, "What record? One junior executive is the same as another. We rotate from department to department and nobody knows what we are doing or even what we are supposed to do. Using Heather as my starting pitcher is a good way of getting noticed by the right person."

Emotional Insecurity.   Some people resort to political maneuvers to ingratiate themselves to superiors because they lack confidence in their talents and skills. As an extreme example, a Nobel Prize winning scientist does not have to curry favor with the administration of his or her university. The distinguished scientist's work speaks for itself. Winning a Nobel Prize has given this scientist additional self-confidence; he or she is therefore emotionally secure. A person's choice of political strategy may indicate that he or she is emotionally insecure.

Olaf, a laboratory technician, used body language to express approval of statements made by his boss or other managers in the company. In a group meeting, Olaf could be seen nodding with a Yes motion and smiling whenever his boss spoke. His peers joked that Olaf nodded more vigorously and smiled wider, the higher the rank of the people talking. In contrast, he was almost expressionless when a peer or hourly worker spoke.

Eventually, his boss became annoyed with Olaf's insincere head gestures. He asked Olaf why he found it necessary to nod approval at almost everything a manager had to say. Changing from a smile to a worried look, Olaf replied, "I don't care what my co-workers think of me. But I want the people who make decisions around here to like me. I thought a worker was supposed to please his boss."

SOURCES AND TYPES OF POWER

Power, in the context used here, refers to the *ability* to control the actions of others. Closely related is the concept of authority, which refers to the *right* to control the action of others.[3] An insecure vice-president might have the authority to make major decisions, but because of his insecurity he is not able to exercise this authority. How you obtain power in an organization depends to a large extent on the type of power that you are seeking. Therefore, to understand the mechanics of acquiring power, you also have to understand what forms of power exist.

John R. P. French and Bertram Raven[4] have developed a classification of power types that depends upon the basis of the power that one individual has over another. The first three of their power types are those granted by the organization; the fourth and fifth are derived largely from characteristics of the person.

Legitimate Power. Also referred to as position power, legitimate power is the easiest to understand and accept. People at higher levels in an organization have more power than people below them. A president has the right to donate money to charity. A supervisor has the right to reprimand an employee for being late. However, the culture of an organization helps decide the limits to anybody's power. A company president who suggests donating most of the company profits to a subversive group may find his decision overruled by the board of directors. A company supervisor who tells a man in his department not to buy a Corvette may find his orders ignored. People disregard orders (and laws) that they perceive as being illegitimate.

Reward Power. This type of power is based on the leader's ability to reward a follower for compliance. If a sales manager can directly reward his sales representatives with cash bonuses for good performance, he will exert considerable power. A nursing supervisor who can dispense appropriate praise to her subordinates for complying with her also exerts power, assuming that the nurses and ward personnel reporting to her want praise. A leader can only use reward power effectively when he or she has potent rewards (as explained in the earlier discussions of expectancy theory and behavior modification).

Coercive Power. The opposite of reward power, coercive power is the power to punish. It is based upon fear. Even in supposedly sophisticated organizations, some managers attempt to rule by fear, sometimes with good results in the short run. One manager demanded that every professional member of the department work a sixty-hour week. They were told that if they didn't like long hours they could look elsewhere for a job. Once jobs were again plentiful, three valuable members of the department left the company. Four other members requested internal transfers. Finally, the manager who managed by fear was demoted to a nonmanagerial position. Organized crime groups also force compliance by using coercive power.

Expert Power. Highly knowledgeable people have power even when their organizational rank is low. Persons such as B. F. Skinner (the psychologist) or Barry Commoner (the biologist and ecologist) exert considerable power over people (when they wish) because of their knowledge, not their formal position. A lawyer specializing in securities exerts expert power when his or her company is planning to raise new capital through a stock offering. A merchanic who can fix a ski lift exerts expert power when people are stranded on the chair lift owing to mechanical failure.

Referent Power.   Many people identify with leaders because of the latter's personality traits and other personal characteristics. Also called *charisma*, this type of power is helpful in influencing people over whom the leader has no direct control. John F. Kennedy and Jimmy Carter are two examples of political leaders with referent power. Entertainers exert considerable referent power (while popular). For instance, in 1976 Tony Orlando and Dawn (a singing and dance group) were dispensing career guidance to millions through radio advertising and follow-up mail. Their acceptance certainly did not stem from expert power (in the area of career guidance).

METHODS OF OBTAINING POWER

As power and politics in organization life gain more acceptance as a legitimate concern of both popular and academic writers, many of the tactics described next[5] will become public knowledge. You will thus be at a disadvantage if you do not use such strategies or recognize when they are being used against you. Even if you prefer not to "play office politics," it helps to be aware of the tactics chosen by those around you.

Identify and Win Support of Influentials.   Also called "maintain alliances with powerful people," this is the most useful general-purpose method of increasing your power base. If you marry the boss's daughter, son, or the boss, you automatically become a more powerful person in your organization. Astute sales representatives learn to cultivate a good relationship with executive secretaries, because these women (and sometimes men) can exert considerable influence with their executive superiors. Ed Roseman has this advice to offer product managers in their quest for power:[6]

> Who else can you get on your side or at least neutralize? Sometimes outsiders such as the advertising agency can add to your base of power, or a key financial man, or member of the legal staff. These influentials are not always in the higher level jobs. Sometimes they're just people in the organization whom others listen to—successful salesmen, persuasive speakers, or close personal friends of people in influence.

Mutual Back Scratching.   Many of the informal agreements that take place in work organizations are based on the idea of exchanging favors with people. In legislative circles the term for the same behavior is *log rolling*. In relationships between purchasing and selling, the term used is reciprocity. Yet another synonym is "collect and use IOUs." In practicing mutual back scratching, it is best to exchange favors with people of higher rank than yourself. The result may be increased power or simply the granting of an important favor when you need it most.

> An executive in a moving company wanted a friend's personal belongings shipped in a hurry. He worked things out quite effectively with a dispatcher in charge of routing the moving vans. Six months later, the dispatcher called the executive asking for a favorable recommendation for a transfer to Florida. The executive replied, "I'll see what I can do." Within one year the dispatcher who had extended himself (slightly bending company regulations in the process) was transferred to a comparable level position in Tampa, Florida.

Boring from Within. Another descriptive term for this power-gaining maneuver is "plant an ally." If you want your cause championed, it helps to have an insider talk about the advantages of your cause. Many a textbook writer has picked up a valued adoption because a former student of his (who liked him and his ideas) took a teaching position at another university. The student later recommends to other faculty members that they adopt the text written by the professor in question. William H. Newman provides an artful example of boring from within:[7]

> The production manager of one company had no use for these "new-fangled personnel ideas." The personnel director, however, did borrow one of the outstanding young executives in the production department for a special project, and during the period when the young man was on loan thoroughly indoctrinated him and enthused him regarding modern personnel practice. Some time after the junior executive returned to his former job a bad situation developed because a man clearly unqualified had been placed in a foreman position. The junior executive took the opportunity to suggest that they might study the foremen who were successful and those who were not in order to determine what to look for when a new man was to be appointed; thus he began laying the basis for the use of personnel specifications.

Develop Expertise. A person who controls the vital resource of important information automatically becomes a more powerful individual (expert power). Alan N. Schoonmaker notes[8] that "Hundreds of former assistants have succeeded their bosses (sometimes pushing them out) because they were the only people who knew what was going on."

During the 1960s and early 1970s, computer experts were catapulted into high-paying and responsible jobs because of their esoteric knowledge. As more people have acquired knowledge about computer science (and some computer programmers have been replaced by computers), computer expertise has lost some of its power-giving value.

Acquire Seniority. In our society, longevity in an organization still garners some respect and privilege. Labor unions, for instance, have long emphasized the rights of seniority. Although seniority alone will not prevent you from being ousted from the organization or guarantee you more power, it helps. The compulsive job hopper is forever working against the implicit threat of the last in, first out personnel policy, even at the managerial level.

> One manager in the food business accepted a position with a Boston company as the manager of new-product development. Three months after he arrived he was informed that the company had no funds left to invest in new-product development. He was given one month's severance pay and faced with the embarrassment and awkwardness of finding a comparable level position. Eight months later, he found a job as a food-processing engineer at a substantially lower level of pay than his previous two positions.

Be Distinctive and Formidable. An ideal approach to increasing your power base, bringing favorable attention to yourself, and advancing your career is to become distinctive and formidable. Implementing this strategy is not easy. You might distinguish yourself by your accomplishments, speech, or mode of dress. Whatever strategy you choose, it is important to be distinctive for positive reasons.

Owing to the American obsession with professional athletes, many a former professional athlete has used his athletic prowess to help him obtain power inside a business organization. One well-known manufacturing company has an informal policy of recruiting former professional athletes for its management-training program. Former athletes advance much more rapidly in the program than their counterparts lacking a sports background.

Camel's Head in the Tent. A gradual approach is sometimes the most effective means of acquiring power. Just as the camel works his way into the tent inch by inch, you might acquire power in a step-by-step manner until you emerge victorious. An administrative assistant in a furniture company took care, one by one, of all the details relating to a line of office furniture. Finally her boss said, "Rosalin, why don't we make you the product manager for office furniture? At this stage you know more about the product line than I do." Rosalin achieved just the position she wanted. If she had suggested at the outset that she be made product manager, her proposal might have been refused.

Keep on Sawing Wood. Another descriptive term for this strategy is "by their works ye shall know them." It is perhaps the simplest and least devious strategy for acquiring power. When faced with criticism of what you are doing, ignore your critics. As time passes and you accumulate good results, your critics will change their opinion of you and your work. If you have faith in what you are doing and you are not impatient, this approach can work effectively.

Rob, manufacturing engineer in a company that produced small appliances, began to collect scrap material on his own. Although his manager did not stop Rob from his endeavor, he offered him no support and some criticism. At a party he once introduced Rob as "the department junk man." Others kidded him about the fact he was probably selling the scrap to a junk wholesaler for 25 cents per pound.

Rob persisted with his scrap collection. When he accumulated sufficient quantities of scrap, he begged for authorization to attempt a recycling experiment. The material savings were found to be substantial. Eventually as recycling became more fashionable, Rob's ideas paid handsome dividends. He was appointed coordinator of recycling operations, a position that paid for itself and brought the company favorable publicity.

Make a Quick Showing. A display of dramatic results can be useful in gaining acceptance for your efforts or those of your group. Once you have impressed management with your ability to work on that first problem, you can look forward to working on the problems of real interest to you. Home-improvement specialists frequently use this approach. They offer to repair an obvious eyesore at a reasonable price. One such team of workers performed a splendid job on a sagging porch of a property owner's building. They eliminated the sags, patched up holes, and painted the porch. Pleased with their good results, the building owner agreed to have other work done (such as replacing a broken roof), which was more extensive (and expensive).

William H. Newman notes that computer specialists often gain power for themselves by first attacking problems where quick savings for management can be made. For instance, they might computerize a manual payroll function and reduce the number of personnel required for its operation. Once these impressive economies have been effected, they offer to attack tasks of more interest to themselves (and hopefully of more long-range benefit to management). One such grand project would be a management information system.

Control of Vital Information. Depending upon how information is controlled, this power tactic can be devious (and therefore should be discussed in a later section in this chapter devoted to such tactics). It is also closely related to acquiring expertise as a power tactic. Many a former government or military official has found a convenient power niche for himself in industry after leaving the public payroll. Frequently, such individuals are hired as the Washington representative of a firm that does substantial business with the federal government or military. The vital information they control is knowledge of who to speak to to shorten some of the complicated procedures in getting contracts approved. Even the esoteric knowledge of how to write a proposal to overcome government or military objections gives that individual power. Part of these people's expertise is possessing information about which people to contact for what purpose.

When you gain favor in an organization, you also increase the chances of your getting promoted and gaining power. Nevertheless, there is some logic in classifying some strategies as geared primarily toward looking good (gaining favor) in your place of work. All these strategies[9] will fail if they are not used as an accompaniment to good work performance. They supplement, but do not substitute for, merit.

Help Your Boss Succeed. Few experienced workers would dispute the value of this often overlooked strategy. The primary reason you are hired is to help your superior achieve the results that he or she must achieve in order to succeed. Avoid an adversary relationship with your boss. In addition, figure out both subtle and direct ways of ensuring his or her chances for success. One subtle way of increasing your boss's chances for success is to help him or her out when he or she is under attack.[10]

> Ray was a quality-control engineer in a company that manufactured and sold a line of office machines. His department came under attack from production supervisors. The latter complained that quality control was becoming a cog in the wheel for output because they were falling behind on their inspections. A series of meetings were scheduled to work out some of these problems. Ray noted that Peter, his boss, was being roundly criticized because of the generalizations he was making about quality-control problems.
> Ray came to Pete's defense by providing some statistical data to support Pete's generalizations. The production personnel could not logically argue with the statistical facts presented by Ray. Pete recognized the contribution Ray was making and rewarded him in his next performance appraisal by giving him a rating of "outstanding performer."

Display Loyalty. A loyal worker is a valued worker, however traditional the idea. Organizations prosper more with loyal than disloyal subordinates. Blind loyalty, in which you believe your organization cannot make a mistake, is not called for. What is helpful in gaining favor is a willingness to defend your company or your boss in time of trouble. Sometimes an innovative approach to displaying loyalty is called for.[11]

> Mandy, a biologist, read a feature story in the local newspaper about how her company was polluting the major river in town. Believing that the story overstated the amount of damage inflicted upon the environment, Mandy sent a letter to the editor of the paper. She explained her views, noting that she was writing from the viewpoint of a private citizen and not that of a company employee. The company president called Mandy in for a private conference shortly after the letter was published. Loyalty of this nature paid off for the observant biologist. Mandy received a one-step promotion in a much shorter time than she expected.

Volunteer for Assignments. An easily implemented method of winning the approval of your superiors is to become a "handraiser." By volunteering to take on assignments that do not fit neatly into your job description, you display the kind of initiative valued by employers. Among the many possible activities to volunteer for are fund-raising campaigns assigned to your company, membership in committee (for example, a safety committee), and working overtime when most people prefer not to work overtime (for example, on a Saturday in July).

Make Effective Use of Praise. Knowing how and when to praise people is a valuable skill when trying to build your reputation in an organization. Those people who you praise sincerely will find your very presence *reinforcing*, thus giving you a small degree of reward power. One appropriate situation for praising a superior is after he or she has made an effective presentation in a meeting.

Two suggestions about the dispensing of praise should be kept in mind. First, it is generally more effective to praise a person's actions than him or her as an individual. In the situation just cited, it would be better to tell your boss, "You really got your points across to the people," than, "You really are a good speaker." When you point to something specific that a person has done well, it appears more sincere than generalized praise. Second, do not use praise indiscriminately. If you are seen praising your superiors for a wide range of their activities, your praise loses its reward value.

Laugh at Your Boss's Jokes. Closely related to praising your boss, is laughing at his or her jokes (when you find at least some humor in them). When you indicate by your laughter that you appreciate your boss's sense of humor, it helps to establish rapport between you and him or her. One of the signals we get from other people that the two of us are communicating well is when the other person catches our subtle points. Most humor expressed in the office deals with subtle meanings about work-related topics. Few career-minded people tell standard jokes during working hours.

Become a Crucial Subordinate. A variation of "help your boss succeed," this strategy means that you help your superior with a task upon which his or her performance depends. You are crucial because you help your superior with crucial assignments. Unless a superior is emotionally insecure (and therefore fearful of capable subordinates), this tactic helps you gain favor in the organization. Your task in becoming a crucial subordinate is to identify crucial tasks facing your superior and then to demonstrate your interest in helping.

Cal worked as a registrar's assistant in a private university. His superior, the associate registrar, had overall responsibility for the registration system at the university. Cal soon learned that the registration system in current use was perceived as disastrous by students and faculty. Students were frequently billed for courses they had never taken. Many class sections were overcrowded, while others meeting at equally desirable times were so small that they were eligible for cancellation.

Assuming that his boss must be under pressure to improve the registration system, Cal volunteered to head up a task force to develop a new system. His boss happily gave Cal the opportunity to help him out with this vexing problem. Cal's task force produced a system that was a vast improvement over the current one. When his boss became the registrar in an organizational shuffle, Cal was selected over two other candidates for promotion to associate registrar. His boss had given Cal outstanding praise for the system he developed and helped implement.

DEVIOUS POLITICAL APPROACHES

Any technique of gaining power or favor can be devious if practiced in extreme. A person who supports his boss by helping him carry company property out the door for his personal use is being devious. Some approaches are unequivocally devious, such as those described next. Each one of them is *precisely what we are recommending not to be followed.*

Blackmail. Extortion has been a long-standing criminal activity. It has also been used by company politicians to gain power and/or favor. A curious aspect of company blackmail is that one deviant person threatens to make public the deviant behavior of another, unless the former makes certain concessions to the latter. Blackmailers, however, lead a hazardous existence.

Dan, an accountant, noticed a few major irregularities in the expense report submitted by an executive in his firm. One abnormality he noticed was that the executive's daily expenses were higher than those of others taking similar trips. A more pronounced problem Dan discovered were two hotel receipts with smudged-in areas over the dates. In addition, the hotels seemed unusually far from any company location. Dan called these hotels to verify the receipts submitted by the executive. Dan's hunch was correct. The executive was submitting phony hotel receipts that he had collected while on private travel. He had apparently stayed with friends in place of using a public hotel. Dan even suspected that the executive might be submitting expenses for phantom trips.

Dan confronted the executive with his findings. He demanded a promotion into his department and threatened to disclose the expense account irregularities if his demands were not met. Dan did receive a promotion to a supervisory position. Four months later he and the executive were both fired. The executive was caught receiving a bribe from a company supplier. On his way out, he revealed Dan's act of extortion.

Character Assassination. According to Ed Roseman, a careful observer of job politics, character assassins are as skillful and lethal as underworld "hit men." Rarely are they openly critical of their victims. Instead they drop innuendoes:[12]

> The salesman I worked with in the field used the visual aid as instructed, but I had the definite impression that he didn't completely understand what we were trying to accomplish. I wonder if the sales manager is failing to explain this to him properly?

In this situation, the product manager making these derogatory hints about the sales manager has some particular reason to have the latter removed from the scene. Perhaps he believes that the sales manager in question is not giving him enough support.

Remove the Opposition.   The ultimate weapon in outdistancing a rival for promotion, or ridding the company of a key person who has a negative opinion of you, is to have that person physically removed. Precipitating a rival's dismissal by making negative comments about another individual rarely leads to a person's dismissal. Unless there is other supporting evidence, most rational managers will not fire one person upon the word of another. Anybody who tries to physically remove another by resorting to "framing" risks being faced with a libel suit.

A still devious, but less criminal-like approach, to removing others is attempting to have a rival transferred or promoted out of your area. At high levels this tactic can take the form of bringing your rival's name and credentials to the attention of an executive employment agency or search firm. Or the manager from another department, division, or firm can be told about the virtues of the "really promising person who is being underutilized where he (or she) is now."

Divide and Rule.   An ancient military and governmental strategy,[13] this tactic is sometimes used in business. The object is to have subordinates fight among themselves, therefore giving you the balance of power. If subordinates are not aligned with each other, there is an improved chance that they will align with a common superior. One company general manager used this technique to short-range advantage by dropping innuendoes during staff meetings.

> Once in a meeting called to discuss the production schedule on a new product, Vic (the general manager) said to Don (the head of manufacturing), "They tell me engineering isn't holding up its end of getting things ready for production." Two weeks later Vic dropped another conflict-arousing comment, this time to the head of engineering. "It's too bad you're having so many problems with manufacturing trying to figure out how to build the product you've designed."
> Vic's techniques did create rivalry and hard feelings between engineering and manufacturing. Ultimately, his top staff saw through his divide and conquer tactics and his effectiveness as a leader diminished. Realizing he was no longer effective as a leader, he was asked to resign by higher executives in the company.

The Setup.   The object of a setup is to place a person in a position where he or she will look ineffective. A young man considered to have high potential by the company was assigned to a manager's department. Suspecting that this new arrival might be intended as his replacement, the manager set up the young man to fail. He placed him in charge of an operation he knew nothing about. In a short period of time the acclaimed individual was in trouble on the job. Believing that they perhaps had overrated this man's potential, they transferred him to another department. He was also relegated to lesser tasks.

Receive Undue Credit.   A devious approach widely practiced by managers is to receive credit for work performed by subordinates and not allow them to share in the praise. The same technique can be used with peers, as practiced by Sam who worked in a computer printing department[14]:

> For each job that was processed, the operator had to log the start and stop time of the job. This list was used to check for responsibility of printing quality and to some extent as a measure of job performance. As each job was set up, Sam would log his operator number even if the job was not processed by him. However, when he observed that the print quality did not measure up to standards, he would change the operator log number to that used by one of his co-workers. He did not, however, adjust the printers to produce the proper print quality.

STEMMING THE TIDE OF JOB POLITICS

Carried to excess, job politics can hurt an organization and its members. Too much politicking can result in wasted time and effort, therefore lowering productivity. Human consequences can also be substantial, including lowered morale and the turnover of people who intensely dislike playing office politics. Three particularly helpful approaches to combatting job politics will be mentioned here.[15]

Provide Objective Measurements of Performance.   As suggested earlier in this chapter, a primary reason we have so much politicking in some organizations is that those organizations do not provide objective methods of measuring performance. When a person knows exactly what it is he or she has to do in order to qualify for promotion, there is less need for political maneuvering. Even more fundamental, you tend to curry favor with a superior when there seems to be no other way to determine if you are competent in your job.

Providing an Atmosphere of Trust.   Several management observers have noted that this is the best overall antidote to excessive playing of politics.

If people trust each other in a company, they are less likely to use devious tactics (or even slightly devious tactics) against each other. People often resort to cover-up behavior because they fear the consequences of telling the truth about themselves. In Chapter 13 we shall return to the topic of creating trust and openness in work organizations.

Set Good Examples at the Top. When people in key positions are highly political, they set the tone for job politicking at lower levels. When people at the top of the organization are nonpolitical (straightforward) in their actions, they demonstrate in a subtle way that political behavior is not desired. A new vice-president squelched job politicking in a hurry through an unusual confrontation:

> Brad called his first official staff meeting as vice-president of finance. After a few brief comments about his pleasure in joining the company, he said bluntly: "I've been here only two weeks, yet I've noticed some strange actions that I want stopped right now. I know it's part of the American culture to please the boss, but don't be so naive about it. I'm not pointing the finger at any one person in particular, but you people have been milling around my office like birds waiting for crumbs. If you have some official business and you want to make an appointment with my secretary, Betty, fine. But if you don't have a legitimate business purpose in seeing me, don't drop by my office. We've got too many things to accomplish to spend time in coffee klatches."

HOW POLITICAL ARE YOU?

To gain some tentative insight into the extent of your political orientation, answer the questionnaire shown in Figure 6.1.

Directions: Answer each question "mostly agree" or "mostly disagree," even if it is difficult for you to decide which alternative best describes your opinion.

	Mostly Agree	*Mostly Disagree*
1. Only a fool would correct a boss's mistakes.	_____	_____
2. If you have certain confidential information, release it to your advantage.	_____	_____
3. I would be careful not to hire a subordinate with more formal education than myself.	_____	_____
4. If you do somebody a favor, remember to cash in on it.	_____	_____
5. Given the opportunity, I would cultivate friendships with powerful people.	_____	_____

6. I like the idea of saying nice things about a rival in order to get that person transferred from my department. ___ ___

7. Why not take credit for someone else's work? They would do the same to you. ___ ___

8. Given the chance, I would offer to help my boss build some shelves for his or her den. ___ ___

9. I laugh heartily at my boss's jokes, even when they are not funny. ___ ___

10. I would be sure to attend a company picnic even if I had the chance to do something I enjoyed more that day. ___ ___

11. If I knew an executive in my company was stealing money, I would use that against him or her in asking for favors. ___ ___

12. I would first find out my boss's political preferences before discussing politics with him or her. ___ ___

13. I think using memos to zap somebody for his or her mistakes is a good idea (especially when you want to show that person up). ___ ___

14. If I wanted something done by a co-worker, I would be willing to say "If you don't get this done, our boss might be very unhappy." ___ ___

15. I would invite my boss to a party at my house, even if I didn't like him or her. ___ ___

16. When I'm in a position to, I would have lunch with the "right people" at least twice a week. ___ ___

17. Richard M. Nixon's bugging the Democratic Headquarters would have been a clever idea if he wasn't caught. ___ ___

18. Power for its own sake is one of life's most precious commodities. ___ ___

19. Having a high school named after you would be an incredible thrill. ___ ___

20. Reading about job politics is as much fun as reading an adventure story. ___ ___

FIGURE 6.1
Political orientation questionnaire.

Interpretation of Scores. Each statement you check "mostly agree" is worth 1 point toward your political orientation score. If you score 16 or over, it suggests that you have a strong inclination toward playing politics. A high score of this nature would also suggest that you have strong needs for power. Scores of 5 or less would suggest that you are not inclined toward political maneuvering and that you are not strongly power driven.

Our customary caution is again in order. This questionnaire is designed primarily to encourage you to introspect about the topic under study. The political orientation questionnaire lacks the scientific properties of a legitimate personality test.

JOB POLITICS AND PERSONAL FAILURE

People who do not achieve their personal objectives in organizations frequently attribute their lack of success to job politics. They feel that favoritism has worked against them—that a less deserving person has been promoted to a key job. Such contentions are not necessarily the product of paranoid thinking. If you are politically naive you probably will not achieve the success you desire. The antidote from the author's standpoint is for you to practice ethical and sensible politics. One such strategy would be for you to become recognized by upper management for your willingness to volunteer for assignments and your participation in company social functions. Under such circumstances, politics might work in your favor.

Summary
of Key Points

1. Job politics, as the term is used here, refers to a variety of approaches other than strictly merit for gaining power, impressing others, or advancing your career.
2. Some political tactics are generally considered ethical, whereas others are clearly devious (such as discrediting others).
3. Among the reasons we have job politics are (a) the competition for power found in a pyramid-shaped organization, (b) lack of objective standards of performance, and (c) the emotional insecurity of people.
4. Power can be granted by the organization or can stem from characteristics of the person (such as charisma).
5. Methods of obtaining power include (a) winning the support of influentials, (b) mutual back scratching, (c) boring from within, (d) developing expertise, (e) acquiring seniority, (f) being formidable, (g) camel's head in the tent, (h) keep on sawing wood, (i) make a quick showing, and (j) controlling vital information.
6. Strategies for gaining favor include (a) helping your boss succeed,

(b) displaying loyalty, (c) volunteering for assignments, (d) praising others, (e) laughing at your boss's jokes, and (f) becoming a crucial subordinate.

7. Three ways of decreasing job politics (they can never be eliminated) are (a) providing objective measurements of performance, (b) establishing an atmosphere of openness and trust, and (c) setting good examples in top management.

1. How do you think the following people would score on the political orientation questionnaire? (a) Jimmy Carter, (b) Mohammed Ali, (c) your instructor.
2. Which tactic of job politics is practiced the most where you work now (or where you last worked)? In what way was it used?
3. What technique of job politics have you seen in action or heard about that was not mentioned in this chapter?
4. Which tactics described here does the Mafia allegedly use?
5. What types of power do the top executives at General Motors probably possess? Use the types mentioned in the chapter section called Sources and Types of Power.
6. If a friend said to you, "I want to someday be an executive, but I refuse to play office politics," what advice would you offer him or her?

A Human Relations Incident
THE COPYING MACHINE EXTORTIONIST

One early spring afternoon you suddenly realize that you have forgotten to take care of an important chore. As coach of the Little League Panthers, it's your job to make sure that all twenty members of your team have a copy of the season baseball schedule. Noticing that the Xerox machine in your office is not being used, you decide to make the necessary copies. Quickly you complete the chore and turn off the machine. As you are finishing the task, Alfie, a clerk in your department, approaches you.

He says with a sly grin, "I couldn't help but noticing those Little League schedules you were running off on the company machine. Shame, shame, and you a management trainee. I tell you what, I'll bet you twenty-five dollars that I don't turn you in to management."

"What are you talking about," you reply.

"Okay, I'll run it by you again," says Alfie. "If I don't turn you in to management, you owe me twenty-five dollars. You must agree, twenty-five dollars is a pretty cheap price to pay for protecting your honor in this company. Who wants to be accused of using the Xerox machine for their personal business?"

Would you give Alfie his twenty-five dollars? Why or why not? What would you do?

A Human Relations Case
MURDOCK THE MANEUVERER*

John Murdock has worked as an industrial engineer for the Bandex Corporation for over five years. During that time span he has rotated through four major assignments and received one modest promotion. John has spent the last eighteen months working with the same group in the area of indirect labor measurement. Although John had been interested in and enthused about his job in its initial stages, lately he has noticed himself becoming somewhat dissatisfied and bored.

John attributes this change in attitude to two factors. First, the type of work he performs has become repetitive and routine. As John states, "Once you've made one hundred measurements of white collar work units, the next one hundred become a dreadful bore." Second, and most important, John had compiled a consistently high work appraisal over the past two years. Performance reviews with both his prior and present managers indicated that he was qualified for promotion. It was patiently explained to Murdock that, considering present group assignments and responsibilities, there would be no promotions for anyone in the group within the next year to year and a half.

After carefully reviewing the situation, John proceeded to take corrective steps within the established corporate framework. He applied for several senior engineer positions within the company utilizing the internal job positioning system. To further increase his chances of finding a suitable new position, John submitted his resumé to a private placement service.

Murdock was surprised at the good results these simple steps achieved. Three interviews within the company were forthcoming from his internal search. However, the interviews only led to an awareness on other people's part of John's promising background and his interest in advancement. Too many equally talented engineers with more experience than John's, were themselves searching for new positions. Interviews generated from John's external search produced similar results. The several warm leads he did turn up were job situations that offered a promotion in title only, while requiring additional responsibility with less pay. Bandex, John quickly learned, is a high-paying company.

At this point, John decided to circumvent the formal system and try a few quiet maneuvers of his own. He began his quest for a bigger position by reviewing his work history and identifying those areas that he could bargain with and utilize in obtaining the senior engineer position that he

* James D. Christie researched and wrote this case.

sought. From this analysis, four key factors emerged: (1) John was regarded as a self-starter who required very little direction from a manager; (2) he worked well with a wide range of people from hourly production workers to executives; (3) he was highly regarded as an individual who could complete a given assignment in a timely manner regardless of the complexity; (4) John had acquired a comprehensive amount of direct and indirect work measurement experience.

Murdock concluded from his introspective analysis that he should search for a job situation containing two essential characteristics: a job situation calling for a person of proven results in getting things done in a short time frame, and simultaneously one in which the knowledge required dealt with labor measurement systems.

John's next step was to make telephone calls to all the managers and engineers he knew personally in other product areas in order to determine on his own what jobs were available. Utilizing this procedure, Murdock located a manufacturing engineering department that looked promising.

The department in question had been asked to develop indirect labor indicators for their plant—an eight person-month task for which they had a five-month deadline. It had become evident that the current engineer assigned to the job would not be able to complete it on time. In John's assessment, this was precisely the opportunity he was seeking. His first step was to arrange a meeting with the manufacturing engineering manager.

During the meeting the manager verified that the problem did indeed exist, but that the product could not afford to allocate two engineers to the task. John Murdock now made his move. He offered to take over the assignment, develop all the indicators to the best of his ability, obtain approval of the indicators from financial control, and do all this within the five-month time frame alloted by the company. In return for his services, he made the following request: "Should I be able to fulfill my promise, I want to be retained by the product and promoted to the rank of senior engineer." After considerable thought, the manager of manufacturing engineering agreed to the proposal. Murdock's superior was contacted and he begrudgingly agreed to "loan" him to the new department.

Things worked out well for John Murdock. He accomplished the task on time, sold the indicators to financial control, and in all respects turned in a high-quality performance. Six months after John took over the assignment, and one month following its completion, he became a senior engineer. Shortly thereafter, his assignments were changed and a new job was created with greater responsibility and authority. John Murdock is now project leader, advanced manufacturing engineering concepts.

Al Blake, a former department colleague of John Murdock's, asked him, "What kind of a corporate stunt did you pull off? Eight months ago you were a straight engineer, moaning and groaning about being locked into your position. The company has been in a budget squeeze. And now you have leapfrogged into a fancy project leader slot. How about sharing your secret with an old friend?"

1. Comment upon the ethics of John Murdock's method of finding himself a new position.
2. Did Murdock rely more heavily upon his technical capability or his

political skill in achieving his promotion to the position of senior engineer? Explain the basis for your answer.

3. What should management do about individuals who circumvent formal channels in getting themselves promoted?

4. Was Murdock justified in searching outside the company for a new position before first exhausting all internal possibilities?

5. What do you think of the ethics of the manager of manufacturing engineering negotiating with Murdock first before speaking to his boss?

FOOTNOTES

[1] Abraham Zaleznik, "Power and Politics in Organizational Life," *Harvard Business Review*, May–June, 1970, p. 47.

[2] Andrew J. DuBrin, *Fundamentals of Organizational Behavior: An Applied Perspective*, Pergamon Press, 1974, p. 140.

[3] Rolf E. Rogers, *Organizational Theory*, Allyn and Bacon, 1975, p. 167.

[4] The power types discussed in this section are found in John R. P. French and Bertram Raven, "The Basis of Social Power," in Dorwin Cartwright and Alvin Zander (eds.), *Group Dynamics: Theory and Research*, 3rd ed., Harper & Row, 1968.

[5] The ten strategies mentioned in this section are based on information in the following sources: Strategy one, Ed Roseman, "The Myth of the Powerless Product Manager," *Product Management* (now called *Product Marketing*), Feb. 1976, p. 34. Strategies two, three, seven, eight, and nine, William H. Newman, *Administrative Action: The Techniques of Organization and Management*, 2nd ed. Prentice-Hall, 1963, pp. 86–98. Strategies four, five, and ten, Alan N. Schoonmaker, *Executive Career Strategy*, American Management Association, 1971, pp. 110–118.

[6] Roseman, *op. cit.*, pp. 34–35.

[7] Newman, *op. cit.*, p. 88.

[8] Schoonmaker, *op. cit.*, p. 103.

[9] Strategies one, two, and four are based on Andrew J. DuBrin, *Survival in the Office: How to Move Ahead or Hang On*, Mason/Charter, 1977, Chapter 1. Strategy six is from Eugene E. Jennings, *The Mobile Manager: A Study of the New Generation of Top Executives*, University of Michigan Press, 1967.

[10] David Crane conducted the research for this case example.

[11] Case example quoted from Andrew J. DuBrin, *Survival in the Sexist Jungle: A Psychologist's Program for Combating Job Discrimination Against Women*, Books For Better Living, 1974, p. 38.

[12] Ed Roseman, "How to Play Clean Office Politics," *Product Management*, May 1976, p. 33.

[13] Newman, *op. cit.*, p. 89.

[14] Case example contributed by Gerard A. Santelli.

[15] An expanded discussion of this topic is found in DuBrin, *Fundamentals of Organizational Behavior*, pp. 164–168.

DONNELLY, CAROLINE. "Warding Off the Office Politician," *Money*, Dec. 1976, pp. 70–74.

DUBRIN, ANDREW J. *Fundamentals of Organizational Behavior: An Applied Perspective*, 2nd ed., Pergamon, 1978, Chapter 5.

DUBRIN, ANDREW J. *Survival in the Office: How to Move Ahead or Hang On*, Mason/Charter, 1977, Chapters 1–3.

FARNSWORTH, TERRY. *On the Way Up: The Executive's Guide to Company Politics*, McGraw-Hill Book Company (UK) Limited, 1976.

HEGARTY, EDWARD. *How to Succeed in Company Politics*, rev. ed., McGraw-Hill, 1976.

JENNINGS, EUGENE E. *Routes to the Executive Suite*, McGraw-Hill, 1971.

KORDA, MICHAEL. *Power! How to Get It. How to Use It*, Ballantine, 1975.

MCMURRY, ROBERT N. "Power and the Ambitious Executive," *Harvard Business Review*, Nov.–Dec. 1973, pp. 140–145.

ROBBINS, STEPHEN P. *The Administrative Process: Integrating Theory and Practice*, Prentice-Hall, 1976, Chapter 5.

ROSEMAN, ED. "How to Play Clean Office Politics," *Product Management* (now *Product Marketing*), May 1976, pp. 30–32, 36.

STERN, WALTER. *The Game of Office Politics*, Henry Regnery, 1976.

ZALEZNIK, ABRAHAM. "Power and Politics in Organization Life," *Harvard Business Review*, May–June, 1970, pp. 47–60.

PART THREE
WORKING WITH SMALL GROUPS

A substantial share of human relations takes place within the context of a small group. This section of the text concentrates on those aspects of small-group behavior that the author feels are the most important for understanding and practicing human relations. Several of the processes that we describe involve groups of two (superior–subordinate interactions). The chapters on communicating with people and counseling subordinates are designed to provide the reader with suggestions for acquiring job-related skills. The final chapter in this section provides an overview of popular techniques for improving interpersonal effectiveness.

7
LEADERSHIP
AND SUPERVISION

Learning Objectives

After reading and studying this chapter, you should be able to

1. Understand why most people obey (follow) leaders.
2. Summarize key leadership traits and behaviors that are related to successful managerial leadership.
3. Summarize the major ways in which the situation influences leadership.
4. Explain the relationship between McGregor's theory X and theory Y analysis of work motivation and leadership behavior.
5. Understand the meaning of participative leadership.
6. Recognize how you can develop your leadership potential on your own.

Leadership is the process of influencing other people to achieve certain objectives. The key word in understanding the concept of leadership is *influence*. If influence is not necessary, an act of leadership has not been performed. Note the contrast between the following two situations:

Clem, a bus driver, navigates his bus over the same route every day for five years. He is known for his punctuality, courtesy, and dependability. He is so well liked by his passengers that several of them take up a collection to buy him a present at Christmas. When asked by one of his fans why he is such a courteous and cheerful bus driver, he claims, "It's just my nature, I guess."

Luke, another bus driver working for the same transit company, is discourteous and rude toward passengers. An inspector notes his behavior and makes an official report. Several months later, Luke mellows in his attitude toward passengers. Although still not lovable, he is tolerable. Asked by a friend, why he has changed, he comments, "I had a good talk with my boss."

Clem would presumably act the way he does no matter who his boss might be. He enjoys his work and he enjoys people. Leadership is not required to keep his performance at a high level. Clem's only requirement of a supervisor is that he or she take care of administrative matters such as Clem being paid, receiving salary increases, and having his bus serviced.

Luke needs leadership. His superior heard about Luke's misbehavior and took remedial steps. Luke's conversations with his boss led to a change in his work behavior. Luke was influenced to achieve an important objective—providing an acceptable service to bus passengers.

Leadership, Management, and Supervision. Unfortunately for the student of human relations, these key terms have different connotations and meanings. Not every manager or scholar has the same thought in mind when he or she is talking about the concepts of leadership, management, or supervision. For the purpose of this book, the following distinctions are drawn:

Leadership is the process of influencing the activities of an individual or a group in efforts toward goal achievement in a given situation.[1] You can exert leadership whether or not you have the official job title of "manager" or "supervisor."

Management is working with and through individuals and groups to accomplish organizational goals. It involves the coordination of human and material resources toward objective accomplishment. "Management is the primary force with organizations which coordinates the activities of the subsystems and relates them to the environment."[2]

Supervision is essentially first-line management. It involves overseeing the work of others with a particular emphasis upon leadership.

The concepts of leadership, management, and supervision are thus not identical. Management or supervision involves a wide variety of activities such as planning, controlling, organizing, scheduling, negotiating, and directing (synonymous with leading). Many people are effective with the administrative aspects of a supervisory or managerial job, but few people are effective leaders.

WHY DO PEOPLE COMPLY WITH LEADERS?

Leadership would not be possible if people did not comply with orders, directives, or suggestions of leaders. An act of leadership has not been completed until the person or persons you are attempting to lead actually carry out a command or suggestion. If you try to lead your subordinates to clean a warehouse, your best proof of leadership is a clean warehouse. People comply with leaders for a number of reasons.

The Psychological Contract.   People in an organization will "go along with" a leader because of an unwritten contract between themselves and the organization. If your company pays you on time, provides you a pleasant working atmosphere, gives you opportunities to socialize with people, and so forth, you will be willing to comply with many favors that they ask in return. Among these are to produce work, conform to dress codes, complete most assignments on time, and be physically present at least 95 percent of the time. Edgar H. Schein[3] states the psychological contract in the following terms:

> The individual has a variety of expectations of the organization and the organization a variety of expectations of him or her. These expectations not only cover how much work is to be performed for how much pay, but also involve the whole pattern of rights, privileges, and obligation between the worker and the organization.

As long as the requests of the organization or your superior seem like a reasonable bargain, you will probably comply. The surly bus driver mentioned earlier was probably willing to tone down his surliness because he enjoyed working as a bus driver.

When the organization goes way beyond the boundaries of the psychological contract, compliance stops. A computer programmer may be willing to get out of bed at 3 A.M. to debug a program if it does not happen too often. But if such an emergency occurs too often (especially on Sunday mornings), he or she may refuse to comply with these nocturnal requests. However, that same programmer might find it within the bounds of the psychological contract for the company to ask him or her to learn a new programming language.

Early Cultural Conditioning.   Most, if not all, cultured people are taught early in life to obey authority.[4] Perhaps more so in the past than today, people in positions of authority, such as the teacher, policeman, boss, judge, or learned authority, are obeyed out of respect to their position. When a superior asks you to perform a work-related task, you thus do so out of habit or past learning. It is part of your early conditioning to want to please authority. People vary dramatically in their automatic acceptance of authority. Some people are pathologically opposed to accepting authority; others are unnecessarily deferential. Most people generally accept what they perceive as *legitimate* authority.

The concept of legitimate versus illegitimate authority is similar to the psychological contract. People, in general, only obey the authority that they perceive as being rational and reasonable. When orders are given that are followed without question, they fall into the *zone of indifference*.[5] For example, a lab technician might be asked to use a new sterilizing procedure for cleaning test tubes. He or she would probably accept such a directive without question; his or her attitude would be indifference. However, if that same lab technician were asked to fake results of laboratory analyses never performed, he or she might say, "The heck I will." People will often quit rather than accept illegitimate use of authority.

Satisfaction of Dependency Needs. Another normal human need is dependency, the desire to have another individual take responsibility for you. In personal life we come to depend upon key people such as spouses or parents to satisfy some of our emotional needs. In a strange city we find it reassuring to ask several people for the same set of directions. Most people find it comforting (satisfying) to depend upon the advice and wisdom of a superior. We also find it satisfying to have rules to govern many aspects of our behavior. It makes order out of chaos. Some people are much more dependent than others:

> Sherman was considered to be an excellent bank teller by his boss, Kathleen. He responded quickly and efficiently to orders given him by Kathleen or other bank officers. One of the guiding principles suggested to him by Kathleen is that "the customer is always right, particularly if he or she is a major depositor." Once Sherman asked Kathleen if it was all right to give a customer 200 one dollar bills in exchange for his $200 social security check. Kathleen invoked the "customer is always right" principle.
>   Several weeks later, a bank customer fell victim to a con game. At the request of a new-found lover, an old woman withdrew $5000 in cash. The woman was assured by her new boyfriend that her money would be doubled within days. Both the money and the boyfriend disappeared. The victimized woman told her tale to a bank officer. Kathleen then reprimanded Sherman for allowing an aged customer to withdraw so much money in cash. Sherman said in self-defense, "I knew it was kind of unusual, but just last month, you told me to go along with any legal request made by a big depositor."

Fear of the Consequences of Noncompliance. Yet another reason people obey leaders is that they are concerned that something negative will happen to them if they do not comply. As discussed in Chapter 6, this is the use of coercive power. People will obey a leader when he or she is in control of powerful negative sanctions. Many people will even expand their zone of indifference when jobs are scarce. Facing the threat of a layoff, a stockbroker might be more willing to sell high-risk stocks to naive investors than he or she would be in boom economic times.

One might argue, "If fear of the consequences of noncompliance is one reason people go along with leaders, then an armed robber is a leader. You give him (or her) the money, or he (or she) clobbers you." Theoretically, the use of extreme negative sanctions is an act of leadership, but it is short lived. The armed robber may wind up in jail; the organizational leader who leads people through coercion will not keep capable subordinates for long. Coercive leadership is usually self-defeating (aside from being unethical).

During the last two decades there has been a declining interest in understanding the traits, characteristics, and behaviors of leaders themselves. Substantial research has shown that leadership is best understood when the leader, the followers, and the situation in which they are placed are analyzed. Nevertheless, the leader remains an important consideration in understanding leadership. Without effective leaders, most organizations cannot prosper. Another practical reason for studying the traits and behaviors of leaders is that without such knowledge leadership selection is left to chance.

A realistic view is that certain leadership traits and behaviors contribute to effective leadership in a wide variety of situations. Correspondingly, similar leadership situations require similar leadership traits and behaviors. To illustrate, a person who was effective in running a production operation in a newspaper could probably run a production operation in a book bindery. There would be enough similarity among the type of subordinates and machinery to make the situations comparable. In contrast, a high school football coach might fail dismally as the managing editor of a fashion magazine. The two situations would call for dramatically different kinds of leadership. Edwin Ghiselli has conducted extensive research about traits, characteristics, and behaviors that contribute to effective leadership in a wide variety of situations.[6] Several of his major findings are included in the following discussion.

Intelligence level is widely used in the selection of people for leadership positions. Effective leaders tend to be bright but not brilliant. They are intelligent enough to be good problem solvers, but not so intelligent that their interests lie primarily in solving abstract problems and puzzles. This author's personal experience has been that successful executives usually score at the top 5 percent category of mental ability tests. Leadership positions in modern organizations place a continuously increasing demand upon problem-solving ability.

Situation sensitivity is a leadership requirement in virtually every leadership position. An effective leader is able to size up a situation and see what leadership practice should or should not be used. A sensitive leader, for instance, would recognize that in an emergency people want unilateral, decisive leadership commands. If a company is approaching bankruptcy, its employees want a leader to say, "Follow my instructions and we'll survive." If a fire breaks out, people want to hear a leader say, "Follow me this way to safety." Being sensitive to situations allows a leader to adapt to different leadership roles and situations. A good leader can effectively manage people of different cultural and educational backgrounds by sensing what needs to be done in different situations. Some leaders are less fortunate:

> Rudy was an effective master sergeant. Often placed in charge of recruits, Rudy could push his troops without engendering much resentment

or any rebellion. Proud of his leadership skills, Rudy volunteered to coach Little League baseball. His hard charging, harassing techniques literally brought tears to the eyes of many of his youngsters. Once he verbally attacked a ten year old for dropping a pop fly in the last play of the game. Parents complained and children quit. Rudy finally resigned, still wondering why young children cannot accept discipline.

Effective work habits are helpful, if not essential, in most leadership situations. Even if directing the activities of artistic, free-spirited individuals, the leader contributes to organizational effectiveness if he or she is well organized. In a rock and roll band somebody needs to keep track of engagements, expenses, contracts, and travel arrangements. If the leader of the group is unequal to the task, then a business manager or agent must accept that responsibility. As modern organizations become more paper-work oriented (forms, budgets, and so forth), good work habits and careful organization become all the more important.

Peter F. Drucker, a renowned management authority, places more blame for executive failure on poor work habits than on inappropriate personality characteristics.[7] An important component of effective work habits is effective time management. A successful executive (or other type of leader) knows where his or her time goes and invests it wisely. A factory supervisor might seem to be wasting time when he joins his work group for a cup of coffee. Yet he might be using that time to help establish rapport with the workers and to learn about departmental problems.

Initiative is a two-faceted characteristic that helps a leader function effectively. Ghiselli[8] notes that initiative on the one hand refers to "self-starting ability"—taking action without support and stimulation from others. A person aspiring toward leadership roles should recognize that initiative (or motivation and drive) is a characteristic looked for in potential leaders. If you do not appear well motivated to people above you, you probably will not be selected for a leadership position.

The second facet to initiative is problem (or opportunity) finding ability. An effective leader looks for things that need doing or tasks that need performing. An effective leader works on problems that could have a big potential payoff. An ineffective leader might spend the week cleaning and rearranging files. A more effective leader in the same situation might try to determine how his or her department could make a bigger contribution to the company.

Self-confidence is an important leadership characteristic in virtually every setting. A leader who is self-assured without being bombastic or overbearing instills confidence in his or her subordinates. Aside from

---

SOME FOLKLORE AND FACT ABOUT THE MANAGER'S JOB

Classic statements about the role of the manager (such as those made by Peter Drucker about effective work habits) have not gone unchallenged.

Henry Mintzberg* has conducted cross-cultural research of his own and synthesized that of many other researchers. He concludes that there are four myths about the manager's job that do not bear up under careful scrutiny of the facts.

A. **Folklore:** *The manager is a reflective, systematic planner.*

   Fact: *Study after study has shown that managers work at an unrelenting pace, that their activities are characterized by brevity, variety, and discontinuity, and that they are strongly oriented to action and dislike reflective activities.*

   One piece of supporting evidence for this fact is a diary study of 160 British middle and top managers which found that they worked for a half-hour or more without interruption only about once every two days.

B. **Folklore:** *The effective manager has no regular duties to perform.*

   Fact: *In addition to handling exceptions, managerial work involves performing a number of regular duties, including ritual and ceremony, negotiations, and processing of soft information that links the organization with its environment.*

   "One study of field sales managers and another of chief executives suggest that it is a natural part of both jobs to see important customers, assuming the managers wish to keep those customers."

C. **Folklore:** *The senior manager needs aggregated information, which a formal management information system best provides.*

   Fact: *Managers strongly favor the verbal media—telephone calls and meetings.*

   "In two British studies, managers spent an average of 66% and 80% of their time in verbal (oral) communication. In my study of five American chief executives, the figure was 78%."

D. **Folklore:** *Management is, or at least is quickly becoming, a science and a profession.*

   Fact: *The managers' programs—to schedule time, process information, make decisions, and so on—remain locked deep inside their brains.*

   "The executives I was observing—all very competent by any standard—are fundamentally indistinguishable from their counterparts of a hundred years ago (or a thousand years ago for that matter.) The information they need differs, but they seek it in the same way —by word of mouth. . . . Even the computer, so important for the specialized work of the organization, has apparently had no influence on the work procedures of the general manager."

---

* Excerpted from Henry Mintzberg, "The Manager's Job: Folklore and Fact," *Harvard Business Review*, July–Aug. 1975, pp. 49–61.

being a psychological trait, self-confidence or self-assurance refers to the behavior exhibited by a person in a number of situations. It might be concluded that Jack is a confident supervisor if (1) he retains his composure when a worker threatens to file a grievance, and (2) he calmly helps a worker fix a machine failure when the department is behind schedule.

Individuality is another characteristic associated with effective leadership. It can express itself both in the unique pattern of traits possessed by the person and in work habits. Ghiselli's research indicated that those managers who displayed the greatest individuality in the way they did their work were also judged to be the best managers. Individuality is important in understanding leaders because it contributes to charm or charisma.

Supportive behavior toward subordinates is frequently associated with leadership effectiveness. A supportive leader (one who gives encouragement and praise to subordinates) usually increases morale and often increases productivity. Supportive behavior comes about because of a group of personal characteristics such as empathy, warmth, and flexibility.

THE TRAIT AND INTERPERSONAL LEADERSHIP QUESTIONNAIRE

A questionnaire is frequently used to study leadership traits and attitudes. Situational approaches at times also rely upon questionnaires to study leadership.[9] Figure 7.1 provides you the opportunity to sample the types of questions often used in leadership research.

> *Directions:* Following are a list of statements about people in supervisory and management positions. Indicate whether you "mostly agree" or "mostly disagree" with each statement. Make a choice even if your most accurate answer would be "it depends upon the situation."

Give yourself a score of 1 for each item scored in the leadership direction. (The leadership direction for each item was established by comparing the responses of experienced leaders with those of followers.) The scoring key is as follows:

1. Agree	8. Agree	15. Disagree
2. Agree	9. Agree	16. Agree
3. Disagree	10. Agree	17. Disagree
4. Disagree	11. Agree	18. Disagree
5. Disagree	12. Agree	19. Disagree
6. Agree	13. Disagree	20. Agree
7. Disagree	14. Disagree	21. Agree

1. The members of my group think I can get them what they want. _____ _____

2. If the members of my group took a poll, I would be voted the leader. _____ _____

3. My authority comes from the people under me. _____ _____

4. I try to keep things as they are. _____ _____

5. I always get the job done. _____ _____

6. I am successful in maintaining team spirit among the members of my group. _____ _____

7. I'm pretty well able to size up my own assets and liabilities. _____ _____

8. I am accepted and noticed by the people under me. _____ _____

9. My acts increase my understanding of and my knowledge about what is going on in the group. _____ _____

10. I stress making it possible for members of an organization to work together. _____ _____

11. I exert more influence in goal setting and goal achievement than most other persons in my organization. _____ _____

12. An important part of my job is to keep group members informed. _____ _____

13. I help individual members adjust to the group. _____ _____

14. Mixing with the people under me is an important part of my position. _____ _____

15. I plan my day's activities in detail. _____ _____

16. I put group welfare above the welfare of any member. _____ _____

17. I maintain definite standards of performance. _____ _____

18. I am successful in getting other people to follow me. _____ _____

19. I work hard all the time. _____ _____

20. I find working with my group interesting and challenging. _____ _____

21. I consider the organization part of me. _____ _____

FIGURE 7.1
The trait and interpersonal inventory.

The higher your score, the more your thinking parallels that of experienced leaders. An unusual research finding here is that experienced leaders tend to agree with items having to do with the interpersonal aspects of leadership.[10] For instance, "An important part of my job is to keep group members informed," and "I put group welfare above the welfare of any member." In contrast, the experienced leaders are less prone to agree with statements which suggest that they have very strong individual traits. For instance, experienced leaders disagree with the statements "I work hard all the time," and "I always get the job done."

One conclusion reached in research with the trait and interpersonal inventory is that leaders, in contrast to nonleaders, may be characterized as more modest, more insightful, and more group-centered than self-centered.

HOW THE SITUATION INFLUENCES LEADERSHIP

Leadership theories in vogue all point to the importance of understanding the situation in order to decide which leadership style should be practiced. They are called *contingency* theories because they attempt to determine upon what factors the best leadership approach depends. Evidence about the exact nature of these contingency factors is limited. Next we present a brief discussion of those factors that seem to exert a major influence on which leadership approach or style works best.

Favorability of the Situation (Fiedler's Contingency Model). The most widely quoted and researched contingency theory of leadership is that developed by Fred E. Fiedler.[11] Underlying his theory is the concept of favorability of the situation. A situation is the most favorable when

1. The leader's personal relationship with members of the groups is good (for example, he or she is well liked and appreciated).
2. The position held by the leader carries considerable formal power and authority (for example, a company president or professional football coach).
3. The task to be performed by the group is well structured and well defined (for example, manufacturing 100 television sets using carefully drawn plans).

Fiedler contends that a permissive, lenient, or considerate (relationship-oriented) leadership style works best when the situation is moderately favorable or moderately unfavorable. Following this theory, if you were moderately well liked by a group of stock brokers, possessed an average degree of power, and their task was somewhat vague, you should use a relationship-oriented approach with them to achieve best results.

In contrast, when the situation is highly favorable or highly unfavorable, a task-oriented approach (emphasis on getting the task at hand accomplished) usually produces better results. A professional football coach usually works in a favorable leadership situation because he is well liked, has high power, and the task to be performed (winning) is well defined. He can therefore be quite task oriented (hard-nosed). A project manager who finds herself with a group of team members who are antagonistic toward her, and who has limited power and a vague task might also have to be task oriented to be effective.

Personal Characteristics of Subordinates. The type of people you are leading heavily influences which leadership style works best. In general, competent people—those who are well trained, intelligent, and well motivated—need a minimum of guidance or emotional support from a superior. The leader in such a situation is best advised to "get out of the way" of subordinates. In other words, a loose approach to leading the group would work the best. As described in the tri-dimensional leadership effectiveness model developed by Paul Hersey and Kenneth H. Blanchard,[12] the low-task and low-relationships leader when effective fits this description: "Often seen as permitting his subordinates to decide how the work should be done and playing only a minor role in their social interaction."

Another characteristic of subordinates that influences the most effective leadership style is their degree of authoritarianism.[13] Authoritarian (strict and unyielding) people have a tendency to prefer directive or authoritarian leaders. Also, they tend to dislike or even distrust a permissive or democratic style of leadership. Authoritarian people prefer to have things spelled out for them in precise detail.

The optimum leadership style can be influenced by how well the subordinates think that they can perform the assigned task: "The higher the degree of perceived ability relative to the task demands, the less subordinates will view leader directiveness and coaching behavior as acceptable."[14] In simple terms, if you are confident in what you are doing, you might even resent a boss telling you how to perform your job.

Environmental Pressures and Demands. Factors related to the job itself and the conditions surrounding the job are a third set of contingency ("it depends") factors influencing the best leadership style.[15] An effective leader takes these into account in adapting to the leadership situation.

Under conditions of heavy stress, threat, or pressure, most people want a leader to take forceful charge of the situation. In crisis situations, people are pleased to have the leader give specific orders and directives. A troubled business corporation elected a new president with a firm belief in financial controls. Although he made many enemies in the process, the company was successful in averting disaster. A middle manager in the company commented:

> At first we all hated the guy. He was almost ruthless about laying off long-term employees. He cut the corporate staff in half. He increased our workload and decreased our staff. In the end though we realized that he saved the company from bankruptcy. Without his take-charge attitude, we would all be out of jobs.

Ambiguous assignments also influence which leadership style is best. When a person cannot tolerate ambiguity (such as unclear assignments) very well, he or she would prefer to have a leader provide much structure. The result for the person would be less tension. But those who like ambiguity (so that they can provide their own structure) prefer a leader who does not meddle in their work. A research associate was asked by her superior if she wanted clarification on a vague assignment. She answered, "No, the fun is in figuring out what it is that you're supposed to be doing."

As the size of the work group increases, subordinates may prefer that the leader play a more active role in coordinating activities. In addition to lowering the frustration of subordinates, clarifying and coordinating activities may improve performance. When work groups are smaller, the group members themselves can divide up responsibilities without much help from their leader.

The type of technology is another influence that helps determine (or mediate) which leadership style is best. One extreme in technology would be the supervision of a craft-like operation, where the workers are highly skilled and self-sufficient. They would need a minimum of guidance and structure, particularly about technological matters. A leader in such a situation should therefore emphasize giving the workers autonomy (freedom to make their own decisions).

The other technological extreme is a mass-production operation where the contribution of one department is interdependent with the contribution of other departments. An automobile assembly plant would be one such operation. Deviations from standard cannot be tolerated, so the managers involved have to ensure that policies and procedures are rigidly enforced.

In discussing a sampling of the many possible contingency factors in determining leadership style, the conclusion should not be reached that leadership traits are unimportant. No matter what the situation, intelligent problem-solving behavior on the part of the leader is required. Sensitivity to people is also required to some extent in every situation. Even an authoritarian leader must recognize when he or she is being too rigid and demanding. As one authoritarian plant manager said to his consultant, "Let me know when I'm squeezing the troops too hard."

An important result of the formal study of leadership has been a recognition of the importance of participative leadership. A participative leader, manager, or supervisor is one who shares decision making with members of the group. Among the many concepts that basically refer to this leadership approach are "employee centered," "subordinate centered," "group centered," "permissive," "relationships oriented," "people oriented," and "theory Y."

McGregor's Theory X and Theory Y. Participation as a management style owes its historical roots to the classical Hawthorne experiments mentioned in Chapter 1. One of the many conclusions reached in these studies was that workers produce more and gain more satisfaction from their work when they feel that their work environment is supportive. One important aspect of support is that power is shared between superior and subordinates. A person feels support (or at least recognition) when he or she is trusted enough to share in decision making.

Although he did not specifically intend to build a case for participative management, McGregor's theory X and theory Y aroused interest in a more participative approach to leading people. McGregor's true intent (as revealed in his later writings) was to challenge managers to question the traditional assumptions made about workers (theory X). Instead, he wanted managers to take more of a *contingency* approach (theory Y). (The reader should note that most students of human relations believe that McGregor held the assumptions made under theory X to be always invalid.) Theory X, the traditional view of direction and control, makes these assumptions about people[16]:

1. *The average human being has an inherent dislike of work and will avoid it if he or she can.* The use of time cards reflects this point of view.

2. *Because of this human characteristic of dislike of work, most people must be coerced, controlled, directed, and threatened with punishment to get them to put forth adequate effort toward the achievement of organizational objectives.* A life insurance manager is acting under this assumption when he says to his sales trainees, "Anybody who fails to sell one new policy in the first month will be fired."

3. *The average human being prefers to be directed, wishes to avoid responsibility, has relatively little ambition, and wants security above all.* So believes the political candidate who says, "If we don't tighten up on welfare laws, we'll have half the population on relief. Who wants to work when you can get paid for doing nothing?"

McGregor then indicated that "the accumulation of knowledge about human behavior in many specialized fields has made possible the formulation of a number of generalizations which provide a modest beginning for new theory with respect to the management of human resources." The assumptions of theory Y are as follows:

1. *The expenditure of physical and mental effort in work is as natural as play or rest.* This is particularly true when somebody intensely enjoys his or her work, such as a violinist, dress designer, or builder of custom automobiles.

2. *External control and the threat of punishment are not the only means for bringing about effort toward organizational objectives. Man will exercise self-direction and self-control in the service of objectives to which he is committed.* For example, when an employee shares in the profits of a small company, he or she usually feels this way.

3. *Commitment to objectives is a function of the rewards associated with their achievement.* Many a person who was considered "lazy" while working in a bureaucracy suddenly becomes ferociously motivated when he or she starts a small business. When you own your own business, rewards are closely tied to effort.

4. *The average human being learns, under proper conditions, not only to accept but to seek responsibility.* Part of the proper conditions, of course, is having a supervisor and company who care about your welfare and help you succeed.

5. *The capacity to exercise a relatively high degree of imagination, ingenuity, and creativity in the solution of organizational problems is widely, not narrowly, distributed in the population.* One supporting example is the success of some suggestions systems. People in low-skill-level jobs sometimes make suggestions that save (or earn) the company thousands of dollars.

6. *Under the conditions of modern industrial life, the intellectual potentialities of the average human being are only partially utilized.* In fairness to modern industry, very few jobs anywhere make close to full utilization of a person's potential. However, some people of limited potential are the most likely to be fully challenged by their jobs. For example, an intellectually retarded man might be fully challenged as a factory janitor.

Results of Participative Management. Under the right circumstances, participative management can provide benefits to both organizations and individuals. As such, participative management is a contingency approach to leadership. Among the right circumstances for participative leadership to be effective are these:[17]

Leaders must have the required skills, subordinates must have favorable attitudes toward participation, and the task must be complex, nonroutine, and require a high quality decision or subordinate acceptance, or both. It therefore seems only fair to say that the effects of participative leadership are often positive but situational.

In actual practice, the full use of participative management is limited. In a study of 49 of *Fortune's* top 500 business organizations,[18] it was found that the preponderance of decisions appears to be made by the manager alone. The observation of the present author is that few companies have formal policies or programs relating to participative management (except management by objectives). However, individual managers may consult extensively with subordinates depending upon both the manager's style and the willingness of subordinates to participate.

To conclude our introduction to participative management, here is how a personnel vice-president of a major aerospace company described one of its participative management projects:[19]

> Work groups were called together for meetings in which impediments to production were examined and corrective actions sought. The psychologists ensured that there was follow-up on each item. As appropriate, "multilevel" meetings were held in which workers representing the work group fed their suggestions to higher management levels who were present, and these were explored on a problem-solving basis. These meetings were almost entirely work related, as opposed to concentrating on working conditions, employee policies, etc. Preliminary results showed that cost savings resulting from the meetings were equal to twelve times the cost of the program. Present plans call for almost 2800 employees to be involved over the next two years, as the program is moved from work group to work group.

DEVELOPING YOUR LEADERSHIP POTENTIAL (ON YOUR OWN)

The next three chapters deal directly with information that can assist a person in developing his or her leadership potential. Chapter 11 describes programs and procedures that are used to enhance leadership effectiveness. Chapter 13 about organizational development also describes programs that are used to develop leaders. For now it is worth noting that no program of leadership improvement can be a substitute for leadership experience. Because leadership is situational, a conceptually sound approach to improving leadership effectiveness is to attempt to gain leadership experience in different settings. A person who wants to become an executive is well advised to gain supervisory experience in at least two different organizational functions (such as marketing and manufacturing).

First-level supervisory jobs are an invaluable starting point for developing your leadership potential. It takes considerable skill to effectively manage a McDonald's restaurant or direct a public playground during the summer. A first-line supervisor frequently faces a situation where subordinates are poorly trained, poorly paid, and not well motivated to achieve company objectives.

Summary
of Key Points

1. Leadership is the process of influencing other people to achieve objectives. Leading (or directing) is one function of management and supervision.
2. People comply with leaders for many reasons. Among them are (a) the psychological contract between the organization and the individual, (b) the fact that people are taught to obey in childhood, (c) the natural dependency of people, and (d) a fear of the consequences of noncompliance.
3. Leadership is situational, yet some traits and characteristics contribute to leadership effectiveness in many situations. Among them are high intelligence, sensitivity to the situation, effective work habits, self-motivation and problem-finding ability, self-confidence, individuality, and supportiveness.
4. A major influence on leadership is the favorability of the situation. Favorability depends upon three factors: (a) the leader's relationship with subordinates, (b) the power of the position, and (c) how well the task is defined.
5. Three major influences on the leadership situation are (a) the personal characteristics of the subordinates (such as ability and motivation), (b) environmental pressures and demands (such as the presence of crisis), and (c) type of technology.
6. Participative leadership occurs when the leader shares decision-making power with subordinates. In many instances, participative management has led to increases in employee satisfaction and productivity. For participative management to work effectively, people must have the desire and ability to participate in decision making.
7. A useful approach to developing your leadership potential is to acquire leadership or supervisory experience in several different situations.

Questions
for Discussion

1. What are the provisions of the psychological contract that you have formulated between yourself and the instructor of this course?
2. Describe the leadership approach of the president of the United States, using concepts found in this chapter.
3. Think of one particular ineffective leader that you have known. How

did he or she rate on the traits and behavioral characteristics described in the section Leadership Traits and Behaviors?

4. Would participative leadership work effectively for a field supervisor working on the installation of the Alaskan Pipe Line? Why or why not?

5. Describe a leadership situation in which the assumptions made in McGregor's theory X are valid.

6. What implications do contingency or situational theories of leadership have for the selection and training of leaders?

A Human Relations Incident
THE REJECTED LEADER

Randy was elated to learn that Fox Drugs offered him the store manager position at a busy location. He was surprised that a twenty-one-year-old man with limited business experience would be offered such an important job. Randy realized the hours would be long and the pay modest, but the experience would be invaluable for building a career in retail store management. Within the first month, Randy encountered a couple of problems he did not anticipate when hired into the position.

Randy noticed that the cashier left the check-out counter unattended for a few minutes while she attended to a task in back of the store. He politely asked the woman not to repeat that infraction of store rules. She replied, "Sonny, don't push me too hard. You're not the owner. You're just a worker here like anybody else."

Randy noticed another situation that he felt needed to be corrected. Bert, the pharmacist, was holding lengthy conversations with customers about their physical ailments. Randy advised him that long conversations lowered his productivity. Bert responded, "Since when does a twenty-one-year-old manager tell a professional pharmacist how to conduct his business? You go mind the store."

How should Randy strengthen his position as a leader?

A Human Relations Case
WE HAVE TO STAY PROFITABLE

"Something has been bothering me," said Bart, a company general manager, to Jack, his assistant general manager. "We seem to be losing our flexibility in this division. Our people don't seem to be able to roll with the punches the way they used to. At times I think we've spoiled our people. We've been running so efficiently for so long that some of us have lost our ability to shift gears."

"Bart, could you be a bit more specific? You seem to be dealing in generalities. Are you talking about any managers in particular?"

"Jack, I'm not trying to pinpoint any one manager or group of managers. It's just that I think some of us cannot accept a sound business decision when it makes us change a sloppy habit.

"It's hard for some of our managers to accept the fact that one way to increase profits is to cut down on the cost of doing business. The way consumers are tightening up on their spending, cost cutting may be our key to profit growth.

"I'm beginning to wonder if we have raised a generation of managers who don't realize that even a company as well entrenched as ours has to be more responsive to change.

"The way I see management, from my vantage point, is that I'm the symphony conductor for change. Everybody below me in the company has a crucial job to perform. If anybody is out of tune, we all look bad. But, nevertheless, somebody has to move the baton. If it looks as if we need to change the pace of the way we are doing things, the conductor has to sense the need for change and see that the changes are made.

"I don't doubt that fifty managers in this company have more leadership talent than I do. Yet, it's not just talent that counts. It's your vantage point. From my perch I can see what is happening on the inside and the outside. I can see the need for change while not everybody below me has the same advantage.

"A mature manager can understand that there are some directives from above that have to be accepted because the people on top are in a position to decide what change is best for the company."

"Bart, I've got an idea. In my next run through the field, I'll broach this topic with a sampling of our managers. I'll try to determine if I, too, see this loss of flexibility."

"Fine idea, Jack. But don't make this look like an inquisition or an attitude survey. I'd like another input on my assessment. Let me know if you see the same problems I see."

The following week Jack visited with Milt, a general manager of one of the company's largest markets. "Milt," said Jack, "have you noticed any differences in the way the company is handling its people or doing business lately?"

"Curious that you should ask, Jack. I have noticed something that doesn't seem to fit with company philosophy. I've felt pressure from above not to give people too much leeway when offered a transfer. Top management thought that we should rotate some of our regional sales managers to help prepare them for bigger jobs. I passed the order on down for three of our sales managers to play musical chairs. Two of them said they were too well established in their own communities to consider moving. I told them that it was for the good of the company, but still they balked.

"One of the sales managers begrudgingly accepted. The other fellow became a real problem. I finally had to tell him that his job with the company was now in Dallas. He told me that he thought the company was putting him under too much pressure; that he really didn't have a choice."

Later that day Jack lunched with Tony, a district sales manager. Jack explained to Tony, "As a member of top management, I'm trying to get a finger on the pulse of the organization. I'm trying to learn what we at head-quarters are doing right and wrong. Tell me what is the most irksome thing top management has done in the last year?"

"I guess there's not too much for me to worry about Jack. My brother-in-law has a prosperous insurance agency. He's been bugging me to enter the business for years. If what I say leads to a pink slip in the mail for me, I'll become an independent insurance agent."

"I admire your candor," said Jack with a smile, "but nobody ever got hurt in this company for telling the truth."

"I wasn't really worried. I think I can speak for my sales representatives and my fellow district sales managers when I tell you that the company is squeezing too hard on expense accounts. For years I had the power to call my reps together for a luncheon or dinner conference. Since I called the conference, the company paid the tab. The sales reps looked forward to these conferences and came to expect them. Embarrassingly, the plug has been pulled out. Now if we want a sales conference during the day, my fellows and gals pay for their own lunches.

"What concerns me the most is that somebody in top management who hasn't run a district in twenty years suddenly thinks that he can save the company a fortune by taking some nickels and dimes out of the hands of the district sales manager. Are we just robots at the district level?

"A major problem as I see it, Jack, is that the company may be moving toward a management approach that is in stark contrast to the way I do business. I try very hard to give each person working for me the feeling that he or she is running a piece of the company. I use the approach with both my sales reps and the inside support staff.

"It works very simply. I don't try to monitor the amount of money a salesman chalks up to expenses, within the broad outer limits set by the company. I tell the rep that he is essentially the president of his territory. If he buys the idea, he looks upon expense money as an investment in future business. If he thinks ordering three shots of Chivas Regal for himself at a working lunch is a good investment for the company, then let him do it. It's his decision.

"After a while, he is likely to catch on to the idea that what is good for the company is in his best interests. If he doesn't catch on to the idea, we may have to let him go; but only after repeated violations of the 'it's your business' philosophy.

"The only way for the company to stay profitable, in the long run, is for people to really believe that this is their company. All the management controls ever developed can't be a substitute for that attitude.

"But hold on Jack," said Tony, "let me introduce you to Lucille back at the office after we finish lunch. She is building quite a reputation for herself out in the field. Her sales performance is outstanding. She has some strong opinions about the problems company policies are causing her. She's outspoken enough to want to talk to a top executive like yourself."

"I'm flattered that you would be interested in talking to a sales representative," said Lucille. "I'm divinely content with my job. There is a certain status involved in carrying the company flag. So long as you asked about possible gripes, I have one small one. It seems that a skinflint has been placed in charge of monitoring the company car system. We have more regulations now for using the company car for personal business than the Interstate Commerce Commission has for regulating truckers.

"Just the other day, I had to drop my daughter off at the dentist on my way to an account. It took me a half-hour with a pocket calculator and a city map to figure out that I owed the company seventy-five cents on my weekly mileage allowance. The way I figured it, my side trip to the dentist was five miles out of the way. I think the company could have profitably consulted field people to help draw up regulations about using a company car for personal business. Things are getting pretty picayune. We are supposed to be professional sales representatives. Why not treat us like professionals?"

As Jack began his flight back home, he thought to himself, "Bart and I have a lot to discuss. We're doing something wrong. What we see as sound business decisions, the front-line people see as arbitrary changes. We need high morale and a good company image, but yet we have to stay profitable."

1. Should Bart and Jack be concerned about the various negative comments expressed in regard to changes made by the company? Why or why not?
2. What do you think are the positive and negative aspects of Tony's leadership style?
3. To what extent is Bart justified in making the statement, "We seem to be losing our flexibility. . . ."
4. How would you characterize Milt's leadership style?
5. What leadership approach should top management use to facilitate better acceptance of policy changes?

FOOTNOTES

[1] Paul Hersey and Kenneth H. Blanchard, *Management of Organizational Behavior: Utilizing Human Resources*, 3rd ed., Prentice-Hall, 1977, p. 68.

[2] Fremont E. Kast and James E. Rosenzweig, *Organization and Management: A Systems Approach*, 2nd ed., McGraw-Hill, 1974, p. 110.

[3] Edgar H. Schein, *Organizational Psychology*, Prentice-Hall, 1970, p. 12.

[4] The discussion of early cultural conditioning and zone of indifference is based on David R. Hampton, Charles E. Summer, and Ross A. Webber, *Organizational Behavior and the Practice of Management*, Scott, Foresman, 1968, pp. 441–442.

[5] This concept traces back to Chester Barnard, *The Functions of the Executive*, Harvard University Press, 1938, p. 167.

[6] Our discussion of traits and characteristics is based partially on the findings of Ghiselli reported in Edwin E. Ghiselli, *Exploration in Managerial Talent*, Goodyear, 1971.

[7] Peter F. Drucker, *The Effective Executive*, Harper & Row, 1966, p. 23.

[8] Edwin E. Ghiselli, "Managerial Talent," *American Psychologist*, Oct. 1963, p. 639.

[9] Andrew J. DuBrin, "Trait and Interpersonal Self-Descriptions of Leaders and Non-Leaders in an Industrial Setting," *Journal of Industrial Psychology*, June 1964, pp. 51–55.

[10] *Ibid.*, p. 54.

[11] A well-written, nontechnical overview of Fiedler's theory is Fred E. Fiedler, "The Leadership Game: Matching the Man to the Situation," *Organizational Dynamics*, Winter 1976, pp. 6–16.

[12] Hersey and Blanchard, *op. cit.*, p. 107.

[13] Alan C. Filley, Robert J. House, and Steven Kerr, *Managerial Process and Organizational Behavior*, 2nd ed., Scott, Foresman, 1976, p. 255.

[14] *Ibid.*

[15] This discussion of environmental pressures and demands is based on information found in Elmer Burack, *Organization Analysis: Theory and Applications*, Dryden, 1975, pp. 315–318.

[16] The italicized statements about theory X and theory Y are quoted from Douglas McGregor, *The Human Side of Enterprise*, McGraw-Hill, 1960, pp. 33 48.

[17] Filley, House, and Kerr, *op. cit.*, p. 229.

[18] Donald F. Crane, "The Case for Participative Management," *Business Horizons*, Apr. 1976, pp. 15–21.

[19] *Ibid.*, p. 19.

SUGGESTED READING

CRANE, DONALD F. "The Case for Participative Management," *Business Horizons*, Apr. 1976, pp. 15–21.

FIEDLER, FRED E. "The Leadership Game: Matching the Man to the Situation," *Organizational Dynamics*, Winter 1976, pp. 6–16.

FIEDLER, FRED E., and CHEMERS, MARTIN M. *Leadership and Effective Management*, Scott, Foresman, 1975.

GREINER, LARRY E. "What Managers Think of Participative Management," *Harvard Business Review*, Mar.–Apr., 1973, pp. 111–117.

HALL, JAY. "What Makes a Manager Good, Bad or Average?" *Psychology Today*, Aug. 1976, pp. 52–53, 55.

HELMICH, DONALD L., and ERZEN, PAUL E. "Leadership Style and Leadership Needs," *Academy of Management Journal*, June 1975, pp. 397–402.

HESPE, GEORGE, and WALL, TOBY. "The Demand for Participation Among Employees," *Human Relations*, May 1976, pp. 411–428.

MCGREGOR, DOUGLAS. *The Professional Manager*, Caroline McGregor and W. G. Bennis (eds.), McGraw-Hill, 1967.

PLUNKETT, W. RICHARD. *Supervision: The Direction of People at Work*, William C. Brown, 1975.

STOGDILL, RALPH. *Handbood of Leadership*, The Free Press, 1974.

8

THE NATURE
OF WORK GROUPS

Learning Objectives

After reading and studying this chapter, you should be able to

1. Identify at least five different types of groups.
2. Explain a few major reasons why some groups succeed and others fail.
3. Identify several positive consequences of group membership and group effort.
4. Identify problems sometimes created by groups.
5. Recognize the conditions under which a committee meeting is likely to be effective.
6. Develop insight into whether you would prefer to work by yourself generally or in a group effort.

Groups are the basic building blocks of the larger organization. The department you are assigned to, the division your department belongs to, the people you share a coffee break with, and the members of your industrial softball team are among the many groups found in an organization. A group has an identity of its own that transcends that of its members. A group of people may laugh at a comment that its members individually would not find humorous. A group can accomplish a task that could not be accomplished by combining the individual contributions of its members.

Precisely defined, a group is "a collection of individuals who regularly interact with each other, who are psychologically aware of each other and who perceives themselves to be a group."[1] Two policemen in a squad car would thus constitute a group. So would the executive committee of an oil corporation. However, ten people waiting for a bus would not be a real group. Although they might talk to each other, their interaction would not be on a planned or recurring basis.

Work groups can be further understood by examining a few ways of classifying or typing groups. Although these types may overlap, they point to different characteristics or aspects of group functioning. For instance, the reason that a particular informal group (such as the people in your department you lunch with regularly) is important to you is that they also represent a *reference* group (their opinion counts for you).

Primary Groups.   A group such as a family or commune where the members have immediate and often intimate contact with each other is called a primary group. In any primary group the relationships among members are personal. Friendship groups or cliques are also considered primary groups. Written rules and regulations are rarely found in primary groups. One modern exception is the detailed marriage contract that many couples are now writing before entering into marriage. These contracts sometimes have clauses such as "He shall prepare dinner two nights per week" or "She shall wax the car once per month."

Primary groups can also be work groups when families or friends enter into business relationships. A primary group then also develops properties of a secondary group.

Secondary Groups.   A secondary group is one in which the members may only get together because of some outside circumstance (such as working for the same company). They tend to be larger than primary groups and are usually governed by rules and regulations. When we refer to work groups, we are usually referring to secondary groups. Many people spend more of their waking hours in secondary than primary groups. A man who lives by himself, has few friends, and works fulltime is one such example. His only contact with a primary group may be at holiday time when he visits his family.

Formal Groups.   A formal group is one deliberately formed by the organization to accomplish specific tasks and achieve objectives. Formal groups are designated by the organization chart or at times indicated on the bulletin board or through office memos (for example, "The undernamed people are hereby assigned to the safety committee"). The duration of a formal group is an important consideration in understanding its nature.

A *command* group, in addition to being specified on the organization chart, consists of a supervisor and a group of subordinates.[2] The formal organization is composed of a group of interconnected command groups. Command groups are easy to identify; they usually have names such as accounting department, sales order department, or radiology lab.

A *task* group is composed of a group of employees who are assigned to complete a particular project or task. In getting their task accomplished, it is necessary for group members to coordinate their efforts. Often members of the task group are from different departments. In some instances, members of a command group have a minimum of interaction. Two clerks in an insurance claims department might be handling completely different work. By definition, the members of a task group must work cooperatively.

A *committee* is basically a temporary task group. The committee members are assigned a project that they work on in addition to their normal duties. Once the committee has finished its work, its recommendations are given to a high-ranking official.

A temporary *task force* is another type of formal group. It is best visualized as a committee with power whose members devote fulltime to a problem until it is resolved. A task force might be assigned to start up a new branch store. Once the store was successfully in operation, the task force would leave and the newly trained personnel would take over.

Informal Groups. An organization cannot be understood by studying its organization chart alone. A large number of groups evolve naturally in an organization to take care of people's desire for friendship and companionship. Informal groups are generally thought of in relation to production and clerical workers, but they can form at any level in the organization. Here are three examples of informal groups:

1. Five secretaries from the marketing department meet once a month for lunch to discuss mutual concerns and to seek relief from the tedious aspects of their jobs.
2. Four computer operators form a jogging club that meets three days per week at lunch time to run two miles.
3. Three managers from different parts of the company commute to work together every business day when they are all in town. Often discussing current events and the stock market, they also discuss company business while commuting to work.

As illustrations 1 and 2 suggest, informal groups are often work related. One function of the informal organization is to fill in the gaps left by the formal organization. Few organizations have a job description written for the "coffee pot tender," yet such a person arises on a rotating basis in a good many offices. Similarly, when somebody in your department is absent for legitimate reasons, you might take care of his or her emergency work, even though it is not a formal part of your job. Informal groups have been divided into two specific types.[3]

Interest groups are informal groups that have come together because of some common concern of people. A group of laboratory technicians banding together to demand better laboratory uniforms would be one such interest group. These technicians might be from different command or task groups, yet they have a common interest in comfortable and neat work clothes.

Friendship groups are often formed in organizations because members have something in common, like outside of job responsibilities or job interests. An example would be a bowling or snowmobile club formed by people who met at work.

Reference Groups. Certain groups have an influence over our lives because we use them to guide our perceptions. We *refer* to those groups in making decisions. For example, in trying to decide whether a given occupation has high status, we use certain key groups as a reference (or standard of comparison). If you lived in a neighborhood where people had low education and low incomes, a job as a factory supervisor would bring you high status. Yet a friend of yours who was raised in a high-income, high-education neighborhood might regard a factory supervisor job as having low status.

Reference groups are important in understanding work groups because many of a person's attitudes toward work are shaped by his or her reference groups. If a worker tries to "beat the system" (for example, cheat on expense accounts), it might be because his or her reference groups considers such behavior acceptable.

When a person's key reference group is outside of an organization, that person is called a *cosmopolitan*.[4] A hair dresser, for example, might feel that he or she is an independent artist who is not dependent upon any one beauty salon. Therefore, he or she might not be as docile as the beauty salon operator would like. Scientists, too, are generally cosmopolitans.

A *local* is a person who identifies himself or herself with a reference group inside the organization. A local thus generally becomes dependent upon the organization because he or she views himself or herself as being tied to the organization. A clerk is often a *local* because he or she has accumulated knowledge that is useful primarily to one particular organization.

WHY SOME GROUPS SUCCEED AND OTHERS FAIL

Although thousands of studies have been aimed at discovering why some people succeed and others fail in their work, much less research has been conducted about the success and failure of work groups. Later in this chapter we shall examine some of the characteristics of an effective meeting. For now, we shall reach some conclusions about success versus failure in general work groups. These conclusions should apply equally well to groups as diverse as hockey teams and ecology task forces.

Proper Leadership. An inescapable conclusion about small groups is that they are more likely to achieve their goals under the proper type of leadership. The nature of the work performed by the small group and its membership influence which leadership style is best (as discussed in Chapter 7). Nevertheless, the nature of small groups usually requires a leader who is directive and task oriented.[5] People in groups need definite guidelines for performing their task, and usually require occasional assistance from the leader.

What we have said does not imply that the more authoritarian or tyrannical the leader, the better the welfare of the group. Based upon years of research, Rensis Likert notes that an effective small-group leader typically engages in behaviors such as the following[6]:

1. Listens carefully and patiently.
2. Has patience with progress made by the group, particularly on slow problems.
3. Gives the group members ample opportunity to express their thoughts.
4. Is careful not to impose a decision on the group.
5. Frequently puts his or her contributions in the form of questions or states them speculatively.

Right Mix of People. In some situations a group of people with similar backgrounds is best suited to accomplishing the group goals. This is particularly true when cooperation among members is important. In one federal government Medicare processing office, a 300 percent increase in claims had to be processed in without a time extension or the addition of additional group members. The task was arduous and repetitive. One reason the group was able to accomplish its mission is that the members were friendly toward each other. They joked about their common plight.

Several factors appeared to underlie their camaraderie. The group members were of similar age and education. Of more significance, they shared a spirit of professionalism. Rather than feeling exploited because they had to work harder than usual, they looked upon the work overload as a professional challenge.

In group problem situations where a high degree of creativity and problem-solving ability is called for, a heterogeneous group is generally the most effective. People with different backgrounds (such as educational specialty or cultural values) help bring fresh perspectives to the problem. A case in point is a new-product committee used quite successfully by a national food manufacturer. People are invited to serve on the committee on a rotating basis. Members are carefully chosen from a diversity of educational and ethnic backgrounds. Among the new products successfully marketed by the company in the last five years are a line of dog food desserts and a soft food for senior citizens with denture problems.

High Degree of Cooperation. Logic would suggest that, when group members cooperate with each other, the group is more effective than when considerable competition or infighting exists. Cooperation is particularly important when different group members are dependent upon each other's work. Should a team approach be used in building a stereo set at the factory, a high degree of cooperation would be required. If the same group of people were all transferred to the radio department of that company, with each person building radio speakers, a new factor would be introduced. Competition among the workers might raise output because the workers would be competing against each other, but they would not be interfering with each others work. Also, their output could be measured individually.

Worker satisfaction (another important output of groups) tends to be higher when people are more cooperative than competitive. Many people are looking for serenity while on the job.

Cohesiveness. When group members are mutually attracted to one another and feel proud to belong to that group, we say the group is cohesive. Successful groups are usually cohesive groups. However, there can be times when a cohesive group is unsuccessful in the eyes of management: when a cohesive group is angry at management, the results can be lowered productivity and, in extreme cases, sabotage. One such example is "bottling an automobile," as described by Mary Lou:

> When we were told by the steward that the company wasn't going to meet the demands we asked for in the new contract, we went into action. All of us would agree to perform a few little tricks that would later give the dealers and the company one giant headache. Our favorite was to "bottle" a few of the cars. We did this by inserting a Coke bottle into the frame of the car. The bottle would create a loud rattle when the car was driven over bumpy roads. There would be no way to remove it because it was sealed into the frame. If a complaint ever got back to our department, we would all give the supervisor an innocent "who, me?" stare.

Emotional Support to Members. A major benefit people derive from working in groups rather than by themselves is support and reassurance. People come to expect encouragement and ego bolstering from the other members of their group. It is not surprising then that effective work groups typically provide emotional support to members. As one retail saleswoman expressed it, "I don't mind hassling with the customers so long as the other women in my department will listen to my problems. At times I get so mad I could punch a customer in the nose. My supervisor usually sympathizes with me when I tell her about the incident. Without her encouragement, it would be hard to face the customers day after day."

Mutual Trust and Confidence.   Closely related to emotional support as a characteristic of an effective work group are mutual trust and confidence. When the group members trust each other and are confident in each others skills, the group tends to be more productive. Member satisfaction is also higher. Imagine how ineffective a surgical team would be if the members did not trust the technical skills of each other. Edgar H. Schein has observed that only when groups achieve mutual trust and confidence are they more effective than individuals in solving problems and making decisions.[7]

A university professor was asked by a former student why his department seemed so disorganized. The latter noted that several substantial overlaps existed among a few of the courses. Asked why this happened, the professor replied:

> That's because we don't talk to each other. At one time we could sit down together and discuss common concerns and problems. But bit by bit we came to suspect each other of intellectual pirating. I would mention some idea that I was researching or using in the classroom. The next thing I knew some other professor was using the idea and claiming it as his. Things have gotten so bad that I won't have any ideas typed or reproduced in the department. I'm afraid some other professor will steal them.

Optimum Size.   Who could argue with the proposition that effective groups are the *right size?* The dilemma only presents itself when we try to specify what we mean by the concept "right size." What is the right size for one type of task may be the wrong size for successfully completing another task. Five is the right number of people to work an automobile racing pit. But five people may be too small to erect a one-family building in thirty days. One general conclusion is that about five to seven people are the desired maximum when you need considerable interaction among people in the group.[8] When a lot of work has to be accomplished and people are not highly dependent upon one another, the group size may be increased (without worrying about a loss of effectiveness).

ADVANTAGES OF GROUP MEMBERSHIP AND GROUP EFFORT

Grouping of people both at work and in social gatherings would not be so common if groups did not offer some benefits over individual effort. Even if you prefer working alone to a team effort, it is still of value to look critically at some of the advantages that groups can offer.

Synergy. As is widely recognized, the productivity of a group often exceeds the contribution that would have been possible by having the group members working separately. Synergy is readily visualized with respect to physical tasks. Five people constructing a house as a group would be far more productive than five people trying to construct a house by themselves. A person working alone perhaps could never accomplish such tasks as erecting the framework or inserting joists in the basement. But five people working together cooperatively should be able to build a house (assuming that they have the right technical skills).

Synergy also applies to intellectual tasks. Five people working together to solve a business problem might accomplish more than the combined output of the same five people working independently. Many advertising firms claim that they are synergistic—the unique combination of talents gathered in their firm produces a certain chemistry that could help clients.

As with any other advantage to group effort discussed in this section, synergy does not always take place. Whether or not a particular group experiences the potential advantage of being a group depends upon its unique circumstances. In general, groups that possess the characteristics of effective work groups experience these potential benefits.

Generation of New Ideas. In many situations, group problem solving is superior to individual problem solving. When this occurs, one underlying factor seems to be the larger amount of ideas generated in a group setting. As in brainstorming, the typical work group provides for multiple inputs to a problem. The group not only allows for the generation of ideas, it provides immediate feedback and refinement of the ideas generated. Jake, an assistant store manager, describes how group membership helped improve one of his ideas:

> A couple of my friends and I decided to develop a business sideline aside from our regular jobs. We met twice a week for two months before we hit upon a workable idea. I suggested we sell cattails—those funny looking weeds that grow in a swamp. My idea was to place an advertisement in several magazines and take orders for them directly. My two partners convinced me that such an approach would be too costly. We decided to approach a few mail-order houses with our product idea. One of them is now stocking our cattails. The reorders continue to trickle in. We seemed to have made the right decision. We're having fun and making a few dollars.

Satisfaction of Individual Needs. A major reason people join groups and retain their membership is that groups satisfy several important psychological needs.[9] Among these are needs for affiliation, security, esteem and self-fulfillment. Many people (if not most) prefer working in groups to individual effort because of the opportunity the former provides for socializing with other people. One man who switched positions from an insurance underwriter to a field claims investigator was asked how he liked his new assignment. He commented, "It's all right, but I miss the give and take of the office atmosphere. It's kind of lonely out there in the field."

Satisfaction of security needs is possible because of the emotional support provided by group membership. Particularly when a person is establishing himself or herself in the world of work, the group offers a source of help. It is more comfortable for some people to consult peers rather than a boss about minor work-related problems.

Esteem needs can be satisfied in at least two important ways by group membership. First, your work group often provides positive feedback when you do something right. In baseball, the player who hits a home run receives a good deal of congratulatory pats on his (or *her* in some leagues) back (or rear end) immediately after the accomplishment. When a new-car sales person chalks up a banner month, he or she might be named "sales person of the month" by the dealership. Such recognition satisfies a need for recognition, but it also adds to a person's worth in the eyes of others—a major source of esteem.

Work groups add to a person's professional or technical development by providing the person with a chance to communicate about job-related skills. If you are a photographer who works with a group of photographers, you can converse with these people about new developments in your field. This is not as feasible when you are the only photographer in your department. Need satisfaction enters the picture, because improving your skills and knowledge leads toward self-fulfillment.

Reduction of Tension. Group membership has the mental health advantage of reducing tension for many people. The emotional support provided by the group helps you control tension. A study conducted by Stanley E. Seashore of 228 industrial work groups in a machinery company showed that tension and anxiety were least pronounced in the highly cohesive groups.[10]

It is a common practice in work groups for members to share problems (both personal and job related) with each other. When faced with a major problem, having a sympathetic listener often reduces tension. The advice offered by a co-worker might lead to a solution to your problem, further reducing your tension. One woman was becoming increasingly tense about funding her child's college education. A co-worker suggested that she apply for a long-term tuition loan offered by a local bank. The troubled woman was able to secure such a loan and her level of tension was reduced.

Dissemination and Exchange of Information. Formal groups are well suited to communicating important information. The give and take possible in a staff meeting, for example, would be difficult to achieve by memo alone. The leader would have to write every person a memo. He or she, in turn, would have to write every other group member a memo giving his or her reaction.

Groups can be used to discuss information that has already been disseminated to individuals prior to the group meeting. Such a process short-circuits the proliferation of large numbers of intraoffice and inter-office memos. Book publishers often use an editorial committee to decide upon the worth of a proposed book. Assuming that no one strong personality ramrods his or her opinion upon others, the exchange of information in the editorial committee will contribute to a sound decision. In such a meeting the comments of one person may spark the thinking of another. Such a benefit would not have been possible if people made the final decision about the various book proposals while sitting alone in their offices or cubicles.

Greater Risk Taking.   A curious phenomenon called the *risky shift*[11] suggests that many people are more bullish (greater risk takers) working in a group setting. For example, people who belong to stock investment clubs might recommend that the group invest in a stock of higher risk than those which they would purchase individually. Here is an example of a risk-taking situation that has been used to demonstrate the risky-shift phenomenon:

> Julie, a commercial artist employed by an automobile manufacturer, inherits $20,000 (after inheritance taxes) from her parents' estate. Julie is divorced and has two children, ages nine and twelve, who live with her. Her former husband has moved out of state and infrequently sends his child-support payments.
>
> Julie discusses her inheritance with Rod, a salesman who sells ad space for magazines. The two of them have been dating regularly for three months but do not have an exclusive relationship. One week after the discussion, Rod suggests that Julie and he open a commercial art studio, using $15,000 of her inheritance as the initial investment. According to Rod's plan (1) Julie will be president of the studio, (b) Rod will be the administrator and be responsible for soliciting business for the studio, (3) Julie will perform the art work assisted by as many artists (on a sub-contract basis) as the workload requires, (4) Julie will retain 75 percent of the profits and Rod 25 percent, and (5) they will each receive an equal salary, geared to cover their basic living expenses.

Which one of the following alternatives should Julie choose?

1. Tell Rod to get lost and forget the deal.
2. Wait until Rod makes a marriage proposal before even considering entering into a business relationship with him.
3. Agree to the general idea except that she invest $5000, and that they begin business on a part-time (evenings and weekends) basis. Neither would resign their positions until the studio was big enough to justify a fulltime effort.

4. Accept the general idea, but insist that Rod put up one half of the investment. He could then share equally in the profits.

5. Totally accept Rod's proposition, recognizing that "opportunity only knocks once." And of course, have a lawyer scrutinize the formal partnership contract.

In experiments such as these, people tend to choose a less risky course of action when they choose the alternatives individually. When such problems are discussed in small groups, the average risk-taking score tends to be higher. One explanation for the risky shift is that certain cultural values favor taking a risk. In the situation described above, owning your own business is said to be part of the Great American Dream.

When making their first judgment, group members believe that they are making a risky choice. In the group discussion sessions, they may discover that in reality other people are riskier. So they become more adventuresome (with Julie's inheritance). Another plausible explanation is that in a group responsibility for the possible loss is spread out over a few people. People are more willing to take chances when they will not be totally responsible for things that may go wrong.

Improved Policy Decisions. Improved policy making is a specific benefit of group decision making in the executive suite. A number of major business corporations now use executive committees to make any major decision facing the corporation. The company, in effect, is run by a committee rather than by one top executive. Such an approach to decision making usually results in a wider perspective on the problem at hand.

An important reason that policy making is improved by use of the executive committee is that occupying the role of chief executive officer of a major corporation (or country) is too big a job for one person. Even if one person is held accountable for the results of the committee decisions, the benefit of balanced judgment is retained by using group decision making.

A Means to Obtain Ends. People often join groups as a means of achieving certain ends that they want outside of the group.[12] One study conducted many years ago showed that college women often joined sororities in order to increase their prestige in the college community. Workers at professional and employee levels may join labor unions in order to obtain higher wages and improved working conditions. In both examples, the ends (prestige or more money) are more important to the individuals than is group membership itself.

Industrial work groups may also serve as a vehicle for group members attaining an end outside of the group. The career-minded person will often volunteer for a committee assignment in order to be "discovered" by a member of top management. As described in Chapter 16, certain groups are advantageous to your career because they make you *visible* to influential people. Many a junior executive has distinguished himself or herself while on loan to the Community Chest fund-raising campaign. A favorable report goes back to the company that loaned the executive to the campaign, enhancing his or her reputation.

Increased Job Satisfaction.   Considerable evidence exists that when people are members of a work group that accepts them they experience a high degree of job satisfaction.[13] When the opportunity for interaction with other workers decreases, job satisfaction suffers. Many people seem to experience their peak moments of job-related pleasure when in conference with others or in coffee breaks. A counselor from an employment agency made the following comment about secretarial help's preference for working in groups:

> The most difficult slot for us to fill is a secretary–receptionist for a one-person office. Some women think they would like to work alone by themselves, but they usually find that it doesn't work. One lawyer who was in practice for himself had three women quit in one year. He spent most of his time out of the office. His secretary would be by herself with very little to do. We finally found that lawyer the right person. She is an older woman who basically doesn't like people.

PROBLEMS SOMETIMES CREATED BY GROUPS

Despite their many virtues, work groups sometimes create problems for management and members of the group. Almost every advantage of group membership cited above could also be a disadvantage in some situations. For instance, people might find interacting with their peers so satisfying that they neglect to concentrate on their work. As recognized by elementary and high school teachers, when good friends work together, productivity often decreases. Here we shall concentrate on four problems that are a by-product of group effort.

Shirking of Individual Responsibility.   For those people not strongly work oriented, group assignments are sometimes an invitation to shirk responsibility. Unless assignments are carefully drawn and both group and individual objectives exist, an undermotivated member can often squeeze by without contributing his or her fair share. The responsibility shirker risks being ostracized by the group, but may be willing to pay this price rather than work hard. Shirking of individual responsibility is commonly found in groups such as committees, task forces, and group project teams. A professor conducting a business research seminar met with a class member one day who had a few candid comments to make:

I've waited as long as I could before coming to you. It's about Jack. The guy is doing nothing for the group. In fact, he's messing up our whole project. He was supposed to interview ten people and so far he has only turned in two questionnaires. I suspect he faked the questionnaire answers. His answers came out too perfect. We're afraid of not making our deadline because of him. Can you help us out?

In this situation, the professor confronted the student with the perceptions of his work held by the other members. The student admitted that he had fallen behind schedule and expressed a willingness to be transferred to another group. Instead, he was assigned an individual research project. All situations dealing with shirking of responsibility are not so readily detected or remedied.

Pressures Toward Conformity. The most frequent criticism of group effort is that the individual may be forced to act and think like other group members. In some situations such conformity can be detrimental. For instance, one design engineer in a group of five may believe a car-braking mechanism is unsafe. After learning that his co-workers think that the braking mechanism is safe, he may say to himself, "If the other members of the group disagree with me, I'm probably wrong. Why be an odd ball? I'll call the mechanism safe."

Such an act of conformity has two negative consequences. First, the conforming design engineer may be right. His pronouncement about the unsafe features of the braking mechanism could save lives if brought to the attention of management. Second, by not casting his opinion and going along with the group, his contribution is almost zero. As one manager said about his staff members, "If they all agree with me, why do I need all of them?"

The subject of pressures toward conformity has been of long-standing interest to social psychologists. Widely quoted experiments conducted by Solomon Asch indicated that people will change their opinions about highly objective matters when faced with group pressures.[14] His most famous experiments had to do with subjects determining which among three straight lines was the longest. Asch brought together groups consisting of one legitimate subject and various numbers of other subjects who were actually confederates of the experimenter.

These confederates were told beforehand to deceive the legitimate subject by unanimously agreeing on the "wrong answer" in a series of visual judgments. Twenty-seven percent of the legitimate subjects gave judgments distorted in the direction of the false group consensus. Subjects yielded for a variety of reasons. A few came to believe that the smaller lines actually were longer. Others yielded because they believed that perhaps they must have misunderstood the instructions. Others yielded because they did not want to be seen as a deviate by the rest of the group. These people conformed in order to avoid disapproval from the other group members.

It must be recognized that conformity can be beneficial to the group and its members. When all the fork-lift operators in a factory agree to drive no faster than 5 miles per hour, the net result is a safer atmosphere. When patients and visitors conform to the No Smoking signs surrounding oxygen tents, explosions are avoided.

Norms and Conformity.   A major reason we have conformity (both beneficial and detrimental) in groups is the existence of norms. Group norms refer to the unwritten set of expectations for group members—what the people "ought to do." Norms become a standard of what each person should do or not do within the group. People learn about norms both through simple observation and conditioning from other group members. Stephen J. Carroll and Henry L. Tosi provide a cogent explanation[15]:

> When a new member works at too fast a pace the first day on the job, he may be subjected to derogatory comments such as "Look at old speed king there," "Look who's trying to make us look bad," "Look who's trying to impress the foreman," "Look at who's trying to make us lose our jobs," and so on. A little of this goes a long way in obtaining compliance with group norms.

Norms are enforced by punishing violators in a number of ways. The person who exceeds or does not live up to group norms may find himself or herself ostracized from the rest of the group. Disapproval and even physical attacks are not unheard of in a group's attempt to "keep members in line."

Pressures Toward Mediocrity.   A potential hazard of being well accepted by your work group and identifying with its members is that your performance (and career) may be held back in the process. To the extent that you try to remain "one of the boys" or "one of the girls," you will not be able to distinguish yourself from others. Your allegiance to the group may make it difficult for you to advance into management or to perform your job in a superior manner. Groups sometimes foster mediocre performance.

> Nancy took the best job she could find for the summer, a chambermaid position at a resort hotel. As she perceived the situation, the pay was good, the hours delightful, and the beach superb. However, Nancy was subject to some uncomfortable group pressures. She explains what happened: "I felt some kind of obligation to do my best for the hotel owners. They were treating me fine and I wanted to reciprocate. I charged into my jobs, literally singing as I went about my chores. Within a week I found that the other chambermaids were almost forcing me to take a coffee or cigarette break with them. They told me I was cleaning too many rooms an hour. They wanted me to slow down so they wouldn't look bad. My decision was to tell them to do what they wanted and I would do what I wanted. My decision was the right one. I was invited back the next year as a supervising chambermaid.

Breeding of Conflict.   At their worst, groups foster conflict in an organization. Intergroup conflict occurs when group members develop the attitude that their work group is more important than the organization as a whole. Rivalries develop, and "beating the opposition" becomes more important than trying to reach goals important to the organization. The folly of trying to outwit the opposition, rather than solving bigger problems, is illustrated by the comments of a marketing executive to a market researcher on his staff:

> What I want you to do is build a convincing story showing how manufacturing screwed us again. Let's convince top management that manufacturing won't respond to customer demands. Dazzle management with charts. Fudge figures a little if you have to. It's time we nailed those bastards to the wall.

THE EFFECTIVE COMMITTEE MEETING

Committees represent an important form of group effort in both profit and nonprofit organizations. Despite the many criticisms and jokes made of them, committees will endure. They are particularly well suited to working on projects that do not justify the creation of a permanent department. For instance, developing an employee pension plan is well suited to a committee assignment. Committees (or task forces) that produce results and provide satisfaction to members generally have five distinguishing characteristics.[16]

1. Members of effective committees are well qualified for their assignment from the standpoint of knowledge and interest. For example, if a young man were planning to quit a company in six months, he would have little interest in serving on the profit-sharing committee and therefore would make a meager contribution. Many people are assigned to committees with limited knowledge of the subject at hand. The result is usually frustration for themselves and the other members.

2. A specific agenda is planned for each meeting, and committee members are given advance notice of the agenda. This avoids the time wasting characteristic of so many committee meetings. When a member asks, "What are we supposed to talk about today?," time wasting is the most probable result.

3. Effective committee meetings are characterized by a balanced contribution from the members. A skillful leader often has to gently curtail the contributions of verbose and domineering members. Equally important, the chairperson has to coax more reticent members to contribute their ideas. Without a balanced contribution, a committee fails to achieve its fundamental goal of being a democratic process.

4. A vital attribute of an effective committee is power sharing by

the chairperson. Unless power is shared, the committee members believe that the real purpose (hidden agenda) of the meeting is to seek approval for the chairperson's ideas. Ideally, the chairperson should not have preconceived ideas about what should be the ultimate recommendations of the committee.

George M. Prince has summarized the beliefs and attitudes of the type of manager who is able to successfully share power with his or her subordinates.[17] Those attitudes especially suited to a committee meeting are noted in Figure 8.1.

- The most efficient mode is to make use cooperatively of the varied talents available.
- The best decision will emerge if I combine my power with that of implementers.
- I must use my power to help each subordinate develop his or her autonomy.
- I share my power so that my subordinates can grow as I grow.
- When subordinates express themselves or act in unacceptable ways, I assume they had reasons that made sense to them and explore the action from that point of view.
- Even mature people are distressed to some degree by put downs and criticism, and this makes cooperation difficult.
- My role is to join my subordinates to make sure that they succeed.

SOURCE: George M. Prince, "Creative Meetings Through Power Sharing," *Harvard Business Review,* July–Aug. 1972, p. 52.

FIGURE 8.1
Attitudes and beliefs of a power-sharing manager.

5. After a committee has deliberated and reached its recommendations, these recommendations must be taken seriously by the organization. People come to believe that committees are futile and powerless if they are bodies for discussion only and no action.

*Summary
of Key Points*

1. A group is a collection of people who meet regularly, interact with each other, and realize that they are a group.

2. Organizations are essentially composed of a collection of small groups.

3. Many different types of groups exist in an organization. A major classification of groups is formal versus informal. A formal group is one deliberately formed by the organization to accomplish specific tasks. An informal group is one that evolves naturally to take care of people's desire for companionship. However, it may also serve organizational purposes.

4. Effective work groups have certain characteristics in common: (a) proper leadership, (b) the right mix of people, (c) high degree of cooperation, (d) cohesiveness (members attracted to each other), (e) emotional support to members, (f) mutual trust and confidence, and (g) small in size, but this varies with the task.

5. Groups serve many useful purposes: (a) they accomplish more than people working alone (synergy); (b) new ideas are generated; (c) individual needs such as belongingness are satisfied; (d) they reduce tension of members; (e) information is readily exchanged; (f) people take higher risks, sometimes beneficially; (g) policy decisions are improved; (h) important ends such as improved working conditions can be achieved; (i) job satisfaction increases for many people.

6. Groups also may create some problems. Among the potential hazards are (a) shirking of individual responsibility, (b) pressuring individuals toward undesirable conformity, and (c) pulling performance down to mediocre levels.

7. An effective committee meeting is characterized by (a) qualified members, (b) planned agenda, (c) balanced contribution from the members, (d) a chairperson who shares power, and (e) use of its recommendations by the organization.

*Questions
for Discussion*

1. Is an employee's credit union a formal or informal group? Explain your reasoning.
2. Describe any informal group to which you belong. Why and how did it come into being?
3. What reference group influences you the most? How does it affect your actions and attitudes?
4. Is the class for which you are reading this book an effective group? Use the ideas developed in the section Why Some Groups Succeed and Others Fail to analyze the class as a group.
5. Think of any group which you belonged to that failed. What factors were responsible for its failure? How might the failure have been prevented?
6. Think of the group that you have belonged to for the longest period of time. How has it helped you? How has it harmed you?

THE MEDIOCRE OUTPUT FIGURES*

You are the key-punch supervisor in your company. Standard rates have been established for key-punch operators in terms of cards keypunched and verified per minute. The number of cards punched and the elapsed time are recorded by the keypunchers after each job. Totals are accumulated daily and a productivity rate is calculated for each operator.

Cindy, a woman who joined your group two months ago, asks to see you in private. She says with conviction, "I'm not going to put up with the shenanigans going on in the key-punch room any longer. Do you know what they are pulling down there? Those girls are manipulating productivity totals. The fastest women are helping the lower performing operators by giving them cards in order to increase their productivity rate. The card counts and the time taken to complete many of the jobs are therefore wrong. I want to get paid for what I can do, not for what that gang of thieves thinks I should do."

How would you handle this situation?

* Researched by Craig A. Happ.

THE UNSTOPPABLE COFFEE KLATCH

Jim Lyons, the newly appointed manager of operations at Gulf Coast Insurance Company, confided to Wendy McPherson, his executive secretary, "We're going to see a lot of changes around here. Last year the company just about broke even. I don't see any need to lay off people, but I do see a need for us to become more efficient.

"What irks me the most is the time being wasted in the office while people sit around in coffee klatches. Around ten in the morning, the place is deserted. About ninety percent of the staff is down in the cafeteria whiling away time, drinking coffee. We could get by on less staff if we could cut down on those coffee breaks. We could lose about five percent of our office staff due to attrition and not have to replace them if we could stop the time leak created by the coffee break."

Jim's first management action to curtail the coffee break was to prepare an edict that from now on no coffee breaks would be allowed in the cafeteria. Instead, coffee- and tea-vending machines would be installed at two key locations in the office building. Any employee who wanted coffee or tea could purchase a beverage in the machine and take it back to his or her work station.

One month later the vending machines were installed and the cafeteria was declared off limits to employees except during their lunch break. Shortly thereafter, Jim received a phone call from Mickey, the head of maintenance.

"Mr. Lyons," said Mickey excitedly, "I think we have a major fire hazard on our hands. Since you ended the cafeteria coffee break and installed the vending machines, the employees have found a new way to serve coffee. All of a sudden we have a collection of hot water heaters, Silexes, and those new coffee makers around the office. I first got on to it when one of them shorted and blew a fuse. I understand that the vending machine is losing money. That's what the route man told me."

"Mickey, I appreciate your having brought this problem to my attention," replied Jim, "I'll get on it right away."

The next day Jim Lyons had a memo affixed to every bulletin board and sent to every supervisor. It read in part, "From now on, no unauthorized coffee- or tea-making equipment will be brought into this office. Any employee caught using unauthorized coffee-making equipment will be subject to suspension."

Two weeks later, Jim asked Mickey to make a secretive night inspection of the office. His task was to discover if any coffee pots were still being used in the office. Mickey's investigation turned up no such evidence. Jim also phoned a few supervisors to see if the edict was receiving full compliance. Again, the report was positive. Jim thought to himself that the coffee klatch problem had finally been resolved. Three weeks later, Jody, the personnel manager, came forth with a disconcerting comment:

"Jim, I thought your edict might have been a little heavy handed. And I told you so. I now have evidence that your removal of the coffee pots has created a new problem."

"What's that? I haven't heard of any problems," said Jim.

"Perhaps, then, you haven't been making recent tours of the office at any time from nine to eleven in the morning. You can find little pockets of people drinking coffee in the strangest of places. We found five women from underwriting sitting on the steps of a fire exit. Three fellows and two gals from the claims department were found gathered around the Xerox machine drinking coffee. Worst of all, five people were sitting under a tree on the front lawn with paper cups in their hands. That's hardly what you had in mind with your no coffee pot edict."

"Jody, let me think about this problem for a while longer," mused Jim. Three days later, he sent out a new memo:

"Because of disappointment with certain aspects of the service, the coffee-vending machine will be removed from the building. Therefore, all employees who so desire are allowed a fifteen-minute break per morning to have coffee or other beverage in the cafeteria. Please make sure that this fifteen-minute limit is not exceeded."

1. Why didn't Jim Lyon's plan to stop the time spent on coffee breaks work?
2. How sound was Jim's decision to reinstate the cafeteria coffee break?
3. What does this case tell us about informal groups?
4. What does this case tell us about Jim's managerial skills?
5. What does this case tell us about vending-machine coffee?

FOOTNOTES

[1] Henry L. Tosi and Stephen J. Carroll, *Management: Contingencies, Structure, and Process,* St. Clair Press, 1976, p. 97.

[2] James L. Gibson, John Ivancevich, and James H. Donnelly, Jr., *Organizations: Structure, Processes, Behavior,* rev. ed., Business Publications, Inc., 1976, p. 150.

[3] *Ibid.,* pp. 150–151.

[4] Alvin W. Gouldner, "Cosmopolitans and Locals: Toward an Analysis of Latent Social Roles," *Administrative Science Quarterly,* Sept. 1957, pp. 281–306.

[5] Alan C. Filley, Robert J. House, and Steven Kerr, *Managerial Process and Organizational Behavior,* Scott, Foresman, 1976, p. 157.

[6] Rensis Likert, *New Patterns of Management,* McGraw-Hill, 1961.

[7] Edgar H. Schein, *Organizational Psychology,* 2nd ed., Prentice-Hall, 1970, p. 95.

[8] Filley, House, and Kerr, *op. cit.,* p. 147.

[9] An expanded discussion of this point is found in Gibson, Ivancevich, and Donnelly, *op. cit.,* pp. 151–152.

[10] Stanley E. Seashore, *Group Cohesiveness in the Industrial Work Group,* Survey Research Center, University of Michigan, 1954.

[11] Rolf E. Rogers, *Organizational Theory,* Allyn and Bacon, pp. 129–131. An original source here is J. A. F. Stoner, "Risky and Cautious Shifts in Group Decisions: The Influence of Widely Held Values," *Journal of Experimental Social Psychology,* vol. 4, 1968, pp. 442–459.

[12] Marvin E. Shaw, *Group Dynamics: The Psychology of Small Group Behavior,* McGraw-Hill, 1971.

[13] Tosi and Carroll, *op. cit.,* p. 110.

[14] Solomon E. Asch, "Opinions and Social Pressure," *Scientific American,* 1955. Summarized in Audrey Haber and Richard P. Runyon, *Fundamentals of Psychology,* Addison-Wesley, 1974, pp. 556–568.

[15] Stephen J. Carroll and Henry L. Tosi, *Organizational Behavior,* St. Clair Press, 1977, p. 106.

[16] The first three points are mentioned in Herbert J. Chruden and Arthur W. Sherman, Jr., *Personnel Management,* 5th ed., South-Western, 1976, p. 66.

[17] George M. Prince, "Creative Meetings Through Power Sharing," *Harvard Business Review,* July–Aug. 1972, pp. 47–54.

SUGGESTED READING

DROUGHT, NEAL E. "The Operations Committee: An Experience in Group Dynamics," *Personnel Psychology,* Summer, 1967, pp. 153–163.

FRANKLIN, JEROME F. "Relations Among Four Social–Psychological Aspects of Organization," *Administrative Science Quarterly,* Sept. 1975, pp. 422–433.

LAU, JAMES B. *Behavior in Organizations: An Experiential Approach,* Irwin, 1975, Part Two.

LEAVITT, HAROLD J. *Managerial Psychology,* 3rd ed., University of Chicago Press, 1972, Part Three.

MAIER, NORMAN R. F. *Problem Solving and Creativity in Individual and Groups,* Brooks/Cole, 1970.

PRINCE, GEORGE M. "Creative Meetings Through Power Sharing," *Harvard Business Review,* July–Aug. 1972, pp. 47–54.

ROSENBERG, M, "Which Significant Others?" *American Behavioral Scientist,* Dec. 1973, pp. 829–860.

SCHEIN, EDGAR H. *Organizational Psychology,* 2nd ed., Prentice-Hall, 1970.

SHAW, MARVIN E. *Group Dynamics: The Psychology of Small Group Behavior,* McGraw-Hill, 1971.

TOSI, HENRY L., and HAMNER, W. CLAY. *Organizational Behavior and Management: A Contingency Approach,* St. Clair Press, 1974, Part Four.

9
COMMUNICATING WITH PEOPLE

Learning Objectives

After reading and studying this chapter, you should be able to

1. Identify the basic steps in the communication process.
2. Identify the major reasons we have communication problems.
3. Understand how to overcome barriers to communication.
4. Identify the major informal communication pathways in organizations.
5. Develop a plan for improving your written and spoken communication skills.
6. Make more effective use of nonverbal communication.

Communicating with people is an inescapable requirement of all but the most routine jobs. Even people whose work does not primarily involve interpersonal relations (such as a laboratory technician) must communicate with people to ask questions or explain their work. Communications is also the basic process by which managerial and staff people accomplish their work. A manager can coordinate the work of others only if he or she receives information from some people and transmits it to others. A staff specialist can only have his or her recommendations implemented if they are communicated in a useful manner to line management.

Despite the importance of good communications in getting tasks accomplished, it remains a major problem facing most organizations. Although it may seem incredible to a person removed from life in large organizations, the following incident is not atypical:

The president of a textile company was away from his office for a one-month tour of the company's European facilities. One week before his return, Billy, the president's administrative assistant, telephoned a work request to Carmen, the head of office maintenance: "Make sure everything is spick and span by the time the president gets back." Carmen, in turn, relayed this order to Tom, one of the office maintenance workers. Said Carmen, "The top boss is coming home. Make sure his office is spick and span, including that very fine mahogany furniture."

When the president returned, he was horrified to see that all his furniture had a dull glow. In place of the highly polished mahogany he had left behind, there was furniture that looked like it had been left in the rain and then wiped dry. At the president's request, Billy investigated what had happened. Carmen contended that he had simply relayed Billy's request to Tom. Although Tom was a new employee, he appeared to be quite reliable. Carmen and Billy confronted Tom about the problem. Tom gave his explanation: "I thought that was a strange request but I figured the boss knows best. You told me to clean the mahogany furniture with Spic and Span—the stuff we use for floors and walls. It did take some of the shine off the furniture, but if you said 'Spic and Span,' I figured you meant it."

The information presented in this chapter is aimed toward reducing communication problems between people. A discussion of how an individual can improve his or her communication skills—a success factor for managerial and staff positions—is also included.

STEPS IN THE COMMUNICATION PROCESS

A convenient starting point in understanding how people communicate is to examine the steps involved in the transmission of a message. A popular conception of this process is shown in Figure 9.1.[1] Assume that a man named Conrad wishes to communicate to his boss, Barbara, that he wants a salary increase.

Step one is *ideation* by Conrad. He organizes his thoughts about this sensitive problem. This stage is both the origin and the framing of the idea or message in the sender's mind. Conrad says to himself, "I think I'll ask for a raise."

Step two is *encoding*. Here the ideas are organized into a series of symbols (words, hand gestures, body movements, drawings) designed to communicate to the intended receiver. Conrad says, "Barbara, there is something I would like to talk to you about if you have the time . . . ."

Step three is *transmission* of the message orally or in writing. In this situation the sender chose the oral mode.

Step four is *receiving* of the message by the other party. Barbara can only receive the message if she is attentive to Conrad.

Step five is *decoding* the symbols sent by the sender to the receiver. In this case decoding is not complete until Barbara hears the whole message. The opening comment, "Barbara, there is something I would like to talk about. . . . ," is the type of statement often used by employees to

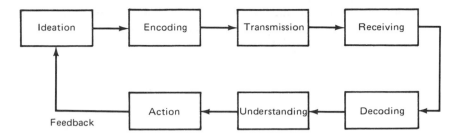

FIGURE 9.1

A basic model of the communication process.

broach a sensitive topic such as discussing a resignation or salary increase. Barbara therefore listens attentively for more information.

Step six, *understanding*, follows upon the decoding process. Barbara has no trouble understanding that Conrad wants a salary increase. When communication barriers exist (as described in the next section of this chapter), understanding may be limited.

Step seven is *action*. Barbara understands Conrad's request, but does not agree. She acts by telling Conrad that he will have to wait three more months until his salary will be reviewed. Action is also a form of feedback, because it results in a message being sent back to the original sender from the receiver.

WHY WE HAVE COMMUNICATION PROBLEMS

Communication problems are ever–present, both in work and personal life. A romantic young man said to his girlfriend "I won't love you any more if you lose weight." She replied, "Why wouldn't you love me if I were thin?" The intention of his communication was that he would not love his girlfriend an additional amount just because she were thinner. His present love for her transcended physical beauty. Communication problems exist because there are so many barriers to communication. A few major ones will be discussed next.

False Assumptions on the Part of the Sender.   In sending messages (communicating) to people, we make a few automatic assumptions. When these assumptions are incorrect, the transmitted message may not get through in the manner intended.[2] One such assumption made by a sender is that the receiver will listen to logic (at least his or her conception of logic).

Rex, a life insurance salesman, expanded his business activities by selling annuities that served as a tax shelter. A purchaser of this plan would be able to realize substantial tax savings in his or her years of highest earnings. During retirement years, the annuity would produce an income at a low tax rate because the recipient would usually be earning very little money during retirement. Rex made an impassioned pitch to every high school teacher he knew. He became frustrated when few teachers would accept the logic of his argument. However illogical to Rex, many people would prefer to get as much cash as they could from their current salary.

Another false assumption often made by a communicator in a work organization is that everybody is well motivated and interested in their work. Thus an executive was surprised when few people changed their behavior in response to his message: "If we all dig in and work hard and take a voluntary pay cut, I know we can avert disaster." In analyzing why nobody stepped forth to take a pay cut, this executive thought that perhaps his message was not worded in a dramatic enough fashion.

Improper Transmission by Sender.   Communication breakdowns occur sometimes because the sender of the message chooses a poor medium for transmitting the message. At times, a written message may be the most effective; at other times a spoken message is best. Paulette, a landlord, discovered this barrier to communication through firsthand experience.

> Paulette invested a medium-sized inheritance into a four-family apartment building. In the process of acquiring the building she introduced herself to the tenants and instructed them to mail her the rent each month. The system worked for the first month. By the second month one tenant, Clancy, was ten days late with his rent. The next month he was fifteen days late. Paulette responded by sending a stern letter about the importance of paying the rent on time. By the twentieth day of the third month, Clancy had still not sent the rent. Paulette wrote an even sterner letter.
> In despair, Paulette made several in-person visits in order to find Clancy (his phone had long been disconnected). Finally locating him, Clancy paid the rent in cash. Paulette asked Clancy why he did not answer her letters. He replied, "I didn't think a letter really counted. It's only when a landlady visits you in person that she means business."

Defensive Behavior by the Receiver.   When people are threatened by a message, they react defensively as a method of reducing tension and protecting their ego. In extreme, they may even deny information (the defense mechanism of denial) that is contrary to a strongly held belief. You might attempt to communicate a message such as this to a subordinate: "If you don't come to work on time more regularly, I'm going to fire you. This is a final warning." When asked by his wife how are things going on the job, that same individual may respond: "Pretty good, except that the boss thinks I could be more punctual." He doesn't hear the painful message that his job is in jeopardy.

Closely related to defensive behavior is the distorting of messages because of stereotyped beliefs about the sender. Behavior that contradicts our stereotypes makes us tense or anxious, so we often deny reality. The role of stereotypes in distorting communication is illustrated by an event that took place at a personnel conference.

> The vice-president of finance was invited to address a conference of personnel workers from a large company. During his talk he emphasized the importance of appropriately valuing the human contribution to a corporation. The speaker emphasized that, unless some quantitative value is attached to the caliber of management and employees, the true worth of a corporation would not be known.
>
> During the luncheon following the talk, the topic of conversation turned to the financial executive's talk. One personnel specialist commented, "What else could you expect from a bean counter? Now he wants to put a dollar and cents value on people, just as if they were machines."

Different Frames of Reference. People perceive words and concepts differently because their vantage points and perspectives differ. Such differences can create barriers to communication. For instance, a registrar might communicate "good news" to a college professor by saying, "Wow, we can expect some crowded classrooms this semester." The professor would interpret this as bad news. An amusing example of different frames of reference creating a communication problem took place in a life insurance agency.

> Jeb, a second-year salesperson, showed his sales figures for the month to his boss, Gary. Proud of his good results, Jeb said, "Well, what do you think of this kind of production for a man of my age?" Gary replied, "That's fine if you want to make $20,000 a year for the rest of your life." (Note: comment made in February 1977.) Jeb was visibly enthused.
>
> Gary looked at him quizically and said, "you mean you'd be happy making $20,000 a year for the rest of your life? I made that comment to shake you up a bit." Jeb answered, "No disrespect, Gary, but where I come from $20,000 a year is one big lump of money. And it still is today."

Different Interpretation of Words. As the reader is already probably aware, the varying meaning people attach to words (semantics) also creates barriers to communication. A word that you think is simply descriptive (such as calling somebody obese) might create a communications barrier between that person and yourself. A continuing problem with word connotation is that the meaning of some words changes over time. Even more baffling, different generations may attach different meanings to the same word at the same point in time.

One such problem word is "girl."[3] To a feminist, and many other modern women, the word girl should be restricted to females under the age of sixteen. In their frame of reference, the term girl applied to an adult female is a sexist put down. Yet many female production operators want to be referred to as "girls." To call a female production operator a "woman" suggests that she is elderly. Adding to the confusion, people who shape public opinion, such as Helen Gurley Brown (the editor of *Cosmopolitan*), refer to adult females as "girls." One hedge when addressing a mixed audience is to say "Hello, everybody," rather than "Hello, men and women," or "Hello, fellows and girls."

Another word that currently creates a communications barrier is "organization." To a human relations specialist, an organization is a system of small groups working in reasonable unity. Thus we have people who study organizational behavior. However, to people in general, an organization is a club or association. The yellow pages in your city telephone directory undoubtedly list social groups and clubs—not businesses, or hospitals, or schools—under the category "organizations."

OVERCOMING BARRIERS TO COMMUNICATION

The most general strategy for overcoming barriers to communication is to be sensitive to the presence of these barriers and act accordingly. If you wanted to communicate with a group of people unfamiliar to you, it would be helpful to conduct some informal research. Discover (1) the words that they perceive as being emotionally loaded and (2) their preferred mode of communication. One young woman using such an approach found out that people in a nursing home particularly disliked being talked to as if they were preschool children.

Another general strategy for overcoming barriers to communication is for organizational members to become more effective communicators. Methods of improving your communication skills are discussed later in this chapter. Now we shall overview five methods of circumventing communication barriers.

Communicate Honestly. A major reason that many communicators (including people in public office and business executives) are not taken seriously (do not get their messages across) is that they lied in the past. Persistent lying has been cited as a major form of deviant behavior in management.[4] To the extent that people lie, a communication barrier is erected. The type of lying that creates communication problems in organizations is described by one subordinate:[5]

> Don is clearly the biggest liar I've met in corporate life. During our last performance review together, he told me that he rated my performance as excellent and that he had recommended me for promotion to a manufacturing manager position in one of our biggest plants. That surely would have been a big position for me at this stage of my career. He told me that he would be back to me within about thirty days on the details. I was told that even if I didn't receive that promotion, I would be receiving a fifteen percent salary increase. I was so elated that I went around the company telling people what a pleasure it was to work for Don. I figured his reputation for telling half-truths was undeserved.

Then things hit like a bombshell. About a month later, Don called me into his office to tell me the company was undergoing a retrenchment and that my services would no longer be required. My successor, it turned out, was a friend of his from another company who was recently recruited into my department at Don's suggestion. When I tried to confront the liar about his plans to have me promoted to another plant, he told me business was no place to show emotion.

Reinforce Words with Action.   A concrete way of demonstrating that you are honest in what you say is to back up your verbal behavior with action.[6] Stated in another way, keep your promises and you will eliminate one more barrier to communication. Reinforcing your words with action is a *proactive* process. You enhance your communications ability as your reputation develops in a positive manner. John, a vice-president in charge of mergers and acquisitions, became an effective communicator following this principle.

Shortly after John joined the company, he made a presentation to the management group describing what he would be doing for the company. He told people that his job was to help the company find small businesses to purchase. John claimed that, by acquiring companies, new opportunities would be created for middle management. He also contended that nobody in the parent company would be replaced with a manager from an acquired company.

At the end of two years many people from the company were promoted to attractive positions in several acquired companies. Furthermore, nobody was replaced by a newly acquired manager. John's reputation as a reliable person was now among the highest in the executive ranks. Whatever message John presented in speech or writing, people took seriously.

Use Multiple Channels.   Repetition usually enhances learning. Repetition also enhances communication, particularly when different channels are used to convey the same message.[7] Effective communicators at many job levels follow up verbal (spoken) agreements with written documentation. Since most communication is subject to at least some distortion, the chances of a message being received as intended increase when two or more channels are used. It has become standard practice in several large companies for managers to use a multiple-channel approach to communicating the results of a performance appraisal. The subordinate receives a verbal explanation from his or her superior of the results of the review. He or she is also required to read the form and indicate by signature that he or she has read and understands the meaning of the review. A personnel manager comments on this practice in regard to communication:

We get much less griping now about the performance reviews than we did in the past. Before we had subordinates sign their reviews, we would get way too many distortions. A few years ago I remember a situatio in which an engineering technician claimed that she was told by h boss that she was doing an outstanding job. Yet she found out later th she was rated slightly below average. We have very few of these misinterpretations now. Aside from having improved communications in the review process, we're also keeping the boss more honest.

Use Verbal and Nonverbal Feedback.   To conclude that your message has been received as intended, it is helpful to ask for feedback. A frequent managerial practice is to conclude a conference with a question such as "Okay, what have we agreed upon today?" Unless feedback of this nature is obtained, you will not know if your message has been received until the receiver later carries out (or fails to carry out) your request. After speaking to a group that you are trying to influence, it would be helpful to ask them to state what message they thought you were trying to convey.

Nonverbal cues are sometimes more revealing than verbal cues. Included in nonverbal language are facial expressions, bodily movements, and hand signals.[8] Here are three examples of nonverbal behavior that could help you interpret whether or not your comments were being accepted:

1. You are making a sales pitch about encyclopedias to a family. Both the husband and the wife move forward in their chairs toward you, while the two adolescent children lean back on their chairs. You probably have the parents about sold on the proposition, but you need to work more with the children.
2. You ask a person of the opposite sex to go on an overnight camping trip with you. He or she firmly squeezes your hand while saying, "Let me think about it for a few moments." His or her answer will probably be "Yes."
3. You ask your boss when you will be eligible for a promotion and he looks out the window, cups his mouth to cover a yawn, and says, "Probably not too far away. I would say your chances aren't too bad." Keep trying. He is not yet sold on the idea of promoting you in the near future.

Appeal to Human Motivation.   A close relationship exists between communication and motivation. People tend to listen attentively to those messages that show promise of satisfying an active need.[9] The hungry person who ordinarily does not hear low tones readily hears a whispered message, "How would you like a pizza with everything on it?" Much advertising strategy is based upon the straightforward assumption that the most effective way to communicate with people is to appeal to an unsatisfied need (even if you have to create that need). The same principle has been applied successfully to situations outside of advertising:

A professional engineering union was having considerable difficulty attracting new members. Part of their organizing appeal was directed toward providing workers with higher wages and better working conditions. Later the union changed its appeal to one of job security. The union did not guarantee job security, but they expressed a willingness to work with management toward hiring practices that would allow for more stability in employment. Their revised appeal worked. As job security became more of a problem to engineers, the union gained in membership.

FORMAL COMMUNICATION PATHWAYS

Two important determinants of the direction in which communication flows are (1) the official pattern of authority relationships (the formal structure) and (2) the design of the work flow (technological needs).[10]

Organization Structure. When the company president wants a task accomplished, he or she is usually aware of the communications path that will take care of the problem. He or she might issue an order to his or her secretary (a lateral flow of communication); or he or she might call upon the appropriate subordinate (a downward flow of communication). The president knows where to direct the message because such authority relationships have been spelled out by the organization chart and/or the policies and procedures manual.

The formal organization chart shapes boss–subordinate–staff relationships and thus dictates communication pathways. In large organizations, these pathways can be complex. Twelve levels of management are often found in major corporations and large governments. Assume that a board chairman is emotionally touched by a message from Health, Education and Welfare that hiring the physically handicapped is a corporate responsibility. He or she reflects, "This is a very worthy cause. Our corporation has been negligent in this regard." A policy statement is then made that everybody in a managerial position should make an effort to hire and train qualified people with physical handicaps. Figure 9.2 shows the major formal communication pathway for this message. The formal pathway indicates the least complicated route over which the message will be transmitted. In practice, the route may be much more circuitous.

Technological Needs. Formal communication pathways are also profoundly influenced by the actual flow of work. In some instances the flow of work may proceed in an opposite direction to the chain of command. A person of low organizational rank may initiate work for a person or persons of higher organizational rank. One germane example is the flow of communications in a busy pediatric office. A receptionist takes the name of a patient. In turn he or she then tells a nurse's assistant which chart to pull. The nurse's assistant alerts the nurse. He or she dictates to the pediatrician which patients are to be seen.

Although the lowest ranking organizational member, the receptionist,

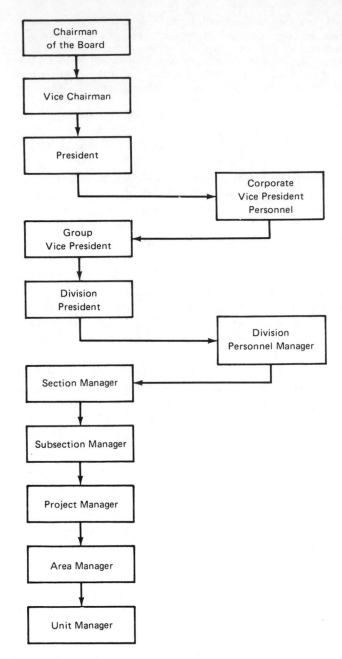

FIGURE 9.2
Formal communication pathway for message from top to bottom of a large business organization.

initiates the work flow and organizes the pattern of communications in two other vital ways. First, the medical receptionist often screens patients for the office. On busy days she might inform a parent to "give your child an aspirin and call us back tomorrow if the problem persists." The highest ranking organizational member (physician) is usually not even aware of how his or her work is being controlled in this manner. Second, when a legitimate emergency exists, as when an unconscious or bleeding child is rushed into the office, the receptionist may tell the doctor directly to work immediately on the case.

INFORMAL COMMUNICATION PATHWAYS

The paths by which messages travel from person to person are more numerous than those designated on the organization chart. A researcher would have to spend months in one department of a complex organization attempting to unravel the thousands of communication links used by people. Two major influences on informal (unwritten) communication paths are the *grapevine* and personal characteristics of people.

The Grapevine. The grapevine is the major informal communication network in an organization. It represents a source of information that bypasses the formal chain of command. Often, the grapevine transmits incorrect information, but official channels also transmit distortions. Keith Davis, a person long identified with research about the grapevine, describes it in this manner:[11]

> Being flexible and personal, it spreads information faster than most management communications systems operate. With the rapidity of a burning powder train, it filters out of the woodwork, past the manager's door and the janitor's closet, through steel walls or construction glass partitions and along the corridors. Moreover, well over three fourths of company rumors are accurate.

Harold Sutton and Lyman W. Porter extended some earlier research by Davis about the grapevine.[12] They studied the transmission of information in a regional tax office of a state government. All 79 employees of the office participated, ranging from the regional director to auditors, tax representatives, and clerical help. Over a period of seven months, nine pieces of information (grapevine items) were studied. One such item might be, "How did you learn about a cost of living adjustment for state employees?" For each grapevine item, each subject independently completed a questionnaire, which provided data about where, when, and how he or she learned or did not learn about the piece of grapevine information.

Analysis of responses to the questionnaires revealed two major results. First, the higher a person's place in the hierarchy (rank), the more he or she had access to grapevine information. This finding refutes the idea that the grapevine is used primarily by lower-ranking employees. Second, a relatively small percentage of individuals (about 10 percent) function as liaison individuals—people who transmit information to others. This finding supports the commonsense notion that only certain people in an organization are useful information sources.

Characteristics of the Individual. Which person is chosen as a source of information depends upon both his or her formal role and personal characteristics. As discussed in the chapters about job politics and leadership, a person's knowledge and personal characteristics contribute to his or her influence. Sometimes a noncharismatic person who is simply a sympathetic listener represents a good informal communication source. People may communicate useful tidbits of information to this person without worrying that he or she will use the information indiscriminately. An individual who has a personal relationship (relative, lover, social friend) with a key person in the organization represents yet another informal communication channel. In short, your personal power influences the extent to which you are relied upon as an information source.

A large proportion of informal communication takes place in a lateral direction. People with technical and professional jobs tend to consult colleagues when they need technical assistance. As logic would suggest, research has shown that the most technically competent people are consulted the most frequently.[13] Sometimes the process of consulting a knowledgeable peer can be overdone.

> Chet, a senior engineer, was asked to furnish an example of lateral communication in his organization. He said with conviction, "Unfortunately, that's me. I get paid to do my own work and provide some help to others in the department. At first it was an ego trip helping so many people out with so many problems. But it's becoming a bother. I spend so much time helping others that I have to do much of my own work at night.

IMPROVING YOUR COMMUNICATION SKILLS

Any serious student of human relations could not deny the importance of improving his or her communication skills. Aside from helping you to overcome barriers to communication, effective communication skills are a success factor in organizational life. Unless you own a business or receive a political appointment, it is difficult to occupy a managerial or staff position without having adequate communication skills. A person intent upon improving his or her communication effectiveness should take a course, attend a workshop, or read a few books geared toward that purpose.[14] Here we shall suggest a few strategies and add a few perspectives for improving your communications effectiveness.

Face-to-Face Speaking. Most people could use improvement in public speaking, but only high-level executive positions require that the incumbent give speeches. What most people do need is improved ability to express their ideas in face-to-face encounters, such as conferences and two-way discussions. Any course in conference leadership would help you achieve this end. Four experience-based suggestions (if carried out) should help the reader to improve his or her face-to-face speaking skills.

1. Take the opportunity to speak in a meeting whenever it arises. Volunteer comments in class and committee meetings, and capitalize on any chance to be a spokesman for a group.
2. Obtain feedback by listening to tape recordings or dictating equipment renditions of your voice. Attempt to eliminate vocalized pauses and repetitious phrases (such as "OK" or "you know") that detract from your communication effectiveness. Ask a knowledgeable friend for his or her opinion on your voice and speech.
3. Use appropriate models to help you to develop your speech. A television talk show host or commercial announcer may have the type of voice and speech behavior that fits your personality. The goal is not to imitate that person but to use him or her as an approximate guide to generally acceptable speech.
4. Practice interviewing and being interviewed. Take turns with a friend conducting a simulated job interview. Interview each other about a controversial current topic or each other's hobby.

Listening. Listening is a basic part of the communication process. Unless you receive messages as they were intended, you cannot properly perform your job or be a good companion. Ralph C. Nichols, a person long identified with serious research about listening, notes that white-collar workers, on the average, spend 40 percent of their workday listening, yet they listen at an average of 25 percent efficiency. He has formulated ten suggestions about listening that can serve as a checklist for improving listening skills.[15]

1. *Find areas of interest.* No matter how boring the message seems, search for something that you can put to use. (Even if it is a lecture on improving your listening skills!)

2. *Judge content, not delivery.* Even if a person stutters and stammers, the content of his or her message might be valuable. Think of how intently you listen to any method of delivery when you are lost and a stranger offers you directions. Take the attitude when listening, "Does this person talking to me have some information that I need to know?"

3. *Hold your fire.* Learn not to get too excited about a speaker's point, pro or con, until you are sure you understand it. Do not make up your mind immediately whether the message sender is "good" or "bad."

4. *Listen for key ideas.* Facts serve as documentation for ideas of broader significance. When your boss tells you your desk is messy, he or she may also be telling you that you are disorganized in a number of ways. Simply cleaning up your desk will not cure the problem.

5. *Be flexible about note taking.* When listening to a talk, note taking is often helpful. However, it should be done with selectivity. Since most speakers are disorganized, attempt to jot down key points. Do not try to outline a disorganized speech.

6. *Work at listening.* Expend effort to concentrate upon what the speaker is saying. Establish eye contact, and attempt not to think of other topics while a person is trying to get a message across to you.

7. *Resist external distractions.* Aside from distractions taking place inside your head, external distractions also have to be resisted. While listening to the receiver, try to ignore the low-flying plane or that physically attractive person adjacent to you. As Nichols states, "A good listener intuitively fights distractions."

8. *Exercise your mind.* Improve your listening ability by tuning in on a variety of material that is more difficult to comprehend than information familiar to you. If you are a dining-room manager, listen to a presentation on computers.

9. *Keep your mind open.* As Nichols cogently notes,[16] "Parallel to the blind spots which afflict human beings are certain psychological deaf spots which impair our ability to perceive and understand. These deaf spots are the dwelling place of our most cherished notions, convictions, and complexes. Often, when a speaker invades one of these areas with a word or phrase, we turn our mind to retraveling familiar mental pathways crisscrossing our invaded area of sensitivity."

10. *Capitalize upon thought speed.* The average rate of speech is 125 words a minute (for English). We think, and therefore listen, at almost four times that speed. Be careful not to let your mind wander while you are waiting for the person's next thought. Instead, try to listen between the lines—interpret the speaker's body language. For instance, did he or she look sincere when he or she said, "You're doing great"?

Writing. Every reader of this book has probably already taken one or two courses designed to improve writing skill. Nevertheless, four brief suggestions are in order to at least serve as a refresher.

1. Read a book about effective business report writing and attempt to implement the suggestions it offers.[17]

2. Read material regularly that is written in the style and format that would be useful to you in your career. *The Wall Street Journal* and *Business Week* are useful models for most forms of job-related writing. Managerial and staff jobs require you to be able to write brief, readily understandable memos and reports. If your goal is to become a good

technical report writer, read continuously technical reports in your field or specialty.

3. Practice writing at every opportunity. As a starting point, you might want to write letters to friends and relatives or memos to the file. Successful writers constantly practice writing. Many people who become an overnight success with a first book have already published a large number of articles.

4. Get feedback on your writing. Ask a colleague to critique a rough draft of your reports and memos. Offer to reciprocate; editing other people's writing is a valuable way of improving your own. Feedback from a person with more writing experience and knowledge than you is particularly valuable. For instance, comments made by an instructor about a submitted paper would be highly valued.

Nonverbal Communication. Body language and other forms of nonverbal communication can also be improved. Published information related directly to this topic is difficult to find. Here are four suggestions to tentatively consider.

1. Obtain feedback on your body language by asking others to comment upon the gestures and facial expressions that you use in conversations. Have a video tape prepared of you conferring with another individual. After studying your body language, attempt to eliminate those mannerisms and gestures that you think detract from your effectiveness (such as moving your knee from side to side when being interviewed).

2. Learn to relax when communicating with others. Take a deep breath and consciously allow your body muscles to loosen. The tension-reducing techniques discussed in Chapter 4 should be helpful here. A relaxed person makes it easier for other people to relax. Thus you are likely to elicit more useful information from other people when you are relaxed.

3. Use facial, hand, and bodily gestures to supplement your speech. (But do not overdo it.) A good starting point is to use hand gestures to express enthusiasm. You can increase the potency of enthusiastic comments by shaking the other person's hand, nodding approval, smiling, or patting him or her on the shoulder.

4. Avoid using the same nonverbal gesture indiscriminately. To illustrate, if you want to use nodding to convey approval, do not nod with approval even when you dislike what somebody else is saying. Also, do not pat everybody on the back. Nonverbal gestures used indiscriminately lose their communications effectiveness.

1. Communication is the basic process by which most work is conducted, yet communications among people is a major problem facing most organizations.

2. Communications among people can be divided into several stages:

ideation, encoding, receiving, decoding, understanding, and action.

3. Among the many reasons we have communication problems are (a) false assumptions made by the sender, (b) improper transmission by the sender, (c) defensive behavior by the receiver, (d) different frames of references, and (e) different interpretations.

4. Among the methods of overcoming these barriers are (a) honest communication, (b) reinforcing words with action, (c) using multiple communication channels, (d) using verbal and nonverbal feedback, and (e) appealing to human motivation.

5. Formal communication pathways are determined to a large extent by the organization structure and the technological requirements of the situation.

6. The grapevine is the major informal communication network in an organization. Characteristics of an individual such as his or her competence and personal contacts also influence communication patterns.

7. You need effective communication skills in order to succeed in managerial and staff positions. Four different modes of communication require attention: (a) face-to-face speaking, (b) listening, (c) writing, and (d) nonverbal communication such as facial expressions and hand gestures.

Questions
for Discussion

1. What major communication problems exist in the place where you work or attend school? What communication problems seem to be underlying this problem?

2. Provide two examples of how you have exhibited defensive behavior in response to a sender's message.

3. How does the concept of frame of reference help explain why the use of the term "boy" in reference to adult males often arouses negative feelings?

4. Billy Graham, the evangelist, is generally regarded as an effective communicator. What is he doing right from a communications standpoint?

5. You purchase a new automobile. After driving it 1000 miles, you conclude that the car fails to start about one in ten times. The service department of the dealer where you purchased the car tells you there is nothing wrong mechanically. What are the formal communication pathways that exist for resolving your problem?

6. How does the grapevine operate in your place of work? (In other words, what is the informal path over which information is transmitted?)

A Human Relations Incident
MAKE THEM LAUGH, BUT ALSO MAKE THEM THINK

Cynthia Baldwin, U.S. District Court judge, receives a telephone call one day from a local high school principal, Mr. Alstair Bainbridge. He asks Judge Baldwin if she would be willing to serve as the high school commencement speaker in June. She replies, "I would be honored. I've always wanted to be a commencement speaker. But one problem, Mr. Bainbridge. What should I talk about?"

"Ms. Baldwin, it's very difficult for me to tell you what to say. A person of your vast experience must have loads of good ideas stored up in her head."

"But I need some direction, some guidelines," said Baldwin. "Who will the audience be?"

"Oh, I can tell you that. We'll have the graduates of course. We will also have a number of their younger brothers and sisters. Since it's a central school nestled in the valley, you can expect a certain percentage of farmers. Grandparents like to attend these things too. But don't forget that you can also expect a goodly number of professional people in the audience.

"As I mentioned, the theme is up to you. But don't forget that you should entertain the people but also deliver a serious message. I guess what I'm really saying is that I want you to make them laugh, but also make them think."

If you were Judge Cynthia Baldwin, what key ideas would you incorporate in your commencement talk? What communication barriers might be confronting you?

A Human Relations Case
WHY DON'T PEOPLE TELL ME THESE THINGS?

Scott, vice-president of marketing at Prompto-Car, announced some plans at lunch to his assistant, Karen: "Finally, Karen, I'm in a position to say that our little car rental company is ready to hit the big time. After one year of operation I think we are ready to compete with the likes of Budget Rent-A-Car and Thrifty. Our price structure is just too much for them to handle. Sometimes I even wonder how we can afford to rent cars at the prices we do.

"Let me tell you more about the expansion plans. I'm thinking of a computerized system for tying in with airplane reservations. The big three in the car rental business have gotten in bed with the airlines and I think we can too. I'm even thinking of tying in with low-priced motels and hotels. A person renting from us can rent a car and sleep cheaper than he or she could by doing business with the majors. We may have to extend our line of credit to its outer limits to pull this off, but it will be worth it in the long run. We're poised for the big jump."

Karen replied, "Scott, it's curious that you should be talking about expansion at this time. I have some recent information that is hardly optimistic. It seems that business is taking a sudden downturn. Our rentals are off by thirty-five percent in the Midwest, and down twenty-five percent in the East."

Scott countered almost defensively, "Hold on, there's been a slight downturn in the airline business lately. We're tied pretty much to their business cycle. It's nothing serious. In a couple of months, demands will be right back up higher than ever."

"I have an idea," said Karen. "Let's call Bud, our midwestern regional manager, and see if he notices any real problems."

Over the telephone, Bud said angrily, "I wish I did know more about the problems. But it's me alone trying to cover ten states. Business doesn't look too good, but I can't be sure of the causes. I hear a few grumblings here and there about customer complaints. But customers would complain if we rented them Rolls Royces at fifteen cents per mile and twenty dollars per day. They would say the ashtrays were dirty or the tires weren't properly inflated."

After Scott and Karen discussed Bud's comments, they agreed to obtain some firsthand information. Together they paid a visit to the metropolitan airport to speak directly with a reservations clerk. Karen and Scott reassured the clerk, Melissa, that their mission was a genuine one; they were making the visit to uncover problems not to find out who should be blamed.

Melissa was surprisingly candid: "Quite frankly, we have more problems out here than you can expect a reservations clerk to handle. Customers may be willing to try us once because of our low prices, but we aren't getting much repeat business. One experience with Prompto-Car is about all most people can take."

"Why is that?" asked Scott.

"No offense, sir, but perhaps you should rent one of our cars and see some of the problems. People have complained to me about filthy ashtrays, finding combs in the seat, broken windshield washers, unwashed cars, and cars that won't climb a hill. As instructed, I smile and say that we guarantee them that problem will not happen again. But it's hard to be sincere, because I know the same problem, or worse, will show up."

Karen interrupted: "How do you know that problem will repeat itself?"

"Simply because we don't have the employees we need to run this operation. Our two maintenance men are so overworked that I hesitate to ask them to take care of a problem. Besides that we're kind of left to float on our own with very little supervision."

"Melissa, do you think you're exaggerating? Are our problems really that bad?"

"Yes, they are that bad," answered Melissa. "In fact the name Prompto-Car is a joke around the airport. The last wisecrack I heard about our company is that if you want the thrill of seeing an odometer move from 99,999 to 100,000 miles, rent a Prompto-Car."

1. Why is this case included in a chapter on communications among people?
2. What should Scott do next from a business standpoint?

3. How can Scott prevent future situations from getting so far out of control?

4. What job or job responsibility might be created for Karen that would enable her to receive early warning of customer dissatisfaction?

5. How unique are the problems of Prompto-Car?

FOOTNOTES

[1] One of many textbook discussions of communications using an approximation to this general model is Herbert J. Chruden and Arthur W. Sherman, Jr., *Personnel Management,* 5th ed., South-Western, 1976, p. 288. Our model also contains some elements from David R. Hampton, Charles E. Summer, and Ross A. Webber, *Organizational Behavior and the Practice of Management,* rev., ed., Scott, Foresman, 1973, p. 67.

[2] An expanded discussion of this topic is found in Hampton, Summer, and Webber, *op. cit.,* pp. 68–69.

[3] "The Unisex Job Title" is a case history about this type of problem. See Andrew J. DuBrin, *Casebook of Organizational Behavior,* Pergamon, 1977, Chapter 9.

[4] Andrew J. DuBrin, *Managerial Deviance: How to Handle Problem People in Key Jobs,* Mason/Charter, 1976, pp. 20–22.

[5] *Ibid.,* p. 21.

[6] James L. Gibson, John M. Ivancevich, and James H. Donnelly, Jr., *Organizations: Structure, Process, Behavior,* Business Publications, 1973, p. 187.

[7] *Ibid.,* p. 184.

[8] A primary popular source of information about nonverbal communication is Julius Fast, *Body Language,* M. Evans, 1970.

[9] Chruden and Sherman, *op. cit.,* p. 290.

[10] Elmer H. Burack, *Organization Analysis: Theory and Applications,* Dryden Press, 1975, pp. 180–181.

[11] This composite definition is derived from Davis's statements in Keith Davis, *Human Relations in Business,* McGraw-Hill, 1957, p. 244, and "Tending the Grapevine," *Time,* June 18, 1973, p. 67.

[12] Harold Sutton and Lyman W. Porter, "A Study of the Grapevine in a Governmental Organization," *Personnel Psychology,* Summer 1968, pp. 223–230.

[13] Supporting research for this generalization is quoted in Gibson, Ivancevich, and Donnelly, *op. cit.,* p. 177.

[14] See the Suggested Reading section of this chapter. The "communication skills" section of most libraries and large bookstores have ample information on this topic.

[15] The italicized suggestions are quoted directly from Ralph G. Nichols, "Listening is a 10-Part Skill," in *Managing Yourself,* presented by the editors of *Nation's Business,* not dated.

[16] *Ibid.,* p. 26.

[17] One such book particularly well suited to a work environment is David W. Ewing, *Writing for Results in Business, Government, and the Professions*, Wiley, 1974.

SUGGESTED READING

ESTRADA, DAN. "Does Your Writing Communicate?" *Industry Week*, June 18, 1973, pp. 49–50.

EWING, DAVID W. *Writing for Results in Business, Government, and the Professions*, Wiley, 1974.

FAST, JULIUS. *Body Language*, M. Evans, 1970.

Managing Yourself, presented by editors of *Nation's Business*, not dated.

A Manual of Style, 12th ed., University of Chicago Press, 1969.

OKUN, SHERMAN K. "How to Be a Better Listener," *Nation's Business*, Aug. 1975, pp. 59–62.

ROSEMAN, ED. "How to Sell Your Ideas," *Product Management*, Nov. 1975, pp. 43–46.

SUTTON, HAROLD, and PORTER, LYMAN W. "A Study of the Grapevine in a Governmental Organization," *Personnel Psychology*, Summer 1968, pp. 223–230.

TURABIAN, KATE L. *A Manual for Writers of Term Papers, Theses, and Dissertations*, 4th ed., University of Chicago Press, 1973.

VINCI, VINCENT. "How to Be a Better Speaker," *Nation's Business*, Aug. 1975, pp. 59–62.

10
COUNSELING AND COACHING SUBORDINATES

Learning Objectives	After reading and studying this chapter, you should be able to

1. Understand the control model for counseling and coaching.
2. Understand how to confront a subordinate about a problem and develop a plan of improvement.
3. Appreciate the importance of day-to-day coaching for improving subordinate performance.
4. Summarize the conditions under which performance-appraisal coaching is likely to be effective.
5. Recognize how a manager should handle the problem of alcohol or drug addiction on the job.
6. Appreciate the difference between those employee problems a manager can and cannot handle.

An effective supervisor spends considerable time counseling and coaching subordinates. Few supervisors face a situation in which all of his or her subordinates are so well trained and so skillful in their work that no assistance is required. Counseling or coaching is often necessary to assist a generally effective subordinate to improve his or her performance. To illustrate, if you were a maitre d'hotel, you might need to show a waiter how to carry a tray with his left hand to facilitate his making a smooth exit and entrance through the dining-room door.

Sometimes counseling and coaching is required to assist a subordinate overcome maladaptive behavior that results in substandard job performance. Assume that you are an accounting supervisor. An alcoholic bookkeeper is making critical mistakes because of her impaired concentration. If you ignore this problem, departmental effectiveness (and your job) will suffer. In addition, successful intervention by you might save this woman's career.

Counseling and coaching are similar but not identical processes. A counselor listens more than a coach does, and is more concerned with feelings than with actions. A coach might give you a tip on how to properly prepare tax depreciation schedules on a piece of office machinery. A counselor might listen to you complain how filling out tax depreciation schedules does not exactly fit your career objectives. Counseling, in general, involves the long-term development of an employee, whereas coaching deals with present job performance. Felix M. Lopez, Jr., draws a sharp difference between job counseling and job coaching:[1]

> The supervisor's function is to coach, not counsel. The proper object of *coaching* is to improve present job performance; the proper object of *counseling* is the realization of potential. The former emphasizes *doing*, the latter, *becoming*.

A CONTROL MODEL FOR COUNSELING AND COACHING

A general plan of attack or framework is useful for counseling and coaching subordinates. One such convenient game plan is the control model of human performance,[2] shown in Figure 10.1. It provides a systematic approach to dealing with any deviations from acceptable or standard job performance. A later section of this chapter discusses specifically the

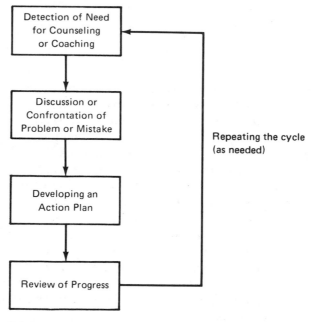

FIGURE 10.1
Control model for counseling and coaching subordinates.

problem of handling extreme deviations, such as alcoholism and drug addiction.

Detection of Need for Coaching or Counseling. To counsel or coach somebody about improvement, you first need a workable definition of what constitutes adequate performance. For well-structured, repetitive jobs, the definition of standard performance is relatively clear cut. An insurance rater might be expected to process an average of ten automobile insurance policies per hour. A water-meter reader might be expected to cover 100 houses per five-day work week. However, it is more difficult to determine when a retail salesclerk is performing in a substandard manner. Factors such as parking problems in the downtown area could be reducing traffic in the store. When a worker displays a consistent pattern (rather than a one-time deviation) from standard performance, counseling or coaching is usually required.

One important exception to the "consistent-pattern" principle exists. Some departures from acceptable performance or behavior are so significant that they must be immediately brought to the attention of the subordinate. A bank teller who borrows $100 for a lunch hour visit to an off-track betting parlor must be coached (or disciplined) upon his or her return to work. A lab technician who leaves a Bunsen burner on overnight must also be the recipient of on-the-spot coaching the next morning.

Detection is the process of noting when a person's performance deviates from an acceptable standard. In order to make such detections the supervisor must stay in contact with the activities of the department. The laboratory supervisor who arrives to work promptly will be able to detect the lit burner by simple observation. Another approach to detection is for the supervisor or higher level manager to have frequent discussions with subordinates about their job performance. Straightforward questioning may uncover unacceptable deviations from performance.

Discussion or Confrontation of Problem or Mistake. After detecting the problem, the manager or supervisor must bring it to the attention of the subordinate. Supervisors have a general tendency to dislike confronting subordinates because of the defensive or hostile reaction confrontation may elicit. A general principle here is for the supervisor to focus on the substandard behavior itself, and not upon the individual. People usually become defensive and uncooperative when they believe their trait or personal characteristics are under attack. According to this principle, the errant bank teller mentioned above might be approached in this manner:

> We have something serious to talk about. A routine audit showed that you borrowed one hundred dollars from your cash drawer before leaving for lunch. Apparently it was returned by the end of the day. Borrowing money from the bank without making formal application for the loan is absolutely forbidden. It could lead to a person's immediate dismissal.

A less effective approach would be to confront the teller about his or her "loan," and simultaneously insult the teller's character. To illustrate:

> I caught your little act of petty thievery. You were very sneaky about it. Don't use any lies to cover up for your dishonesty. You've been caught.

Douglas McGregor formulated the red-hot-stove rule, which provides a set of workable suggestions for dealing with situations of employee criticism and discipline. A stove metaphor is used because "when you touch a hot stove your discipline is *immediate,* with *warning, consistent,* and *impersonal.*"[3] The principle can be applied in the following manner:[4]

> Assume that Herb, a systems analyst, has been telling various people in the organization that he has the power to ask that they be fired if they do not cooperate with him in his studies. His manager learns of this deviant behavior and confronts Herb, stating that such behavior will not be tolerated (*immediate*). Herb realized when he took this position as a systems analyst that the position involved limited formal power. Herb knew he would have to *ask* for the cooperation of people, not use implied authority (thus he received *warning*). He has been treated *consistently* with others in the organization. Any other systems analyst who abused power would be similarly advised of his or her unacceptable behavior.
>
> *Impersonality* is generally difficult to convey when administering punishment, but Herb's boss makes an effort in that direction. He criticizes Herb's behavior rather than attacking his character. For example, the statement, "Herb, you're a devious person without conscience," would have been taken quite personally.

Developing an Action Plan.   An action plan essentially describes what should be done to bring performance back to an acceptable standard. In some instances, the plan might be as simple as "Don't blow smoke in the president's face" or "Refrain from taking office supplies home for personal use." At other times the action plan might be more complex, because new skills or behaviors are required in order to bring about acceptable performance. An organization member might be preparing disorganized, clumsily written reports. Part of his or her action plan might be to take a home-study course in report writing.

Underlying any effective action plan are specific improvement goals that specify what kind of terminal (end) behaviors are required. (The topic of setting specific improvement goals or *objectives* will be returned to again in Chapter 13.) Improvement goals that are vague, such as "Become a more productive" employee, do not give the person a specific improvement target. More helpful would be an improvement goal such as "Do not leave a customer inquiry unprocessed for more than twenty-four hours." Following are five improvement goals that specify the type of behavior that constitutes improved performance. As such, they can serve as a guide to action.

1. *Retail clerk:* Decrease the number of bogus checks you accept by insisting upon proper identification before accepting a check.
2. *Personnel specialist:* Volunteer only for those projects that you have the time to take care of properly.
3. *Computer programmer:* Consider no programming assignment complete until you have run the program twice without error.
4. *Newspaper reporter:* Include no "facts" in your stories that cannot be authenticated by a second party.
5. *Truck driver:* No hitchhikers allowed unless the person given the ride is an accident victim.

Review of Progress.   After a subordinate is coached or counseled about improvement, some form of systematic follow-up is required. At an elementary level, the follow-up could consist of the supervisor checking to see that the desired actions have been taken. If the employee were coached not to wear blue jeans to staff meetings, his or her compliance with the request could readily be detected.

When the new behavior required is more complex, formal review sessions are in order. To illustrate, a draftsman might be coached about his relationships with engineers. An improvement goal might have been "Decreases incidences of conflict with engineers over technical matters." After three months, the draftsman and his manager might discuss progress toward this goal. The manager might have inquired in the engineering department about incidences of conflict, while the draftsman might have reached his or her own conclusion about his or her relationship with the engineers. When both agree that substantial progress has been made, the manager might conclude: "It looks like we have this problem licked. We can touch base on the problem six months from now. In the meantime, proceed as you have been doing. It's working."

Use of Positive Reinforcement.   The comments made by the manager above illustrate the use of positive reinforcement (see the discussion of behavior modification presented in Chapter 2). Giving people encouragement, or other forms of positive reinforcement, is one of the most effective tools for coaching and counseling at the disposal of a manager. Making rewards contingent upon good performance increases the probability that the improvements made will be lasting. A major purpose, then, of the review sessions is for the manager to dispense rewards for tangible progress toward the improvement goals established earlier.

When progress has not been made, it may be necessary to administer discipline (a form of punishment) in the manner described earlier in the chapter. An important general principle of reinforcement theory is that positive reinforcement works more effectively than punishment. It is better to reward people for the improvement that they have made than to punish them for the improvement they have not made.

Listening is an instrumental part of the review process. The superior must listen carefully to problems that might be hampering the coached person from making the necessary improvements. In one situation a quality-control inspector persisted in allowing too many citizen-band radios to pass inspection that were in fact defective. Rather than chastising the inspector for persisting in his errors, the manager asked, "Why is it that you cannot make the agreed upon improvements?" The inspector replied, "My problems with my wife are still making it difficult for me to concentrate." A community resource was identified (a family service agency) that proved helpful to the inspector in resolving his marital problems. He was then able to overcome much of his distractability, thus improving his job performance.

Repeating the Cycle. The counseling and coaching process is rarely completed. After progress is made in overcoming one aspect of deficient performance, channels of communication must remain open. Linda, a babysitter working at a day-care center, was coached by her superior about not feeding children candy or cookies between meals. She complied with these regulations. The following week, a toddler in Linda's charge was screeching. Recognizing the problem as one of a thirsty child crying for water, the supervisor came to the rescue. Linda was asked why she failed to recognize that the child needed water. She replied, "I thought I wasn't supposed to give a child anything between meals."

Another important reason for keeping counseling channels of communication open is that improvements are rarely permanent. A person who overcomes a specific form of substandard performance may readily slip back into his or her previous behavior, particularly under stressful conditions. An automobile service manager was criticized by his boss for telling people who brought their cars for servicing at close to quitting time to return the next day. He agreed to mellow in his approach. However, when the season for changeover to snow tires came back, so did the service manager's abruptness. Three customers complained to the agency owner that they were treated rudely by the service manager. Additional counseling was necessary to correct an old problem. Changes in behavior are rarely permanent.

DAY-TO-DAY COACHING

Coaching and counseling of subordinates should not be an activity confined to formal review periods. An effective supervisor coaches subordinates as soon as feasible after the need for coaching is evident. Coaching a person shortly after a mistake has been made capitalizes upon the principle of learning called *immediate feedback*. Counseling should also be conducted close in time to when it is needed. Because counseling takes more time than coaching, formal sessions often have to be arranged. Following is one illustration each of the use of coaching and counseling on a day by day basis:

1. *Coaching incident:* During a staff meeting, Kevin, the advertising and sales promotion manager, says, "If it weren't for our stingy president, we could launch a campaign that would guarantee the success of our new product." Returning from the conference, Kevin's boss Ned says to him, "Let's get together in my office. I want to talk about your criticism of the president."

2. *Counseling incident:* Larry, a final assembly supervisor, notices that one of his assemblers, Emil, is visibly upset to the point of tears rolling down his cheeks. Larry says, "Emil, I think you need a couple of hours off the line with pay. Let's you and I meet in the personnel conference room at ten A.M." In the conference room Larry says, "OK Emil, let's have it. What's troubling you?" Weeping heavily, Emil talks steadily for thirty minutes about his favorite hunting dog having developed a cancerous tumor.

COACHING AND COUNSELING DURING PERFORMANCE APPRAISAL

Virtually all large organizations, and most small ones, have some formal system of reviewing employee performance. In the typical format, the boss discusses with the subordinate how well he or she has reached certain agreed-upon work objectives (such as conducting seventy-five correct laboratory analyses per month). The worker is then given a formal rating similar to a "report card." Aside from fulfilling such administrative requirements, the performance-appraisal process is well suited to coaching and counseling subordinates about improving their performance. Even if the subordinate has fulfilled job expectations, there is usually room for some improvement.

Considerable skepticism exists[5] about the utility of most appraisal systems for improving employee performance. However, when performance-appraisal sessions are conducted with a counseling and coaching orientation, the chances for improved performance are increased. Several of the suggestions presented next about coaching and counseling during a performance appraisal session[6] apply equally well to day-to-day coaching.

1. *The subordinate takes an active role in the appraisal process.* Effective job-performance interviews are characterized by an extensive amount of listening on the superior's part. He or she attends carefully to the subordinate's feelings and observations about the latter's work performance. Rather than diagnosing the reasons that a subordinate failed

to reach a particular objective, the coaching-style superior asks questions. Observe the difference between the two approaches:

Diagnosis-giving approach: "The reason you didn't sell enough vacuum cleaners is that you have a lousy attitude. You really don't like selling vacuum cleaners for a living. Tell me I'm wrong."

Coaching approach: "You fell behind quota again. I see that as a problem. What seems to have gone wrong? What roadblocks are you running up against?" Using the coaching approach, the manager allows the subordinate to participate in the review session. While answering the manager's question, the subordinate may reveal the true nature of the underlying problem. In this instance the vacuum cleaner salesperson replied, "My attitude has been down lately because I've been getting discouraged. My territory is a very poor neighborhood. I think my quota is too high for such an area."

2. *The superior conveys a helpful and constructive attitude.* By being helpful and constructive, the superior provides emotional support to the subordinate. A coaching session should not be a cross-examination or an interrogation. An effective way of providing emotional support is to use positive rather than negative motivators. Assume that Max, a cub reporter, mismanaged an assignment. He was to cover a fire on Elm Avenue, and instead he showed up on Elm Street. By the time he worked his way back to Elm Avenue on the other side of town, most of the fire-related activity had subsided. During the next performance review, his boss might use a positive or negative motivator in relation to this incident:

Positive motivator: "Your photos have been quite good whenever you get to the assignment on time. Do you see a trend as to why you've missed out on a couple of assignments?"

Negative motivator: "Get yourself a good city map and use it before running off half-cocked. What good is having fancy equipment if you don't get to the scene on time?"

3. *The superior and subordinate jointly set specific short-range goals.* By jointly setting goals, the subordinate feels psychologically involved in the review process. By setting short-range goals, the subordinate can readily see whether or not he or she is making progress. Assume that a manager is reviewing the work performance of a budget analyst whose reports are invariably late. The improvement goal for the next month might be for her to turn in three out of five reports on time. If this target is reached, she and her boss might make the goal four out of five on-time reports for the following month. For the third month, the goal might be five out of five timely reports—if superior and subordinate agree.

At times the principle of mutual goal setting must be preempted by organizational realities. Assume that in the above instance management needs all five reports on time before the third month. The manager would then be forced to impose goals upon the subordinate with an explanation of why these goals, or objectives, are necessary. Similarly, management might be forced by a financial crisis to tell (order) people to cut operating

costs by a specified amount. Although the manager might counsel with
the subordinate about how to achieve these cost-reduction goals, the goals
themselves are not negotiable.

Goal setting of this type is crucial to any personal development in a
job setting. Without clear, concise, and unambiguous improvement goals,
very little change is likely to take place. Following are three additional
examples of the type of improvement goals under discussion here. In each
case both superior and subordinate have agreed that change is necessary.
They have also agreed upon the type of change that is required.

1. *Office supervisor:* Within sixty days, eliminate all instances of "out
   of stock" on vital supplies such as typing paper, typewriter ribbons,
   and photocopy paper.
2. *Service manager:* Shorten the average time customer automobiles
   are in shop from seven to five hours. Improvement must take place
   within thirty days.
3. *Industrial engineer:* Within ten days, take initiative to ask manufacturing supervisors their opinion on manufacturing changes you
   plan to recommend to the standards department.
4. *Job problems are solved that may be hampering the subordinate's
   job performance.* When placed in a coaching or counseling role, the
   manager must not neglect technological and organizational factors.
   Many problems of poor work performance are caused by factors beyond the employee's control. By showing a willingness to intervene
   in such problems, the superior is simultaneously displaying a helpful and constructive attitude. One boss helped his advertising and
   sales promotion manager improve performance through a simple
   remedy:

   Marketing manager: The main job objective that you missed this review
   period was having the flyers sent out on time to introduce our new line
   of desk-top computers. What happened?

   Advertising and sales promotion manager: As I've hinted at several times
   in the past, our budget for clerical help is too tight. It was virtually
   impossible to have those flyers out on time without more help.

   Marketing manager: Then I'll get you more help if I have to lend you my
   own secretary one day per week.

5. *Managers with the right personal characteristics and skills conduct
   the coaching and counseling.* A fortunate few managers are intuitively good coaches or counselors. Most other managers need training in interviewing and coaching techniques. One characteristic that
   interferes with effective coaching is compulsive talking. A compulsive talker cannot listen long enough to effectively coach. Some people are so naturally hostile or fearful of confronting others that they

are unequal to the coaching task. A hostile plant manager made the following comment to a subordinate during a performance-appraisal session:

> You messed up again. One more mistake like that and you're going to know what a demotion feels like. I'm going to station you so far out on the plant floor that you're going to need a map to get to work.

6. *Improvement goals established during the review sessions lie within the subordinate's capacity to change.* A goal or objective that a person cannot reach because of insufficient education, training, or native ability is both unrealistic and frustrating. A sales manager leaned heavily upon one of his best sales representatives to produce almost flawless reports that would be sent to the market-research department. After failing to make the improvement desired by his manager for two consecutive review periods, the salesman commented:

> Sorry, there is just nothing I can do to make my reports any better. One of the reasons I went into sales twenty years ago is that I hate paper work. I want to cooperate with the market researchers. Let them interview me instead of my doing their work for them. I'm at my best dealing with customers, not doing staff work.

COACHING ALCOHOLIC AND DRUG-ADDICTED EMPLOYEES

As described in Chapter 4, alcoholism and drug abuse among employees and managers constitutes a significant management problem. An alcoholic or drug abuser cannot and should not be treated for the problem on company premises, yet the manager plays an active role in the rehabilitation process.

The recommended procedure for coaching or counseling such maladaptive behavior stems directly from the guidelines outlined in the control model depicted in Figure 10.1. Assume that Marty, a maintenance mechanic, has been ingesting large quantities of amphetamines ("uppers"). Elmo, his boss, *detects* the need for coaching or counseling. Marty acts giddy and he is subject to manic-like overactivity. Elmo *confronts* Marty about the problem: "The way you've been acting lately, I can't trust you with our machinery. When you are off on one of your excited episodes, you use very poor judgment. Go get help, or I'll have to recommend that you be fired." Elmo and Marty then develop an *action plan* whereby Marty attends a drug-abuse center. A *review of progress* is made weekly. Marty seems to be able to control his drug intake to the point where he is "clean" when on the job. If at any point Marty's drug abuse affects his job behavior, Elmo will *repeat the cycle.*

J. David Else, a specialist in rehabilitating alcoholic employees, has developed a set of positive steps he recommends that a manager can take to help an alcoholic. His suggestions fit the coaching and counseling suggestions presented throughout this chapter. They also are consistent with other recommended procedures[7] for handling alcoholic employees. Else suggests:[8]

Review records. Attempt to identify employees with drinking problems.

Talk with the person. Ask for explanations. Don't be satisfied with obviously misleading answers. "You say you're having problems at home? Do you know what's causing them? Why does your wife (or husband) nag you? Is drinking at all related to your problem?"

Explain the seriousness of the problem. Many alcoholics, now sober, say that they wish that someone had been honest with them and had also told them about possible treatment programs. "I knew I had a problem but I needed someone else to tell me." And "I was willing to admit I needed help, but I didn't know that any real help was available."

Ask the person to take a leave of absence. Special leaves should be abolished for alcoholics. The policy could provide for hospitalization, for continuance of the employee's benefits, and for an accumulation of a certain percentage of his or her pay to be paid after the person has received adequate help.

Avoid the pep-talk syndrome. A good heart-to-heart talk, alone, is merely a way for the alcoholic to exercise his or her artistry in "conning" others. Recognize that alcoholism is an illness and as such needs professional treatment.

Assure him that he will have a job if he gets help but that he or she will not have a job if he or she refuses to seek help.

Maintain a list of agencies that will help. It's good to know such resources as the central Alcoholics Anonymous office, the nearest alcoholism clinic, those hospitals which provide detoxification services, halfway houses, mental-health centers, and other such facilities in your vicinity or even at some distance. It is best to have one person who can most effectively treat the individual involved.

Use sober alcoholics as resource persons. Do so only with their permission.

Don't back away. Once you decide on a course of action, follow through. The alcoholic is accustomed to empty threats. He or she needs to know you mean business.

Follow through when the alcoholic is ready to return to work. He or she will need support and encouragement. He or she will need an understanding supervisor and co-workers. Often a boss or co-worker will encourage the man or woman to take that first drink. Encourage the person to attend AA. Allowances regarding shift work are important. Most AA groups meet between 8 and 11 P.M., once a week. During the initial recovery stage, the alcoholic may need to attend a meeting almost every night. Encourage the person to do so and make allowances.

1. Counseling and coaching of subordinates is an important part of a supervisor's job. Both satisfactory and substandard performers may require coaching and counseling.

*Summary
of Key Points*

2. Coaching deals primarily with current job performance, whereas counseling deals primarily with the long-term development of an individual.

3. A control model is proposed for counseling and coaching that consists of five phases or stages: (a) detection of the problem, (b) discussion or confrontation, (c) developing an action plan, (d) review of progress, and (e) repeating the cycle.

4. The red-hot stove is recommended for disciplining subordinates. Discipline should be immediate, with warning, consistent, and impersonal.

5. Most superior–subordinate coaching should take place on a day-by-day, as needed basis.

6. Coaching and counseling as part of the performance-appraisal system should lead to improved performance under certain conditions: (a) the subordinate plays an active role; (b) the superior is helpful and constructive; (c) specific short-range goals are jointly set; (d) job problems interfering with performance are solved; (e) the superior is psychologically suited for counseling or coaching; and (f) realistic improvement goals are set.

7. The control model also applies to the counseling of alcoholic and drug-addicted employees. Alcoholics and drug abusers must be confronted with the job-related implications of their behavior and encouraged to accept outside treatment.

Questions
for Discussion

1. Does discussing an employee's feelings about a work-related problem constitute an invasion of privacy? Discuss.

2. What should you do if your boss enters your office in an obviously intoxicated condition?

3. Show how you could apply the control model to improving the typing skills of a secretary reporting to you.

4. For what reasons do many managers dislike confronting subordinates?

5. Develop two objectives each for improving your school and work performance.

6. Why is it true that most people respond better to positive than negative motivators?

Joe Toby, director of management services, schedules a coaching session with Herman Sutherland, a management consultant on his staff:

Joe: As you know, Herman, I've scheduled this meeting with you because I want to talk about certain aspects of your work. And my comments are not all that favorable.

Herman: Since you have formal authority over me, I guess I'll have to go along with the session. Go ahead.

Joe: I'm not a judge reading a verdict to you. This is supposed to be a two-way interchange.

Herman: But you called the meeting, go ahead with your complaints. Particularly any with foundation. I remember once when we were having lunch you told me that you didn't like the fact that I wore a brown knitted suit with a blue shirt. I would put that in the category of unfounded.

Joe: I'm glad you brought appearance up. I think you create a substandard impression to clients because of your appearance. A consultant is supposed to look sharp, particularly at the rates we charge clients. You often create the impression that you cannot afford good clothing. Your pants are baggy. Your ties are unstylish and often food stained.

Herman: The firm may charge those high rates. But as a junior the money I receive does not allow me to purchase fancy clothing. Besides, I have very little interest in trying to dazzle clients with my clothing. I have heard no complaints from them.

Joe: Nevertheless, I think that your appearance should be more business-like. Let's talk about something else I have on my list of things in which I would like to see some improvements. A routine audit of your expense account shows a practice that I think is improper. You charged one client for a Thursday night dinner for three consecutive weeks. Yet your airline ticket receipt shows that you returned home at three in the afternoon. That kind of behavior is unprofessional. How do you explain your charges for these phantom dinners?

Herman: The flight ticket may say three P.M. but with our unpredictable weather, the flight could very well be delayed. If I eat at the airport, then my wife won't have to run the risk of preparing a dinner for me that goes to waste. Food is very expensive.

Joe: But how can you eat dinner at three P.M. at the airport?

Herman: I consider any meal after one in the afternoon to be dinner.

Joe: Okay for now. I want to comment on your reports to clients. They are much more careless than they should be. I know that you are capable of more meticulous work. I saw an article you prepared for publication that was first rate and professional. Yet on one report you misspelled the name of the client company. That's atrocious.

Herman: A good secretary should have caught that mistake. Besides, I never claimed that I was able to write perfect reports. There are only so many hours in the working day to spend on writing up reports.

Joe: Another thing that requires immediate improvement is the appearance of your office. It's a mess. You have the worst-looking office in our branch. In fact, you have the worst-looking office I have ever seen in a C.P.A. or management-consulting office. Why can't you have a well-organized, cool-looking office?

Herman: What's the difference? Clients never visit me in this office. It's just a work place. Incidentally Joe, could you do me one favor?

Joe: What's that?

Herman: Get off my back.

If you were Joe, how would you handle this situation?

A Human Relations Case
THE DIFFICULT CRITIC

Brett, features editor at the *Herald Globe*, confided to his friend and colleague Shirley, "I've got a sensitive problem that I would like to talk over with you. As office manager, you're supposed to help us handle personnel problems, and I think I have a major problem in that category."

"Be my guest. The only problems that don't fall into my lap around here are when the printing machines get stuck or if a news carrier calls in sick. What's your problem?"

"It concerns Vance, our illustrious movie critic. Somehow he thinks he's working on the staff of the *New York Times*. The guy is unreal. He can't get it into his head that we're a medium-sized paper who can't afford superstars or even super specialists. Everybody has to chip in and do his or her share of scut work."

"What do you mean by that comment, Brett?"

"Vance seems to think that any assignment except writing movie reviews is outside his bailiwick. He has an implied arrogance about him that irks me, yet he is a first-rate critic. He has the guts to call films as he sees them whether or not the film producers have assaulted the public with favorable publicity.

"But Vance is even selective about the films he shows a willingness to review. He just about threw a temper tantrum when I asked him to do a review of a new Walt Disney film about a bear who could read people's minds. He finally did the review in a haphazard fashion and concluded something to the effect that he highly recommended the film to any person under ten who cared about mind-reading bears."

"Brett, I think it's about time you and Vance had a long serious talk. You and he should have some dialogue. That should take care of your problem with him. Be specific about your complaints, and let him know how you feel."

"Good advice, Shirley, I'll do just that."

Brett took the initiative to arrange a luncheon meeting with Vance to discuss a few of his concerns about Vance's attitude and performance.

"Vance, how do you like your job? Sometimes you don't seem so happy to me."

"How sweet of you to ask," replied Vance in an almost sarcastic tone. "Some things I like and some things I don't like."

"What is it that you don't like?" queried Brett.

"The absolutely trashy assignments you often hand me. It would seem I must remind you that I am a movie critic, not a cub reporter."

"What are you talking about Vance?"

"Let's look at two of the assignments I've been given this month. One involved doing a rewrite on the Muscular Dystrophy Telethon. I have nothing against crippled children, but I can't see wasting the talents of a professional movie critic by having him perform such routine tasks.

"Another winner was the Planned Parenthood Conference. There was absolutely nothing worth covering at that event. They were asking the paper to give them publicity, when they should have been paying for advertising. I think Planned Parenthood is a fine thing, but the fact that those people are holding a routine conference is hardly a newsworthy event. Even if it were, that's hardly my area of professional interest. Would you send a brain surgeon out to fix a leaky sink?"

"Somebody has to cover such events," countered Brett.

"That's an area where you and I disagree. The *Herald Globe* might be better off if we only wrote stories about newsworthy events. Had you ever thought of furnishing doodling space for the readers in lieu of copy about vapid happenings?"

"Be careful, Vance, you might be pushing me too far."

"Oh, excuse me, Mr. Features Editor. I thought your concern for freedom of the press implicitly meant that you had an equal concern for freedom of speech. Despite our little heart-to-heart talks, I do what's expected of me, even if I don't relish a few of the miscellaneous assignments you throw my way."

"Vance, I don't want to give you the impression that I don't think you are a first-rate movie critic. Every paper needs an acid-tongued, witty critic on board. I'm just concerned about your attitude and the spillover effect it can have on others."

"Tell me more about this spillover effect."

"A third party, whom I will not identify, told me that you ridiculed Rachel for her willingness to cover the circus. I heard that you told her a music reporter should be immune from covering mundane events like that. You told her that, if you were in her shoes, you would have declined the assignment. That's kind of incompatible with developing a team spirit around here."

"Your informant may be exaggerating the true nature of what happened. Besides, I refuse to be held responsible for undocumented charges made about me by a third party."

"Okay, I'm willing to forget that incident for now, but I still think you could show a more cooperative attitude. You should be willing to take both the good and the bad. Learn to roll with the punches a little more. You're too temperamental."

"Brett, you're forgetting one thing. I am an artist. A true artist is a professional. He should not be subject to the same demands as the ordinary working person. You hired me for my creative talents; therefore, you must respect my professionalism."

"Vance, let's you and I just drop things for now. Do the best you can, and you'll hear from me again later."

As Brett picked up the check he thought to himself, "I must do something about this problem, but I'm not sure what."

1. What should Brett do about Vance?
2. What specific improvement goals (or objectives) should Vance establish?
3. What did you think of Brett's strategy of holding a coaching session over lunch? What are the advantages and disadvantages of such an approach?
4. Should Vance be handled differently than a business reporter? Why or why not?
5. What errors, if any, has Brett made so far in his handling of Vance?

FOOTNOTES

[1] Felix M. Lopez, Jr., *Evaluating Employee Performance*, Public Personnel Association, 1968, p. 112.

[2] This control model, is found in Andrew J. DuBrin, *Managerial Deviance*, Mason/Charter 1976, p. 109. It is based on a model found in John B. Miner, *Personnel Psychology*, Macmillan, 1969, p. 238.

[3] McGregor's principle is explained in George Strauss and Leonard R. Sayles, *Personnel: The Human Problems of Management*, 3rd ed., Prentice-Hall, 1972, p. 267.

[4] The illustration of the red-hot-stove principle is quoted from DuBrin, *op. cit.*, pp. 149–150.

[5] A useful analysis of the pitfalls of most performance-appraisal systems is found in William J. Kearney, "The Value of Behaviorally Based Performance Appraisals," *Business Horizons*, June 1976, pp. 75–83.

[6] This section follows closely the outline presented in Andrew J. DuBrin, *Fundamentals of Organizational Behavior: An Applied Perspective*, Pergamon, 1974, pp. 249–255.

[7] Useful guidelines to the problem of alcoholism are found in Harrison M. Trice, "Alcoholism and the Work World," *Sloan Management Review*, Fall 1970, pp. 67–75.

[8] J. David Else, "Treat or Treatment for Alcoholics," *Industry Week*, Apr. 26, 1971, p. 50.

CHAMBERS, CARL D., and HECKMAN, RICHARD D. *Employee Drug Abuse: A Manager's Guide for Action,* Chaners Publishing Co., 1972.

DWYER, JAMES C., and DIMITROFF, NICK J. "The Bottoms Up/Tops Down Approach to Performance Appraisal," *Personnel Journal,* July 1976, pp. 349–353.

ELSE, J. DAVID. "Treat or Treatment for Alcoholics," *Industry Week,* Apr. 26, 1971, pp. 48–50.

KEARNEY, WILLIAM J. "The Value of Behaviorally Based Performance Appraisals," *Business Horizons,* June 1976, pp. 75–83.

KOLB, DAVID A., and BOYATZIS, RICHARD E. "On the Dynamics of a Helping Relationship," in David A. Kolb, Irwin M. Rubin, and James M. McIntyre, *Organizational Psychology: A Book of Readings,* Prentice-Hall, 1971, pp. 339–355.

LAU, JAMES B. *Behavior in Organizations: An Experiential Approach,* Business Publications, Inc, 1976.

LEWIS, EDWIN C. *The Psychology of Counseling,* Holt, Rinehart and Winston, 1970.

LOPEZ, FELIX M. *Personnel Interviewing: Theory and Practice,* 2nd ed., McGraw-Hill, 1975, Chapter 13.

TRICE, HARRISON M. "Alcoholism and the Work World," *Sloan Management Review,* Fall 1970, pp. 67–75.

WHITEHEAD, ROSS. "The Incredible Cost of Booze," *Industry Week,* Sept. 2, 1974, pp. 28–32.

11
IMPROVING HUMAN RELATION SKILLS

Learning Objectives

After reading and studying this chapter, you should be able to

1. Understand the framework for human relations training.
2. Summarize the major potential benefits and harmful consequences of encounter groups.
3. Describe several characteristics of an effective interview.
4. Identify and explain the key concepts of transactional analysis.
5. Explain the difference between *passive*, *aggressive*, and *assertive* behavior.
6. Understand the current magnitude of your sexist beliefs.

Human relations is the art and practice of using systematic knowledge about human behavior to achieve organizational and/or personal objectives. Thus any experience that would increase your effectiveness with people would also improve your human relations skills. Much of management training and development is essentially an attempt to improve human relations effectiveness. This chapter concentrates upon a sampling of modern techniques and approaches designed to increase the interpersonal skills of organizational members. A discussion is also included on improving interviewing skills because of its importance in a wide range of job situations.

FRAMEWORK FOR HUMAN RELATIONS TRAINING AND DEVELOPMENT

Improving personal effectiveness is best accomplished when guided by a framework or plan. Figure 11.1 suggests that improving the human rela-

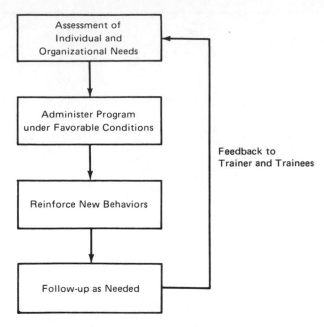

FIGURE 11.1
Framework for human relations training and development.

tions skills of organizational members should proceed in a systematic manner that allows for correction and renewal. An effective program of improving human relations skills usually incorporates elements similar to those shown in our framework for human relations training and development.

Assessment of Individual and Organizational Needs. Before embarking upon any program of training or development, it is important to diagnose what kinds of training or development are needed. Applied to the individual, we speak of *developmental needs.* In what particular aspects of human relations effectiveness does this individual need improvement? Some people may have poor listening skills; others may be insensitive to people; others may need to become more assertive with people; still others must learn to behave in a less assertive manner. A person's developmental need should influence what particular human relations improvement program he or she attends.[1]

Organizational requirements also weigh heavily in the choice of a program for improving human relations effectiveness. In one firm, middle managers might be practicing discrimination against women. To help remedy this situation, a program of management awareness training about sexism might be selected. Another firm might conclude from a human resources forecast that much of its future work force will be under age thirty. Encounter group meetings might be used to help managers become more sensitive to the demands of younger workers.

Administer Program Under Favorable Conditions.   Under the appropriate conditions most human relations training programs can contribute to individual and organizational effectiveness. Under the wrong conditions, the program might even be harmful. In general, the program must be technically sound, the participants must have the capacity and willingness to change, and the organization must welcome the changes. A worker who, during an encounter group, learns to be more candid with people must then work for a boss who will accept criticism from subordinates. To determine whether or not a given program of improving human relations skills will be effective, answers must be sought to questions such as the following:[2]

1. Does the participant have the motivation and intelligence to benefit from the program?
2. Does he or she have sufficient emotional stability to benefit from the program?
3. Is the program tied to the developmental needs of the participant?
4. Is the program technically sound and administered by a technically competent person?
5. Is the program tied to the objectives of the organization?
6. Does the participant's boss welcome development among subordinates?
7. Does the organization welcome change?
8. Will the organization provide the participant the opportunity to practice the new skills learned in the program?

Reinforce New Behaviors.   If new learning is not practiced and reinforced, it will be forgotten. A case in point would be the situation of Derek, a chemist who attends an assertiveness training workshop. By the end of the workshop, Derek says to himself, "I agree with everything I've heard. I should learn to express my feelings in a positive, forthright manner. That way people won't take such advantage of me."

Back on the job, he receives no encouragement for attempting to be more assertive. He says to his boss, "My opinion as a chemist is that we cannot properly perform these experiments unless we purchase the equipment I recommended." His boss replies, "Accept the working conditions as they are or we will find somebody else to do your job. There are loads of good chemists out looking for work these days." After one or two more episodes like this, Derek decides to discontinue his attempts at being more assertive on the job.

How rewards are administered for displaying new behaviors influences their effectiveness. W. Clay Hamner has formulated a set of rules based on research for administering positive reinforcement in a work environment.[3] A manager or staff person may use these rules in encouraging people to use the skills that they have acquired in a human relations training program. Of greater importance, these suggestions for administering positive reinforcement may be used in any situation where constructive changes in behavior are desired.

Rule 1. *Don't reward all people the same.* Managers who reward all people the same are encouraging average performance. If one person makes a substantial improvement after attending an interviewing workshop, he or she should receive more recognition (or other reward) than somebody who made only token progress.

Rule 2. *Failure to respond has reinforcing consequences.* If a manager ignores any changes in behavior that a subordinate has made as a result of a human relations training program, that subordinate will probably no longer repeat the new learning. Similarly, if exceptional performance goes unnoticed, an employee may lose his or her enthusiam for performing in an exceptional manner.

Rule 3. *Be sure to tell a person what he or she can do to get reinforced.* The employee who has a standard against which to measure his or her job will have a built-in feedback system. He or she will automatically know how he or she is doing. A manager might tell a subordinate, "After attending that workshop on overcoming sexism, I want you to be able to give males and females in your department equal opportunity to bid on better jobs."

Rule 4. *Be sure to tell a person what he or she is doing wrong.* By patiently explaining to a subordinate what he or she is doing wrong, the subordinate will then know what needs to be done to get *rewarded*. A person participates in an interview training program and upon returning from the program still alienates interviewees. He or she needs to change interviewing techniques in order to receive positive reinforcement. Once the deficiency is overcome (in this case, antagonizing interviewees) the person is one step closer to receiving rewards.

Rule 5. *Don't punish in front of others.* The punishment (for example, reprimand) should be enough to extinguish the undesired behavior. By administering the punishment in front of the work group, the worker may feel ridiculed or humiliated. In response, he or she becomes defensive and counterhostile.

Rule 6. *Make the consequences equal to the behavior.* Fair rewards are best. "Punishment should fit the crime," and rewards should fit the good deed. A person who learns to behave assertively with customers should be rewarded with encouragement of a reasonable sort. Perhaps telling him or her, "I think you've become the greatest salesperson in the region" would be overdoing praise. It would lose its effectiveness because the praise would seem ungenuine.

Follow-up as Needed. A common failing of most job-oriented human relations programs is that they are "one-shot affairs." A person attends the program, perhaps tries out the new skills, and after awhile returns to his or her former ways of doing things. A convenient way of circumventing this problem is for the organization to sponsor periodic "refresher" or "reminder" courses.

Feedback to Trainer and Trainees. As new skills are developed, they often create the need for the development of additional skills. Irma, a first-line supervisor, might attend an interviewing workshop. She becomes more proficient as an interviewer. Because of it, subordinates begin to confide in her more about work-related personal problems. Irma now decides that she could benefit from a developmental program that would enhance her skills in coaching and counseling subordinates. As a person improves his or her human relations skills, he or she often begins to identify additional areas for growth.

ENCOUNTER GROUPS

Encounter groups have shown an explosive growth over the past three decades. Perhaps 3 million people in the United States and Canada have participated in some type of group experience with the general goal of trying to learn more about themselves in relation to other people. An encounter group includes a wide variety of group activities designed to improve human relations effectiveness, including T-groups (the core part of sensitivity training). Among the many other forms of encounter groups are gestalt therapy, personal growth laboratories, interpersonal effectiveness laboratories, marathon groups, Esalen groups and executive effectiveness groups sponsored by the American Management Association. A discussion of encounter groups—particularly T-groups—is typically presented in a chapter about organization development because of their application to improving organizational effectiveness. Yet from the standpoint of the individual, encounter groups are seen as a way of improving his or her human relations effectiveness.

Goals and Purposes. People vary in what they expect to derive from an encounter group experience, and encounter group leaders vary in what they hope the groups' members will achieve. Despite this diversity, a few consistent purposes emerge. These include the following:

1. Make participants more sensitive to how they are perceived by others and how their behavior affects others.

2. Acquire knowledge about the processes that help and hinder group functioning.

3. Help participants become more aware of their own feelings and how these feelings influence behavior.

4. Help participants, in general, achieve greater self-understanding, including insight into their conflicts, feelings, defenses, and impact on others.

5. Develop specific behavioral skills such as improved listening ability, praising and criticizing others, and communicating with body language.

What Actually Happens During an Encounter Group? In a pure form of T-group, the leader provides no direction at the start of the session. It is hoped that by providing no rules or agenda people will begin to talk about the here and now. Such groups often begin as generalized bull sessions until people get the point that the encounter group is a unique experience. The group then begins to focus on each other and what is happening to them. Because a completely unstructured group takes so long to "get moving" and so many people find it frustrating (including some group leaders), a variety of semistructured exercises are now used in encounter groups. A sampling of two such encounter group exercises is presented next.

> *Group Leader:* To get things started everybody will tell everybody else what kind of first impression they have made. We'll do this in a clockwise manner, starting with Jack sitting to my left. Everybody, beginning with Alison, will tell Jack what he or she thinks of him. Of course, if Jack has made absolutely no impression on you, if he is the invisible man, you can pass [group laughs]. Okay, Alison, look Jack straight in the eye and tell him what you think.
>
> *Alison:* I don't know Jack very well at all. I just met him an hour ago. But he looks kind of pleasant and intelligent to me.
>
> *Chuck:* That mustache of his kills me. It looks like something from the turn of the century. Do you use mustache wax on it, Jack? [group laughs]. Other than that you look like a regular guy.
>
> *Aaron:* Any guy who wears baggy pants and white socks must not care what other people think of him. I can't think of anything else right now.
>
> *June:* Jack, you give me the impression of being an ambitious person. I like the way you're taking in what everybody is saying. I like the expression in your eyes.
>
> *Steve:* Jack reminds me of a boss I once had that fired me. So I really can't be objective about him [group laughs in a tense way].
>
> *Bob:* Jack, you give me the impression that you came here to get your head on straight.

Gil: I'll have to pass. Jack doesn't affect me one way or another.

Peggy: Jack, I think you're kind of cute. Not too supermasculine. Just sensitive and nice.

Rolf: Jack looks like the kind of guy I wouldn't mind having a beer with.

Group Leader: Jack, tell us how you feel about what has just happened to you.

Jack: I feel great. Thanks for all the compliments. I think I am ambitious and sensitive. Okay, Aaron, wait until it's your turn. I don't think too much of what you're wearing either.

Group Leader (much later on in the session): I get the impression we are becoming more candid with each other. Everybody has received some feedback on how he or she is perceived by everybody else. Now I would like everybody to share with the group the most pressing problem that you are facing. But it must be a problem you don't feel uncomfortable telling others about. Let's begin with Alison. It's Jack's turn to be last.

Alison: My biggest problem is that I love so many people and I like to do so many things. Sometimes it's difficult to make choices. I hope to be a magazine editor in a large city, but that would mean leaving behind my parents and friends.

Chuck: Money is my big hassle. I have two dollars in my pocket right now to last me until Friday. I need more money.

Aaron: I have a real hang-up with my parents. They want me to be a religious freak, and I'm not into that in a big way. My dad's a rabbi. I love him and wouldn't want to disappoint him, but I'm just not cut out of that cloth.

June: My future in-laws are driving me crazy. My fiancé is Italian and they want a tremendous Old World wedding. When I tell them I'm not interested in such a big wedding, they tell Mario he should have never become engaged to a girl who wasn't Italian.

Steve: My biggest problem is my height. I'm afraid I'm being discriminated against because I'm five feet four. Every executive in my company is six feet or over. I feel I'm being held back because of my height. But nobody will level with me.

Bob: My bowling score is five points below where it should be. That's a real problem.

Group Leader: Bob, I think you mean that right now you are not willing to share anything personal about yourself with the group.

Bob (blushing): You're right, Doc. I don't feel too comfortable telling other people my feelings. Okay, here's a problem. I hate my job, yet I can't get up enough courage to quit.

Gil: I'm very much in love with a wonderful woman whom I've been dating for three months. Yet she doesn't want an exclusive relationship with me and she doesn't want to marry me.

Peggy: I'm a very aggressive person. I'm also very ambitious. Because of it people may think I'm a woman's libber. I wish people would realize I'm just being me.

Rolf: I've been out working for awhile and I'm getting discouraged.

There are so many talented people out there that I wonder if I can hack it.

Jack: I'm twenty-five and I've never really had a long-term job. I just don't know where I'm headed. I wish I were one of these kids whose parents decided for him at age twelve that he should be an engineer or a doctor. I'm aware of a lot of things I don't want to do, but I have no good fix on what it is I want to do.

Duration, Frequency, and Group Composition.   The above sample of encounter group happenings took place during one three-hour session. Encounter groups vary widely in the duration and frequency of meetings. Job-oriented encounter groups tend to meet less frequently than some social–personal groups, which might meet regularly for a year or more. Many sensitivity training groups meet for ten or more hours per day for a full week. This is often followed up by a weekend reencounter about six months later. A frequent practice is for trainers to conduct encounter groups over a weekend, often meeting only once.

Are encounter groups conducted with strangers or co-workers? A correct answer is "both." Some group leaders believe that a family group (co-workers or cohorts) is best because (1) less time is spent getting acquainted, and (2) these are the people with whom you must learn to deal more effectively. More work organizations are moving toward family and away from stranger groups. Family groups are particularly useful when a purpose of the encounter group is to foster teamwork among group members.

Effectiveness and Precautions.   Encounter groups are controversial procedures. Proponents believe that participants receive many important short- and long-range benefits. Opponents of the approach believe that the benefits some people derive from participation in encounter groups are far outweighed by the damages done to others. Research evidence exists about both the benefits and potential hazards of encounter groups.

On the positive side, Peter B. Smith[5] reviewed studies of sensitivity training that used both control groups and repeated measures on the same individuals. All programs ran for not less than twenty hours. Of one hundred studies using measurement immediately after training, seventy-eight detected beneficial changes to individuals significantly greater than those shown by people who did not attend sensitivity training. Of thirty-one studies using measures completed one month or more after training, twenty-one also found significant change.

The changes most frequently brought about by the encounter groups included a more favorable self-concept, reduced prejudice toward people, and changed behavior as perceived by others not present during training (such as co-workers, superiors, and subordinates).

On the negative side, Morton Lieberman, Irwin Yalom, and Matthew Miles[6] conducted a large-scale investigation of encounter groups that cast doubt on the effectiveness of such experiences. In this research 210 student volunteers were assigned to eighteen encounter groups and sixty-nine students were assigned to a control group. Sixteen professionally qualified and experienced leaders were selected to conduct the experimental groups. A variety of different encounter groups was used, ranging from T-groups to psychoanalytically oriented groups. The encounter group experiments lasted for one semester.

A general conclusion reached by the investigators (two psychologists and one psychiatrist) was that a third of the participants gained benefits from the encounter groups, one third gained nothing, and one third reaped negative outcomes—in some cases sustaining significant psychological injury.[7] Some encounter group casualties found themselves experiencing what is commonly called a nervous breakdown.

Another conclusion drawn was that, although encounter groups sometimes offer temporary relief from alienation and loneliness, groups can be dangerous, and the danger is not counterbalanced by high gain.

What then can be said of the future of encounter groups if so much negative evidence has accumulated about their effectiveness? Under appropriate conditions, encounter groups can be beneficial. First, the people conducting the groups should be qualified professionals, such as clinical psychologists or psychiatrists with specialized training in conducting groups. Too often people conducting encounter groups are nonprofessionals who are looking more for thrills than for ways to help others develop their potential. A qualified group leader, for instance, can usually prevent a group from exerting too much pressure upon one individual.

Second, people who participate in encounter groups should be carefully screened. Encounter groups are not therapy groups designed to help emotionally ill people. People who need individual or group psychotherapy should get such help before participating in encounter groups. Some psychologists interview people individually before allowing them into an encounter group. Third, encounter group participation should be voluntary. Offering people an option to leave the group anytime the experience becomes uncomfortable is also a helpful precaution. One man exited from a group when people were asked to describe what animal each other group member reminded them of. He stated, "It gets me too tense to be described as an animal."

Payoff to Management.   The quip has been made that encounter groups make better husbands and fathers out of male managers, but it doesn't make them more productive. A fair generalization about the impact of T-groups and other encounter groups is that such experiences make managers more sympathetic to the problems of subordinates and more open in dealing with problems and controversial issues. However, the payoff of encounter groups in terms of increased organizational effectiveness is still uncertain.[8] A modified version of encounter groups, team-building sessions, appears to have more promise in terms of improving both productivity and satisfaction. Team building will be discussed in Chapter 13.

Interviewing skill is called for in hiring, employee coaching and counseling, and in gathering information for research or report-writing purposes. Twelve suggestions follow for conducting an interview.[9] A person intent upon improving his or her interviewing skills should also make use of technology such as recording equipment and video taping. Such equipment provides crucial feedback to both the learner and the experienced interviewer. Another general suggestion is to obtain frequent interviewing practice. Interviewing is an art, thus requiring substantial experience to perfect.

1. *Be relaxed during the interview.* A tense, tight interviewer makes it difficult for the interviewee to relax, thus interfering with an easy flow of conversation. Frequent interviewing practice is a prime way of learning to relax as an interviewer.

2. *Avoid excessive warm-up.* Many interviewers waste time discussing travel arrangements, professional supports, and mutual hobbies. Two or three minutes of general conversation is all that is generally required to work into the central purpose of the interview. Interviewees are eagerly waiting for the real interviewing to begin while the interviewer discusses general topics.

3. *Encourage interviewees to talk.* By assuming a listening posture—talking very little yourself—the interviewee will get the message that he or she is expected to talk. Nodding approval when the interviewee talks or making comments such as "Tell me more" are effective conversation-inducing techniques.

4. *Proceed from the general to the specific.* Called the narrowing technique, you begin by asking a general question about a topic and then following up with more specific inquiries. To illustrate: "What is your financial situation? How much do you earn from your job? How much outside income do you have? How far in debt are you? Do you have any judgments out against you?"

5. *Ask controversial questions after rapport has been established.* Early in an interview, the experienced person asks noncontroversial, objective questions for which answers are readily available: "What school did you attend? Where do you live?" Later on in the interview, once rapport has been established, more controversial questions can be asked such as, "How much time have you spent in prison?" (Questions like that may destroy the interview atmosphere and thus must be saved for the very end!)

A serious disadvantage of asking "controversial" questions during an employment interview is that they may have questionable legal status. Similar to psychological tests, interview questions should be related to job performance. Since it is impossible to conduct studies on every question asked during an interview, the conservative course for management is to avoid questions that people may perceive as being offensive or an invasion of privacy. A useful general guideline is that questions on interviews (as well as on tests and application forms) "pertaining to personal habits, attitudes about sex, etc., when not related to job requirements are considered to constitute an unwarranted invasion of the applicant's right to privacy."[10]

6. *Ask questions one at a time and wait until that question is answered before proceeding on to the next.* Inexperienced interviewers have a tendency to ask questions requiring multiple answers, such as "How well are you doing on your job and how do you like what you are doing?" It is preferable to break a question of this nature into two separate short questions.

7. *Use open-ended questions.* Open-ended questions require that the respondent provide information rather than give yes or no responses. For example, "How do you like laboratory work?" is a more effective question than "Do you like laboratory work?" Also, "What are your qualifications for this job?" is a better question than "Are you qualified for this job?"

8. *Use probes to elicit more information.* As the interviewee submits information of interest to the interviewer, the latter should use probes to dig for more specifics. Here is one example:

Interviewer: What problems are you having on the job?
Interviewee: The pace is getting awfully fast.
Interviewer: In what way?
Interviewee: It's hard to keep up with the workload.
Interviewer: How far behind are you?
Interviewee: I think I'll be late with all my reports this month.

9. *Avoid advice giving.* Giving people unsolicited advice tends to short-circuit information flow and may cause resentment. Save your constructive suggestions for the end of an interview. Wait until you get the entire story before moving in with advice. Never say, "I think I know what your problem is," until you have heard the other person's version of the story.

10. *Avoid premature judgment.* Interviewers have a tendency to reach an early conclusion about an interviewee, often in the first few minutes. One interviewer known to this author would make the notation "thumbs up" or "thumbs down" shortly after a job candidate entered his office.

11. *Use reflective summaries.* Originally designed as a technique of nondirective psychotherapy, reflective summaries are now used by interviewers in a wide range of situations. A reflective summary is essentially a concise statement of the interviewee's feelings about a particular interview topic. A subordinate might be ranting about the high scrap rate in his department. You might comment, "You are concerned about the

quality of work in your department." His response would probably be, "Yeah, yeah, that's exactly what I think," thus encouraging more useful dialogue.

12. *Close interview on a positive note.* Good human relations practice and common sense dictate that all interviews, even those of a disciplinary nature, end on a constructive note. Assume that you were coaching a subordinate about her need to make sure that all accounts were paid within thirty days. You might conclude, "Alice, don't forget I'm very satisfied with the fact that you are paying 80 percent of our bills on time. Just bring around the other 20 percent."

Value of the Interview as a Selection Device. As stated earlier, the interview is a multipurpose instrument. It is indispensable for such purposes as gathering information from other people and conducting performance review sessions. *Under the right circumstances,* the interview can be used to make accurate predictions about future job behavior. In general, the right circumstances refer to using a carefully guided or *structured* interview.[11] An interview of this type follows a series of questions of know relevance to job behavior. Several of these patterned interviews are available commercially. For many years the Dartnell Corporation of Chicago has been a leader in the field of furnishing patterned interview forms.

Following are four examples of the types of questions typically asked on a patterned interview form. Without conducting research for a particular occupation or within a particular firm, it cannot be determined whether or not the selection interview is an accurate predictor of job performance.

1. What experience have you had that qualifies you for this position?
2. How successful have you been in selling in the past? Please tell me specifically how you did in your last sales position?
3. What criticisms have been made of you in the past by your superiors?
4. Why should we hire you?

TRANSACTIONAL ANALYSIS WORKSHOPS (BECOMING AN OK BOSS OR SUBORDINATE)

Transactional analysis (TA) has blossomed from its original intent as a form of psychotherapy to a technique for improving interpersonal relationships both on and off the job. A general goal of TA training is to help people relate to each other in a mature, adult manner, thus easing tensions and getting important things accomplished. An overview of key TA concepts is necessary to understand how TA can be applied to making you a more effective subordinate or boss.[12]

Ego States.   According to the TA framework, the human personality is composed of three parts, called ego states. As defined by Muriel James in *The OK Boss,* "An ego state is a system of feelings and experiences related to the pattern of behavior that a person develops in the stages of growing up." They are perceptions based on real-world behavior. A healthy person moves from one ego state to another, depending upon the demands of the situation.

The *parent* ego state dictates that we act as our parents once did. It is a body of recordings in the brain that reflects the unquestioned events perceived by a person during his or her childhood. A person acting in the parent state will display such characteristics as being overprotective, distant, dogmatic, indispensable, and self-righteous. "Physical and verbal clues that someone is acting in the parent state include the wagging finger to show displeasure, reference to laws and rules, and reliance on ways that were successful in the past."[13]

When people are acting and thinking rationally, when they are gathering facts and making judgments based upon these facts, they are in the *adult* ego state. The adult is an information seeker and processor. In this ego state, the person functions as a computer processing new data, making decisions, and updating the data in the original recording of the parent and child ego states. You can tell a person is being an adult when he or she concentrates and engages in factual discussion.

When people feel and act as they did in childhood, they are in their *child* ego state. It is the data that are recorded in the brain as a result of experiences taking place through ages one to five. Characteristics of the child include creativity, conformity, depression, anxiety, dependence, fear, and hate. Because childhood experiences are so varied, people show varied behavior when in their child state. Despite this variation, a clue that a person is being a child is when he or she is nonlogical and demands immediate gratification of impulses. Other clues are temper tantrums, giggling, coyness, attention seeking, and stoney-faced silence.

Analysis of Transactions.   To apply TA to relationships between people, it is necessary to identify the transactions taking place between the different ego states. Much of what takes place in a TA workshop involves the analysis of transactions. Recognizing the ego states of the two people involved in the transaction can help a person communicate and interact more effectively. Transactions are classified into complementary and crossed (noncomplementary). When transactions between people are complementary (positive strokes), effective interaction is the result. When transactions are crossed (when one person gives negative strokes to the other), we have ineffective interaction.

Complementary transactions are shown in Figure 11.2.[14] All are

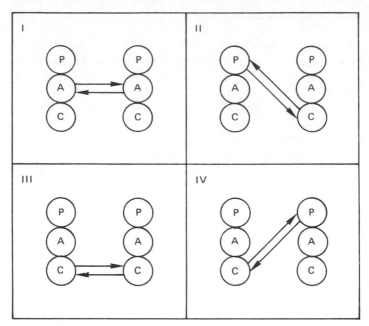

P is parent; A is adult; C is child

FIGURE 11.2

effective transactions because both people receive the positive stroking that they want. In cell I a boss acting in an adult state might say to a subordinate, "When will I get my report?"; the subordinate replies, "It will be ready tomorrow at three o'clock." In cell II, the boss, in a parent state, says, "Be here early tomorrow, it's an important day." To which the subordinate replies, "Don't worry, I'll be here." In cell III, the child-acting boss says, "Let's have a few drinks at lunch." The subordinate replies, "Maybe we can even drink right up to quitting time." In cell IV the child-acting boss says, "We're so overwhelmed with work in this department, I don't think we'll ever catch up." In a parent-like fashion, the subordinate responds, "I'll get things under control."

Crossed transactions, shown in Figure 11.3, result in negative strokes and ineffective interactions between people. In cell I the boss in a child state says, "I desperately need your cooperation," hoping for a parent response. Instead, the boss hears, "I'm doing all I can right now. What more can you expect?" In cell II, the parent boss, hoping for a child response from his subordinate, says, "Your work is sloppy and needs immediate correction." Instead a parent-like subordinate says, "I'll be the judge of the neatness of my work." In cell III an adult boss, hoping for an adult response, says, "Have you ever thought of attending sensitivity training?" Acting as a parent, the subordinate says, "That, sir, constitutes an invasion

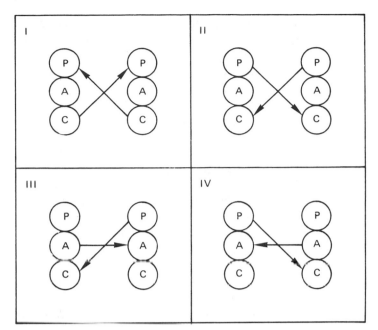

P is parent; A is adult; C is child

FIGURE 11.3

of privacy." In cell IV, a parent-acting boss says, "You are totally without self-discipline." Instead of acting as a whipped or obedient child, the subordinate responds in an adult manner; "In what way am I lacking in self-discipline?"

Life Positions.   Another important set of key concepts of TA are the four life positions, as follows:

1. I'm not OK—You're OK; the anxious dependency of the immature that leads to feelings of depression.
2. I'm not OK—You're not OK; the surrender or despair position that can in extreme situations lead to schizophrenic withdrawal.
3. I'm OK—You're not OK; the criminal position that hints of paranoid thinking.
4. I'm OK—You're OK; the response of the mature, healthy adult, and the only truly constructive life position. An OK boss has this attitude.

Life Scripts.   TA theory contends that people usually live their lives according to elaborate and consistent (although often unconscious) game plans called scripts.[15] There are winner's scripts for people who generally receive a goodly share of life's rewards. Loser scripts are for those who almost inevitably fail. If you latch on to the right life position (I'm OK—You're OK), you too can be a winner (so contends the TA cult).

Transactional analysis emphasizes that people have a choice in selecting a life position or script. Once we have gained some insight into our life positions, we can deliberately and rationally decide to change. We therefore must accept responsibility for our own behavior. Transactional analysis has no sympathy for the person who blames his alcoholism on his mother's insistence upon an early weaning!

Seven Different OK Bosses.   Muriel James has developed a framework that helps bosses realize that they can function effectively (be **OK**) even if they don't all use the same leadership style.[16] Her concepts also apply to subordinate behavior. Once you recognize your basic leadership style, you can liberate yourself to use a different style (if a change is warranted). Through TA you can make a contract with yourself to use a healthier script. Three bossing styles are found in the parent state; *critic, coach,* and *shadow.* Each has an **OK** and a not **OK** aspect.

A *critic* can be a dictator or an informed critic. A not-**OK** critic is a dictator who is typically opinionated and who insists that everything be done his or her way.

A *coach* is a parental boss who enjoys being helpful, but may at times overdo it. Because he or she does so much for subordinates, there is danger of becoming a benevolent dictator: "Underneath the nurturing mask is the paternalistic, condescending attitude—you're not OK—of someone who feels threatened by the talents and achievements of anyone else."[17] The OK coach does a superior job of helping people develop their fullest potential. An OK coach cares about people's feelings and helps them with different problems. Subordinates of an OK coach feel understood and respond with increased productivity.

A *shadow* is a boss who stays uninvolved. When he or she is not OK, his or her typical behavior is one of aloofness from the team. When a loner is an OK boss, he or she lets people alone to develop by themselves.

An adult-state boss is an *analyst.* As such, he or she is always rational, asking who, what, why, when, where, and how? When an analyst is not an OK boss, he or she acts too much like a computer, primarily processing financial data. Frequently, they are inadequate in handling human relations problems because they think too much in terms of statistics. Also, they tend to regard feelings as too personal to deal with on the job.

Child-state bosses are categorized into three types by Muriel James: pacifiers, fighters, and inventors. Again, a boss can be OK or not-OK, no matter what type.

A pacifier is OK when he or she is a supernegotiator who knows how to avoid conflict through fairness and negotiation. A not-OK pacifier is a Milquetoast who is soft, bland, compliant, and who tries to please everybody. He or she is an overcompromiser.

A fighter varies from being a punk to a partner who scraps for success. James notes that the not-OK fighter is sulky, rebellious, and hostile. He fights dirty. In contrast, OK fighter bosses use their aggressiveness to foster teamwork. As partners, aggressive bosses fight for their department and share information with subordinates.

A child-like boss is often an *inventor* who flits around from one project to another, half-processing each idea. An OK inventor boss is a true innovator and often a successful entrepreneur. He or she is adept at thinking up imaginative solutions to problems and creating an exciting work atmosphere.

In summary, TA is designed to help people in ways that lead to effective communications and productive relationships with others. Although TA has built a clever terminology of its own, it is not radically different in its goals or methodologies from other forms of human relations training.

ASSERTIVENESS TRAINING

Another important by-product of the human potential movement has been training programs designed to teach people methods of appropriately asserting themselves in work and social situations. As with transactional analysis, assertiveness training is derived from a technique of psychotherapy. The goals of assertiveness training include (1) know how you feel, (2) say what you want, and (3) get what you want.[18]

Passive, Aggressive, and Assertive Behavior. The true goal of assertiveness training is to help an individual make a clear statement of what he or she wants, or how he or she feels in a given situation, without being abusive or obnoxious. It is also implied that the individual will learn to avoid the passive mode of suppressing feelings and actions. From another perspective, the nonassertive (passive) individual is stepped on and the aggressive person steps on others, whereas the assertive person deals with a problem in a mature and explicit manner. A frequent situation in organizational life—that of being appointed to a committee—can be used to illustrate these differences.[19]

Opening his morning mail, project manager Lloyd notices a letter from another project manager, which says in part: "Congratulations, you have been appointed area captain to collect money for the Veterans of Foreign Wars. You will find it both an honor and a privilege to serve your country in this manner."

Unfortunately, Lloyd is already heavily committed to community activities, including serving as a precinct worker in upcoming elections. He can respond in three different ways:

Passive behavior: Lloyd does nothing and awaits further instructions. He is simmering with anger, but grits his teeth and hopes that the assignment will not be as time consuming as he now estimates.

Aggressive behavior: Lloyd grabs the phone, calls the other project manager, and says, "Who do you think you are assigning me to your cockamamie committee? When I want to be on a committee, I'll volunteer."

Assertive behavior: Lloyd calls the other project manager and says, "I appreciate your thinking of me in connection with your committee. But I choose not to serve. Good luck in finding another captain."

Training Exercises. Assertiveness training workshops utilize a number of different techniques to help participants develop more assertive responses to situations. A helpful beginning is for the workshop participant to learn the basic steps to assertion. One such list has been prepared by the authors of *The New Assertive Woman*[20]:

Steps to Assertion: A Checklist

1. Clarify the situation and focus on the issue. What is my goal? What exactly do I want to accomplish?
2. How will assertive behavior on my part help me accomplish my goal?
3. What would I usually do to avoid asserting myself in this situation?
4. Why would I want to give that up and assert myself instead?
5. What might be stopping me from asserting myself?
   a. Am I holding on to irrational beliefs? If so, what are they?
   b. How can I replace these irrational beliefs with rational ones?
   c. (For women only) Have I, as a woman, been taught to behave in ways that make it difficult for me to act assertively in the present situation? What ways? How can I overcome this?
   d. What are my rights in this situation? (State them clearly.) Do these rights justify turning my back on my conditioning?
6. Am I anxious about asserting myself? What techniques can I use to reduce my anxiety?
7. Have I done my homework? Do I have the information I need to go ahead and act?
8. Can I
   a. Let the other person know I hear and understand him/her?
   b. Let the other person know how I feel?
   c. Tell him/her what I want?

Fogging is a technique developed by Manuel J. Smith[21] that provides insight into the techniques of assertiveness training. In fogging, you respond to manipulative criticism as if you were a fog bank. You are thus virtually unaffected by the criticism and you will be able to get across your point. The learner is instructed to offer no resistance to the criticism. Here are three examples of fogging styled after the elaborate training program offered by Smith:

Critic: I see that you are as sloppy looking as usual.

Learner: That's right. I look the same today as I usually do.

Critic: How atrocious! You made five errors in preparing that corporate tax return.

Learner: That's true. I counted the errors you red circled. There were exactly five.

Critic: Have you ever thought of giving up your career and dropping out of college to become a beachcomber?

Learner: I could see some merit in dropping out of college and becoming a beachcomber.

Another popular technique of assertiveness training is for the learner to rehearse an assertive response to a hypothetical situation. By imagining how you would handle them, you should increase your skill in handling similar situations in real life. Here are two such situations:

1. You are waiting in line at a bank to cash a paycheck. An angry looking man, weighing about 250 pounds, steps in ahead of you. Rehearse your response to this situation.

2. You diligently prepare a term paper for a course in human relations. With considerable pride, you submit your report. It is returned one week later with a grade of "D+" and the comment, "Incoherent paper, shows very little effort." Rehearse your response to this situation.

SEXISM AWARENESS TRAINING

The thrust toward equal opportunity for women in business has led to a number of training programs designed to make male (and often female) managers aware of their own prejudices and discriminatory tactics against women.[22] In the typical format of such programs, a feeling-laden discussion is held about the topic of sexism in business. Frequently, facts and figures about job discrimination against females are also presented (such as only 1 out of 600 key executive positions in American industry is occupied by a female).

As a starting point in sexism awareness training, the participants are asked to assess the extent of their sexist thinking. The sexism rating scale, shown in Figure 11.4, has been used in a wide variety of such programs.[23] Take the scale yourself to assess the current status of your sexist beliefs and attitudes. Although this scale has much more statistical support than others presented in this text, it still must be regarded as an experiential exercise, not a scientifically developed scale. Your score may not be a valid indication of the extent of your sexist thinking.

Directions: Read each question and check in the appropriate space whether you "mostly agree" or "mostly disagree." Answer each question even if you think the real answer *depends upon the situation.* Candor on your part will result in a score that could tell you something meaningful about yourself. Be honest and learn something new about the magnitude of your sexist attitudes and beliefs.

		Mostly Agree	Mostly Disagree
1.	A female executive would probably cry if a decision did not go her way.		
2.	Women reporters should be assigned only to stories about women, children, society, and real estate.		
3.	It is natural for the female member of a committee to take care of getting the coffee.		
4.	I would have a difficult time calling a woman by the title Doctor.		
5.	Secretaries should not be required to run errands for their bosses.		
6.	Allowing men and women to travel together on business creates many problems.		
7.	Book reviewers should not comment upon the sex of the author whose work is being reviewed.		
8.	Women should be paid less than men for the same job because women are a high-turnover risk.		
9.	Males and females performing comparable work should receive identical pay.		
10.	The current underuse of women in business and government is a waste of human resources.		
11.	It is unfeminine for a woman to be aggressive on the job.		
12.	Men should be paid higher wages than women because men have families to support.		
13.	The best women managers think like men.		
14.	Given a fair chance, many executive secretaries could probably take over their bosses' jobs.		
15.	Women are poor decision makers because they are so subjective.		
16.	Women make up 38 percent of the work force.		

Therefore, they should hold about 38 percent of executive jobs. _____ _____

17. A woman's place is in the home. _____ _____

18. Few women would be willing to be examined by a female doctor. _____ _____

19. At "certain times of the month," women would be too irritable to make good decisions. _____ _____

20. Women are treated unfairly in most places of work. _____ _____

21. Give a woman a good job and she begins to act in a very authoritarian manner. _____ _____

22. Sex (gender) is an irrelevant characteristic in evaluating people for professional and managerial jobs. _____ _____

23. Women who are successful in their careers are probably sexually frustrated. _____ _____

24. A woman middle manager would have an advantage over a man because she would use charm and sex to get ahead. _____ _____

25. Women are concentrated in low-paying dead-end jobs because society has forced them into that situation. _____ _____

26. Women waste more time than do men, even at the same type of job. _____ _____

27. Women should receive full pay and benefits while on maternity leave. _____ _____

28. Women should be considered as individuals, not as "women." _____ _____

29. Women are quite often as ambitious as men. _____ _____

30. It makes good sense to use such words as chairwoman, spokeswoman, or saleswoman, in place of chairman, spokesman, or salesman (when a woman is holding the position). _____ _____

31. Most men and women resent working for a female boss. _____ _____

32. I have yet to meet a woman qualified to hold a top executive position. _____ _____

33. Women, because of their humanistic values, are well suited to holding leadership positions in business and industry. _____ _____

34. Women are really the underprivileged class in the United States. _____ _____

	Mostly Agree	*Mostly Disagree*
35. It just wouldn't work out if the United States had a female president.	_____	_____
36. More men should be encouraged to enter nursing.	_____	_____
37. Doctors, on the average, earn four times as much money as nurses. This situation is unfair and unjust.	_____	_____
38. It is natural for the female member present at a meeting to take notes for the group.	_____	_____
39. Women should be invited to attend the same management-development programs as men.	_____	_____
40. Men who have worked for a woman boss realize it creates no particular problem.	_____	_____
41. More women should be encouraged to enter medicine and law.	_____	_____
42. The practice of supplying potential customers with call girls makes good business sense.	_____	_____

Finding Your Score. Every question among the forty-two you have just answered is worth 1, 2, 3, or 5 points toward your total sexism rating. Follow the straightforward scoring key presented next to arrive at a total score on the sexism rating scale. Record your score value in the space provided after each question. For example, if you answered the first question "mostly disagree," you would receive 3 points toward your total sexism score. If you answered "mostly agree," you would receive zero points for that question.

Question Number	*Enter your score for each question in this column*
1. Mostly agree is worth 3 points:	_____
2. Mostly agree is worth 5 points:	_____
3. Mostly agree is worth 3 points:	_____
4. Mostly agree is worth 3 points:	_____
5. Mostly disagree is worth 1 point:	_____
6. Mostly agree is worth 1 point:	_____
7. Mostly disagree is worth 1 point:	_____
8. Mostly agree is worth 3 points:	_____
9. Mostly disagree is worth 5 points:	_____
10. Mostly disagree is worth 2 points:	_____
11. Mostly agree is worth 2 points:	_____

Question Number

*Enter your score
for each question
in this column*

239
*Improving Human
Relations Skills*

12. Mostly agree is worth 3 points: _____
13. Mostly agree is worth 3 points: _____
14. Mostly disagree is worth 1 point: _____
15. Mostly agree is worth 3 points: _____
16. Mostly disagree is worth 2 points: _____
17. Mostly agree is worth 5 points: _____
18. Mostly agree is worth 2 points: _____
19. Mostly agree is worth 3 points: _____
20. Mostly disagree is worth 3 points: _____
21. Mostly agree is worth 3 points: _____
22. Mostly disagree is worth 1 point: _____
23. Mostly agree is worth 3 points: _____
24. Mostly agree is worth 3 points: _____
25. Mostly disagree is worth 2 points: _____
26. Mostly agree is worth 3 points: _____
27. Mostly disagree is worth 2 points: _____
28. Mostly disagree is worth 2 points: _____
29. Mostly disagree is worth 1 point: _____
30. Mostly disagree is worth 1 point: _____
31. Mostly agree is worth 1 point: _____
32. Mostly agree is worth 3 points: _____
33. Mostly disagree is worth 1 point: _____
34. Mostly disagree is worth 3 points: _____
35. Mostly agree is worth 3 points: _____
36. Mostly disagree is worth 1 point: _____
37. Mostly disagree is worth 1 point: _____
38. Mostly agree is worth 3 points: _____
39. Mostly disagree is worth 3 points: _____
40. Mostly disagree is worth 2 points: _____
41. Mostly disagree is worth 1 point: _____
42. Mostly agree is worth 3 points: _____

Now add your scores for each question to arrive at your total score: _____

FIGURE 11.4
Sexism rating scale.

SOURCE: Andrew J. DuBrin, *Survival in the Sexist Jungle: A Psychologist's Program for Combatting Job Discrimination Against Women,* Books For Better Living, 1974, pp. 215–221.

Assuming you answered the sexism rating scale with as much candor as possible, and also assuming that you are aware of most of your attitudes about career women, your score can be interpreted with reasonable accuracy. Generally accepted methods of attitude scale construction were used in the development of this scale.

Outrageously sexist: Scores of 51 or more strongly indicate that you are a rabid sexist. You believe quite strongly in different roles for males and females in a work and home environment.

Sexist: A score between 36 and 50 points on this scale suggests that you are sexist in your thinking. You probably use terms such as "unladylike" and "unfeminine" to describe the activities of ambitious and successful women. Young people would probably describe you as "old-fashioned," "traditional," or "straight" in your thinking—whether you are young or old.

Moderately sexist: A medium score on this scale—approximately 16 to 35 points—suggests that you are moderately sexist in your thinking. You probably believe that men and women should be considered equal in some areas, but not in others. People with attitudes similar to yours are usually willing to accept most of the demands of women liberationists, providing they are not seen as too extreme. A statement frequently made by the moderate sexist is, "I think every woman is entitled to a career providing she doesn't work until all her children are in school." Moderately sexist male professionals and managers encourage women to get ahead in business, providing these women do not compete for *their* jobs.

Nonsexist: A low score on this scale, 0 to 15, suggests clearly that you are very nonsexist (or feminist) in your thinking. You tenaciously cling to the notion that the world of work should be egalitarian. From your point of view, capability and interest, not gender, should determine what kind of work a person performs.

Summary
of Key Points

1. A program for improving human relations effectiveness should first determine what kind of improvement is necessary. The program should be administered under favorable conditions, and new learning should be reinforced by the organization.

2. Encounter groups are useful as a way of developing better insight into yourself and others. Misapplication of these groups, however, can result in psychological harm. Both encounter group leaders and participants should be carefully screened.

3. Interviewing skill is important in a variety of work situations. Frequent practice plus following the suggestions of experienced interviewers should improve your interviewing effectiveness.

4. Transactional analysis is now widely applied to improving communication among people in work situations. Applying TA to the job

requires that you learn its jargon and be able to analyze the transactions that take place between yourself and others.

5. Transactional analysis helps you to recognize your "script" (roughly, pattern of success or failure) and change it to your advantage.

6. You can be an **OK** (effective) boss using a wide variety of leadership styles.

7. Assertiveness training helps you learn how to recognize and constructively state your true feelings in both work and social situations. An assertive person is neither passive nor obnoxiously aggressive.

8. Sexism awareness training helps you recognize the extent of your sexist thinking. One goal of such training is to help both males and females better accept women in key positions.

1. How could you accurately determine what type of human relations training you needed?

2. How would you determine what kind of human relations training best suited the needs of an organization?

3. Would you send a computer programmer with a severe stutter to an encounter group? Why or why not?

4. Which one of the training programs described in this chapter is needed the most by the current president of the United States? Why?

5. Which of the human relations training programs described in this chapter would be the most beneficial to you? Why?

6. What seems to be your life "script"? In what way would you like to change it?

Questions
for Discussion

A Human Relations Incident
THE ASSERTIVE BOSS

You are employed as a systems analyst. Mandi, your boss, has just returned from a four-day encounter group as part of a management-development program. You pass by her in the hall and she comments, "My gosh, those slacks you are wearing sure don't go well with your shirt. By the way, I'm glad we met. Meet me in my office at three this afternoon. There is something heavy I want to discuss with you."

Puzzled by both her comments, you have some concern about the meeting. Three minutes into the meeting Mandi says to you, "I'm going to have to lay it on the line to you. I'm beginning to wonder if you are cut out for systems work. I mean your thinking is so unsystematic, so haphazard. Don't you think you would be better off as a kindergarten teacher?

"But I'm not trying to write your script for you. Do what you think is best."

How should you respond to Mandi? How should her comments affect your career planning?

A Human Relations Case
WHAT WE NEED AROUND HERE IS BETTER HUMAN RELATIONS

Hank called his three highest-ranking managers together for a surprise luncheon meeting. "Have a drink on United Mutual," said Hank, "you may need it to loosen up your thinking about an important topic I want to bring to your attention."

After Madeline, Raymond, and Allen ordered their drinks, Hank launched into the agenda:

"As office manager, I think we have to move into a rigorous human relations training program for our front-line supervisors. It's no longer a question of whether we should have a program, it's now a question of what kind and when."

Allen spoke out, "Okay, Hank, don't keep us in suspense any longer. What makes you think we need a human relations training program?"

"Look at the problems we are facing. Twenty-five percent turnover among the clerical and secretarial staffs; productivity lower than the casualty insurance industry national standards. What better reasons could anybody have for properly training our supervisory staff?"

Madeline commented, "Hold on Hank. Training may not be the answer. I think our high turnover and low productivity are caused by reasons beyond the control of supervision. Our wages are low and we expect our people to work in cramped, rather dismal office space."

Hank retorted, "Nonsense. A good supervisor can get workers to accept almost any working conditions. Training will fix that."

"Hank, I see another problem," said Allen. "Our supervisors are so overworked already that they will balk at training. If you hold the training on company time, they will say that they are falling behind in their work. If the training takes place after hours or on weekends, our supervisors will say that they are being taken advantage of."

"Nonsense," replied Hank. "Every supervisor realizes the importance of good human relations. Besides that, they will see it as a form of job enrichment."

"So long as we're having an open meeting, let me have my input," volunteered Raymond. "We are starting from the wrong end by having our first-line supervisors go through human relations training. It's our top management who needs the training the most. Unless they practice better human relations, you can't expect such behavior from our supervisors. How can you have a top management that is insensitive to people and a bottom management that is sensitive. The system just won't work."

"What you say makes some sense," said Hank, "but I wouldn't go so far as to say top management is insensitive to people. Maybe we can talk some more about the human relations program after lunch."

1. Should Hank go ahead with his plans for the human relations training program? Why or why not?
2. What do you think of Raymond's comment that top management should participate in human relations training first?
3. What is your opinion of Hank's statement that good leadership can compensate for poor working conditions?
4. If you were in Hank's situation, would you try to get top management to participate in a human relations training program?
5. What type of human relations training program would you recommend for first-line supervision at United Mutual?

FOOTNOTES

[1] See Chapter 15 in Henry L. Tosi and Stephen J. Carroll, *Management: Contingencies, Structure, and Process*, St. Clair Press, 1976. A more expanded discussion of matching development programs to individual and organizational needs is found in Andrew J. DuBrin, *The Practice of Managerial Psychology*, Pergamon, 1972, Chapter 3.

[2] DuBrin, *op. cit.*, p. 82.

[3] W. Clay Hamner, "Reinforcement Theory and Contingency Management in Organizational Settings," in Henry L. Tosi and W. Clay Hamner, *Organizational Behavior and Management: A Contingency Approach*, St. Clair Press, 1974, pp. 96–98.

[4] George F. Wieland and Robert A. Ulrich, *Organizations: Behavior, Design, and Change*, Irwin, 1976, p. 482.

[5] Peter B. Smith, "Controlled Studies of the Outcome of Sensitivity Training," *Psychological Bulletin*, July 1975, pp. 597–622.

[6] Morton Lieberman, Irvin Yalom, and Matthew Miles, *Encounter Groups: First Facts*, Basic Books, 1973. A nontechnical report of these findings is found in *Time*, April 30, 1973, p. 65.

[7] Lieberman, Yalom, and Miles, *op. cit.*, p. 147.

[8] Alan C. Filley, Robert J. House, and Steven Kerr, *Managerial Process and Organizational Behavior*, Scott, Foresman, 1976, p. 501.

[9] Our discussion of interviewing suggestions follows closely several suggestions offered in George Strauss and Leonard Sayles, *Personnel: The Human Problems of Management*, 3rd. ed., Prentice-Hall, 1972, Chapter 11.

[10] Herbert J. Chruden and Arthur W. Sherman, Jr., *Personnel Management*, 5th ed., South-Western, 1976, p. 162.

[11] *Ibid.*, p. 134.

[12] Two worthwhile sources of information about TA applied to job settings are Charles Albano, *Transactional Analysis on the Job*, Amacom, 1974; and V. P. Luchsinger and L. L. Luchsinger, "Transactional Analysis for Managers, or How to Be More OK with Organizations," *MSU Business Topics*, Spring 1974, pp. 5–12.

[13] Muriel James, *The OK Boss*. Addison-Wesley, 1975, p. 32.

[14] The diagrams presented in Figures 11.2 and 11.3 are based upon those in Luchsinger and Luchsinger, *op. cit.*, p. 6; and James, *op. cit.*, pp. 92–95.

[15] An original source of information about life positions and life scripts is

Thomas A. Harris, *I'm OK—You're OK*, Harper & Row, 1969. A concise source is Donald D. Bowen and Raghu Nath, "Transactions in Management," *California Management Review*, Winter 1975, pp. 76–87.

[16] Muriel James, "The OK Boss," *Psychology Today*, Feb. 1976, pp. 32–34.

[17] *Ibid.*, p. 33.

[18] Lynn Z. Bloom, Karen Coburn, and Joan Pearlman, *The New Assertive Woman*, Dell, 1976, p. i.

[19] The nonassertive, assertive, and aggressive behavior categorization was developed originally by Robert E. Alberti and Michael L. Emmons, *Your Perfect Right: A Guide to Assertive Behavior*, Impact, 1970.

[20] Bloom, Coburn, and Pearlman, *op. cit.*, pp. 175–176.

[21] Manuel J. Smith, *When I Say No, I Feel Guilty*, Bantam, 1975, pp. 104–115.

[22] An original source of information about sexism awareness training is Rosalind Loring and Theodora Wells, *Breakthrough: Women into Management*, Van Nostrand Reinhold, 1972, pp. 197–200.

[23] Reproduced with permission from Andrew J. DuBrin, *Survival in the Sexist Jungle: A Psychologist's Program for Combating Job Discrimination Against Women*, Books for Better Living, 1974, pp. 215–220.

SUGGESTED READING

BENNE, KENNETH, BRADFORD, LELAND, GIBB, JACK, and LIPPITT, RONALD. *The Laboratory Method of Learning and Changing: Theory and Applications*, NTL Learning Resources Corporation, 1975.

BLOOM, LYNN Z., COBURN, KAREN, and PEARLMAN, JOAN. *The New Assertive Woman*, Dell, 1976. Originally published by Delacorte Press, 1975.

BOWEN, DONALD D., and NATH, RAGHU. "Transactions in Management," *California Management Review*, Winter 1975, pp. 73–85.

FRENCH, WENDELL L., and BELL, CECIL, JR. *Organization Development: Behavioral Science Interventions for Organization Improvement*, Prentice-Hall, 1973.

JAMES, MURIEL. *The OK Boss*. Addison-Wesley, 1975.

JONGEWARD, DOROTHY. *Everybody Wins: Transactional Analysis Applied to Organizations*, Addison-Wesley, 1973.

LORING, ROSALIND, and WELLS, THEODORA. *Breakthrough: Women into Management*, Van Nostrand Reinhold, 1972.

LUCHSINGER, V. P., and LUCHSINGER, L. L. "Transactional Analysis for Managers, or How to Be More OK with OK Organizations," *MSU Business Topics*, Spring 1974, pp. 5–12.

SMITH, MANUEL J. *When I Say No, I Feel Guilty*, Bantam, 1975. Published originally by Dial Press, 1975.

SMITH, PETER B. "Controlled Studies of the Outcome of Sensitivity Training," *Psychological Bulletin*, vol. 82, July 1975, pp. 597–622.

PART FOUR
WORKING WITH THE ORGANIZATION

Total organizations rather than individuals or small groups are the *primary focus* of this part of the book. Although we emphasize such topics as the nature of effective organizations and improving organizations, individuals cannot be disregarded. People are the basic building block that contribute to effective and ineffective organizations. An entire chapter is devoted to coping with problems created by a bureaucracy. Our justification for including this chapter is that countless numbers of people are trying to find constructive ways of easing the frustrations that they experience in either working for or dealing with bureaucracies.

12

THE EFFECTIVE ORGANIZATION

Learning Objectives

After reading and studying this chapter, you should be able to

1. Know the difference between an *effective* and an *efficient* organization.
2. Understand the relationship between environmental demands and organizational effectiveness.
3. Describe at least six measures of organizational effectiveness.
4. Identify and explain several factors that contribute to organizational effectiveness.
5. Explain the meaning of an *organic organization*.
6. Understand the relevance of Parkinson's law and the organizational multiplier to organizational effectiveness.

Your reaction to many places of work you know about has probably been, "I wonder how they stay in business." About other places you may have commented, "What a smooth running outfit. No wonder they are tops in their field." This chapter examines the issue of what and who determines organizational effectiveness. In addition, reference will be made to organizational practices so ineffective that they have become the subject of satire.

A useful distinction can be made between organizational *effectiveness* and organizational *efficiency*.[1] Generally speaking, an effective organization is one that reaches its goals and objectives. A cannery that reaches its profit objective and supplies health-giving food to people is effective. Organizational efficiency refers to the amount of resources an organization consumes to achieve its output. If that same cannery destroys a large supply of crops per unit of useful food and simultaneously pollutes an entire river in meeting its production goals, we say the organization is inefficient. Armies that "win" wars are thus effective but inefficient organizations.

The nature of an organization cannot be properly understood without an appreciation of how its two major subsystems, or components, operate. Every organization has both a formal and an informal structure. (In this context the term system can be used interchangeably with structure.) When the formal and informal structures work together harmoniously, the overall organization has the capacity to operate effectively. When the formal and informal organizations clash, ineffectiveness (and sometimes chaos) is the result.

Our discussion of formal versus informal groups in Chapter 8 referred to the same type of phenomenon under consideration here. The formal organization is the organization as it exists on paper. It is the official, sanctioned way of doing things. The formal organization tells you who reports to whom (see the organization chart) and how various problems should be handled (see the policies and procedures manual). A modern definition states, "The formal structure is composed of job descriptions, organization charts, procedures, and other written documents which describe and define how individuals should work with each other."[2]

The informal organization refers to a pattern of relationships that develops to both satisfy people's social needs and get work accomplished. Accordingly, "The nonformal structure is the pattern of relationships that emerges among people that are not specified in written documents. It is their behavior."[3] A successful integration of the formal and informal structures is illustrated by an incident that took place in a medium-sized company.

A company that manufactured snow shovels found itself suddenly faced with an unprecedented backlog of orders during the winter of 1976–

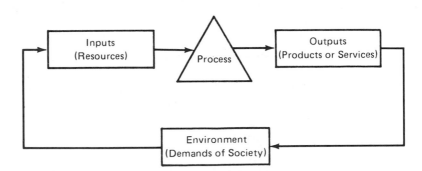

FIGURE 12.1
Organizations are part of a larger system.

SOURCE: James L. Gibson, John M. Ivancevich, and James H. Donnelly, Jr, *Organizations: Structure, Process, Behavior,* rev. ed., Business Publications, 1976, p. 62.

1977. Reliance on the formal structure alone would have made it very difficult to meet such demand. A company policy states, "We shall not incur additional manufacturing costs due to shipping charges levied by suppliers. Suppliers are therefore not authorized to charge us shipping costs for any method of special delivery."

Literal application of this rule would have made it impossible to receive a rush shipment of plastic needed for shovel blades. The head of manufacturing therefore sought an ethical and constructive way around this policy. His decision was to rent a truck for purposes of picking up 1000 pounds of plastic at their usual supplier. The truck rental fee was then allocated to "business travel." By this informal bending of the formal structure, an emergency situation was solved without violating a company rule. This judicious use of the informal organization was possible because the manufacturing head had not used up his business travel budget for the quarter.

A SYSTEMS VIEWPOINT

A modern perspective for understanding the nature of organizational effectiveness is that of systems theory.[4] As diagrammed in Figure 12.1, an organization is seen as part of a larger system (society itself). An effective organization makes wise use of natural resources (inputs) by processing them (process) into something useful (outputs) for society. As these outputs are placed in the environment, the effective organization changes in response to new demands from the environment. Often this means using different inputs.

A business analogy will help explain these relationships further. An automobile dealership uses the *inputs* of (1) new and used automobiles and (2) people in the form of office, shop, and sales personnel in order to provide a service to the public. The cars taken into the dealership are *processed* to the extent that they are prepared for sale and displayed on a lot or in a showroom. Offering financing and insurance programs to the public is part of the process that takes place in the dealership. The *output* is private transportation for the public. As tastes and requirements change (for example, a demand for more energy-efficient autos), the dealership receives *feedback*. Such feedback helps inform the dealer and the manufacturer what types of inputs (new cars) the dealer should be offering next. As long as the dealership responds to the tastes of the public in an efficient manner (without going bankrupt), it will be able to meet its objective of delivering cars to the public (organizational effectiveness).

The Organization as an Open System. In recent years, the systems perspective of organizations has become dominant. Fremont E. Kast and James E. Rosenzweig have contributed heavily to this view of organizational life. Their concept of the organization as an open system is particularly helpful in trying to comprehend the complexities of an effective or efficient organization. No organization exists in isolation. Its effectiveness and survival are contingent upon how it relates to the world outside. Kast and Rosenzweig explain:[5]

> The organization can be considered in terms of a general open systems model . . . . The open system is in continual interaction with its environment and achieves a "steady state" or dynamic equilibrium while still retaining the capacity for work or energy transformation. The survival of the system, in effect, would not be possible without continuous inflow, transformation, and outflow . . . . The system must receive sufficient input of resources to maintain its operations and also to export the transformed resources to the environment in sufficient quantity to continue the cycle.
>
> For example, the business organization receives inputs from the society in the form of people, materials, money, and information; it transforms these into outputs of products, services, and rewards to the organizational members sufficiently large to maintain their participation. For the business enterprise, money and the market provide a mechanism for recycling of resources between the firm and its environment. The same kind of analysis can be made for all types of social organizations . . . .

SELECTED MEASURES OF ORGANIZATIONAL EFFECTIVENESS

No single measure or *criterion* determines whether or not an organization is effective. A criminal group may meet all its objectives of providing money for itself, yet the harm done to people in the process negates its effectiveness. A fish and tackle shop in the Rocky Mountains may satisfy its customers, refrain from polluting the environment, and operate at a slight loss. Few people would view this as an effective organization. Ultimately, what constitutes an effective organization depends upon a person's values—what he or she thinks is important. A variety of measures of organizational effectiveness is described next to help you appreciate the complexity of defining what constitutes an effective organization. It is much like defining what constitutes an effective person.

Goal attainment is the most general measure of effectiveness. When an organization accomplishes what it sets out to accomplish, it can be said to be effective. Assuming that its goals are not destructive or harmful to others, there is much to be said for this criterion.

Making a profit is often considered to be the single most important measure of organizational effectiveness for a business. Unless an organization makes a profit, it cannot afford to accomplish other objectives, such as making charitable contributions or providing job training to culturally disadvantaged people. Yet an overemphasis on profit can result in such practices as firing people indiscriminately or overworking employees. It would be difficult to call a business organization effective that did not turn a profit, yet profit cannot be the sole criterion.

Staying within budget is a nonprofit organization's equivalent of making a profit. Unless an organization stays within its budget, it risks losing much of its public support. People who work for nonprofit organizations must be as budget conscious as those employed by businesses. Nonprofit organizations that overspend risk "going out of business."

Social responsibility has become an important criterion of organizational effectiveness. Corporate social responsibility has been defined as the serious attempt to solve social problems caused wholly or in part by the corporation.[6] One example is a distillery that chooses to attack the social problems of alcoholism. If it were not for distilleries, people would not have a legal means of consuming alcoholic beverages.

Making efficient use of inputs relative to outputs is a systems theory measure of efficiency.[7] The production of pacemakers (devices to trigger the heart back to normal functioning when it stops beating) would represent an efficient act. The amount of materials, money, and human resources consumed is small in relation to the output—a life-saving device.

Producing outputs of services or goods is another commonsense measure of an effective organization. An organization that provides what it is designed to provide is justifying its own existence. If a singles club affiliated with a church turns out large numbers of events (such as picnics and dances) where singles can meet, that club is effective in that one important respect.

Performing technical and administrative tasks rationally can be an index of an effective organization. "Rationally" in this context means that the most satisfactory means are used to attain an objective. In an aircraft company studied by one researcher this meant (1) investing time and money into aeronautical research and (2) using a decentralized organization structure.

Societal values influence whether or not an organization can be considered effective. When certain key groups in society are satisfied, we can say that the organization is doing its job. In one study of ninety-seven small businesses,[8] the researchers identified seven different groups (parties at interest) who have a vested interest in the welfare of the company. To the extent that these parties at interest are satisfied, the organization can be classified as effective.

The seven groups are customers, creditors, suppliers, employees, owners, the community, and the government. Many of the expectations these groups have of a small business are similar; for example, all groups want the company to stay in operation. Other concerns are more meaningful to one group than another. The government is strongly interested in a given company obeying safety regulations, whereas a creditor would be more concerned about prompt payment of bills.

Stability refers to an organization's ability to maintain its basic character and size over time.[9] A company such as Prudential Insurance is considered stable because it continues to be a dominant influence in the life insurance business and is not subject to wide fluctuations in employment. A company like Lockheed Aircraft is much less stable, and therefore less effective from that criterion.

Integration has been defined as the *ability of the organization to avoid conflict among its members*. A company may require some conflict to be effective (as described in Chapter 5), but too much conflict detracts from effectiveness. When people conform to the same code of conduct, conflict is usually held in check.

Voluntarism is the extent to which people want to continue as members of the organization. When most of the members want to leave at the earliest opportunity, it can be concluded that the organization is ineffective. Among the exceptions are hospitals and prisons, where most of the employees want to remain, but the patients and prisoners, respectively, want an early exit.

Number of products or services has some utility as a measure of an effective organization. A company with a limited product line may be in a perilous condition. A fund-raising organization that collects money for only one disease may also be in trouble. A cure might be suddenly found that would necessitate an intensive search for a new disease to conquer.

Number of clients leaving under favorable circumstances has also been used as a measure of effectiveness. Hospitals, schools, and prisons must all stand up against this criterion. Ideally, a long-range measurement should be taken several years after a client leaves to determine if the organization was successful. If 95 percent of "cured" people return to a drug rehabilitation center within six months, we might conclude that the center is not effective.

Survival is a comprehensive criterion of effectiveness. When an organization survives over time, it can be concluded that it in some way is meeting the needs of some section of society. A 100-year-old college is probably performing a legitimate service. A 100-year-old bank can probably be trusted. A home-building company that has been in business in the same community for forty years has undoubtedly earned a favorable reputation.

FACTORS CONTRIBUTING TO ORGANIZATIONAL EFFECTIVENESS

So far we have been concerned with output measures of effectiveness. To achieve favorable outputs, such as productivity, profits, or favorable discharge of clients, organizations must possess favorable characteristics. A key issue is to identify those characteristics of a favorable versus unfavorable organization. Broadly conceived, this task is the study of human relations. Most of what has been said or will be discussed in this book is related to organizational effectiveness. To illustrate, an organization will probably be effective when it successfully handles such processes as motivating employees, leading them, minimizing harmful job politics, managing conflict, providing appropriate training, and communicating accurately.

To limit our discussion of factors contributing to organizational effectiveness to manageable proportions, attention will be directed to a selected number of characteristics that have been associated with healthy, adaptable organizations. The characteristics chosen refer to the psychological rather than the physical or financial aspects of an organization.

Organizational Mental Health. An organization, similar to a person, tends to be effective when it possesses what amounts to good mental health. The following are four such characteristics of a healthy organization:[10]

1. *Adaptability:* problem-solving ability combined with the capacity to react with flexibility toward changing environmental demands.

2. *A sense of identity:* an organization has a sense of identity when it is aware of what it is and what it is trying to accomplish. When people in the organization see it as it is seen by others, a sense of identity is fostered. The Mayo Clinic and the Boston Celtics represent organizations with a strong sense of identity.

3. *Capacity to test reality:* the ability to see the environment as it objectively exists, particularly in matters that concern the organization. When Sears & Roebuck realizes its stronghold lies with Middle America, it shows a good sense of reality testing.

4. *Integration among the subparts of the organization:* when the subparts are not in severe conflict or working at cross purposes, integration is achieved. When employees believe that they can prosper in an organization only by lying and stealing, the opposite of integration has occurred. When the various departments of a company realize that only through teamwork will they all succeed, integration occurs.

Effective Coping. An effective organization has good coping mechanisms. When problems arise, the organization rises to the occasion and makes the necessary adjustments. Edgar H. Schein[11] has identified four organizational conditions he believes are associated with effective coping:

1. The ability to take in and communicate information reliably and validly. An active market-research department could help an organization in this regard.

2. Internal flexibility and creativity to make the changes that are demanded by the information obtained. One hospital recognized that the demand for child delivery would be shrinking drastically in the forth coming decade. By closing its obstetrical ward and converting it to a surgical ward, the hospital improved its financial position.

3. Integration and commitment to the goals of the organization from which comes the willingness to change. When members take seriously the organization's desire to trim costs, effective cost cutting can be achieved. They will save money wisely, but not do things that could injure the organization—such as diluting the quality of the product.

4. "An internal climate of support and freedom from threat, since being threatened undermines good communication, reduces flexibility,

and stimulates self-protection rather than concern for the system." When the threat of being fired is held over those who fail to perform adequately, the result is often minimum compliance (doing just enough to get by) and high voluntary turnover.

Organic Organizations. The opinion that an effective organization is one that adapts readily to change is further reinforced by the observations of John B. Miner.[12] His list of the characteristics of an *organic* organization is similar to the favorable internal organizational conditions just mentioned.

1. A close and direct relationship between the expectations of people and organizational goals. A college that has a specific fund-raising department would fit this characteristic.

2. Continual redefining of what is expected of people through discussion with the people most intimately involved. As times change, so would job descriptions.

3. Rejection of the "it's not my responsibility" response as an excuse for failures. In an effective organization people are eager to enlarge their contribution.

4. The feeling of wanting to contribute to the larger organization without having to always receive specific inducements for accomplishing specific tasks. Under these conditions people take pride in making a worthwhile contribution.

5. The presence of needed information at appropriate places in the organization. When a few key people attempt to monopolize all the information and dispense it in small doses, many inefficiencies occur.

6. Emphasis on horizontal as opposed to vertical communication. People consult with each other rather than place demands on each other according to their rank (formal power). In an effective organization, peers identify problems and take care of them without the impetus of orders issued from above.

7. A strong commitment to goals that further the organization rather than to goals that involve simply maintaining what already exists. Similarly, a tendency not to be too ingrown; instead a tendency to look favorably toward outside reference groups. A manager who spent excessive time on "housekeeping" instead of figuring out how he or she could further the company would thus in a small way be contributing to organizational ineffectiveness.

WASTEFUL ORGANIZATIONAL PRACTICES

A general reason that many organizations fail to attain a state of effectiveness is that they engage in many wasteful practices.[13] Several of these practices have been the subject of satire. Although as satire they are exaggerated, a discussion of organizational efficiency warrants some mention of these practices.

Parkinson's Most Famous Law. Almost anyone who has worked in a complex organization has heard about C. Northcote Parkinson's statement that "Work expands so as to fill the time available for its completion."[14] Parkinson also formulated several other satirical observations, called *laws*, about the waste and inefficiency taking place is so many organizations. His most famous law can be illustrated by several incidents.

1. Parkinson found that between 1914 and 1928 the number of officers and enlisted men in the British Royal Navy decreased from 146,000 to 100,000.[15] Over the same period the number of large ships decreased from 62 to 20. Paradoxically, the number of officials in the British Admirality Headquarters increased during this period at the average annual rate of 5.6 percent.

2. One steno pool was asked to increase its workload about 20 percent, and simultaneously decrease the number of typists from seven to five. The manager at first complained stating that such demands were exorbitant. After two months experience with the new arrangement, she found that typing efficiency (measured in amount of work processed that met company requirements) actually increased. In the past, typists and stenographers simply took more time to perform routine functions such as changing typewriter ribbons and filing correspondence.

The Organizational Multiplier. Herbert G. Hicks and C. Ray Gullett use the term *organizational multiplier* to denote a wasteful practice in which an organization feeds on itself more than serving its real purpose.[16] Unlike Parkinson, they are not speaking tongue in cheek. Essentially, the practice refers to a condition in which many people in the organization wind up taking care of each other rather than clients or customers. Many fund-raising organizations, for example, spend about 90 percent of contributions on administrative costs. When an organization begins to hire additional staff people just to serve other staff people, the multiplier is at work.

An organizational multiplier can work in this fashion: a company grows from 200 to 300 people on the basis of a substantial new contract. No longer can the office manager handle all the personnel problems. So a full-fledged personnel department is formed. The new personnel department of five people soon recognizes that it needs more office space. Since conditions are cramped already, a temporary building (a mobile-home-type building) is purchased to house the personnel department. The addition of one more building to the company complex now requires that one more worker be added to the maintenance staff. The addition of the new temporary building has also created so much paper work for the facilities planning department that another clerk is added. In larger organizations, the multiplier effect is even more devastating.

The Administrative Waltz. Two organizational satirists, G. Singer and Meredith Wallace, have formulated the idea of the administrative waltz, which they define as "A queer sort of trance dance where the dominant partner is always an administrator. He or she performs all the leading steps and you have no option but to follow."[17] Basically, the waltz refers to the overintrusion of administrators into organizations, thus leading to inefficiency and ineffectiveness. Two aspects of the waltz can be used to illustrate its nature.

1. *The doctrine of functional autonomy* states that an administrative unit will tend to develop until it becomes completely independent. Singer and Wallace cite the example of an audiovisual unit in a school system, which is originally set up to improve communications:[18]

> The head of one such unit in a large university found that as the popularity of the service grew the staff had to be doubled. As the demand started to snowball, he devised a multiplex system of writing requests designed to make more equitable use of the service he offered. New systems for storage and maintenance of equipment and materials, spare parts, and stock records kept on growing. Demands on space, vehicles, and computers increased proportionately. It was fortunate that during this period requests for assistance from the academic staff declined sharply. This falloff occurred because waiting time for audiovisual equipment had escalated from one day to five months and because members of staff found that the filling in of request forms and provision of statistics of usage exceeded their mental and physical capacities.

2. *The doctrine of conservation of matter* states that once an administrative unit has been set up it becomes indestructible.[19] For example, a tea-tasting bureau of the U.S. government lived some 100 years beyond its needed purpose.

Summary of Key Points

1. In broadest terms, an effective organization is one that achieves its goals. An efficient organization is one that uses a minimum of resources to get things accomplished.

2. To remain effective, an organization must change in response to feedback from the environment.

3. A useful way of determining organizational effectiveness is to use multiple measures or criteria. These include the following:
   a. Goal attainment.
   b. Making a profit.
   c. Staying within budget.
   d. Social responsibility.
   e. Efficient use of resources.
   f. Production of goods or services.
   g. Rational performance of tasks.
   h. Meeting societal values.
   i. Stability of function and size.
   j. Avoidance of conflict (integration).
   k. Voluntarism.
   l. Number of products or services.
   m. Number of people "graduating."
   n. Survival.

4. Certain factors or intervening variables contribute to organizational effectiveness. Among the many factors in this category are the following:
   a. Organizational mental health: adaptability, a sense of identity, capacity to test reality, and integration among the subparts.
   b. Effective coping characterized by (1) valid processing of information, (2) flexibility and creativity, (3) commitment to organizational goals, and (4) high emotional support and low threat.
   c. Being an organic organization, one that adapts readily to change.
5. Wasteful organization practices detract from organizational effectiveness. These include (a) Parkinson's laws, (b) the organizational multiplier, and (c) variations of the administrative waltz, such as the doctrine of functional autonomy.

1. Suppose that you were asked to head a task force to determine if a particular hospital were an effective organization. How would you go about finding an answer to this question?
2. Provide an example of an organization familiar to you that is effective but not efficient.
3. Provide an example of an organization familiar to you that is efficient but not effective.
4. Identify the *most* effective organization you know of. On what basis did you reach your conclusion?
5. Identify the *least* effective organization you know of. On what basis did you reach your conclusion?
6. In your opinion, what characteristics of an organization are the most influential in determining whether or not it will be effective? Do not necessarily confine yourself to factors mentioned in this chapter or book.

A Human Relations Incident
THE FUEL-HUNGRY FURNACES

You are working as an administrative assistant to the manufacturing vice-president at Allied Heating Equipment Company. After eight months on the job, you have learned to admire the manufacturing efficiency of the company and its impressive earnings records. One day you ask your boss why Allied has become so successful in a field you think is competitive. He answers:

"No mystery there. Through certain economies in manufacturing we are able to price our furnaces about twenty-five percent below the competition. This way we are the favorites of the large home developers who are trying to cut corners."

Still curious about the reasons for the success of your company, you decide to conduct some informal market research. After speaking to about ten homeowners who have Allied furnaces, one consistent complaint is sounded: the furnaces consume much more fuel than the owners believed they would. You inform your boss of your findings. He now comments:

"Why should we care at Allied? It's hard to please both the builder and the homeowner. It's the builders whom we are trying to impress. They want to save dollars and don't care too much about their customers' fuel bills. When we get complaints from the builders, I'll start worrying."

You begin to wonder if you are really working for an effective organization. What should you do about your concerns?

A Human Relations Case
MANAGEMENT INSISTS UPON CERTAIN STANDARDS OF PERSONAL CONDUCT

A company listed on the New York Stock Exchange currently circulates a document about rules of personal conduct to its manufacturing employees. It is presented next without any editing or paraphrasing.

COMPANY STANDARDS OF PERSONAL CONDUCT

It is our belief that our employees desire to be efficient in their work and conduct themselves with a proper regard for the rights of others. Therefore, these standards are not designed to restrict the rights of anyone, but rather to define them and thus protect the rights of all.

ATTENDANCE

1. Be at your work station on time.

2. Do not punch in or out for anyone else except yourself.

3. Do not punch in sooner than 15 minutes before the starting of your shift nor more than 10 minutes after it ends.

4. Report absences promptly.

5. Employees must notify their supervisor before they leave the plant or their work place. They must punch out when they leave the plant.

6. Do not be tardy or absent unless absolutely necessary.

7. Absences for three or more days without notice will result in disciplinary action.

HOUSEKEEPING AND REFRESHMENTS

1. Food and beverages must be obtained when production schedules and working conditions permit. It must be consumed only in designated areas.

2. Dispose of all trash in provided containers.

3. Dispose of cigarettes, cigars, and matches only in ashtrays or approved receptacles. Observe all no smoking signs and smoke only in designated areas.

4. Possession of or drinking of liquor or any alcoholic beverage while on company property or reporting for work under the influence of alcohol is not permitted.

SAFETY AND SECURITY

1. Observe all safety rules and practices and follow instructions regarding the use of safety equipment and devices.

2. All employees must enter and exit through the employee's entrance.

3. The theft or unauthorized use of any property (tools, equipment, records, confidential information) of other employees of the company is not permitted.

4. Do not operate machines, tools, or equipment unless authorized.

5. No visitors are allowed in the plant without prior approval of a management official. All visitors must obtain a pass.

6. Weapons are not allowed on company property.

7. Physical violence or fighting is not permitted.

8. Possessing, using, distributing, or selling narcotics, drugs, marijuana, or the like on company premises or reporting for work under the influence of drugs, narcotics, marijuana, or the like or otherwise in a condition which makes work performance doubtful or hazardous is not permitted. (Possession or the use of a narcotic while on company premises pursuant to a doctor's prescription and with the advance approval of the Plant Manager shall not constitute a violation of this standard.)

COMMUNICATIONS

1. Posting or removal of notices, signs, or written material of any form on bulletin boards or company property at any time must be authorized by the Plant Manager in writing.

2. Collecting contributions or soliciting for any purpose during work hours must be authorized by the Plant Manager in writing.

3. Distribution of written or printed matter of any description in the plant during working time is not permitted without specific written authorization from the Plant Manager.

4. Making or publishing false, vicious, or malicious statements concerning any employee, supervisor, the company, or its products is not permitted.

5. Do not refuse to do a job assigned or to obey an order of a supervisor.

6. Do not threaten, intimidate, coerce, or interfere with fellow employees.

7. Incoming personal phone calls will be received and messages forwarded to the individual's supervisor.

8. Emergency calls will be relayed to the individual's supervisor and then to the employee immediately.

9. Outgoing calls may be made with permission of the super-

visor, but should be made only when necessary and usually at breaks or lunch periods. Company phones must not be used for personal business unless authorized by the supervisor.

GENERAL

In addition to the above, the following are of a serious nature and, although not an exhaustive list, represent the type of conduct which may result in disciplinary action up to and including discharge.

1. Falsification of work, attendance, personnel, or other records.

2. Gambling on company property.

3. Failure to observe all rules governing traffic, speed, and parking while on company premises.

4. Failure to perform work according to instructions or established procedures, both as to quality and quantity.

5. Deliberate damage, destruction, or abuse of the property of others or of the company.

6. Negligence or carelessness resulting in damage or destruction to or loss of company property or the property of others.

Should disciplinary action become necessary in applying these rules, it will only result after full consideration of the nature of the offense, all facts surrounding it, and the work history of the individual. Disciplinary action may include verbal and written reprimand and warning, disciplinary layoff, or discharge. Such discipline is intended to be corrective rather than punitive with the purpose of instilling self-discipline in all employees.

1. How useful do you think the foregoing document is in fostering organizational effectiveness?

2. How useful would this document be in minimizing wasteful organizational practices?

3. What contribution do you think this document would make to increasing the level of employee motivation?

4. What might be the negative consequences to morale and productivity stemming from this document?

5. How would you personally react to these "standards of personal conduct" if you worked for the company?

FOOTNOTES

[1] This distinction has been made by several writers. An original source is Amitai Etzioni, *Modern Organizations,* Prentice-Hall, 1964, p. 8. See also E. J. Miller and A. K. Rice, *Systems of Organizations,* Tavistock Publications, 1967.

[2] Henry L. Tosi and Stephen J. Carroll, *Management: Contingencies, Structure, and Process,* St. Clair Press, 1976, p. 18.

[3] *Ibid.*

[4] James L. Gibson, John W. Ivancevich, and James H. Donnelly, Jr., *Or-*

ganizations: Structure, Process, Behavior, rev. ed., Business Publications, 1976, p. 62.

[5] Fremont E. Kast and James E. Rosenzweig, *Organization and Management: A Systems Approach*, 2nd ed., McGraw-Hill, 1974, p. 110.

[6] H. Gordon Fitch, "Achieving Corporate Social Responsibility," *Academy of Management Review*, Jan. 1976, p. 38.

[7] This and the following two measures are taken from Bertram M. Gross, "What Are Your Organization's Objectives? A General Systems Approach to Planning," *Human Relations*, Aug. 1965, pp. 195–215. Reprinted in Walter R. Nord (ed.), *Concepts and Controversy in Organizational Behavior*, Goodyear, 1972, pp. 297–319.

[8] Hal Pickle and Frank Friedlander, "Seven Societal Criteria of Organizational Success," *Personnel Psychology*, Summer 1967, pp. 165–178.

[9] Stability and the following two measures are mentioned by Theodore Caplow, *Principles of Organization*, Harcourt Brace, 1964, pp. 119–124.

[10] Edgar Schein, *Organizational Psychology*, 2nd ed., Prentice-Hall, 1970, p. 118.

[11] *Ibid.*, p. 126.

[12] John B. Miner, *The Management Process; Theory, Research, and Practice*, Macmillan, 1973, p. 270.

[13] The concept of wasteful organizational practices is developed at length in Herbert G. Hicks and C. Ray Gullett, *The Management of Organizations*, 3rd ed., McGraw-Hill, 1976, pp. 360–376.

[14] C. Northcote Parkinson, *Parkinson's Law*, Houghton Mifflin, 1957, p. 2.

[15] *Ibid.*, pp. 4–7.

[16] Hicks and Gullett, *op. cit.*, pp. 363–369.

[17] G. Singer and Meredith Wallace, *The Administrative Waltz*, Pergamon, 1976, p. xiii.

[18] *Ibid.*, p. 2.

[19] *Ibid.*, p. 3.

SUGGESTED READING

CAPLOW, THEODORE. *Principles of Organization*, Harcourt Brace, 1964.

GROSS, BERTRAM M. "What Are Your Organization's Objectives? A General Systems Approach to Planning," *Human Relations*, Aug. 1965, pp. 195–215.

FITCH, H. GORDON. "Achieving Corporate Social Responsibility," *Academy of Management Review*, Jan. 1976, p. 38.

HIRSCH, PAUL M. "Organizational Effectiveness and the Institutional Environment," *Administrative Science Quarterly*, Sept. 1975, pp. 327–342.

MACY, BARRY A., and MIRVIS, PHILIP H. "A Methodology for Assessment of Quality of Work Life and Organizational Effectiveness in Behavioral Economic Terms," *Administrative Science Quarterly*, June 1976, pp. 212–223.

MOTT, PAUL E. *The Characteristics of Effective Organizations,* Harper & Row, 1972.

PARKINSON, C. NORTHCOTE. *Parkinson's Law,* Houghton Mifflin, 1957.

PRICE, JAMES L. *Organizational Effectiveness: An Inventory of Propositions,* Irwin, 1968.

"Report of the Committee on Non-Financial Measures of Effectiveness," *The Accounting Review,* 1971, pp. 165–211.

SINGER, G., and WALLACE, MEREDITH. *The Administrative Waltz,* Pergamon, 1976.

13
ORGANIZATIONAL DEVELOPMENT

Learning Objectives

After reading and studying this chapter, you should be able to

1. Define in your own words, the term organization development (OD).
2. Explain how team building can help an organization.
3. Know the five key positions on the managerial grid.
4. Write three questions that could be used in a survey feedback approach to OD in your place of work or school.
5. Summarize the basic features of an MBO program.
6. Provide several important criticisms of OD.

Organization development (OD) is a general strategy for achieving the type of efficiency and effectiveness discussed in the last chapter. The term OD refers to both a variety of techniques for improving individual, small-group, and organizational effectiveness and a way of thinking about the quality of working life. Originally, OD referred to a strategy for improving organizational effectiveness by use of behavioral science techniques such as sensitivity training and organizational confrontation meetings. Today, OD practitioners include in their offerings such far-reaching techniques as organization restructuring, job enrichment, management by objectives, and transactional analysis.

The growth of OD is part of the human potential movement in work organizations. The vast majority of OD programs are designed to improve organizational effectiveness by helping people achieve more authentic (honest and open) relationships with each other. A composite formal definition[1] of OD will help the reader appreciate its scope:

OD relates to a large and diverse body of concepts and tools and techniques for improving an organization's effectiveness. At the heart of OD is the concern for vitalizing, energizing, activating, and renewing of organizations through technical and human resources.

Several OD techniques, such as organization confrontation meetings and encounter groups, have been described in earlier chapters. Here we shall examine five additional OD approaches. Equally important, we shall discuss the role of the OD practitioner and some important criticisms of organization development.

ROLE OF THE CONSULTANT OR CHANGE AGENT

A large group of people apply OD concepts and techniques to organizations. Originally, OD practitioners were organizational psychologists who worked with clients on a consulting basis. Now a wide variety of human relations specialists consider themselves "OD consultants." Included in their ranks are 1300 members of the OD network, a group of practitioners who meet twice a year to keep up with the latest in OD.[2] Outside consultants have now been joined by a large group of internal consultants who practice OD exclusively with their own organizations. Many of these people have job titles, such as organization development specialist.

Organization development practitioners are also referred to by such titles as "interventionist," "change agent," and "process consultant." Although confusing, such a diversity of titles does point to the two primary roles of the OD specialist. The traditional role is that of an observer who helps people solve their own problems. He or she does not give expert advice but encourages people to diagnose the true nature of their problems and arrive at workable solutions. Using this approach, the OD consultant will say to a client, "Here is what I see you doing. You talk to each other about budgets when the real issues are those of personality clashes. What are you going to do about it?" To be effective in such a role, the consultant must have a humanistic perspective—believe in both people's desire and capacity for constructive growth.

A newer role for the OD consultant is one of expert advisor (the traditional consulting role). He or she diagnoses the client's problems and then suggests a course of action that should remedy that problem. Acting in this role, an OD consultant might say, "My diagnosis of your problem is that your sales personnel are undermotivated. My solution is a program of job enrichment. The motivation of the sales force will increase if their jobs are made more exciting and meaningful." As W. Warner Burke[3] has noted, "The consultant himself has changed from a nondirective, purely process oriented practitioner to an authoritative specialist."

Many people believe it is difficult for an OD practitioner to be effective when he or she is part of the power structure that he or she is trying to change. People are more likely to trust you when you seem to be a neutral observer. A change agent from remote company head-quarters can thus work more effectively than a person permanently as-signed to that particular division. Several professors of human relations or organizational behavior have learned through experience that it is difficult to bring about organizational change in their own college. However, to the extent that the OD consultant deals in mostly technical changes (such as redesigning jobs)—and not personal issues—being an outsider is a much less significant factor.

TEAM BUILDING

The most popular form of OD (unless MBO is considered part of OD) is approaches geared toward improving the effectiveness of regular work groups. Top management readily sees the relevance of a program that promises to help people work more effectively with each other. Under-lying team building are two assumptions about group behavior.[4] First, in order for groups to work productively, they must cooperate and coordi-nate their work toward getting specific tasks accomplished. Second, the personal welfare and emotional needs of the group must be met. Team building works on both these aspects simultaneously. A general strategy is for the team builder (consultant, change agent) to help the group con-front the underlying issues that group members find frustrating. Once these are uncovered, it is hoped that tasks will more readily be accom-plished.

Team Building in a Food-Service Company.   Saga, a California institu-tional feeding contractor, emphasizes team building in their approach to OD. This involves grouping a manager at any level with his or her sub-ordinates into a team, usually 6 to 12 people. For instance, a food-service manager at a campus and his or her staff make up a team. "Every person is involved in two teams," says the vice-president of human relations, William Crockett,[5] "one with his boss and one with his subordinates. In most organizations you can get feedback only from your boss. In our groups, it works both ways. The concept of boss is to find the needs of one's subordinates and serve them."

A team-building session at Saga was reported in this manner:

> Attending the 10-hour session—the group's second—were nine female clerks and supervisors, their department manager, and a group leader. The group leader asked the participants to give their objectives for the session. After an OD film was shown, a clerk said she needed "to be ac-cepted by the group." The manager responded, "I've got a need to be-

long, too. I try to make people feel they are working with me rather than for me."

Rating sheets on how the group functioned as a team were filled out, and "feeling charts" were prepared on which members drew their relationships with colleagues. One clerk drew a tree topped by three coconuts labeled with the supervisors' names. "I think you are like coconuts—set high up and hard to get to," she said. A secretary told the manager she disliked his reading letters on her desk. "Seriously," he answered, "the next time it happens, slap my hand."

Although the costs and benefits of Saga's OD program would be difficult to measure, a company executive claims that the economics are very sound. He states that "Profitability is borne out by increased productivity." (Evaluating OD will be discussed later in this chapter.)

A Management Team Examines Communications Barriers. An OD consultant met with the management staff of a medium-sized company to help improve their functioning as a team. The president has asked the consultant to "Help my company get moving at the top." An approach to team development was agreed upon by the consultant, president, and

---

The reader should note that the team concept advanced at Saga fits exactly that proposed by the famous psychologist and management theorist, Rensis Likert. According to the *linking-pin concept*, "The capacity to exert influence upward is essential if a supervisor (or manager) is to perform his or her supervisory functions successfully." To be effective in leading his or her own work group, a boss must be able to influence his own boss. He needs to be effective as both a superior and a subordinate. This relationship is illustrated symbolically in Figure 13.1.

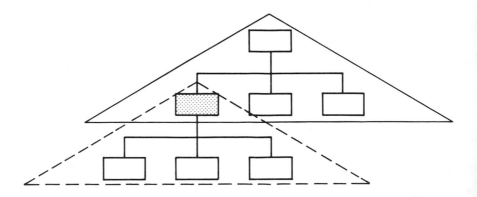

FIGURE 13.1
The linking-pin concept whereby the supervisor represents the group in the next level of management.

SOURCE: Rensis Likert, *New Patterns of Management*, McGraw-Hill, 1961, p. 14.

personnel manager that involved overcoming communications barriers among the staff. The group met for three 3-hour sessions to accomplish their objective of lessening communication barriers among themselves. Next is a sampling of the interchange that took place during the second session.

Consultant: We've been batting around the periphery for too long now. Let's get down to specifics about the communication barriers that you are facing. I want each person to let the others in the group know specifically the nature of the biggest communication problem facing you in your work.

Fred (sales manager): I'll be first. I'm not trying to get rid of our beloved president [nervous laughter from the group] but I do have a bone to pick with Bernie. Because you were a sales manager yourself Bernie, you tend to second-guess me on my decisions. You have an irresistible impulse to modify my plans. That's why I hesitate to come to you on most problems. I'm not really looking for my mind to be changed.

Gerry (production manager): Now that Fred has leveled with our president, I guess there's no reason for any of the rest of us to hold back. Gloria makes it very difficult for me to get new employees into the shop. She sets up so many tight restrictions that nobody seems good enough to work for us. Angelo, my shop superintendent, was really miffed when Gloria said his nephew wasn't qualified for our tool and die maker apprentice training program.

Gloria (personnel manager): I have a comment similar to the one Fred made about Bernie. I think Bernie makes far too many personnel decisions. Bernie are you the president or the personnel manager?

Bernie (president): At this point I think I may apply for a foreman's position out on the floor [group laughs]. Seriously Gloria, and the rest of you, my impression has always been that you people should learn to act more independently. You seem to want my approval on even minor matters. Communications would be much smoother here if you didn't come to me with so many picayune problems.

Holly (engineering manager): The biggest communication problem I have relates to Fred. I'm a straightforward person. As you all know, I'm certainly not a politician. Fred is so devious at times that I have a hard time working with him. When Fred tells me something, I'm never sure if that's the same story he has told Bernie or a customer.

The above interchange led to an improvement in team functioning. A major misperception that surfaced related to relationships with Bernie. Fred and Gloria thought that Bernie wanted to influence most decisions, while Bernie thought his staff demanded such behavior. Gloria and Gerry spent more time together reviewing hiring standards. As a result, a few workable compromises were made. For instance, the high school diploma requirement for a few jobs was dropped. One minor casualty

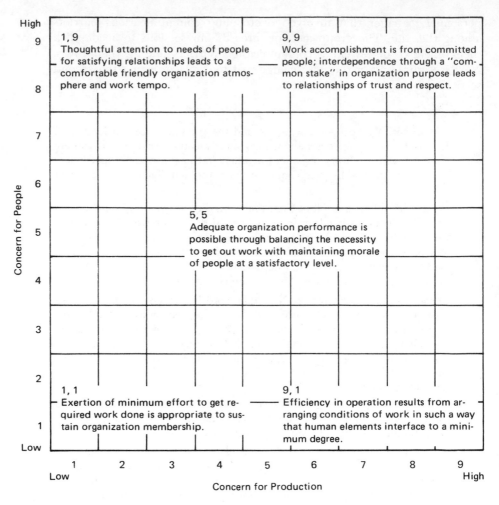

FIGURE 13.2
The managerial grid ® Scientific Methods, Inc.

SOURCE: Robert R. Blake and Jane S. Mouton, *Corporate Excellence Through Grid Organization Development,* Gulf, 1968, p. 15. Reproduced with permission.

from the sessions was that the relationship between Fred and Holly became more cool and distant.

GRID ORGANIZATION DEVELOPMENT (THE MANAGERIAL GRID)

The popular grid approach to organization development endeavors to make individuals and organizations more effective by bringing about changes in attitudes and values.[6] The OD program is built up on a framework for understanding leadership styles, as shown in Figure 13.2.

Leadership styles in the grid system are classified according to one's ratings on two key dimensions of leadership behavior: concern for production and people. These two dimensions are extensions and popularizations of the concepts of *initiating structure* and *consideration* stemming from a long series of studies conducted at the Ohio State University.[7]

Initiating structure is used to describe the degree to which the leader initiates structure for subordinates by activities such as assigning specific tasks, specifying procedures to be followed, scheduling work, and clarifying work of subordinates. Traditional management functions such as planning, organizing, and controlling are aspects of initiating structure.

Consideration describes the degree to which the leader creates an environment of emotional support, warmth, friendliness, and trust by engaging in such behaviors as being friendly and approachable, looking out for the personal welfare of the group, keeping the group abreast of new developments, and doing small favors for the group.

In the grid system, concern for production, which reflects the amount of emphasis the leader places on task accomplishment, is represented on the horizontal scale. Concern for people, or the amount of emphasis the leader places on responding to the requirements of people, is represented on the vertical scale. Five key positions are found on the grid, each representing a different combination of concern for people and production:

Lower right corner (9, 1): indicates a great deal of concern for output (production) and a minimum of concern for the people who are expected to produce. A manager using this style assumes people basically dislike work, so he or she pushes hard to make them produce.

Lower left corner (1, 1): indicates a manager with little concern for production or people. He or she has psychologically surrendered, having little hope that things will improve.

Middle of the grid (5, 5): indicates the compromising style in which there is medium concern for both people and production. This leadership style assumes that there is conflict between the needs of the organization and its members. His or her solution is to resolve conflict through compromise.

Upper left corner (1, 9): represents a maximum concern for the welfare of people, but little concern for the production or output requirements of modern organizational life. A manager using this style assumes that pressing for output is incompatible with the basic needs of people.

Upper right corner (9, 9): represents the ideal—maximum concern for both production and people. A manager using this style assumes that people are basically responsible. Given rewarding work to which they are committed, maximum output will result. The developers of the grid are careful to point out that there is no one best way to manage people.

Under certain circumstances the 9, 9 approach may not be best. For example, there is no 9, 9 best way of getting prisoners who are going over the wall back into their cells. Similarly, a 9, 1 style might be useful in leading people who are forced to work in jobs that they basically dislike. Effective managers generally have a regular and a backup style to use in emergencies or unusual circumstances.

Phase 1 consists of managerial grid laboratory–seminar training, emphasizing the theory of effectiveness that underlies the grid program. Concepts about the various leadership styles are taught at this stage of the program.

Phase 2 gives managers a chance to develop and analyze their managerial styles and group practices. Building upon these skills, phase 3 involves an examination of the interrelationships of related organizational units. An important objective here is joint problem solving.

Phase 4 involves top management working with lower-ranking groups to develop an ideal corporate model for managing the organization in the future. Phase 5 follows with exercises designed to help the organization move toward the model developed in phase 4. Much of this involves people receiving honest feedback from each other (an essential element of many OD approaches).

In Phase 6, the capstone, the achievements of earlier phases are evaluated, with the objective of working through problem areas and taking corrective action.

THE SURVEY FEEDBACK APPROACH

A well-structured, well-organized approach to organization development with a long history of good performance is the survey feedback technique. In essence, it involves (1) taking a survey of organizational problems through questionnaires and/or interviews, (2) reporting these results back to the organization, and (3) developing action plans to overcome the problems uncovered.

Administering the Survey. A survey designed by a specialist in attitude measurement is administered to a total organization, a subunit, or a representative sample of either. Both multiple-choice and write-in items are generally used on the questionnaire, as illustrated in Figure 13.3.

Feedback Sessions. After an analysis of the survey results has been conducted, the information is fed back to survey participants. Both items of relevance to most organizations and a few company-specific items are included. For example, if the human relations specialist developing the

	Strongly Disagree	Disagree	Neutral	Agree	Strongly Agree
We have a major communications problem around here.	_____	_____	_____	_____	_____
Few people listen to each other in our company.	_____	_____	_____	_____	_____
Our management makes all the decisions.	_____	_____	_____	_____	_____
Few people leave our company voluntarily.	_____	_____	_____	_____	_____

Sample Write-in Question

In your opinion, what are the two or three biggest problems facing this company? Write your answer in the space provided. Use the back of this page if necessary.

_____

_____

_____

_____

FIGURE 13.3
Sample questionnaire items from an OD survey.

questionnaire knew that tight budgets were recently imposed in the company, a question like this might appear:

Our budgets are realistic and fair.

Strongly
disagree_____   Disagree_____   Neutral_____

Agree_____   Strongly agree_____

When is a good time to conduct an organizational survey? Experience suggests that the best time is when the organization is not undergoing a major change. Also, general conditions should not be unusually good (such as the acquisition of a major contract) or particularly bad (a major layoff). Administering the survey under "normal" conditions helps to provide data that are not basically a reaction to temporary conditions.

The opinion is often expressed that a survey should not be administered unless people in the organization trust each other. According to this reasoning, distrust leads to response bias. Although this opinion is logical, a survey OD technique is designed to uncover such problems. Unless the survey is conducted, the distrust problem may not be resolved. The OD practitioner first meets with members of top management to discuss the findings and some of their implications. Next, meetings are held with organizational families (regular work groups such as departments) to discuss the findings. In years past, more emphasis was placed upon sending written summaries of the results to participants. Such an approach is devoid of emotional involvement, thus losing its effectiveness as an OD technique.

Develop Actions Plans. A major difference between OD and merely "conducting a survey" is contained in this step. Participants are asked their recommendations about how some of the problems uncovered in the survey should be resolved. A final report of the survey is not released until the action plans developed by people at several levels in the organization have been incorporated. At the University of Michigan Survey Research Center, the following rule has been formulated:[8]

> No report containing recommendations based solely on their own analysis of data will be given to the client. Instead, they present data in preliminary form and involve members of the client organization in interpreting the data and deciding on specific courses of action.

A dominant theme uncovered in an OD survey conducted in upstate New York was that employees were unsure of the future of their company. Many people wrote in comments such as "Rumors have it that our plant will be closed within six months. That's no way to live when you have a daughter ready for college." The action plan developed by middle management was straightforward and workable. They suggested an open meeting with top management to discuss the future of the company at that location. Top management complied. In the meeting it was explained that the rumors had a grain of truth, but were essentially incorrect. The company would not close the plant, but all expansion would take place in states with a lower tax rate and utility rates.

Follow-up. Without continuous feedback and correction, OD fails, or at best is a short-lived, interesting experience. Several months after the OD survey is conducted, a check should be made to determine if the action plans developed in the earlier stages are being implemented. In one company an action plan was developed to realign the wage scale of first-line supervision. A three-month checkup revealed that nothing had been done. Prodding by the OD consultant and a representative from first-line supervision helped management begin some long-needed changes.

Management by objectives has gained widespread acceptance in business and nonprofit organizations as a way of improving organizational effectiveness. In recent years, MBO programs have been included in the general category of OD techniques, even though MBO can properly be considered a system of management. A major purpose of MBO is to provide everybody included in the program with specific work targets (objectives). To the extent that managers and nonmanagers reach these objectives, they are considered successful in their work. At its best, MBO is considered a systematic way of managing an organization. An essential feature of MBO is that people have a large say in determining both the objectives that they are striving for and how they will reach them.

Common Elements in an MBO Program. MBO lacks a format that is uniformly applied in every organization, but certain key elements can be found in most programs. A true MBO program always involves people setting some objectives for themselves. However, management frequently imposes key organizational objectives upon people. Five steps are usually followed in sequence:[9]

1. *Establishing organization goals.* Top levels of management set organizational goals to begin the whole MBO process. These goals are usually quite broad and at times philosophical. A group of hospital administrators, for example, might decide upon the general goal of improving health-care service to poor people in the community. After these broad goals are agreed upon, a determination is then made of what must be accomplished by divisions or units in order to meet the organization goals.

2. *Establishing unit objectives.* Unit heads then establish objectives for their units, and this process proceeds on down the line. Objectives set at lower levels of the organization must be designed to meet the general goals established by top management. Lower-level managers and individuals have a say because a general goal usually gives considerable latitude for setting individual objectives to meet that goal. The head of the inpatient admissions department might, for example, decide that he or she must work more closely with the county welfare department if the health-care goal cited above is to be met.

3. *Subordinate proposals.* At this point, subordinates make proposals about how they will contribute to unit objectives. For instance, the assistant to the manager of inpatient admissions might agree to set up a task force to work with the welfare department. Each subordinate is also given the opportunity to set some objectives in addition to those that meet the major organizational goals. Many MBO formats suggest that each person establish some personal and professional objectives in addition to the standard work objectives. Figure 13.4 shows the work objectives jointly set by one person and her boss.

4. *Joint negotiation or agreement.* Superior and subordinate get together in this stage to either agree on the objectives set by the subordinate or negotiate further. In the hospital illustration being used here, one department head might state that she wants to reserve ten beds on the ward for the exclusive use of indigent people. Her supervisor might commend her suggestion but point out that only five beds could be allocated for such purpose. They might settle for seven beds to be set aside for the needy poor.

5. *Reviewing performance.* After an agreed upon review cycle (typically once quarterly or semiannually), a performance review is held. A person receives a good performance review to the extent that he or she attained most of the major objectives. The suggestions for improving employee performance through coaching discussed in Chapter 10 are particularly relevant here. When objectives are not attained, the manager and his or her subordinate mutually analyze what went wrong and discuss corrective action. New objectives are set for the next review period. For example, one hospital manager agreed to establish a task force to investigate the feasibility of establishing satellite health-care facilities in poor sections of town.

Job Title and Brief Job Description

Case worker: Responsible for interviewing welfare applicants for public assistance. Serve as liaison person between agency and client. Provide clients assistance on matters of managing personal resources.

Objectives for Wanda Benjamin

1. By December 31, 1978, 15 percent of my clients will be able to live adequately without benefit of public assistance. I will accomplish this by helping them find employment or additional help from close relatives.

2. Improve my handling of hostile clients by using transactional analysis to achieve this end. I will attend a week-long TA workshop in February.

3. Decrease by 75 percent the number of case reports that I submit to my manager past their due date.

4. Increase by 20 percent the number of clients I serve by spending less time with my most troubled clients.

5. Will coordinate my efforts more closely with utility company to ensure that my clients do not spend cold nights without heat.

FIGURE 13.4
Memo form used in social agency for statement of objectives.

Problems with MBO. As with other forms of OD, MBO encounters numerous problems in practice. Many organizations have discarded their MBO program after an initial burst of enthusiasm. A general problem is that considerable training is required for people to effectively implement such a program. For example, few people are skilled in setting objectives that prove useful. If the objective is set too loosely, it offers small improvement over a job description. If the objective is too precisely defined, it can serve as a straitjacket. Three of the potential problems with MBO are discussed next.[10]

MBO Is a Very Time Consuming Process. For MBO to work well, substantial amounts of time must be devoted to its planning and implementation. Training programs have to be scheduled, elaborate forms have to be drawn, and countless hours have to be spent in superior–subordinate discussions about objective setting and reviews. If you view a manager's job as primarily one of implementing an MBO system, then the time is not excessive. An authoritarian organization in which superiors simply tell subordinates what has to be done and how to do it is a less time consuming system of management than MBO.

Objectives Can Become Obsessions. Under an MBO system, people realize that their job performance will be rated high to the extent that they reach all their objectives. Thus people have a tendency to invest most of their energies in reaching these objectives, even if more important job problems occur. One sales order specialist had agreed upon the objective of having a better organized, neater workplace. He put so much effort into attaining this objective that he resisted doing work that would create a disorganized condition in his work area. Unfortunately, this meant discouraging out of the ordinary inquiries—those that would require foraging through the files.

People Resist Being Measured. Many people who consider themselves professionals or technicians resent having their output measured. As one optometrist said when his medical clinic began to implement an MBO system, "Who needs some forms to tell me how to do my job. If I didn't know what to do when I came to work everyday, I shouldn't be practicing optometry." A related line of reasoning is that the work of many managers, staff, and professional people is difficult to measure precisely. Thus many believe that only people working in jobs where output can be precisely measured (such as a furniture maker) should be subject to MBO.

From this author's standpoint, the statement that MBO is not applicable to professional work is invalid. Although direct measures of professional output cannot always be made, inferred or indirect measures are sometimes a useful substitute. A staff physician might complain that his or her work cannot readily be measured; therefore, MBO does not apply to his situation. Yet, with careful analysis, several indirect measures might be used to measure his performance. Among these are (1) relative number of complaints about his care of patients, (2) ratings of the quality of his patient care by ward personnel such as nurses and paramedics, (3) his participation in medical seminars and the like, and (4) relative hospital stay of his patients.

A similar argument for the use of MBO with professionals and managers is that, if an individual is carrying out an action plan, it can be assumed that he or she is on the way to achieving an objective.[11] If a design engineer is trying to develop a new product, he or she might need to spend six months studying the competition. A review after four months might conclude that he or she is making progress, providing evidence is presented that he or she is in fact analyzing the competition.

The problems of MBO should be regarded as potential problems. Intelligent application of MBO gives an organization a chance of having people working together in a systematic, organized manner. At its best, MBO capitalizes upon the advantages of goal setting described at the outset of this book. Quite often the problems encountered with MBO systems stem from a lack of thorough training in its techniques or an explanation of its underlying philosophy. One engineer complained that, since he was a professional, he did not need to work under a system that kept score of his activities. His manager patiently explained that MBO gives top performers an opportunity to receive credit for outstanding contribution. Quickly the engineer realized that MBO documents good as well as poor performance.

EVALUATION OF ORGANIZATION DEVELOPMENT EFFECTIVENESS

A researcher would rightfully argue that no OD program is complete without an evaluation of the results obtained. In recent years, practitioners of OD have also become concerned with taking formal measurements of their efforts.[12] The subject of measuring the outcome of any training program or OD activity is complex, involving both knowledge of behavioral statistics and experimental design. Here we shall summarize the absolute minimum steps an organization should take to evaluate whether or not a given program of OD is contributing to organizational effectiveness.

Step 1: *Management must set objectives for the program.* Without a careful set of objectives, there is no sensible way to measure progress. Two objectives of an OD program might be to (1) decrease intergroup conflict between marketing and engineering and (2) increase the number of new products offered to the public by the company.

Step 2: *Before-measures must be taken on the relevant variables.* In this situation an attitude survey of the conflict might be taken. Objective questions as well as write-in comments would be used. Objective measures could readily be taken of new products released by the company.

Step 3: *Intervention of the OD activity.* A series of team development meetings and organization confrontation sessions might be held. A goal of these sessions might be to determine the factors that were contributing to conflict and blocking new ideas.

Step 4: *Establishment of control or contrast group.* Ideally, one part of the organization experiencing similar problems would receive the "before measures," but would not participate in the OD program. In practice, such a contrast or control group would be difficult to locate. Splitting the marketing and engineering groups in half would be inappropriate, because a measure such as "new products" involves a total departmental effort.

Step 5: *After-measures must be taken on the relevant variables.* The recommended procedure is to take measures at different time intervals, such as three and twelve months. Most human relations training programs or OD programs have a dramatic, short-range impact that lessens rather suddenly.

CRITICISM OF ORGANIZATION DEVELOPMENT

Organization development programs and practitioners have been subject to much criticism by both managers and management researchers. One division president passed an edict that no more OD programs would be conducted in his division. His objection was that group discussions about problems were stirring up discontent in the company. Researchers criticize OD because not enough solid research evidence supports its widespread application. This same criticism, however, is made by scholars about virtually every approach to improving human relations effectiveness. A student who browses through the *Journal of Applied Psychology* or *Administrative Science Quarterly* will discover that programs of group or individual change usually do not fare well under the scrutiny of a behavioral science researcher.

In defense of the OD practitioner, it is still very difficult to develop sensitive measures of the kinds of changes brought about by OD. Many an individual has said, "My boss is sure a changed person since he (or she) attended that encounter group. He's much easier to work for." Such anecdotal evidence may reflect worthwhile changes, but it is not easily translated into objective measures of improvement.

OD Overemphasizes Confrontation, Feelings, and Attitudes. Most forms of OD (excluding approaches such as job enrichment or MBO, which some might argue are not really OD) place heavy emphasis upon people leveling with each other about feelings, attitudes, and opinions. Such an emphasis on feelings often affords the program participant a temporary emotional lift or "high," but may not improve organizational effectiveness. Properly conducted, most people *feel better* after having been through an exercise such as a team development meeting, but they may not *act* better. In defense of its practitioners, most current OD approaches do emphasize establishing specific improvement goals.

OD Makes People Unfit for the Real World. A predominant value system of people who practice organization development is one characterized by a belief in openness, trust, and sharing of power. They are typically "up-front" people. After attending OD workshops, many people convert to such values and behaviors. Placed back in their own organization, instead of being rewarded for such behavior, they are sometimes punished.

> Karen, an accounting supervisor, spent a weekend at an encounter group designed to improve organizational communications. The message she received from the experience was to be more candid in criticizing subordinates, superiors, and colleagues. Back on the job four days, Karen's boss announced that payments to vendors would be one month late. He informed his staff to answer any complaints with the retort that "We had a computer malfunction, but it should be straightened out shortly." Karen complained to her boss that such a tactic was highly devious. Angrily, he replied, "When I want naive criticism from one of my supervisors, I'll ask for it."

OD Practitioners Are Engulfing Everything. Organization development as a formal activity began with social psychologists applying sensitivity training to business. This spawned offshoots of sensitivity training, such as the managerial grid and team building. Soon OD practitioners included such diverse activities as participative management, organizational design, and even individual counseling under the OD framework. A recent essay titled "A Comprehensive View of Organization Development" lists ten levels of change activities as part of OD.[13] Among these are company policies, and practices, personnel policies and practices, performance appraisal and improvement, and management development. The outsider is left to conclude that OD includes all human relations, organizational psychology, and management! A small group of practitioners that profess expertise in so many things is in danger of losing its credibility.

Summary
of Key Points

1. Organization development (OD) refers to a variety of behavioral science techniques and approaches for improving individual, small-group, and organizational effectiveness.

2. An OD consultant functions in two general ways: (a) as a catalyst

who helps people identify and solve their own problems, and (b) as an expert advisor who prescribes specific solutions to problems.

3. Team building is a popular form of OD aimed at helping natural work groups overcome communication problems, fostering teamwork in the process.

4. The grid approach to OD is a complex training program that has achieved worldwide popularity. An underlying assumption of the grid is that people can learn to manage in such a way that maximum output is achieved from committed people.

5. Another well-structured form of OD is the survey feedback approach whereby (a) organizational problems are revealed through a survey, (b) the results are fed back to people, and (c) plans for improvement are developed and implemented.

6. Management by objectives (MBO) is a system of management that both holds people accountable for results (achieving objectives) and allows them to participate in setting these objectives.

7. Organization development, as with other human relations techniques, has received much criticism. A major one is that confrontation of feelings and attitudes is too frequently prescribed as a solution to most organizational problems.

Questions for Discussion

1. How much job satisfaction do you think you would receive as an OD consultant? Explain.

2. What would you think is the biggest problem an OD consultant faces?

3. If you were in a team-building session with your boss, how candid would you be in criticizing him or her?

4. Where do you think you fit on the managerial grid? What information about yourself did you use to arrive at your conclusion?

5. How honest do you think people are in responding to organization surveys? What factors do you think influence the extent of their honesty?

6. State three personal objectives you might put in writing on an MBO form.

A Human Relations Incident
STOP MANIPULATING ME

You are the chief administrator of a foundling home that receives much of its support from the Community Chest. The Chest decides that every agency receiving support will operate under a management-by-objectives system. You spend one week in a training program on MBO and leave with a good understanding of what is required to operate the system. You hold a conference with your staff to announce the program.

As a starting point, you schedule a conference with Irene, the director of placement, who is in charge of placing children in foster homes. You ask Irene to complete a form that focuses on employee objective setting. You also ask her to meet with you again in one week to discuss her objectives.

On the agreed-upon date, you open the meeting with Irene in this manner, "Thanks for being here so promptly Irene. Could you please tell me what objectives you have established for yourself?" She replies, "Stop trying to manipulate me. They are your objectives and you know it. I won't be part of this deception."

What should be your approach to Irene?

A Human Relations Case
THE TARNISHED COMPANY IMAGE*

The Silverstone Corporation was the brainchild of Gordon Silverstone. Gordon persuaded his older brother John, a certified public accountant, and his younger brother Tom, a computer salesman, to join him in this enterprise. Recognizing that their personal resources were insufficient to really get the company going, they managed to secure financial backing from Brainbridge Corporation, which became the fourth principal stockholder of the company.

The organization of the company was built around the backgrounds of the three brothers. John, the accountant, was named as president and was responsible for the financial functions. Tom, the salesman, was installed as marketing vice-president, and Gordon, the technician, was also titled vice-president with responsibility for recruiting, staffing individual accounts, and generally managing the day-to-day operations.

Early in the company's history, Tom actively searched for business and managed to line up a few small initial programming contracts. Gordon was busy prospecting for some expert technicians (whom he called "eagles") to form the core of the staff; by use of such phrases as "ground-floor opportunity" and "employee stock option plan" he was successful in attracting three capable individuals.

These "eagles" rapidly performed the work called for by the programming contracts. Estimates were consistently beaten, the company began to develop an excellent reputation, and new business was becoming plentiful. As the amount of work grew, Gordon and the other technicians invested time in recruiting new personnel. The new people brought in more people and within two years the company employed thirty systems engineers (or SE's as the technicians were called) on the payroll. The Silverstone Corporation was a profitable operation from its very first year and the future looked bright.

Underrunning estimates became expected, thereby making them even more profitable to the company, which usually worked on a fixed-price

* Case researched and written by Paul R. Paulson.

basis. This resulted in many unpaid overtime hours for the SE's. Sixty-hour work weeks (and more) were common. No one seemed to mind since a true team spirit had developed, and, besides, it would be worth it in the end because, as Gordon would frequently say, "This company will belong to those who build it."

Within four years, the company had grown to 100 people and expanded geographically into five cities. In a number of cases the Silverstone brothers deliberately underestimated contract bids for the purpose of securing a foothold in a new market. They felt this approach was justified by the fact that the Silverstone SE's had traditionally underrun estimates and could be counted on to do so in the future.

The reason for the excellent track record the SE's had established on past contracts was primarily because of overtime effort. The effect of low-balling a contract bid, then, was to plan on this overtime effort and thereby remove the profit–loss cushion that it normally provided. Consequently, any error in the estimating procedure would result in an overrun condition even if the normal overtime effort was expended. This problem was compounded by the fact that many of the SE's were commuting (on a daily or weekly basis depending upon distances involved) from their homes to the client's work site in another city. The travel time involved made it difficult for the SE's to apply even the normal amount of overtime, and almost impossible for them to react to major problems with extended overtime.

The first seeds of discontent among the SE's had taken root and a general pressure for improved working conditions: less traveling and less over-time, higher pay (or at least some form of compensation for overtime), and, most importantly, the as yet unseen "piece of the action" (stock options). Gordon Silverstone's reading of this situation was that he was losing control of the SE's. The company, he reasoned, had grown to the point that he could no longer effectively manage all the SE's, spread around as they were. His response was to install Fred Maxwell (an older and well-liked SE) as SE manager. Fred's responsibility was to keep the SE's happy and productive, and lift from Gordon the burden of dealing with individual SE complaints.

It became apparent to both the SE's and Fred that he was not given the tools to do the job. He had no authority to grant pay increases, modify company policy with respect to overtime pay, or even discuss the stock-option question about which he knew nothing. In effect, Fred's real job was to act as a buffer to shield Gordon from the unhappy SE's. A quote attributed to Silverstone in describing Fred's function spread throughout the SE ranks. "He keeps the cattle off my back."

Within three months, five SE's left the company. Four months later a group of six SE's left to work for a client whose Silverstone contract had expired. Three weeks later all SE's were required to sign a document (the legality of which was questioned, but never tested) stating that no Silverstone SE could go to work for a current or previous Silverstone client within two years of the SE's separation from the company. There was a general acceptance of the idea that those who refused to sign (and there were some) might as well start looking for new jobs, since, although they might not be fired, they certainly had lost a lot of leverage within the company.

After much informal pressure had been brought to bear on the Silverstone brothers, primarily by the original group of SE's who had been with the company longest, the "key employee stock option plan" was announced. This was greeted with high expectations by the SE's, who assumed that their loyalty, hard work, and their long hours were finally being recognized.

As the details of the plan were made clear, however, the high expectations turned to deep disappointment. The company had, immediately before announcement of the plan, diluted the stock through a ten for one split. The stock was being made available to certain employees (at the discretion of the Silverstone brothers) in twenty-five share blocks. Each certificate carried on the back an agreement which said:

> These shares were purchased for investment purposes only. They cannot be sold to anyone without first offering Silverstone Corporation the option to buy them at the price originally paid by the employee. In the event of termination of employment for any reason, the employee must offer the shares to Silverstone Corporation at the original purchase price. These shares cannot be used as collateral for securing any type of debt.

The employees' reaction to this plan was that it was worse than worthless. The number of shares offered was so small as to be insignificant. Even if the stock greatly appreciated in value, the employees could not realize any cash gain if the company elected to exercise its option to buy at the original purchase price. The SE's were close to outrage. They felt cheated and insulted. Distrust of the Silverstone brothers was widespread. This general condition precipitated a new wave of quits, primarily among the older, original SE's, which included Fred Maxwell.

This further depressed morale among those left, who, at the same time, were being called upon to put forth greater effort to make up for the diminishing manpower. This extra effort, for the most part, was not forthcoming. Several important accounts were lost, and six years after its birth the company suffered its first loss. The reputation of the company was severely damaged. It became increasingly difficult to secure new business and more difficult still to attract competent computer professionals to the firm.

1. What do you think can be done to recapture the trust of the system engineers at Silverstone Corporation?
2. What approach to OD would you recommend for Silverstone Corporation?
3. Why do you think the situation at the company was allowed to deteriorate so badly without somebody taking corrective acion?
4. How might Gordon Silverstone have prevented the loss of effectiveness in his company?
5. What is the lesson or moral to be learned from this case?

[1] Based on definitions presented in Alan C. Filley, Robert J. House, and Steven Kerr, *Managerial Process and Organizational Behavior*, 2nd ed., Scott, Foresman, 1976, p. 487.

[2] W. Warner Burke, "Organization Development in Transition," *Journal of Applied Behavioral Science*, Jan. 1976, p. 24.

[3] *Ibid.*, p. 28.

[4] Edgar F. Huse and James L. Bowditch, *Behavior in Organizations: A Systems Approach to Managing*, Addison-Wesley, 1973, p. 293.

[5] "The 'Humanistic' Way of Managing People," *Business Week*, July 22, 1972, p. 48.

[6] Information about the managerial grid is found in virtually every recent text about human relations in business or organizational behavior. Two primary sources are Robert R. Blake and Jane S. Mouton, *Corporate Excellence Through Grid Organization Development*, Gulf, 1968; and Blake and Mouton, *The Managerial Grid*, Gulf, 1964.

[7] An excellent original source of information about this topic is Edwin A. Fleischman, "Twenty Years of Consideration and Structure," in Edwin A. Fleischman and James C. Hunt (eds.), *Current Developments in the Study of Leadership*, Southern Illinois University Press, 1973.

[8] George F. Wieland and Robert A. Ullrich, *Organizations: Behavior, Design, and Change*, Irwin, 1976, p. 504.

[9] The steps presented here are a synthesis of information found in Felix M. Lopez, Jr., *Evaluating Employee Performance*, Public Personnel Association, 1968, pp. 227–229; and Ross A. Webber, *Management: Basic Elements of Managing Organizations*, Irwin, 1975, pp. 347–350.

[10] A thorough discussion of problems with MBO is found in Webber, *op. cit.*, pp. 351–355. An analysis of the effective application of MBO is Robert N. Hollmann, "Applying MBO Research to Practice," *Human Resource Management*, Winter 1976, pp. 28–36.

[11] Stephen J. Carroll and Henry L. Tosi, *Organizational Behavior*, St. Clair Press, 1977, p. 404.

[12] Achilles A. Armenakis, Hubert S. Field, and Don C. Mosley, "Evaluation Guidelines for the OD Practitioner," *Personnel Journal*, Spring 1975, pp. 39–44.

[13] Richard J. Selfridge and Stanley L. Sokolik, "A Comprehensive View of Organization Development," in Henry L. Tosi, *Readings in Management: Contingencies, Structure, and Process*, St. Clair, 1976, pp. 309–328.

SUGGESTED READING

BERNARDIN, H. JOHN, and ALVARES, KENNETH M. "The Managerial Grid as a Predictor of Conflict Resolution Method and Managerial Effectiveness," *Administrative Science Quarterly*, Mar. 1976, pp. 84–92.

BOWERS, DAVID G. "Organizational Development: Promises, Performances, Possibilities," *Organizational Dynamics*, Spring 1976, pp. 50–62.

BLAKE, ROBERT R., and MOUTON, JANE S. *Building a Dynamic Corporation Through Grid*, Addison-Wesley, 1969.

BLAKE, ROBERT R., and MOUTON, JANE S. *Diary of an OD Man*, Gulf, 1976.

BURKE, W. WARNER (ed.). *New Technologies in Organization Development I*, University Associates, Inc., 1975.

FILLEY, ALAN C. *Interpersonal Conflict Resolution*, Scott, Foresman, 1975.

IVANCEVICH, JOHN M. "Changes in Performance in a Management by Objectives Program," *Administrative Science Quarterly*, Dec. 1974, pp. 563–574.

JAMIESON, BRUCE D. "Behavioral Problems with Management by Objectives, *Academy of Management Journal*, Sept. 1973, pp. 496–505.

REDDIN, WILLIAM J. *Effective Management by Objectives: The 3-D Method*, McGraw-Hill, 1971.

WEIHRICH, HEINZ. "MBO: Appraisal with Transactional Analysis," *Personnel Journal*, Apr. 1976, pp. 173–175, 183.

14
COPING WITH A BUREAUCRACY

Learning Objectives

After reading and studying this chapter, you should be able to

1. Understand the difference between the popular and technical meaning of the term *bureaucracy*.
2. Recognize several advantages of the bureaucratic form of organization.
3. Recognize several of the problems created by a bureaucracy.
4. Give your own example of "inversion of means and ends."
5. Identify two ways of coping with the problems of a bureaucracy.
6. Develop insight into your *bureaucratic orientation*.

In its popular meaning, the term *bureaucracy* is associated with a number of negative attributes. Most people think a bureaucracy is an organization rampant with the rigid application of rules and procedures, slowness of operation, buck-passing, repetition of effort, empire building, exaggerated secrecy, and frustrated employees.[1] Yet to a social or behavioral scientist, a bureaucracy refers essentially to a form of organization in which division of effort, rank, rules, and regulations are carefully defined. It is a rational, systematic, precise form of organization. A modern description of a bureaucracy provided by Leonard V. Cordon[2] gives a clue to its true nature:

> The classical bureaucratic model is characterized by a pyramid consisting of positions which are ordered into a hierarchical system of super and subordination. Each position has well-defined activities and responsibilities, demanding specialized competence, and with authority delimited to that necessary for the discharge of its duties. Employees function as representatives of particular positions, which define the degree of formality and the nature of the relationships to be observed.

Ultimate control of the organization rests at the top of the hierarchy. Reliability of behavior is maintained by directives, by rules and regulations, and by standard operating procedures which prescribe the exact manner in which duties are to be performed.

Most readers of this book either work for now or will be working for a bureaucracy. It is thus worthwhile to examine further the nature of bureaucracies, and suggest strategies for coping with several problems created by them.

CHARACTERISTICS OF A BUREAUCRACY

Max Weber, a German sociologist writing in the 1920s, believed that bureaucracy was the pure form of organization, designed for the purpose of maximum efficiency. A bureaucracy exhibits certain identifying characteristics[3]:

1. *A division of labor based on functional specialization.* Thus companies have departments such as engineering, manufacturing, marketing, data processing, accounting, and personnel. People in these departments possess specialized information that contributes to the overall welfare of the firm.

2. *A well-defined hierarchy of authority.* The person granted the most power sits at the top of the hierarchy (chairman of the board or president). As you move down the organization chart, people at each level have less power than those people at the levels above them. As discussed in Chapter 6, there are sources of power other than your place on the hierarchy. For example, a senior scientist of low rank might have power because of his or her valuable contribution to the organization.

3. *A system of rules covering the rights and duties of employees.* In a truly bureaucratic organization each person has a precise job description and knows what he or she can expect from the company. In a few large corporations, you are entitled to an extra day's vacation should you get sick one day during your vacation.

4. *A system of procedures for dealing with work situations.* In a bank, for example, each teller knows exactly what to do when a customer wishes to deposit money in his or her account. No deviation from bank policy is encouraged or allowed.

5. *Impersonality of interpersonal relations.* Even when you smile sweetly at the civil servant in the motor vehicle department, he or she will not renew your registration until you have a certified inspection of your vehicle (in many states and provinces).

6. *Promotion and selection based on technical competence.* To make this characteristic of a bureaucracy true to life, technical competence must also include managerial or administrative competence. Thus in a bureaucracy laughing at your boss's jokes can never be an official reason for your receiving a promotion.

The world could probably not function without bureaucracy.[4] Imagine the chaos in the United States if state and regional telephone companies did not have elaborate procedures established for cooperating about interstate phone calls. When you call from a phone booth in Wisconsin, the operator might tell you, "I'm sorry you cannot call Georgia. The Georgia phone company will not cooperate with us." Imagine also the chaos if each middle manager at General Motors established his or her own pay scale and retirement policies for supervisors.

Personally Given Orders Become Unnecessary. A bureaucratic manager can smugly point to the rule book and say, "Any employee who is late five consecutive days will be docked one day's pay." He or she thus cannot be accused of discriminating against you personally, nor can you legitimately feel that you were unjustly treated. At its best, a bureaucracy prevents people from being treated arbitrarily or unfairly.

Repetition of Orders Is Unnecessary. A bureaucratic manager can tell you that each day at closing time the money in your cash register must be balanced. In the future, this order does not have to be repeated. Somewhere in the back of the store a rule book exists that tells you this must be done everyday. Theoretically, given a carefully designed rule book, employees would need a minimum of supervision (which, of course, works best with competent and well-motivated employees).

Remote Control of People. Top management can control people from a distance when those individuals are governed by a rational set of rules and regulations. When first-line supervisors are given a thorough grounding in machine safety including rules in writing, frequent on-the-spot checks should not be necessary. At the other extreme, when management has not established a clear set of rules, there is need for extensive visitation to remote areas of the organization. An effective set of rules allows people to be managed properly without constant supervision.

Punishment Becomes Legitimate. In some instances, reprimands or punishments are necessary in a complex organization. Since most people resent punishment, they tend to question its legitimacy. A college policy may state that any individual who fails to attain a C average will not graduate. A person with a 1.8 average cannot cry "unjust punishment" when he or she does not graduate. A supervisor has every right to dismiss a fork-lift truck operator who drives his or her truck while drunk. The rules make such punishment legitimate.

Equitable Division of Resources. In a bureaucracy, the job each manager is supposed to perform is well defined. Each manager would prefer that he or she have substantial resources to carry out his or her mission.

Most managers, if given a choice, would prefer that another staff member be added to the department. A bureaucracy usually prevents people over-allocating resources for their own purposes. Managers at the top of the hierarchy try to divide up resources in an equitable fashion. Unfortunately, this advantage of a bureaucracy is sometimes subverted through the practice of empire building—adding people to your group or departments to your organization more to acquire power than to serve the good of the firm.

Machine-like Efficiency. At its best, a bureaucracy is a highly efficient form of organization. Max Weber believed that "the fully developed bureaucratic mechanism compares with other organizations exactly as does the machine with the non-mechanical modes of production . . . precision, speed, unambiguity, continuity, discretion, unity . . . these are raised to the optimum point in a strictly bureaucratic administration."[5]

IBM represents a modern example of what Weber envisioned when he spoke of a methodically efficient organization. A purchasing agent in one company had this comment to make about IBM's penchant for thoroughness: "When we don't know where something is in our company, we call our IBM account representatives. The people from IBM seem to know more about our company than we do."

PROBLEMS CREATED BY A BUREAUCRACY

Several of the problems created by bureaucracies have been discussed earlier in this book. In Chapter 4 we discussed underutilization of abilities as a source of stress found in vast bureaucracies. In Chapter 12, mention was made of Parkinson's law and the organizational multiplier, both observations about what goes wrong in bureaucracies. Next we shall examine a few more problems created by bureaucracies.

High Frustration and Low Job Satisfaction. Untold numbers of people find life in bureaucratic organizations to be frustrating and dissatisfying. Among the sources of frustration and dissatisfaction people point to are the "red tape," loss of individuality, and inability to make an impact on the organization. Pedro, a salesman, provides anecdotal evidence of such frustration:[6]

> Aggravation, aggravation, you would think our twenty million dollar company was General Motors. All I want is some simple information about how many parts my customer in Toledo received. Instead of facts, I get some apologies about the company shifting from one system of inventory accounting to another. Nobody can give me a direct answer on whether or not my customer's order has been filled. I ask myself, what are we in business for?

Research evidence has been collected providing additional support to the belief that working in a bureaucracy creates some job dissatisfaction.[7] The subjects were seventy-eight staff employees drawn from six large manufacturing organizations in the Midwest. They represented the areas of accounting, personnel, engineering, architecture, and market research. Among the information collected were measures of the style of organization (bureaucratic, collaborative, coordinative) and job satisfaction. A major finding was that job satisfaction decreased as the bureaucratic properties of the organization increased. According to the authors of the study, "This can be explained by the lack of individual responsibility and control characterizing bureaucratic structures."

Insensitivity to Individual Problems. A woman attempted to purchase two stereo speakers with her consumer credit card. Because of the size of the purchase, a computer check was made of her available line of credit. The retail clerk reported back to the woman, "I'm sorry, our records show that you are not allowed to charge anymore merchandise until you pay the amount you have past due." The woman protested that a serious error had been made by the computer. Somehow a charge of $556 was entered for a purchase she had never made. She had already spent one hour on the phone trying to resolve this mistake. The clerk said that she knew nothing about the phone conversation; therefore, the woman could not use her credit card to purchase the stereo equipment.

The store clerk just cited had been given specific decision rules by the store management. In a bureaucracy, very few people have the power to allow deviations from the rule. Only a store executive could grant this woman's need for individual attention.

One hospital had rigid rules about identifying a prospective patient's medical insurance policy number before administering medical care to him or her—even an accident victim. Such rigidity has been reduced in severe medical emergencies because many prospective patients hemorrhaged while their friend or relative fumbled for a Blue Cross or Blue Shield card.

Inversion of Means and Ends. Rigid adherence to rules and regulations can sometimes result in a situation whereby obeying rules becomes an end in itself. Under these circumstances, the people involved become more concerned about following rules or carrying out procedures than accomplishing the objectives of the organization.

A local official of the Girl Scouts noted that in her organization an emphasis on recruiting sometimes results in detrimental consequences to the scouts. Many young girls are persuaded to join the scouts who have superficial interest in such activities. Shortly thereafter they drop out, having wasted time and money of both their own and the scouts. An inversion of means and ends has occurred, because recruitment is a *means* to the end of building an effective, large organization. John Knowles, former director of Massachusetts General Hospital (and open critic of American medicine), provides another example of the inversion of means and ends: "In the teaching hospital, it has become set that the patient exists for the teaching programs, and not that the hospital exists for the patient."[8]

Avoiding Responsibility. A bureaucracy is designed to pinpoint responsibility, yet in practice many people use bureaucratic rules to avoid responsibility.[9] Faced with a decision that he or she does not want to make, the buck-passing official will say, "That's not my job," or "That decision lies outside my sphere of influence," or "I'm afraid you will have to speak to my boss about that problem."

Closely related to avoiding responsibility is the avoidance of innovation so frequently found in a bureaucracy. Rather than risk trying a new procedure, the bureaucratic boss may say, "What you are suggesting violates tradition. Around here we don't do things that way." Such was the response a marketing-oriented banker received from his boss when he suggested that the bank hold a "money sale." (It consisted of an advertising campaign offering loan rates lower than the competition.) The young banker whose suggestion was denied became doubly irritated when three months later a competitive bank held a successful money sale.

Delay of Decision. Bureaucracies move painfully slowly on complex decisions. The delay comes about because a number of people have to concur before a final decision is made about issues of importance. In one company a manager wanted authorization to subscribe to a trade newsletter that cost $5 per year.[10] After four weeks of memos and counter memos, the final decision was, "No, there are four months left on your present subscription." About fifteen people were involved in making the decision. At one point a long-distance telephone call was made from California to New York about the newsletter subscription.

The Peter Principle. In the late 1960s an educational psychologist and a professional writer teamed together to formulate an explanation of why (in their evaluation) so many incompetent people are found in bureaucracies. The now famous Peter principle states, "In a hierarchy every employee tends to rise to his (or her) level of incompetence."[11] In other words, many people get promoted once too often. Similar to Parkinson's law, the Peter principle is a satire that contains an element of truth. However, many sophisticated organizations use advanced techniques of personnel selection that minimize people being promoted into positions for which they are unqualified.

An example of the Peter principle in action is when a competent baseball player is promoted to a front-office position and becomes an incompetent administrator. Similarly, many competent technical or sales personnel are promoted into management jobs or administrative assignments for which they are ill suited by temperament.

Although bureaucracies often create problems for their own members and outsiders to the organization, it is illogical to suggest that bureaucracy does not serve a useful purpose in society. A more promising approach to dealing with the problems of a bureaucracy is to make the bureaucracy more adaptable to the demands of a given situation. Two general approaches toward this end are (1) using a more flexible approach to organization design within the bureaucracy, and (2) more careful selection and promotion of people.

Flexible Organization Structures. As described earlier, a bureaucracy is well suited to large-scale, repetitive operations. Yet subparts of the bureaucracy may call for more loosely structured forms of organization. Temporary task forces can be embedded within the bureaucratic structure to carry out special assignments, as mentioned in Chapter 8.

A new area of knowledge, called *organizational taxonomy,* is emerging that shows promise for overcoming the problems created by a rigid organizational structure. A synonymn for organizational taxonomy is *contingency organization design.* As implied by the term, the purpose of contingency organization design is to use the best organization design to meet the purpose at hand.

Alan C. Filley and Robert J. House explain how research-based knowledge can be applied to design a more flexible organization structure. They note that the appropriate form of organizational structure depends on the production technology and external environment. "When the environment and technology are stable and predictable, the traditional pyramidal organization appears to work best."[12] Thus, if you are a production supervisor in a mass-production assembly operation, accept the fact that a bureaucracy is best suited to accomplishing the task at hand.

In contrast, where the product is customized and the environment is unpredictable, a loose, nonhierarchical organization structure appears more appropriate. Should you be assigned to an intelligence operation within the Central Intelligence Agency, your mission would probably be best accomplished by a project or task force organization structure. The ombudsman described in Chapter 5 is another valid example of how a bureaucracy can be made more responsive to the problems of its members.

Improved Methods of Selection and Promotion. Several of the problems of a bureaucracy can be overcome by using sophisticated methods of selecting and promoting people.[13] The Peter principle, for instance, is not nearly so inevitable in organizations where people are carefully screened before being promoted. If it appears that an individual is unsuited to administrative work (because of his or her performance on temporary assignments or on the administrative portions of his or her current responsibilities), that person should not be promoted in the organization.

Another problem of misplacement in a bureaucracy is the "bureaucratic personality" who hides behind rules and regulations in order to avoid responsibility or conflict. If management detects these characteristics early in an individual's career, he or she can be appropriately counseled. Without improvement, that person is ineligible for promotion.

Sophisticated methods of personnel selection and promotion do exist. Much of the field of personnel administration and personnel psychology is concerned with this matter. A number of large organizations, and some smaller ones, make effective use of assessment centers. Aside from using psychological tests and interviews, the assessment-center method measures the performance of people on simulated work tasks. Before a person is promoted to a leadership position, his or her performance as a temporary leader has been carefully observed by several people.[14]

DO YOU HAVE A BUREAUCRATIC ORIENTATION?

A person with a bureaucratic orientation is one who fits comfortably into the role of working in a bureaucracy. Unless the world were populated with people who adjust readily to working for a bureaucracy, organizations such as AT&T or the Ford Motor Company could not function. Other people—those with a low bureaucratic orientation—experience feelings of discomfort working for a bureaucracy. The bureaucratic orientation scale[15] presented in Figure 14.1 gives you a chance to acquire tentative (not scientifically proved) information about your position on this important aspect of work life.

Directions: Answer each question "mostly agree" or "mostly disagree." Assume that you are trying to learn something about yourself. Do not assume that your answer will be shown to a prospective employer.

	Mostly Agree	Mostly Disagree
1. I value stability in my job.		
2. I like a predictable organization.		
3. The best job for me would be one in which the future is uncertain.		
4. The U.S. Army would be a nice place to work.		
5. Rules, policies, and procedures tend to frustrate me.		
6. I would enjoy working for a company that employed 85,000 people worldwide.		

7. Being self-employed would involve more risk than I'm willing to take.   _____ _____

8. Before accepting a job, I would like to see an exact job description.   _____ _____

9. I would prefer a job as a free-lance house painter to one as a clerk for the Department of Motor Vehicles.   _____ _____

10. Seniority should be as important as performance in determining pay increases and promotion.   _____ _____

11. It would give me a feeling of pride to work for the largest and most successful company in its field.   _____ _____

12. Given a choice, I would prefer to make $20,000 per year as a vice-president in a small company to $25,000 as a staff specialist in a large company.   _____ _____

13. I would regard wearing an employee badge with a number on it as a degrading experience.   _____ _____

14. Parking spaces in a company lot should be assigned on the basis of job level.   _____ _____

15. If an accountant works for a large organization, he or she cannot be a true professional.   _____ _____

16. Before accepting a job (given a choice), I would want to make sure that the company had a very fine program of employee benefits.   _____ _____

17. A company will probably not be successful unless it establishes a clear set of rules and procedures.   _____ _____

18. Regular working hours and vacations are more important to me than finding thrills on the job.   _____ _____

10. You should respect people according to their rank.   _____ _____

20. Rules are meant to be broken.   _____ _____

FIGURE 14.1
Bureaucratic orientation scale.

Scoring and Interpretation. Give yourself a plus one for each question that you answered in the bureaucratic direction:

1. Mostly agree
2. Mostly agree
3. Mostly disagree
4. Mostly agree
5. Mostly disagree
6. Mostly disagree
7. Mostly agree
8. Mostly agree
9. Mostly disagree
10. Mostly agree
11. Mostly agree
12. Mostly disagree
13. Mostly disagree
14. Mostly agree
15. Mostly disagree
16. Mostly agree
17. Mostly disagree
18. Mostly agree
19. Mostly agree
20. Mostly disagree

Although the bureaucratic orientation scale is currently a self-examination and research tool, a very high score (15 and over) would suggest that you would enjoy working in a bureaucracy. A very low score (5 or lower) would suggest that you would be frustrated by working in a bureaucracy, especially a large one.

Summary of Key Points

1. In its technical meaning, a bureaucracy refers to a form of organization in which the division of effort, rank, and rules and regulations are carefully defined. At its best, a bureaucracy is a rational, systematic, precise form of organization.

2. A bureaucracy is designed for maximum efficiency. Among its characteristics are (a) a division of labor based on functional specialization, (b) a well-defined hierarchy of authority, and (c) promotion and selection based on technical competence.

3. A bureaucracy offers some potential advantages: (a) personally given orders are unnecessary; (b) people can be controlled from a distance; (c) punishment for rule violation is legitimate; (d) machine-like efficiency.

4. Bureaucracies also create many potential problems: (a) high frustration and low job satisfaction; (b) insensitivity to individual problems; (c) inversion of means and ends; (d) avoiding responsibility; (e) delay of decision making; (f) the Peter principle (promoting people once too often).

5. Two broad strategies for coping with problems created by a bureaucracy are (a) using flexible organizational structures and (b) using improved methods of selecting and promoting people.

Questions for Discussion

1. Why are some people quite content working for a bureaucracy?
2. Bureaucracies were designed with efficiency in mind. What has gone wrong that makes so many bureaucracies seemingly inefficient?
3. What really is "red tape"?
4. If somebody called you a "bureaucrat," would that be a compliment? Why or why not?
5. Is your local McDonald's a bureaucracy? Use the characteristics of a bureaucracy presented in this chapter to help you develop your answer.

6. Are the Cincinnati Reds a bureaucracy? Use the characteristics of a bureaucracy presented in this chapter to help you develop your answer.

THE MISSING PREREQUISITE

During his senior year in high school, mechanically inclined Chris decided that he would like to become an engineering technician. An uncle of his with a degree in engineering technology is happily employed as a field engineer for an office machine company. Chris enters Western Junior College and performs well enough to achieve a 3.4 grade point average. Six months before graduation, Chris meets with a Mr. Wimple, registration official, to plan his last semester's course work.

Mr. Wimple says to Chris, "Young man, I see a serious error in your program. You have received an A in Engineering Statistics, but you are lacking the prerequisite course, Introduction to Statistics. This is a serious omission that will prevent you from graduating on time. Perhaps you can stay on an additional semester to take the course."

Upset, Chris replies, "I can't take that course. I want to work as a field engineer, which requires heavy travel. Besides isn't it kind of silly for a person to take the 'prereq' to a course that he passed with an A?"

"I understand how you feel," replied Wimple, "but you must realize we have certain rules around here. My decision is that you will take Introduction to Statistics before you can graduate."

What should Chris do?

A LOT OF HEADACHES

The following case example of bureaucratic behavior was reported in a metropolitan newspaper serving a community of approximately 700,000 people.

How do you get your neighbor to clean up his or her property when you don't know who he or she is . . . or even if he or she lives in this country?

And how do you get the city of Rochester to stop sending you citations for not mowing the weeds or picking up the trash on property that doesn't belong to you?

Frank Pachla of 67 Milan St. has been trying to figure out answers to those questions for the last nine years. He's been cited twice, at eight-year intervals, for failing to clean up a mess in a vacant lot next to his home. The city apparently thought it was part of his property.

And Pachla has learned that the wheels of city government grind slowly.

"Mr. Pachla is a very patient man," Jerome A. Bonvenzi of the city's Department of Buildings and Property Conservation, said yesterday.

But Pachla said that after talking to twenty city officials in the last week, and getting nowhere, his Job-like patience is wearing thin. He said his patience began to erode late last week after he was told by an unidentified official at the Department of Public Works: "Look buddy, what do you expect? This is a bureaucracy."

Bonvenzi said public works isn't responsible for cleaning up private property, but said the city recently moved a step closer to resolving Pachla's problems—they found out who owns the lot.

After nine years, the property—on which taxes have been regularly paid—has been identified as belonging to Claude Rodrigue, address unknown.

Rodrigue formerly was listed on tax records as c/o Louisa Muoio, at 59 Vinal Avenue, Irondequoit. But the Irondequoit directory lists no occupant at that address.

If the lot isn't cleaned up "within a reasonable time," Bonvenzi said, the city will hire a private contractor to do the job and charge it to Rodrigue's tax bill.

Pachla hopes they don't mail the bill to him.

1. What should Pachla do if he does receive the tax bill?
2. How should Pachla have reacted to the comment, "Lookit buddy, what do you expect? This is a bureaucracy."
3. What should Pachla have done when he received his first citation for failing to clean up the lot adjacent to his property?
4. What should the city do to prevent mistakes like this from happening again?
5. Is Pachla's case an isolated incident that need not be the concern of a serious student of human relations? Comment.

FOOTNOTES

[1] Rolf E. Rogers, *Organizational Theory*, Allyn and Bacon, 1975, p. 3.

[2] Leonard V. Gordon, "Measurement of Bureaucratic Orientation," *Personnel Psychology*, Spring 1970, p. 3.

[3] From Max Weber, *Essays in Sociology*, translated by H. H. Gerth and C. W. Mills, Oxford University Press, 1946. Reprinted in Joseph A. Litterer, *Organizations: Structure and Behavior*, Wiley, 1969, p. 34.

[4] The first four advantages described here are an extension of the reasoning presented in Alvin W. Gouldner, "The Explicational Functions of Bureaucratic Rules," in Alvin W. Gouldner, *Patterns of Industrial Bureaucracy*, Free Press, 1954. Reprinted in Stephen J. Carroll, Jr., Frank T. Paine, and John B. Miner, *The Management Process: Cases and Readings*, Macmillan, 1973, pp. 267–277.

[5] Max Weber, *Essays in Sociology*, quoted in Gary Dessler, *Organization and Management: A Contingency Approach*, Prentice-Hall, 1976, p. 31.

[6] Andrew J. DuBrin, *Survival in the Office: How to Move Ahead or Hang On,* Mason/Charter, 1977, p. 47.

[7] Nicholas Dimarco and Steven Norton, "Life Style, Organization Structure, Congruity, and Job Satisfaction," *Personnel Psychology,* Winter 1974, pp. 581–591.

[8] Quoted in David R. Hampton, Charles E. Summer, and Ross A. Webber, *Organizational Behavior and the Practice of Management,* Scott, Foresman, 1973, p. 530.

[9] This and the following disadvantage are described in Herbert G. Hicks and C. Ray Gullett, *The Management of Organizations,* 3rd. ed. McGraw-Hill, 1976, pp. 380–386.

[10] Case example presented in J. D. Donavid (pen name), "The Bureaucracy Lives," *Dun's Review,* Apr. 1972, pp. 93–96.

[11] Lawrence J. Peter and Raymond Hull, *The Peter Principle,* William Morrow, 1969, p. 26.

[12] Alan C. Filley and Robert J. House, "Management and the Future," *Business Horizons,* Aug. 1972, p. 14.

[13] A standard reference about personnel selection is Ernest J. McCormick and Joseph Tiffin, *Industrial Psychology,* 6th ed., Prentice-Hall, 1974.

[14] The best overview available of the assessment center method is Joseph L. Moses and William C. Byham (eds.), *Applying the Assessment Center Method,* Pergamon, 1977.

[15] The idea for the development of this scale stems from the research of Leonard V. Gordon (see footnote 2).

[16] "9-year Headache a Lot of Trouble," Rochester *Democrat and Chronicle,* June 23, 1976, p. 1A.

SUGGESTED READING

BENNIS, WARREN G. "Organization Development and the Fate of Bureaucracy," *Industrial Management Review,* Spring 1966.

BLAU, PETER M., and MEYER, M. W. *Bureaucracy in Modern Society,* rev. ed., Random House, 1971.

DONAVID, J. D. (pen name). "The Bureaucracy Lives," *Dun's Review,* Apr. 1972, pp. 93–96.

DOWNS, ANTHONY. *Inside Bureaucracy,* Little, Brown, 1967.

DUBRIN, ANDREW J. *Survival in the Office: How to Move Ahead or Hang On,* Mason/Charter, 1977, Chapter 3.

HUMMEL, RALPH P. *The Bureaucratic Experience,* St. Martin's, 1977.

ROGERS, ROLF E. *Organization Theory,* Allyn and Bacon, 1975, Chapter 1.

SORENSON, JAMES E., and SORENSON, THOMAS L. "The Conflict of Professionals in Bureaucratic Organizations," *Administrative Science Quarterly,* Mar. 1974, pp. 98–106.

THOMPSON, VICTOR A. *Modern Organization,* Knopf, 1961.

WEBER, MAX. *The Theory of Social and Economic Organization,* translated by A. Henderson and Talcott Parson, Oxford Univeristy Press, 1947.

PART FIVE
WORKING WITH THE FUTURE

Many books conclude with a chapter about the future. Here a chapter about the future world of work *precedes* a chapter about career management. Our reasoning is that a person's assumptions about the future automatically shape his or her career planning. For example, many people in the early 1970s believed that a strong, seemingly unlimited demand for accountants would continue. By the late 1970s this demand had sharply declined, making it difficult for many new accountants to find professional-level employment. Even if you take a pessimistic view of making predictions about the world of work, this part of the book should help you recognize the importance of managing your future.

15

THE FUTURE WORLD OF WORK

Learning Objectives

After reading and studying this chapter, you should be able to

1. Understand the concepts of *knowledge worker* and *knowledge work*.
2. Understand the concept of *resource conservation industry*.
3. Identify a few trends of organizations of the future.
4. Understand how an *adhocracy* differs from a *bureaucracy*.
5. Understand how values influence the management of organizations.
6. Adapt your career planning to your concept of the future.

To better plan your career, it is helpful to have reliable information about the future world of work. Knowing which jobs and which types of people will be in demand can serve to your advantage. A seventeen-year-old Mexican-American male might be informed by his career counselor that the demand for Mexican-American executives is growing; that by the year 2000 Mexicans will probably occupy two percent of executive jobs in major corporations. The young man in question might pursue life experiences that would help prepare him for executive work if he had faith in the counselor's prediction.

Unfortunately, many predictions about the future are inaccurate. As noted by an ancient Chinese proverb, "To prophesy is extremely difficult, especially with regards to the future."[1] One of the many reasons that forecasts about broad trends in organizational life prove inaccurate is that they fail to anticipate one or two key factors. In the late 1960s and early 1970s many predictions were made that young people were becoming loyal to themselves and their careers, yet disloyal to large organizations. As a consequence, it was believed that the new breed of managers would be high turnover risks. It was predicted they would be particularly impatient while on the job. By the late 1970s, this army of disloyalists had not appeared. Young people in management-training programs, technical, and professional jobs seemed more content than in the past; they even valued and jealously possessed reasonably satisfying jobs.

What went wrong with the prediction? The forecasters overlooked the possibility of a worldwide recession, which decreased young (and older) peoples' opportunity for job switching. As jobs became scarcer, people were more satisfied with holding on to what they had. In the 1970s, economic forces at least temporarily cooled off American obsession with career growth as an end in itself.

Despite the hazards of futurology, we shall make a few extrapolations from the present to the future about major trends influencing tomorrow's jobholder. Such predictions are designed to serve as a backdrop to logically based career planning.

JOBS OF THE FUTURE

A realistic prediction is that new occupations will arise and some fading ones will experience a rebirth. Such a phenomenon has taken place in the 1970s. For instance, in response to federal government requirements for detailed information, hospitals have been forced to increase their administrative staff. Before Medicare and Medicaid became law in the United States, "medicare claims clerks" were nonexistent. Also during the 1970s, a dramatic increase in plant stores was evident in metropolitan areas. For many years the demand for florists was stable, at best. Plant stores led to a surge in the demand for florists, or at least for store clerks who could communicate with people about plants.

Continuing Trend Toward Knowledge Work.   Many readers of this book will lead a productive occupational life without ever helping directly build a product. Today more people are engaged in nonmanufacturing (service occupations such as barber, cardiac surgeon, or computer scientist) than in straight manufacturing jobs. People who work more with ideas than with things are considered *knowledge workers:* managerial, professional, technical, and sales personnel. The percentage of technical and professional workers has approximately doubled in the 1950–1975 time span. About 15 percent of the work force is engaged in professional or technical work.[2] Apparently, this shift away from production and low-level clerical occupations will continue.

Knowledge workers include people in such diverse occupations as bank officer, biochemist, ceramic engineer, claims examiner, employment counselor, comedian, meterologist, podiatrist, and sanitarian. Knowledge worker positions of the future might include interplanetary vehicle pilot, brain transplant technician, industrial behavior modifier, and senior-citizen recreational counselor.

The Resource Conservation Industry. Marvin D. Dunnette, a noted industrial psychologist, boldly predicts the following about future jobs:[3]

> So far, society's maladaptive use of its human and natural resources has been counter to the hope of providing a better life for all. Future efforts to improve the physical and environmental well-being of people, however, will yield millions of new job opportunities—new careers to use fully the human resources available in society.

The resource conservation industry is developing to meet the needs just specified. Air and noise pollution control specialists now help to cope with the unfortunate negative side effects of crowded highways, streets, garages, and parking lots. As cities search for creative ways to dispose of junked cars, appliances, buildings, and paper, a demand will be created for more specialists in the field of waste disposal.

Many new jobs in recreation are created each year to help take better care of human resources. Total employment in the management of public and private recreation areas is expected to reach almost 1.5 million by 1980. As the work week becomes increasingly shorter for some categories of worker, the recreation industry will continue to grow. As an increasing number of people become forced into early retirement, permanently unemployed, or lifetime recipients of welfare, more professional attention may be directed toward helping them cope effectively with leisure time.

Hospitals and other health facilities periodically face austerity drives, yet the long-term trend is a burgeoning of occupations that provide health care services. Dunnette and his associates predict the following:[4]

> Cities and rural areas are in serious need of trained medical personnel. Many people do not go to clinics or hospitals for care because of family responsibilities, the lack of accessible facilities, or simply fear of institutional complexities. Para-professional medical workers are needed to teach out-patients to recognize symptoms of common disorders, do follow-up studies on patients, provide transportation to and from clinics, care for children and older people, allay patients' anxieties, and to listen to complaints. And these medical workers need to be in accessible locations. Hospitals also need more personnel to orient and interview incoming patients and, in general, to give patients more attention.

Increased Demand for Basic Craft and Technical Skills. Large cities do not suffer from the lack of sophisticated technology. Engineers, technicians, and architects are able to ingeniously erect 100-story office towers that do not topple in the wind or crumble with decay. Inside these buildings are usually found modern devices such as computers and related equipment that are too complex for most people to comprehend. The same buildings that house computers usually have leaking toilets that are dribbling away pure water—a precious resource.

Within a few miles from these magnificent towers are shabby, buildings with rotting porches, leaking roofs, faulty electric wiring, and inefficient heating systems. Thousands of buildings are abandoned by landlords every year and turned over to the city as unwanted property. Ultimately, the world may begin to pay more attention to fixing leaky toilets and renovating substandard buildings. Vast numbers of "fix-it persons" will then be in at least as much demand as space-vehicle technicians or Pentagon war-game tacticians.

ORGANIZATIONS OF THE FUTURE

Businesses of today have become highly adaptable to environmental demands. One reason is that consumer preferences for goods and services appear to be increasingly unstable. To illustrate, banks have in recent years found themselves in competitive warfare with financial institutions that in the past provided different kinds of services. In some states, consumers are able to obtain checking account privileges at both savings and commercial banks.

Organizations of the future will probably have to be increasingly adaptable to demands from the environment. Consumer action groups, environmentalists, and the federal government are examples of forces for change. Major ways in which organizations will become more adaptable and flexible are discussed in the next two sections.

Increased Emphasis on Effectiveness and Efficiency. During the 1970s both profit and non-profit organizations placed a growing emphasis on management by results, even in situations where the organization lacked a formal MBO program. The trend of inflation followed shortly by recession has helped foster a climate whereby people at all levels are expected to achieve tangible results. Few jobs are totally secure today, even in school systems or civil service.

Organizations of the future will probably achieve greater effectiveness and efficiency through two general strategies used by more sophisticated organizations of the present. A continued use of rational approaches to management (such as computerized information systems) is the first major approach. More extensive use of computer-based information will mean that many routine middle management and staff jobs will disappear. People who serve basically as an information link between two levels of management will find themselves surplus.

A second major thrust toward organizational effectiveness and efficiency will be more judicious use of human relations techniques and concepts. The company president of tomorrow may look upon human relations knowledge as a sensible way of achieving employee commitment *and* productivity. He or she will not say, "We don't have time for human relations around here." Instead the president might say, "We can't afford not to practice good human relations. If we mismanage human resources, we will be out of business."

Growth of the adhocracy. A consensus of opinion has emerged that organizations of the future will rely more on task (project) teams and less on formal hierarchies to get their work accomplished.[5] The *adhocracy* will replace the traditional bureaucracy. (The term adhocracy stems from *ad hoc* or special purpose.) Construction and aerospace companies have long used such an approach to getting tasks accomplished.

A distinguishing feature of the adhocracy is that people will be assigned to task teams on the basis of their expertise, rather than upon their rank in the organization. A service company might want to start a rodent-control service to be offered to municipalities. The program would start small with a task force of anybody in the company who knew something about rodent control. A young high school graduate who was raised in a rat-infested neighborhood might have more rank on this committee than an older person with a graduate degree who was raised in a suburb.

Task forces help an organization adapt to change because they are so quickly formed and disbanded. Should the company just mentioned find that few municipalities are ready to purchase comprehensive programs of rodent control, the task force can be quickly disbanded. No new Rodent Control Division of the company had been formed. Similarly, if the same company learned that municipalities needed educational programs about rodent control rather than rodent control itself, a new special-purpose (ad hoc) task force could be formed.

WHAT TYPES OF PEOPLE WILL BE NEEDED IN THE FUTURE?

People who succeed in organizations of the future will probably not be markedly different from people who succeed in organizations of today. However, the predicted increase in organizational rationality and adaptability will underscore the importance of a few aspects of behavior.[6]

Increased Capacity for Handling Conflict and Change. An adhocracy will force its members to come into contact with many different people, rather than sticking to the confines of one department. It will be common practice for one person to belong to several different work groups at the same time (one for each project). Adaptability to change will thus become a necessity. Temporary task-force workers also will have to be adept at handling conflict, because conflict is so frequently present in the "free for all" that results when people cannot use formal power (rank) to order each other around. Project leaders also find themselves in frequent conflict with department heads and other project leaders. For instance, three different project leaders may want the same talented computer expert to work on their project.

Greater Tolerance for Ambiguity. An adhocracy will by definition have fewer rules and regulations than a bureaucracy. The rodent-control team mentioned above will not be able to refer to a carefully drawn rodent-control manual to provide them direction. Instead, they will have to establish some ground rules for themselves—still working within general guidelines (such as budget limitations) set by the company.

The knowledgeable worker of tomorrow will have to be able to tolerate ambiguity for another basic reason. Change itself is somewhat ambiguous. One reason new situations (jobs, assignments, or people) make us uneasy is that we are not sure if our past experience will allow us to effectively handle the present.

Increased Importance of Personal Accomplishment. Although office politics will never be completely eliminated, it appears probable that personal accomplishment will be an increasingly important basis for judging people. An emerging (or returning) trend is for a person's record of accomplishment to carry more weight in business than his or her educational degree, sex, or race. As organizations become more rational (efficiency and effectiveness-minded), they must appoint to leadership and higher-level technical assignments those people who have demonstrated ability to achieve results. For example, if you met all your objectives in your last job, that accomplishment might be more help to you in getting promoted than if you lived in a high-income neighborhood.

FUTURE ORGANIZATIONAL VALUES

The goals that an organization pursues depend to a large extent upon its values. One retail store known to this author has the informal policy of encouraging turnover to avoid giving people salary increases. When a competent worker demands a raise, he or she is told that a raise will be "forthcoming." The company recognizes that many people will leave dissatisfied, but that they will save money by having so many new employees working at close to the minimum wage. This organization *values* profits, even when it results in unsound business practices.

Quality of Working Life (QWL). It has been suggested that organization development specialists be called QWL specialists.[7] OD practitioners are essentially trying to achieve a better working environment. Young people of today (as well as many oldsters) have come to prefer a satisfying working environment to high pay or job security.[8]

During a recession many dirty, uncomfortable factory jobs go begging because people refuse to accept these types of working conditions. A cynic might argue that people prefer to receive welfare benefits than to work. However, not everybody who refuses a job with a poor working environment is granted welfare benefits.

At higher-level jobs, people also continue to demand a better quality of working life. Organizations sometimes share these values, as evidenced by an increased concern for employee physical health. A bank in Houston has built a mini-gym on company premises for managerial personnel to help them stay physically fit. Healthy employees at any level, of course, contribute to profitability. Whatever the deepest underlying motive, employee gyms, jogging clubs, and noise-reduced environments suggest an increased concern for the quality of working life.

Democracy.   Participative management (described in an earlier chapter) is the usual way of implementing democratic values. As organizations become more complex and employees become more knowledgeable, a greater emphasis on the democratic approach of participative management may be a necessity. Organizations will come to value democracy because it works. Democracy may also show itself in an increased range of people participating on the boards of businesses and other organizations. The current trend toward actively recruiting blacks and females for board of directorships will probably accelerate, thus extending beyond the fad or *tokenism* stage.

Concessions to the Counterculture.   Every era has its subgroup of people whose values run counter to the mainstream. At one time the counterculture may be opposing armaments; at another time their opposition may be mounted against unsafe consumer products or pollution of natural resources. At first these people are dismissed by the traditional holders of power (the Establishment) as rabble rousers who will probably go away.

Members of the counterculture probably will never go away, and they will continue to have many of their demands met. The growth of consumerism (concern for the welfare of the consumer) is an outgrowth of the counterculture. An increased concern for the demands of students was a productive offshoot of the student riots of the early 1960s. Members of the counterculture were also successful in banning the use of noxious substances in some consumer products, such as the fluorohydrocarbons in aerosol sprays and the red dye in maraschino cherries. As behavioral scientist Joe Kelly notes,[9]

> The great achievement of the counterculture is that it has persuaded the Establishment to challenge the rationality of unlimited economic

growth; to face the evil demon of Science, with its attendant evils of industrialization, urbanization, and technocracy; and to try to formulate new social policies which somehow combine the productivities of the systems approach with the intangible values of man's existential needs.

*Summary
of Key Points*

1. Accurate predictions about the future are helpful in planning your career.
2. Two opposing future trends are (a) an increased emphasis on knowledge workers, and (b) an increased demand for basic craft skills to help deal with urban problems.
3. A new resource conservation industry is emerging to help minimize waste and conserve physical and human resources. This industry may be gaining in importance in the near future.
4. In the future, most large organizations will be characterized by (a) an increased emphasis on effectiveness and efficiency, and (b) a temporary task force or project form of organization (adhocracy).
5. Successful people in these organizations will have to be adept at managing conflict and handling ambiguous (ill-defined) situations.
6. Future organization values may include (a) a greater emphasis on quality of working life, (b) more participative democracy, and (c) increased acceptance of the counterculture.

*Questions
for Discussion*

1. What are you doing to get ready from a career standpoint for the year 2000?
2. What prediction about the future made in this chapter do you think is the least likely to come true? Why?
3. In what way do you think you could apply your skills to the "resource conservation industry"?
4. Do you view yourself as part of the counterculture? Why or why not?
5. What evidence can you present of any current emphasis on an increased demand for basic and craft skills?
6. What evidence do you have that you would or would not enjoy working in an adhocracy?

A Human Relations Incident
THE QWL TECHNICIAN

Reginald Brewster, vice-president of human resources at Aerodynamics Corporation, was scanning the suggestion box. Lately he noticed an increasing number of complaints about general working conditions at Aerodynamics. Among the more representative suggestions centering on this theme were these:

"The year is now 1984 and things are as bad as George Orwell said they would be. I can't take this incessant concern we have about efficiency."

"I feel like a robot. I hope this suggestion is read by a person, not a computer. Our company has no regard for human feelings. I think I'm going to self-destruct if things don't get better."

Brewster thought to himself, "The complaints are getting too consistent. If we don't take action, the Conservation of Human Resources Commission will be on our backs. Maybe Roberta Hanson, our manager of educational services, can help us. She's really concerned about helping people achieve the good life."

Later that day Mr. Brewster met with Ms. Hanson. After reviewing the suggestion box complaints, he said to Roberta, "Congratulations, we've just appointed you the quality of working life manager. Do what you have to do to get rid of these problems."

If you were Roberta Hanson, (1) Would you take on this assignment? (2) What would be your general strategy for tackling the assignment?

A Human Relations Case
THE RAT PATROL

Environmental Associates was founded in 1980 to help cities deal with problems of urban blight. Whatever the problem, EA assigns a task force composed of people with appropriate backgrounds. They have achieved a first-rate reputation for proposing feasible solutions to vexing environmental problems. Among the many task forces currently on assignment is the Rat Patrol, a group assigned to assess the magnitude of rat infestation. In addition, they are charged with the responsibility of making recommendations on how the rat-infestation problem might be solved.

Forrest is the leader of the Rat Patrol. His team members are Gloria, Tim, and Nick. Part of Forrest's management approach is to hold weekly conferences with his team to discuss progress and problems. The scenario at his first conference on a new assignment went something like this:

Forrest: This Thirteenth Ward is a political hotbed. The member of congress responsible for this ward thinks they are being overtaken by rats. But there is a lot of public sentiment that too many funds have already been poured into that district with very disappointing results. We need a highly objective assessment of the rodent problem. How big a problem do you folks think we have?

Gloria: I've been concentrating my efforts on Magnolia Street. I'm using both direct and indirect measures. I've been looking for evidences of rat bites on children and rat-like holes in bags of garbage. Of course, I'm also on the lookout for the little beasts. So far, I get the impression we do have a problem. I see too many suspicious-looking bites on the legs and arms of little children. I have to dig a lot more, but I think we have a problem.

Tim: As you know, I place the greatest faith in the rat-poison approach. I spread the poison around and see what bites. If I see a lot of dead rats in places I've dropped the poison, I have some pretty definitive proof that we've got a rodent problem. I need some more time for the poison to work. I'll have a more reliable answer by next week.

Gloria: Tim, I don't agree with your approach. It's objective but haphazard. The smart rats just don't go for your poison.

Nick: It's a little early for me to reach a conclusion. I'm undecided as to whether or not we have a problem. I'd like to make my report when Gloria and Tim make theirs.

Tim: That's the kind of response we'd expect from Nick. He takes the easy way out and piggybacks on what other people have found.

Gloria: Yeah, Nick, [laughingly] have you been to any good matinees lately?

Forrest: Okay gang, I can see you're getting at each others throats right now. Why don't we plan for another review session next week?

As Forrest drove the Rat Patrol van back toward the home office he thought to himself, "Maybe Gloria and Tim have something. I've gotten the impression from time to time that Nick is kind of a goof-off who doesn't carry his weight on the task force. Yet I can't quibble with results. Our Rat Patrol has developed a terrific reputation. Maybe if we got rid of Nick we'd be disturbing the chemistry of our group. He seems to add just the right amount of conflict to the task force. I'll give some more thought to this problem later."

1. What, if anything, should Forrest do about Nick?
2. Should Tim and Gloria be so concerned about every member of the team performing an equal amount of work?
3. If a task force is getting good results, should the contribution of each member be measured separately?
4. Should the politics of the situation described early in the case influence how the Rat Patrol carries out its work?
5. Should Forrest get personally involved in looking for evidences of rat infestation? Why or why not?

FOOTNOTES

[1] Quoted in Edgar F. Huse and James L. Bowditch, *Behavior in Organizations: A Systems Approach to Managing,* Addison-Wesley, 1973, p. 378.

[2] A brief synthesis of these projections is found in Andrew J. DuBrin, *Fundamentals of Organizational Behavior: An Applied Perspective,* 2nd ed., Pergamon, 1978, pp. 8–9. A source document is the current edition of *Statistical Abstract of the United States, U.S. Bureau of the Census.*

[3] Marvin D. Dunnette, *Work and Nonwork in the Year 2001,* Wadsworth, 1973, p. 91.

[4] *Ibid.*, pp. 92–93.

[5] The term *adhocracy* was coined by Alvin Toffler, *Future Shock,* Bantam, 1971.

[6] The first two characteristics mentioned here are based on a discussion in Huse and Bowditch, *op. cit.*, pp. 398–399.

[7] W. Warner Burke, "Organization Development in Transition," *Journal of Applied Behavioral Science,* Jan. 1976, p. 22.

[8] Research evidence about these values is summarized in Don Hellriegel and John W. Slocum, Jr., *Management: A Contingency Approach,* Addison-Wesley, 1974, pp. 456–457.

[9] Joe Kelly, *Organizational Behaviour: An Existential-Systems Approach,* Irwin, 1974, p. 716.

SUGGESTED READING

BENNIS, WARREN G. "A Funny Thing Happened on the Way to the Future," *American Psychologist,* 1970, pp. 595–608.

DUNNETTE, MARVIN D. *Work and Nonwork in the Year 2001,* Wadsworth, 1973.

EMERY, F. E. "The Next Thirty Years: Concepts, Methods, and Anticipations," *Human Relations,* vol. 20, 1967, pp. 199–236.

HOPKINS, FRANK S. "Humanism, Robotism or Destruction," *The Futurist,* Feb. 1971, p. 23.

JUN, JONG S., and STORM, WILLIAM B. *Tomorrow's Organizations: Challenges and Strategies,* Scott, Foresman, 1973.

KAHN, HERMAN, and WIENER, ANTHONY J. *The Year 2000: A Framework for Speculation on the Next Thirty Years,* Macmillan, 1967.

REICH, CHARLES. *The Greening of America,* Bantam, 1971.

ROSZAK, THEODORE. *The Making of a Counterculture,* Doubleday, 1969.

STEADE, RICHARD D. *Business and Society in Transition: Issues and Concepts,* Canfield Press, 1975.

STEIGER, WILLIAM A. "Can We Legislate the Humanization of Work," in W. Clay Hamner and Frank L. Schmidt, *Contemporary Problems in Personnel,* St. Clair Press, 1974, pp. 499–504.

16

MANAGING YOUR CAREER

Learning Objectives

After reading and studying this chapter, you should be able to

1. Understand how self-motivation fits into career development.
2. Establish short-, intermediate-, and long-range goals for yourself.
3. Summarize at least seven major career-planning strategies.
4. Develop a workable strategy for finding a new job.
5. Write an attention-getting letter for yourself.
6. Recognize and implement strategies that will help you prevent the mid-career crisis.

I'm pleased to be assigned to your department," said a young accountant to his new boss. "But could you tell me where this job will lead? I'm very interested in properly planning my career." His boss replied, "Just do your job, and the company will take care of your career."

However well intended this boss, the accountant should not leave his career development to somebody else. (Career development is the process of creating a pattern of jobs in a series of steps from the initial job to retirement.[1]) Only a small number of large organizations (such as the U.S. Air Force, the U.S. Forest Service, and General Electric) have long-standing programs of this nature. A recent trend in American industry suggests that more attention is now being paid to career development, at least at the managerial and professional levels. Although this trend may continue, the individual must still assume the major responsibility for developing his or her own career. To increase your chances of career success and satisfaction, you must practice *self-motivated career planning*.[2] (Basically, taking the initiative to plan your career.)

This chapter presents a few preliminary insights into the process of career development. As with most information presented in the previous chapters, career development is a field of study within itself. The career-minded person should therefore pursue additional information and guidance.

MAINTAIN SENSITIVITY TO THE EXTERNAL ENVIRONMENT

The most general suggestion for career management is for a person to heighten his or her sensitivity to the external environment. Organizations must adapt to their external environment in order to survive, and so must individuals. Since the external environment is usually unstable, prescriptions of what you should do right now to cope with the environment are of temporary value. Yet the general principle of being aware of the external environment is valid. Several illustrations will suffice for the purposes of this chapter.

The forces of supply and demand exert a profound impact on career planning. In the 1976–77 period about 10 percent of college students graduating with degrees in elementary or secondary education found jobs in teaching (figures are for New York State). A person interested in a career as a high school or elementary school teacher in New York State would have to realize that he or she has a small chance of success.

Geographic shifts in areas of economic prosperity must also be taken into account in career planning. During the present decade the Southeast and Southwest portions of the United States (and parts of Alaska) are on the economic upswing. All things being equal, a person has a better chance for career advancement by gravitating toward a growth industry in a growth area. Only by carefully studying basic sources (government reports) or objective secondary sources (for instance, the *Wall Street Journal*) can such external forces and movements be understood.

Legal constraints also influence career planning. Many an individual has discovered too late that it is difficult to obtain licensing or certification in his or her field in his or her preferred state. Many a physician seeking semiretirement in Florida has found that obtaining licensing in Florida is difficult; too many physicians have the same idea. One successful real estate broker lost a major real estate commission because he closed a deal in a state in which he was not licensed. The opposing attorney informed him, "Your deal was not legal. You are not licensed in the state of ＿＿＿."

ESTABLISHING CAREER GOALS

A person's chances of finding career satisfaction increase if he or she establishes clear-cut goals. The opposite of the goal-setting process is referred to as *occupational floundering*. It occurs "when an individual enters the labor market seeking full-time work without having a chosen commitment to an occupational goal or for one reason or another does not adapt to that goal once it is attained."[3] A fortunate few flounderers find their way into rewarding jobs and careers. One vice-president of marketing began employment in his company as a draftsman. A sales manager asked him to try his hand at selling because he was familiar with the workings of the machines sold by the company. Ultimately, this individual rose to the vice presidency, having no early goal that related to marketing or sales. For most people, goal setting is crucial for success.

Finding a Field. Before setting occupational goals, a person must first find a field compatible with his or her interests. Among the varied ways in which people find a field and occupation to pursue are these:

1. Influence of parent, relative, or friend: "My uncle owned a pharmacy, so I became interested in pharmacy at an early age."
2. Reading and study: "While in high school I read about astronomy, and decided that I wanted to be an astronomer."
3. Natural opportunity: "I was born into the business. Who would give up a chance to be a vice-president by the time I was twenty-five? Our family has always been in the retail business."
4. Forced opportunity: "I had never heard about electronics until I joined the army. They told me I had aptitude for the field. I enjoyed working as an electronics technician. After the army I applied for a job with IBM as a field service engineer. It has worked out well."
5. Discovery through counseling and or testing: "I took an interest test in high school. My guidance counselor told me that I had interests similar to those of a social worker. Not knowing what else to do, I decided to become a social worker."

Levels of Responsibility. After a person finds a field compatible to his or her interests (and then finds an entry-level job), the process of goal setting becomes meaningful. An ambitious, executive-minded person who wants to rise to the top of his or her field might establish goals such as these:

1. Sales representative for three years.
2. Branch manager for three years.
3. Market research analyst in home office for two years.
4. Assistant to regional manager for two years.
5. Regional manager for five years.
6. Marketing vice-president for five years.
7. Executive vice-president for five years.

8. President of medium-sized company for five years.
9. President of large company until forced into retirement.
10. Proprietor of fish and tackle shop until physically unable to continue.

The goals just mentioned include a time element, which is crucial to sound career management. Your long-range goal might be clearly established in your mind (such as owner of an automobile distributorship). It is also necessary to establish short- (for example, get any job connected with the automobile business) and intermediate-range (sales manager of an automobile distributorship by age 30) goals. Goals set too far into the future may lose their motivational value.

Financial Goal Setting. Some people establish income goals, rather than focus on the kinds of work that they want to do. At one time it was fashionable to set a goal of "earning your age in thousand dollar units." It was said that a person is extremely successful if he or she earns $25,000 per year at age 25, $50,000 per year at age 50, and so forth. Such a yardstick is unrealistic for a person entering the job market ($20,000 at age 20). Nor does it take into account the effects of inflation or the differences in wage rates in different fields.

A more realistic approach to income goal setting is to strive for earning levels in comparison to others. For example, people in the top 1 percent of incomes are generally considered affluent. In 1977, this would be about $36,000 per year. However, another person might be financially satisfied if he or she were earning an above average income—in 1977, above $13,000 per year.

Career goal setting that focuses on income has one striking disadvantage: it does not point you toward work in which you will necessarily succeed. People who earn high incomes usually do so because they were successful in their work (even criminals). An advantage of using income goals is that they can point you toward high-paying occupations (and away from low-paying occupations). For instance, if it were very important to you to earn a high income, it would be to your advantage to avoid fields such as retailing or library work. Instead, you might try to look for employment in the business-equipment field. Your only virtual *guarantee* of extremely high pay would be medicine or dentistry.

CAREER-PLANNING STRATEGIES

The strategies of job politics described in Chapter 5 can be regarded as ways of advancing your career. For instance, the person who enhances his or her power will simultaneously be advancing his or her career. Next we shall overview eleven other career-planning strategies that have with-stood the test of time.[4] However, indiscriminate use of any of these tactics may backfire. For instance, if you overdo the strategy of "find the right organization," you may never find a place good enough for you.

Make an Accurate Self-appraisal.   The most important ingredient in mature career planning is to have an accurate picture of your strengths, areas for improvement, and preferences. Feedback of this nature can be obtained professionally (as described later in this chapter) through performance appraisal review sessions or by obtaining peer evaluations. The latter type of information can be achieved in encounter groups or more informally through asking significant people their opinion of you.

One sales representative constructed a brief form asking questions about himself such as, "What have I done that displeased you this year?" He gave this form to customers, his boss, and the clerical staff in his office. The information he received helped him become more effective with others. In this regard he learned that he was standing too close to people (violating their *personal space*) when he talked to them.

Use Occupational Information.   In addition to knowing about yourself, it is important to be aware of the world outside so you can find a good fit between yourself and existing opportunities. Few people take advantage of the voluminous information available about careers or career planning. Most libraries and bookstores are well supplied with this type of information. (See the suggested reading section of this chapter.) The most comprehensive source document of occupational information is the *Occupational Outlook Handbook,* published every two years by the U.S. Department of Labor. Each occupation listed is described in terms of (1) nature of the work, (2) places of employment, (3) training, (4) other qualifications and advancement, and (5) employment outlook. Using the *Handbook,* one can find answers to such questions as "What do zoologists do and how much do they earn?"

The Bureau of Labor Statistics also publishes the *Occupational Outlook Quarterly,* which supplements the *Handbook* with articles on current occupational developments. Another useful source of career information is the "Careers for a Changing World" series distributed by the New York Life Insurance Company,[5] which deals with a wide range of selected careers. Examples are health care, transportation, and visual arts.

Career guidance information is now also computerized. One such application is the *Guidance Information System* (GIS),[6] which is acknowledged to be the most up-to-date and useful source of occupational and educational information available. The system evolved from concepts and experiences developed in a project conducted at Harvard University under the sponsorship of the U.S. Office of Education.

Sending a set of instructions to the computer produces a series of immediate responses in printed form. The information the student obtains allows him or her to see the results of choices and decisions he or she has made, and also to compare them with the results of other choices. The unique aspect of the Guidance Information System is that it makes it possible for the counselee to interact directly with the information. Information is available in about 1200 occupations and fifteen occupational clusters. In addition, the counselee can take into account his or her personal characteristics and educational background.

Using the GIS, a counselee might say, "I like the hospitality and recreation field. I have good verbal aptitudes, good clerical perception, and I have a two-year college degree." One suggestion that might emanate from the computer would be "travel agent."

Establish Meaningful Goals. Chris Argyris observes that goals which lead to personal growth are (1) challenging or stretching, (2) relevant to the person's self-image, (3) set by the person independently or in collaboration with another individual, and (4) implemented by the person's independent effort.[7] A note of caution is in order: occasionally, people do reach seemingly unattainable goals. Robert J. Ringer, author of *Winning Through Intimidation,* contends that one year he made close to $850,000 in real estate commissions. Establishing realistic goals does not preclude such activity. Each time you achieve one set of goals, adjust your sights upward.

Find the Right Organization. A student of human relations might conclude that every organization is run by rational people who do a careful job of managing human and material resources. Such organizations are in fact rare. Many deviant people are found in key jobs[8]:

> A woman accepted a position as the director of publicity for a publisher of general audience books. She was told that she would be given free rein in running the book publicity department. One week after she was hired she was informed that the firm would not authorize spending money for book publicity other than for routine mailings. When this woman made a special request to management, such as asking for prompt shipment of books, she was told, "Don't bother us; we will ship them when we get around to it."

Information about a potential employer can be found through such means as reading annual reports (if it is a business corporation) and asking the opinion of a broker, customer, or supplier. Best of all, seek the opinion of several current or past employees. Choosing the wrong organization can be hazardous to your career. An organization that is "wrong" for you can be "right" for another person, and vice verse. You may not be able to tolerate an organization that expects its higher-level employees to work a fifty-five hour week under intense pressure. Another person might thrive in such an atmosphere.

Outperform the Competition.   Above all else, career advancement is contingent upon good performance. As described in a career management book for women,[9]

> Job competence and talent are still the number one success ingredients in all but the most pathologically political organizations. All other talk about success strategies is fanciful without first assuming that the person on the make is competent in his or her specialty. Before anybody is promoted in any big organization, the prospective new boss asks, "How well did he (or she) perform for you?" Even if you become the most adept office politician (including cavorting with people in power), you still have to exhibit job competence to be assigned more responsibility. I know of no woman manager who, prior to becoming a manager, was not skillful at something specific, be it computer programming, bookkeeping, writing, editing, nursing, or welding.

Stay Mobile.   A widely accepted strategy for advancing in responsibility is to strengthen your credentials by broadening your experience. Broadening can come about by performing a variety of jobs, or sometimes by performing essentially the same job in different organizations. Eugene E. Jennings, a management psychologist, has developed an elaborate set of rules for practicing *mobiliography*—roughly the science of managing your career by judicious job hopping.[10] Two of his many useful suggestions will be noted here:

1. *Don't be blocked by an immobile superior.* If you work for a boss whom the organization thinks is unpromotable, try to get from under that boss. He or she is probably not a good model and will block your upward progress. Tactfully ask for a transfer, or look around the organization for an opening for which you feel you could qualify. If these maneuvers fail, your career progress may be contingent upon finding a job in another organization.

2. *Be prepared to practice self-nomination.* Have the courage and aggressiveness to ask for a promotion or a transfer. Your boss may not believe that you are actually seeking more responsibility. An effective method of convincing him or her is to volunteer yourself for specific job openings or for challenging assignments. A boss may need convincing, because many more people claim to be seeking advancement than the number who will actually accept more responsibility. Verne Walter, a career counseling practitioner, provides this anecdote about the importance of self-nomination:[1]

> A general foreman in a heavy-equipment manufacturing company held hopes for broader and more responsible management experience. He had been a general foreman for approximately five years when he heard of the general manager's plan to create a new position—Manager: Planning and Control. He strongly desired to be considered for it.
> However, he believed it would be presumptuous of him to express his feelings to his superior. He was apprehensive about being perceived as

overstepping his bounds. He rationalized that both his superior and the general manager knew him well, and that undoubtedly the administrative and planning ability he had shown on projects over the past would be recognized by them. As a consequence, he did nothing to convey his desires to management.

Unknown to the foreman, the general manager, in answer to the question, "Had he thought of this man as a prospect," said, "Heavens no. I wouldn't think of it. His strength is in line operations. We'll be expanding his operation within the next three years, and he's looking forward to the added responsibility our expansion plans entail."

Swim Against the Tide. The essence of this strategy is to take an unconventional path to career success. It involves placing yourself in a job environment where competition might not be so overwhelming. A college graduate, for example, might seek employment in a company that is not overloaded with young college graduates. His or her background might then be at a premium. As with any other career-development strategy, it requires good judgment to implement. That same company that has few college graduates might have an informal policy of not promoting college graduates into key jobs!

Find a Sponsor. A swift route to career progress is to find somebody at a high place in the organization who is impressed with your capabilities. Such a person can even be a blood relative or one by marriage. One reason that task-force assignments are helpful to career progress is that they provide you with the opportunity to be seen by a variety of high-ranking people in your organization. Many an individual who performed well in an activity such as the Community Chest has found a bigger job in the process.

Document Your Accomplishments. Keeping an accurate record of what you have accomplished in your career can be valuable when being considered for promotion. An astute career person can point specifically to what he or she has accomplished in each position. Here are two examples from different types of jobs:

1. As ski shop store manager, increased sales to deaf skiers by 338 percent in one year by hiring a deaf interpreter to work in our shop on Saturday mornings.

2. As industrial engineer, saved my company $36,000 in one year by switching from steel to nylon ball bearings in our line of bicycles and baby carriages.

Play Career Ping-Pong. The Ping-Pong theory of career management suggests that you move back and forth from line to staff functions in order to ultimately land an executive position. An industrial engineer using this approach might work as a manufacturing supervisor for three years, followed by one year as an operations researcher (management scientist), then on to a general foreman's job. At that point in his career, he might be ready for a high-level manufacturing assignment. "Ping-Ponging" your way up the organizational ladder may be a valid approach, but it is probably more difficult to implement than some of the other strategies suggested here. Its underlying premise is sound: both line and staff (or generalist and specialist) experience are helpful to a career.

Consider Your Spouse. As the sex-role revolution becomes more engrained into our society, more and more couples will be dual-career couples. When one person is transferred or promoted, the impact on the other partner has to be carefully considered. Today, in families where only the husband works outside the home, the community ties and volunteer-work involvements of the wife are given more consideration than in the past. An increasing number of men are refusing transfers to another city because of its potential adverse impact upon their wives or children. A well-managed career takes into account both family and career well-being.

Manage Luck. Good fortune weighs heavily in most successful careers. Without one or two good breaks along the way (such as your company suddenly expanding and being in need of people for key jobs), it is difficult to go far in your career. The effective strategist to some extent *manages luck* by being prepared for the big break. Douglas T. Hall offers two suggestions about dealing with chance events:[12]

> First, you can anticipate what conditions might arise and develop *contingency plans* for them (e.g., "If we have a recession, I'll go back to graduate school"). Ask yourself, "What are all the things that could go wrong?" And "How would I respond to each course of events?" Second, you can prepare yourself to be ready to take advantage of opportunities when they come along. (A colleague of mine recently said, "Luck is the reward of the diligent").

FINDING A JOB

Anybody intent on finding a job, whether currently employed or unemployed, should make good use of information and services available for such ends. A number of books portray accurately the mechanics of job finding. (See the suggested reading list at the end of this chapter.) College placement offices and career counselors provide professional assistance, as do state and private employment agencies. Here we shall present eight summary suggestions about the job-finding process.[13]

Identify Your Job Objective(s). A proper job search begins with a clear perception of what kind of job or jobs you want. Most people can more readily identify what jobs they don't want than those they do want. Your chances for finding employment are directly proportional to the number of positions that will satisfy your job objective. One woman with a background in writing might be willing to accept only a job as a newspaper reporter (always a difficult position to find). Another woman with the same background is seeking a job as (1) a newspaper reporter, (2) a magazine staff writer, (3) a copywriter in an advertising agency, (4) communications specialist in a company, or (5) copywriter in a public relations firm. The second woman has a better chance than the first of finding a job.

Identify Your Potential Contribution. A man responded by phone to a want ad with this initial comment: "Hello, this is Tom Crawford. I've just got to have a job. I've been laid off and I have a family to support. I need something right away." Poor Tom probably did need the job, but the company he was calling was more interested in *receiving* than in *giving* help. If Tom had used the following approach, he might have increased his chances for being granted an interview (and hopefully getting hired): "Hello, this is Tom Crawford. I see you need somebody to help ship packages. I know how to ship packages in a fast and economical way. When could I talk to you about it in person?"

Use the Insider System. Richard Lathrop, the director, National Center for Job-Market Studies, contends that only one in five of the 1 million job openings in the United States each month is likely to be advertised or listed with employment agencies. He notes, "Employers most often go 'outside' to find personnel only when they have jobs that are hard to fill."[14] Employers traditionally fill the four out of five jobs that are not publicized in this manner:

1. They fill them with their friends or people recommended by their friends.
2. They fill them with friends of their employees.
3. They fill them with people who have applied directly to them without knowing that any opening existed.

A job seeker thus might canvass friends and relatives to learn of openings for which they are qualified. Another approach is to directly cold canvass virtually any prospective employer using an unsolicited letter of inquiry. (See the section about attention-getting letters later in this chapter.)

Use Multiple Approaches. A standard method of job finding is to exhaust all possible approaches. Many an individual has claimed "I've tried everything," when they have only pursued a few job-finding channels. Among the possible approaches are college placement offices, private employment agencies, state employment services, classified ads in local and national newspapers, trade journals and magazines, employment booths at trade associations and conventions, inquiries through friends and relatives, and cold canvassing. Another standard approach is to place a situation wanted ad in local and national newspapers. An ad similar to the following helped one college graduate find a job:

> Pro-Establishment problem solver wants in on your management-training program. Try me, I'll give you a big return on your investment.

Write an Attention-Getting Letter.   Responding to want ads and cold-canvass approaches requires that you submit a letter of inquiry. Most job applicants use the conventional (and somewhat ineffective) approach of writing a letter attempting to impress the prospective employer with their background. A sounder approach is to capture the reader's attention with a punchy statement of what you might be able to do for them. Later in the letter you might give a one-page summary of your education and the highlights of your job and educational experience. Here are two examples of opening lines geared to two different types of jobs:

1. Person seeking employment in credit department of garment maker: "Everybody has debt-collection problems these days. Let me help you gather in some of the past due cash that you rightfully deserve."
2. Person looking for position as administrative assistant in hospital where vacancy may or may not exist: "Is your hospital drowning in paper work? Let me jump in with both feet and clear up some of the confusion. Then you can go back to taking care of sick people."

Prepare an Effective Resume.   No matter what method of job hunting you use, inevitably somebody will ask you for a resume. Most companies require a resume before seriously considering a job candidate from the outside. Resumes are sometimes also required in order to receive a job transfer within a company. The purpose of a resume is to help you obtain a job interview, not a job. Very few people are hired without a personal interview. Effective resumes are straightforward, factual presentations of a person's experience and accomplishments. They are neither overdetailed nor too sketchy. A general rule is that two or three pages in length is best. One page seems too superficial; a four-page (or longer) resume may irritate an impatient employment official. Some writers suggest that a chronological (the standard-type) resume be used; others argue for an *accomplishment* resume. A useful resume should include both your experiences and key accomplishments. A general-purpose resume is presented in Figure 16.1. When sent to a prospective employer, a resume should be professionally reproduced, with particular attention to misspellings, typographical errors, and careful spacing.

To attract attention, some job seekers print resumes on tinted paper, in a menu-like folder, or on unusual-sized paper. If done in a way to attract positive attention to yourself, these approaches have merit.

Resume

Arthur L. Poland
170 Glenview Drive
Dallas, Texas 75243

Born: August 8, 1952
Single: no dependents
(312) 385-3986

Job Objective	Industrial sales position, handling large, complex machinery. Willing to work largely on commission basis.
Job Experience 1976–present	Industrial account representative, Bainbridge Corporation, Dallas. Sell line of tool and die equipment to companies in Southwest. Duties include servicing established accounts and canvassing for new ones.
1974–1976	Inside sales representative, Bainbridge Corporation. Answered customer inquiries. Filled orders for replacement parts. Trained for outside sales position.
1970–1974	Tool and die maker apprentice, Texas Metals, Inc., Dallas. Assisted senior tool and die makers during four-year training program. Worked on milling machines, jigs, punch presses, numeric control devices.
Formal Education 1970–1974	Madagascar College, Dallas, Texas. Associate Degree in Business Administration; graduated with 3.16 grade point average: courses in marketing, sales techniques, consumer psychology, accounting, and statistics. President of Commuter's Club.
1966–1970	Big Horn High, Dallas. Honors student; academic major with vocational elective. Played varsity football and basketball. Earned part of living expenses by selling magazine subscriptions.
Job-related Skills	Competent sales representative. Able to size up customer's manufacturing problem and make recommendation for appropriate machinery. Precise in preparing call reports and expense accounts.

Major Business Accomplishment

In one year sold at a profit $150,000 worth of excess machine inventory. Received letter of commendation from company president.

Personal Interests and Hobbies

CB radio hobbyist, scuba diving, recreational golf player, read trade and business magazines.

FIGURE 16.1
A general-purpose resume.

Present Yourself Favorably But Accurately in the Interview.   Job hunters typically look upon the employment interview as a game-like situation in which they must "out-psyche" the interviewer. Prospective interviewees also want to know in advance answers to "trick questions." A better approach in the long range is to do your best to present a positive, but accurate picture of yourself. Outright deception in the interview, if discovered, will lead to your rejection. If the facts you presented (such as attendance at a particular school) are later discovered to be untrue, you might be dismissed from the job for which you were hired.

A straightforward explanation about something controversial in your background has a good chance of being accepted by the employment interviewer. Lying about that situation is usually grounds for rejection:

> A thirty-eight-year-old man told his prospective employer that his wife would not mind relocating if he were hired for the position in question. During lunch, an offhand comment indicated that the job candidate was in the process of separating from his wife. The company president turned him down for the position because of the discrepancy between his interview comment and his casual comment. The fact of legal separation did not concern the president.

A strongly recommended approach to overcome concern about job interviews is to practice being interviewed for a series of positions by a friend. Practice of this nature will enable you to develop skill in speaking coherently and smoothly about your job and educational experiences and key job-related attitudes.

Questions to Ask During An Employment Interview.   In the process of being interviewed for a position, it is important to also ask some questions yourself. The best questions are sincere ones that reflect an interest in job *content* factors (see Chapter 2). A rule of thumb is to only ask questions of real interest to you. An experienced employment interviewer is usually adept at detecting questions asked simply to impress him or her. Following are five questions of the type that will usually meet with good reception in an employment interview. Ask them during a period of silence or when you are asked if you have any questions.

1. If hired, what would I actually be doing?
2. What kind of advancement opportunities are there in your firm for outstanding performers?
3. Who would I be working with aside from people in my own department?
4. What is the company's attitude toward people who make constructive suggestions?
5. Is there anything I've said so far that requires more elaboration or further explanation?

Expect Some Rejection.   Finding a new job is fraught with rejection. It is not uncommon for a college graduate or an experienced career person to send out 150 letters of inquiry to find one job. When your job search is confined to places that are trying to fill a position that matches your speciality, you still may have to be interviewed many times in order to find one job. Often you will be rejected when it appears to you that your qualifications match perfectly those required for the job opening. The employment interviewer may have interviewed another applicant that he or she thinks is even better qualified than you. In short, do not take rejection personally. It is an inevitable part of job hunting.

MANAGING THE MID-CAREER CRISIS

Part of managing your career is to realize that many people encounter a psychological slump somewhere between the ages of 35 and 55.[15] Theodore A. Jackson describes the *middle-aged middle-management syndrome* (which applies equally well to people engaged in other kinds of work) as[16]

> the general feeling of discontent and unhappiness these executives have concerning their jobs, the feeling of boredom and restlessness, the sense of entrapment, and absence of any significant challenge, and the vague dissatisfaction with the way their careers seem to have turned out. And it's all wrapped up in an overall distaste for getting up and going to work.

At mid-career many people begin to question the meaning of life and what they are doing. They ask themselves such questions as: Who am I? Where have I been? What have I done of value? Where am I headed? What's left for me? Aside from these philosophical concerns, most people at mid-career begin to notice a physical and physiological slowing down. Active participants in sports may realize that they can no longer compete as effectively with younger people. An increased tendency toward fatigue is another problem associated with the mid-career slump. Coping with or preventing mid-career problems encompasses much of career and life planning. Nevertheless, five suggestions are in order here.

Maintain a Growing Edge.   A person who maintains a life-long positive attitude toward self-development and self-improvement will decrease his or her chances of becoming obsolete (and therefore experiencing the mid-career crisis). The individual should not be required to take full responsibility for preventing obsolescence. Company-sponsored training programs along with varied job assignments can help reduce the problem of "going stale." Training programs should be geared toward the particular problem at hand. For instance, a mid-career administrator might begin to realize that he has contributed too few creative suggestions in the last several years. A creativity training program could perhaps help with this situation.

Receive Continuous Feedback.   One reason many people face the mid-career crisis or become obsolete is that they perpetuate the same old errors. Honest feedback from others can help an individual prevent repeating the same mistakes year after year. Feedback of this nature should be part of a performance review system. Effective managers tend to give this kind of feedback spontaneously as the need arises:

> Mack, an administrative assistant, had not received a promotion in three years. His newest assignment was a lateral transfer, working for Bud, manager of systems and procedures. Bud called Mack into his office one month after his starting date. "Mack, I have something sensitive to tell you but I think it will help you. I've noticed that you touch people too much when you are talking to them. As an outside observer, I can see that people wince when you put your arm around them, males and females included." Shocked at first, Mack quickly changed his touching behavior. Gradually, he was better accepted by people he worked with and received a promotion to supervisor one year later.

Realign Goals.   At mid-career many people are frustrated because they have not achieved the goals that they established earlier in life. The secret of success is to lower your goals if you (1) are satisfied with your new goals, and (2) you attain them. Goal changing is not an easy process, but careful reflection about the current appropriateness of your goals can be beneficial. For instance, at age 20 a woman might want to be a leading fashion photographer. After fifteen years of working as a photographer, she might realize that merely surviving in this competitive field is a mark of success! By establishing a new goal of "receiving at least one major magazine assignment a year," she may ward off the mid-career slump.

Develop Outside Interests.   One executive commented, "Some of the people working for me are unreal. They expect more out of their jobs than they do out of their marriages." Many people do expect their careers to be the dominant source of personal growth and satisfaction in life. An individual who can shift more attention to his or her personal life and hobbies at mid-career may be able to soften the impact of unfulfilled career expectations. People in their forties who become grandparents often experience a rejuvenated feeling that detracts their attention from career concerns. Grandchildren can be an ideal diversion because of the love and emotional involvement present. In addition, being an active grandparent is not so time consuming that it interferes with job performance.

A self-defeating example of using outside interests to help circumvent career problems is the person who becomes overinvolved with a hobby:

> At age 45, one staff manager began to enter senior tennis tournaments. Although he had been a tournament tennis player for many years, he did not allow his tennis to interfere with his work. Now his weekend tournaments frequently necessitated that he leave work late Thursday afternoon and return late Monday morning. After two demotions, he was finally asked to resign from the company. His forced resignation only intensified his career problems. Unable to find a comparable-level position, he began a business of his own and went bankrupt in six months.

Find a Second Career or New Job. The New American Dream could very well be finding a satisfying second career when it appears that the first one is going stale. It is not unusual for the personnel office of a community college to receive 500 applications for one opening in the area of business teaching. Most of these applications are from mid-career (or late-career) middle managers and executives who think that teaching would be more rewarding than their present line of work.

Finding a second career requires long-range planning. The economy can only absorb so many ski shop or fish and tackle proprietors or boutique owners. Sometimes a long-term avocation can be converted into an occupation, providing a high level of skill has been developed. One engineer had been customizing automobiles since age 18. By age 43 he felt that corporate life was no longer satisfying. He converted savings plus a Small Business Administration loan to open an automobile customizing shop. He worked longer hours in his new occupation at slightly lower net income, but his psychic income increased dramatically. Finding a new job can also be an antidote to the mid-career crisis, providing the new job is more rewarding and exciting than the one left behind. In some instances, what a person felt was a mid-career problem was in reality an overreaction to a dissatisfying job.

USING A CAREER COUNSELOR

The vast majority of career-minded people manage their careers with no outside professional help. What is common practice is not always the best practice. Using a career counselor *may* be a sound investment in time and money.[17] Counseling services are generally found in college counseling centers. Job counselors and counseling psychologists are also found in private practice. A problem with career counseling, as with any other professional service, is that you may misinterpret the results or be given harmful advice. One man was advised by a counselor to have a mail campaign conducted for him by the career counseling firm. The firm inadvertently mailed his resume to the man's own company. He was fired and experienced considerable difficulty in finding a new job. Two key advantages of career counseling are (1) it might provide you new insights into yourself, and (2) you may become aware of more alternatives in your career life. Next is a sampling of a counseling session that provided the counselee new insights and new alternatives:

Counselor: You say that there is almost nothing else in life a high school biology teacher can do but teach biology.

Biology Teacher: Darn right. That's my problem. As I explained last week, I no longer want to teach. I want to get out of education and do something different. And I know there are no job openings for biologists these days.

Counselor: Okay, so biologists aren't in big demand these days. But what really is a biologist?

Biologist: I guess you could say a biologist is a scientist. At least, I'd like to think of myself as a scientist.

Counselor: You should think of yourself as a scientist. You've been taking a too narrow view of yourself from a career standpoint."

Biologist: Okay, you've waved your magic wand over me. Poof, I'm a scientist. So where does that leave me?

Counselor: What's a scientist?

Biologist: I think I can play this game. A scientist is a person who explores the world in a very logical and systematic manner.

Counselor: Exactly, exactly. That's what I want you to understand and accept. There are lots of things a person who uses a logical and systematic approach to problems can do.

Biologist: That's good to know, but how does that help me find a new job? My contract at the high school expires in sixty days.

Counselor: Many companies are looking for well-educated scientists to work in the systems and procedures area. What you basically need is the right aptitude and a willingness to learn. Systems and procedures work is sometimes just a rigorous application of common sense.

Biologist: Systems and procedures work sounds like something I would very much enjoy. My brother-in-law is a systems and procedures analyst. His work sounds fascinating. I never thought of it as a field for me before today. I think I'll start making some inquires.

1. You must accept the major responsibility for your career development despite whatever help is offered by your organization.
2. An important first step in managing your career is to establish short-, intermediate-, and long-range goals. Goals that focus on levels of

*Summary
of Key Points*

responsibility or type of work are usually more meaningful than financial goals.

3. Twelve major career-planning strategies are as follows:
   a. Make an accurate self-appraisal.
   b. Use occupational information.
   c. Establish meaningful goals.
   d. Find the right organization.
   e. Outperform the competition.
   f. Stay mobile.
   g. Swim against the tide.
   h. Find a sponsor.
   i. Document your accomplishments.
   j. Play career Ping-Pong.
   k. Consider your spouse in your plans.
   l. Manage luck.

4. Finding a new job is an important part of career management that should be carried out in an organized, systematic manner. Four key strategies are (a) identify your job objective(s), (b) use the insider system, (c) use multiple approaches, and (d) write an attention-getting letter.

5. The mid-career crisis can be minimized by a continuous process of obtaining feedback about yourself and a life-long positive attitude toward self-development. Finding a second career or a new job, realigning your goals, or developing outside interests can help you cope with the problem.

6. Career counseling may help you acquire useful insights about yourself and an awareness of a wider range of career alternatives.

*Questions
for Discussion*

1. What steps have you taken to manage your career? In other words, what career planning have you already done?

2. "Winging it" is the alternative to career planning. If some very successful people are "wingers" rather than "planners," why should you plan your career?

3. What are your short-, intermediate-, and long-term career goals? How flexible are they?

4. Which do you think are the two most useful career-planning strategies described in this chapter? Why?

5. An eighteen-year-old female high school senior comes to you for advice? She states, "I want to make $100,000 per year. What field should I enter?" What advice might you offer her?

6. What do you think are the advantages and disadvantages of "practicing self-nomination"? Have you tried it? What were the results?

Charlie's high school classmates nicknamed him "Mr. Straight Lace" because of his dedication to his studies and his forthright attitude about most things. Needing to be self-supporting, Charlie worked as a bank teller while he attended college at night. Within four years, Charlie was promoted to head teller. Three years later he was promoted to assistant loan officer, an accomplishment that made Charlie proud.

The same year as his promotion, Charlie fell in love with Sue, a young woman whose father was a real estate developer (and an influential bank customer). Charlie and Sue were soon to be married, but Charlie cautioned, "Sue, I may have a lot of status as an assistant bank officer, but please recognize that I couldn't afford a house and a family at this stage in my career. Banks just aren't high-paying institutions."

One week before the wedding, Sue's father invited Charlie to lunch at his private club. The soon to be father-in-law made his point explicit over cocktails: "Okay, Charlie, welcome to the family. But let's get something straight right away. You're going to become a vice-president in my company. Forget about this namby-pamby clerical job you have now. Be a real man and join me. For openers, we'll double your present salary. Let's have our agreement in writing before the wedding day."

What would you do if you were Charlie?

What would you do if you were Sue once you were informed about the conversation between your father and fiance?

When Dr. Samuel Stabins first meets his "patients," he takes a history from them. But for the past three years, that history has been a financial rather than a medical one, because Stabins has become a stockbroker.

"I always say patients instead of clients," he said. After 45 years in practice as a surgeon, it's easy to understand.

Stabins, 75, said he never thought about becoming a stockbroker during his years in medicine. "I'd buy a stock and forget about it. It was something I never really thought about."

He made the change when he turned 70 because most local hospitals have a rule that surgeons can't operate after they reach that age. He considered staying on at Genessee Hospital, where he had been surgeon-in-chief, as a consultant, but decided not to.

"I decided if I was away from the hospital, I wouldn't miss it. I get nostalgic," Stabins said. He said his friends at a large brokerage firm convinced him to become a stockbroker, and he took an intensive six month course.

"I had to study ten or eleven hours a day. As you get older, you can absorb it all, but you can't retain it as well," he said.

He said it wasn't difficult to attract investors. Many are his former patients and friends. "I think it's a matter of confidence," he said. And in the same way that he examined a patient's medical history and prescribed the necessary help, he said, he now examines a person's financial history and gives advice.

"I think people should be as knowledgeable about their money as they are about their health," Stabins said.

Stabins said he has to do a tremendous amount of reading to keep up with the stock market. But then he also had a lot of reading to do to keep up with medicine.

He works fulltime as a stockbroker, but also devotes a lot of his spare time to volunteer work. Stabins is on the board of trustees of Monroe Community College, the board of trustees of the Gannett Foundation, an advisory board at Genessee Hospital, the advisory board of Community Savings Bank, and several blood donation committees of the American Red Cross.

"I think it's so important when you retire to do something to use your brain so that you think. Some people put themselves into a closet and don't try to change their routine. One of the great benefits of retiring is to do something," Stabins said.

Stabins was reluctant about publicity because, he said, "I'm not interested in competing with other people. It's not my livelihood. I don't want to hurt my friends."

Asked how long he'll continue as a stockbroker, he said, "If I reach the point where I feel I'm not holding up my end to the company I would resign.

"When you're 75, you take every day as it comes."

1. Is Dr. Stabin's second career a product of planning or luck? Explain your reasoning.
2. Should Dr. Stabin's boss discourage him from calling the people he serves "patients"? Why or why not?
3. Would you accept financial advice from Samuel Stabins?
4. What do you think of the hospital management's policy of prohibiting any surgeon 70 or older from operating on patients?
5. What lesson does this case provide about the relationship between career satisfaction and life satisfaction?

FOOTNOTES

[1] William F. Glueck, *Personnel: A Diagnostic Approach,* Business Publications, 1974, p. 259.

[2] This concept is developed in Verne Walter, "Self-Motivated Personal Career Planning: A Breakthrough in Human Resource Management," *Personnel Journal,* Mar. 1975, pp. 112–115, 136.

[3] Lou Varga, *Occupational Floundering, Personnel and Guidance Journal,* Dec. 1973, p. 225.

[4] The information presented in this section follows ideas presented in two sources: Andrew J. DuBrin, *Fundamentals of Organizational Behavior: An Applied Perspective,* Pergamon, 1974, pp. 147–158; and Douglas T. Hall, *Careers in Organizations,* Goodyear, 1976, pp. 181–189.

[5] Available to professionals in the field by writing "Careers," New York Life Insurance Company, Box 51, Madison Square Station, New York, N.Y. 10010.

[6] *The Guidance Information System,* Time Share Corporation, 630 Oakwood Ave., West Hartford, Conn. 06110.

[7] Quoted in Hall, *op. cit.,* pp. 183–184.

[8] For an extended discussion of this problem, see Andrew J. DuBrin, *Managerial Deviance: How to Handle Problem People in Key Jobs,* Mason/ Charter, 1976.

[9] Andrew J. DuBrin, *Survival in the Sexist Jungle,* Books for Better Living, 1974, p. 30.

[10] Eugene E. Jennings, *Routes to the Executive Suite,* McGraw-Hill, 1971. These strategies are summarized in Hall, *op. cit.,* pp. 186–187.

[11] Walter, *op. cit.,* p. 115.

[12] Hall, *op. cit.,* p. 188.

[13] The information in this section is based on DuBrin, *Survival in the Office, How to Move Ahead or Hang On,* Mason/Charter, 1977, Chapter 16, and Richard Lathrop, *Who's Hiring Who,* Reston, 1976, Chapters 2 and 7.

[14] Lathrop, *op. cit.,* p. 14.

[15] A recent examination of this problem is Robert F. Pearse and Purdy B. Pelzer, *Self-Directed Change for the Mid-Career Manager,* AMACOM, 1976.

[16] Theodore A. Jackson, "Turned Off by Your Job," *Industry Week,* Jan. 29, 1973, p. 41.

[17] A useful manual about using professional assistance in career guidance is Dean C. Dauw, *Up Your Career,* Waveland Press, Inc. (P.O. Box 400, Prospect Heights, Ill. 60070), 1975.

[18] Source: Meryl Gordon, "A Case of Financial 'Patients'," *Democrat and Chronicle,* Rochester, N.Y., Sept. 15, 1976, p. 8D.

SUGGESTED READING

BOLLES, RICHARD N. *What Color Is Your Parachute? A Practical Manual for Job Hunters and Career Changers,* rev. ed., Ten Speed Press, 1975.

DUBRIN, ANDREW J. *Survival in the Office: How to Move Ahead or Hang On,* Mason/Charter, 1977. See Part V, Managing Your Future.

DUBRIN, ANDREW J. *The New Husbands and How to Become One,* Nelson-Hall, 1976. See Chapters 6–8.

GRUSKY, OSCAR. "Career Mobility and Organizational Commitment," *Administrative Science Quarterly,* Nov. 1966, pp. 488–503.

HALL, DOUGLAS T. *Careers in Organizations,* Goodyear, 1976.

LATHROP, RICHARD. *Who's Hiring Who,* Reston, 1976.

Occupational Outlook Handbook, U.S. Government Printing Office, Washington, D.C. 20402.

PIETROFESA, JOHN J., and SPLETE, HOWARD. *Career Development: Theory and Research*, Grune & Stratton, 1975.

SUPER, DONALD E., and BOHN, MARTIN J., JR. *Occupational Psychology*, Wadsworth, 1970.

WALTER, VERNE. "Self-Motivated Personal Career Planning: A Breakthrough in Human Resource Management," *Personnel Journal*, Mar. 1975, pp. 112–115, 136.

GLOSSARY

Action plan.   A description of what needs to be done to achieve an objective or bring performance back to an acceptable standard.

Adhocracy.   An organization composed primarily of special-purpose (ad hoc) teams, as opposed to a bureaucracy that is composed primarily of departments.

Ambiguous assignment.   An assignment that is unclear and uncertain to the person performing it.

Assertiveness training.   A human relations training program derived from behavior therapy that teaches people to express their feelings and act with an appropriate degree of openness and aggressiveness.

Behavior mod (modification).   A system of motivation that aims to change individual responses by changing the person's environment. In general, desired responses are rewarded and undesired responses are sometimes punished.

Behavioral model of human beings.   A framework for understanding how and why a person acts the way he or she does in a given situation. The model also predicts whether or not that behavior will be repeated in a similar situation.

Behavioral science. Any science concerned with the systematic study of human behavior, such as psychology, sociology, and anthropology. Also the study of human behavior that uses whatever body of knowledge is the most relevant.

Biofeedback control. A system of achieving relaxation by receiving information concerning blood pressure and other bodily processes under control of the autonomic nervous system.

Blackmail. Any payment forced by intimidation such as threats of injurious revelations or accusations.

Bureaucracy. A rational, systematic, and precise form of organization in which rules, regulations, and techniques of control are defined.

Career counselor. A professional person whose specialty is to help people overcome career problems or accelerate their career growth.

Career development. The process of creating a pattern of jobs in a series of steps from the initial job to retirement.

Career goals. Specific positions, types of work, or income levels a student or employed person aspires to reach.

Career Ping-Pong. A career advancement strategy in which the person alternates between line and staff assignments in order to gain maximum advantage.

Case. An involved description, usually based on reality, that is useful in illustrating or studying a phenomenon. This book uses human relations cases to illustrate many of the concepts discussed.

Change agent. A person whose formal role is to bring about organizational (or sometimes individual) change. Also called *OD consultant.*

Coaching. Helping an individual overcome a specific, immediate problem by giving him or her advice and encouragement.

Common sense. Sound practical judgment that is independent of specialized knowledge, training, or the like. Natural wisdom, not based on formal knowledge.

Communication. The passage of information between or among people (or animals) by the use of words, letters, symbols, or body language.

Conflict. Simultaneous arousal of two or more incompatible motives. Often accompanied by tension, anxiety, or frustration.

Confrontation. Bringing forth a controversial topic or contradictory material in which the other party is personally involved. To say "You have bad breath" is a confrontation.

Contingency theory of leadership. Any leadership theory that attempts to explain how leadership effectiveness depends upon the demands of the situation.

Counseling. A formal discussion method for helping another individual overcome a problem or develop his or her potential. It involves considerable listening on the part of the counselor.

Counterculture. A separate culture formed in reaction to the established value system. "Hippies" represent the counterculture, as did "beatniks" and "peaceniks."

Creative climate. A work environment that is conducive to or encourages creativity.

Creative potential. A person's basic aptitude for engaging in creative behavior. Virtually everybody has some creative potential.

Creativity. The ability to process information in such a way that the result is new, original, and meaningful.

Cultural conditioning. Patterns of behavior that people learn as a result of growing up in a particular culture.

Developmental need. A weakness or deficit within a person that is currently interfering with his or her present job performance or future progress. For example, a shy sales representative might need to become more assertive.

Doctrine of functional autonomy. An observation that an administrative unit will tend to develop until it becomes completely independent.

Emotion. Any strong agitation of the feelings triggered by experiencing love, hate, fear, joy, and the like.

Encounter group. A small therapy or training group that focuses on expressing feelings openly and honestly.

Expectancy theory. Any theory of human motivation that centers around how much a person believes that effort will lead to a desired outcome, and whether or not that outcome (for example, getting the job done) will lead to a reward (such as a large salary increase).

Feedback. Information that tells you how well or poorly you have performed. Also, knowledge of results of one's behavior that helps you judge the appropriateness of your responses and make corrections where indicated.

Fiedler's contingency model. A popular theory of leadership that emphasizes the importance of three factors in determining leadership effectiveness: (1) personal relationships of the leader, (2) the leader's power and authority, and (3) the clarity of the task to be performed.

Fogging. A way of responding to manipulative criticism by openly accepting the criticism. Such as "Yes, it's true I was one hour late for work today."

Formal communication pathway. A communication route officially designated by the organization.

Formal group. A group that forms in response to the demands and processes of the formal organization.

Frame of reference. A consistent view about something which tends to serve as an intellectual map for guiding your perception and behavior. This book may be evaluated from three frames of references; those of instructors, students, and job holders.

Frustration. Thwarting or blocking of a need, wish, or desire.

Goal. An event, circumstance, object, or condition for which a person (or animal) strives.

Grapevine. The major informal communication network in an organization. Used in both the transmission of rumors and true information.

Group. A collection of individuals who regularly interact with each other, who are psychologically aware of each other, and who perceive themselves to be a group.

Group cohesiveness. The attractiveness of the group to its members, which leads to a feeling of unity and "stick-togetherness."

Human potential movement. The growth of interest in and techniques for helping people fulfill their potential, particularly with regard to self-understanding. The growth of transactional analysis (TA) workshops is one example.

Human relations. The art and practice of using systematic knowledge about human behavior to achieve organizational and/or personal objectives.

Human relations movement. Basically the application of human relations in work organization from the Hawthorne studies (around 1927) to the present.

I'm OK—You're OK. A key concept of transactional analysis (TA) that signifies the life position of the mature, healthy adult.

Incident. A brief description usually based on reality that is useful in illustrating or studying a phenomenon. This book uses human relations incidents to illustrate many of the concepts discussed.

Informal communication pathway. A communication route that develops spontaneously in an organization, such as the grapevine.

Informal group. Natural grouping of people in a work situation that evolves to take care of people's desire for friendship and companionship.

Innovation. A step beyond creativity, in which an original or borrowed idea is applied to a situation where it has not been employed before.

Insider system. A job-finding technique in which you search for nonadvertised jobs that are usually given to company insiders.

Integration. The ability of the organization to avoid conflict among its members. Also, the meshing of individual and organizational goals.

Inversion of means and ends. A situation in which following orders or performing your specialized activity becomes more important than the overall goal you are trying to achieve. An example would be an organization-development specialist who cares more about setting up training programs than helping the company reach its objectives.

Job enrichment. Increasing worker motivation by making the nature of the job more exciting, rewarding, challenging, or creative.

Job motivation. Effort directed toward achieving job goals, thus following the principles of human motivation in general.

Job politics. Achieving your objectives by use of techniques other than strictly merit. Two examples are apple polishing and discrediting the opposition.

Job satisfaction. The amount of pleasure or contentment associated with a job.

Knowledge worker. A person who works more with ideas and concepts rather than things. Generally, managerial, professional, technical, and sales personnel.

Leadership potential. A person's basic capacity or aptitude for carrying out a leadership role. It stems from both inborn and acquired traits and characteristics.

Leadership style. A leader's characteristic approach to leading people in most situations. For instance, some leaders are very demanding, and others are permissive.

Level of drive.   The amount of effort a person puts forth toward reaching a goal.

Life script.   A key concept of transactional analysis contending that people usually live their lives according to elaborate and consistent game plans called scripts.

Line management.   Managers in an organization who have direct responsibility for certain key activities such as sales or manufacturing.

Management by objectives (MBO).   A system of management in which people are held accountable for reaching objectives that they jointly set with their superiors.

Managerial grid.   A framework for simultaneously examining the concern for production and people dimensions of leadership. Also an OD program for teaching leaders team management—getting work accomplished through committed people.

Mid-career crisis.   A general concern career-minded people have between the ages of 35 and 55 about their level of career accomplishment, usually accompanied by feelings of dissatisfaction, boredom, and restlessness.

Motivator.   Job elements or incentives that energize you to action—exert a motivational impact upon you.

Negative reinforcement.   Removing something negative (such as a penalty) when somebody makes the desired response.

Nonverbal feedback.   Body language used by the receiver in response to a message that suggests how well the message is being received.

Objective.   A specific end state or condition aimed for that contributes to a larger goal.

Objective standard of performance.   A precise measure of how well or poorly an individual performs in his or her job, such as achieving an agreed upon objective.

OK boss.   An effective boss in the jargon of transactional analysis. Seven different boss styles exist in this approach, all with an OK and a not-OK variety.

Organic organization.   One that adapts readily to change (versus *inorganic organization*).

Organization confrontation meeting.   A method of resolving intergroup conflict in which the opposing sides tell each other what is bothering them and share perceptions of each other.

Organization development (OD).   A wide variety of techniques for improving organizational effectiveness, primarily focusing on changing the attitudes and behavior of people.

Organizational design.   How an organization is laid out, or its structure.

Organizational effectiveness.   In general, an organization that meets its goals and objectives, but effectiveness can be measured in a variety of ways.

Organizational efficiency.   A measure of the amount of resources an organization consumes in relation to its output. The fewer resources used, the more efficient the organization.

Organizational multiplier. A condition in which many organizational members wind up taking care of each other rather than helping clients or customers. The organization grows in size strictly for internal reasons.

Participative leadership. An approach to leading others in which the subordinates share decision-making responsibility with the leader. Also called democratic leadership.

Perceptual block. An almost rigid tendency to think of an object in a limited way. A person might perceive a tire as serving only transportation ends, but a gorilla might perceive the tire as a toy.

Performance appraisal. A formal system of measuring, evaluating, and reviewing employee performance.

Positive reinforcement. Receiving a reward for making a particular response, such as getting approval from a boss for being prompt.

Proactive. An action or behavior taking place at one point in time that influences a future event. If you communicate honestly now, it will help your future communication effectiveness.

Probe. An interview technique used to elicit more specific information from the interviewee. "Tell me more about that" is a probe.

Psychological contract. An unwritten understanding between you and the organization defining how much you will do for the organization, providing your expectations of an employer are met.

Receiver. The person who is sent the message in an instance of communication.

Resource conservation industry. An emerging industry whose central concern is preserving existing and future resources, both human and nonhuman.

Response predisposition. A learned action likely to be repeated in the future when a similar situation arises. If being assertive in a performance review works once, you will probably be assertive in the next performance review.

Role. Behavior expected of an individual occupying a given position within a group.

Role-based conflict. Conflict aroused because the achievement of your objective is incompatible with the achievement of somebody else's objective. For instance, a traffic policeman giving a ticket to a truck driver.

Role conflict. Anxiety generated in a person when people have incompatible expectations of you or when two or more of your roles conflict with each other.

Self-actualization. Making maximum use of the potential in oneself. Similar to self-fulfillment.

Self-concept. The total view one has of oneself. A positive self-concept leads to self-confidence.

Self-discipline. Discipline or training of oneself, usually for self-improvement.

Self-nomination. Naming yourself as a contender for transfers, promotions, and special assignments.

Sender. The person who attempts to transmit a message in an instance of communication.

Sexism. A set of beliefs indicating that males and females should occupy distinctly different roles in society.

Shaping of behavior. Inducing somebody to achieve the desired response by first rewarding any action in the right direction, and then rewarding only the closest approximations until finally the desired response is attained.

Situation sensitivity. Ability of a leader to size up a situation and act appropriately, that is, do what is required in the situation.

Staff. People in an organization who make recommendations to line management but who do not have the formal authority to implement their recommendations. One example would be a public relations advisor.

Stimulus. Physical energy that arouses an individual and produces an effect on the person.

Stress. Any demand inside or outside the person that requires the person to cope with the demand. Groups and organizations also experience stress.

Survey feedback. An approach to OD in which the results of an attitude survey are fed back to management and workers. Corrective action is taken about problems uncovered in the survey.

Synectics. A group problem-solving technique in which various elements are fitted together to produce novel and creative alternatives with a view to reaching group consensus.

Systems theory. An approach to understanding organizations that emphasizes the input–process–output schema and the relationship between the organization and the environment.

T-group. A popular form of encounter group that is particularly unstructured. T-groups (as part of sensitivity training) were originally developed for training managers to be more open and honest with people, but are now widely used in nonwork settings.

Team building. An OD technique emphasizing small discussion groups that attempts to bring about improved communication and cooperation in work groups.

Territorial encroachment. When one person or group takes over some responsibility that another person or groups thinks is theirs. An example would be a sales manager telling a manufacturing manager how to handle a manufacturing problem.

Theory X. Douglas McGregor's famous statement of the traditional management view that considers people as usually lazy and needing to be prodded by external rewards. A rigid and task-oriented approach to management.

Theory Y. Douglas McGregor's famous statement of an alternative to traditional management thinking. It emphasizes that people seek to fulfill higher-level needs on the job and that management must be flexible and human relations oriented.

Transactional analysis (TA). A technique for improving interpersonal relationships that looks upon every human relationship as a transaction between the ego states (parent, adult, child) of people.

Transcendental meditation (TM). A system of almost total relaxation involving achieving a physiological state of deep rest.

Type A behavior. A behavior pattern that can be observed in any person who is aggressively involved in a chronic, incessant struggle to achieve more in less and less time. An environmental challenge must always serve as the fuse for the explosion of this behavior.

Unit. A subpart of an organization such as a department or division.

Zone of indifference. Area of behavior within which a subordinate is prepared to accept direction or influence. Orders of this type are seen as lawful and within the person's value system.

INDEX

NAME INDEX

SUBJECT INDEX